Kings, Courtiers & Imperium

KINGS, COURTIERS & IMPERIUM

The Barbarian West, 565-725

P.S. Barnwell

Duckworth

First published in 1997 by
Gerald Duckworth & Co. Ltd.
The Old Piano Factory
48 Hoxton Square, London N1 6PB
Tel: 0171 729 5986
Fax: 0171 729 0015

A catalogue record for this book is available
from the British Library.

ISBN 0 7156 2763 5

Typeset by Ray Davies
Printed in Great Britain by
Redwood Books Ltd, Trowbridge

Contents

Contents

Preface

Like its predecessor, *Emperor Prefects and Kings: the Roman West 395-565*, this book had its origins as part of a University of Leeds doctoral dissertation. It is once again a pleasure to record my gratitude to members of the University for their unfailing encouragement and helpfulness, and in particular to the staff of the Brotherton library, to which I have with great pleasure returned after an interval spent elsewhere.

The research on which the present work is based was supervised by Professor I.N. Wood, to whom I remain indebted for continuing interest and support. I have greatly benefited from the criticisms of the earlier version of the material presented here made by the late Professor G.R.J. Jones and Professor J.L. Nelson, while their enthusiasm for the enterprise has played a considerable part in encouraging me to bring it to fruition in the moments left after completion of my day-time employment. None of the above, nor any of the other people who have from time to time kindly offered support and advice, would necessarily agree with the arguments I here present, nor are they responsible for any remaining defects.

The appearance of this volume owes much to the faith of the late Colin Haycraft of Duckworth who readily accepted it as a companion to my earlier book, and to Deborah Blake, who has overseen its production with her customary courtesy and efficiency.

I am once again grateful to Mr A.T. Adams for producing the maps and tables, and to my father for helping to check the typescript. The debt to my father extends beyond the merely practical, as he has patiently listened to my ideas over many years, and has continually encouraged me to pursue my quest for answers. His support was only equalled by that of my late mother, whose interest and encouragement knew few bounds, continuing to provide succour even as she came to realise that she would not see the results of her inspiration: without her, this book would not exist.

P.S.B.

In appreciation of
the life of my mother,
Joan Barnwell

List of Maps and Tables

Maps

Genealogical Tables

Introduction

This book is intended as a companion to my *Emperor, Prefects and Kings: the Roman West, 395-565* (though each of the two volumes can stand alone), and continues the study of western administrative institutions from the late sixth century to varying points in the eighth. As east and west increasingly went their separate ways in the post-Justinianic age, so the relationship between the western rulers and the Empire changed: although diplomatic relations do not form part of the present study, the evolution of the ways in which western rulers thought of, and presented, their authority does. No longer was the Empire seen as the ultimate source of authority and, perhaps spurred by that, kingship came, in varying degrees, to be viewed in a theocratic way: the changing relationship with the Empire is part of the explanation for the inclusion of *imperium* in the title.

There were other changes in the circumstances in which kingship was practised during and after the late sixth century, one of the most notable being that Visigothic and, more particularly, Frankish, kings came to rule much larger areas than they had done before, often exercising hegemony over peoples other than their own. The issues this raised for the 'provincial' administration form one of the themes of the first two parts of this book, and, although the effect on kingship is less explicitly discussed, it provides the *imperium* of the title with a secondary significance, for the term's early medieval meaning is 'wide rule'.[1]

The book is divided into four parts – one for each of the major kingdoms (or, in the case of England, collection of kingdoms) which came to dominate the western European provinces of the former Roman Empire. Primacy is accorded to the Frankish kingdom for several reasons. First, there is a larger and more varied body of evidence concerning the *Regnum Francorum* than for the other kingdoms discussed here. Second, although the nature of the evidence changes after the end of Gregory of Tours' *Decem libri historiarum*, it is possible to write a continuous history of the Frankish people from the late fifth century to the eighth and beyond.

The same cannot be said – for differing reasons – of any of the other kingdoms discussed. Although the Visigoths had been settled in the former Empire since the fifth century, their history during the first two-thirds of the sixth century is almost completely a blank, owing to a lack of extant

1

source material: it is only with the reign of Leovigild and the conversion to Catholicism of his son, Reccared, that the Visigoths again emerge into the record. The Lombards had lived in the former Pannonia since the early sixth century, but their documented history only really starts with their arrival in Italy in 569, while the history of the Anglo-Saxons starts even later, with the conversion of Æthelberht of Kent to Christianity in the years around 600. The extent to which these differences between the histories of the various peoples caused their administrative institutions to vary, and in particular, the question of whether some were less 'Roman' (or 'advanced') than others, forms another of the themes of this work.

The terminal date for the study is not as neat as is suggested by the title. In the case of the Visigoths and the Lombards, there seemed to be little problem: the Visigothic kingdom ceased to exist in 711-12, and the Lombard in 768. For the Franks, the question is more complex: the change of dynasty in 751 might have seemed appropriate, but in the event the end of Chilperic II's reign, thirty years earlier, seemed better. After that not only were the Merovingians increasingly at the mercy of the Pippinids, but the hostility of most of the sources is such that objectivity becomes an increasingly difficult goal to attain, and it has been thought better not to risk distorting the seventh-century picture by including the final years of Merovingian rule. In reality, the loss is not great, since the amount of material for the period after 721 is small. Finally, England, where the combination of the end of the narrative provided by Bede's *Ecclesiastical History of the English People*, with the eighth-century rise of Mercia, suggested that a convenient terminal date would lie somewhere in the 720s.

While the continental kingdoms have often been discussed in a comparative way, each has also been studied in relative isolation according to differing historiographical traditions. England, by contrast, has only infrequently been set in the continental context provided here, and it is hoped that some insights are gained by placing discussion of it in a framework identical to that employed for the continent (this is discussed more fully in the appropriate places). Although they are treated separately (which may engender a small amount of repetition), parallels between the kingdoms, and points where their administrative histories are mutually illuminating, are noted. This approach has, as in *Emperor, Prefects and Kings*, seemed appropriate in order to take account of the varying nature of the sources for each kingdom.

Those familiar with my earlier work will recognise the methodology of the present volume, but it is worth briefly re-stating it for readers who come to this book first. Faced with the small amount of source material for any of the kingdoms under discussion, there has, until recently, been a tendency to use later documents to illuminate the earlier period; there has also been a propensity to allow hindsight to colour views of the seventh century. This has particularly affected interpretations of the Frankish kingdom, since the later sources (in common with some of the contemporary ones) are, for political reasons, hostile to the Merovingians.[2] The fact that the Visigothic kingdom was driven out of existence by the Arabs has similarly led to suggestions that its rulers were ineffective, while the Lombards' absorption into the Carolingian world has sometimes given rise to the same kind of interpretation.

What is attempted here is to take the seventh and early eighth centuries on their own terms and to try to maximise what can be understood of royal government during the period by arriving at a comprehension of the ways in which the nature of each individual source or type of source affects the range of information which can be extracted (archaeological and numismatic evidence is also used as appropriate). Despite the initial appearance of some of the narrative evidence, no source was written to provide answers to the questions modern historians pose: each had its own purpose, in accordance with which the material included was selected and presented. Unless that purpose is understood the significance of the evidence each provides (or does not provide) cannot be assessed, and a distorted picture may be drawn. For this reason, the sources for each kingdom are briefly examined in the initial chapters of the main sections of this book, while the implications of their character in relation to specific topics are discussed in the relevant places. It is believed that this approach, while perhaps slightly restricting the range of subjects which can be treated, allows the issues to be addressed with greater clarity, not only in relation to each individual kingdom, but particularly in terms of comparisons between the geographical and political units covered by different sources.

Much of the ground here covered has formed the subject of research for well over a century, and the secondary literature is large. In order to keep the notes to a reasonable volume, not all the relevant literature has always been cited in them, though an attempt has been made to place some of the more important omissions in the bibliography. The fact that a work is not referred to in the notes is not necessarily a reflection on its usefulness: this applies in particular to the major prosopographies.

PART I

The *Regnum Francorum*

The history of kingship and government in seventh-century Frankia has traditionally been seen in terms of decline, an almost inevitable result of which was the replacement of the Merovingians as the ruling dynasty. Einhard's depiction of the last of the Merovingians as 'rois fainéants', dominated by their *maiores domus*, is too well known to require elaboration,[1] and is supported by the negative image created by other Carolingian writers, notably the author of the *Annales Mettenses Priores*. Such interpretations, however, tend to be those of authors of the Carolingian period, writing at the least with the benefit of hindsight, and often also with the purpose of justifying and glorifying the new ruling dynasty. Their negative view should not be taken uncritically as an indication of what seventh-century Franks thought of their kings, or as a precondition for an objective understanding of the mechanisms of royal government at the time. The obstacles in the way of gaining such an objective view are not inconsiderable, largely owing to the nature of the source material, much of which is more sophisticated than has sometimes been recognised, and requires greater subtlety of interpretation than it has on occasion been accorded. In the following pages an attempt is made to examine seventh-century kings and their courts in their own, seventh-century, terms, constantly seeking to comprehend the impact which the characteristics of the documentary evidence have on the understanding of the period.

Seventh-century Merovingian kingship did not spring from nowhere, and, unlike the history of the peoples discussed in the other parts of this book, there is no break in either its development or the coverage of the sources during the second half of the sixth century. The type of source material changes with the ending of the *Decem libri historiarum* of Gregory of Tours, which is taken as the starting point for the present study, but that date (594) itself has no significance in terms of the development of the kingdom.

It will become clear that the governmental structures of the *regnum Francorum* evolved throughout the seventh century, and that by the end of the period of effective Merovingian rule – Charles Martel's elevation of Theuderic IV in place of Chilperic II in 721 – they appear rather different from their sixth-century predecessors which had, in turn, evolved from Roman provincial administrative institutions. However, the break with

5

the past was not total, and new forms of borrowing from 'Roman' traditions are in evidence (particularly in relation to images of kingship): it is also easier – owing to the survival of different kinds of evidence from the sixth and seventh centuries – to see some borrowings which must have occurred earlier (particularly in relation to the writing office). Thus, for all the change, there was an underlying continuity of development throughout the Merovingian period, as even Einhard unwittingly shows when he mocks the last of the Merovingians for travelling in an ox-cart – which, as J.M. Wallace-Hadrill argued, was descended from a practice of Roman provincial governors who progressed slowly around their provinces collecting petitions.[2]

1

The Sources

Unlike the sources for sixth-century Merovingian royal government,[1] those for the seventh century are not dominated by the *œuvre* of a single author: they are of considerably more diverse authorship and type. The evidence for the seventh century may conveniently be split into two categories – that of an 'official' nature, such as law codes and *diplomata*, which were produced by the government itself as it conducted its affairs, and that produced by chroniclers, propagandists, churchmen, and hagiographers. It is the second category of document with which this chapter is primarily concerned; documents produced by the government itself are discussed in general terms at the end of the chapter, further elucidation concerning their uses being reserved for the next, which treats them as part of the evidence for the nature of kingship.

The seventh century lacks a narrative account to compete with that provided by the *Decem libri historiarum* of Gregory of Tours. The only work which approaches its range is the fourth book of the *Chronicle* of Fredegar. However, it is much nearer in character to the chronicles of the fifth and sixth centuries than to Gregory's work: indeed, the first three books of the *Chronicle* were largely compiled from the writings of Jerome, Hydatius and Isidore of Seville (among others).[2] The purpose of the work seems to have been to provide a survey of world history from a Frankish perspective,[3] but its form means that it is episodic and disjointed. Hence, for example, the events of the period before Chlothar II's victory and the execution of Brunhild (in 613) are narrated in some detail, but the period between then and *c.* 624 is treated considerably more sketchily. This has been interpreted as evidence that the *Chronicle* was produced by more than one author,[4] with the earlier part finishing with the great events of 613. The sparse coverage of the following twelve years is, according to this interpretation, to be attributed to the fact that the second author, who did not write until about 660, could not have been writing from his own experience until after the mid-620s. This view has, however, been challenged, and it is possible to interpret the text as that of a single hand.[5]

That the date of authorship is to be placed *c.* 660 is indicated by the fact that the latest events mentioned in the *Chronicle* relate to 658 (cap. 81). The chapter in which they occur contains an overview of Byzantine affairs between 641 and 658, but the account of Frankish history in the remaining nine chapters ends in 642/3. This probably indicates that the author was interrupted in his work: if that is so, not only is the chronological span shorter than was originally intended, but some of the unevenness in earlier parts of the *Chronicle* may be due to a lack of final revision. Further, given the date of composition, events before *c.* 625 are unlikely to have lain within the author's own adult memory: the period before 613 may have been relatively well remembered during the author's earlier lifetime, and there may also have been some written sources, since it was a period of high-profile faction politics in which strong loyalties and emotions were aroused. By contrast, the first part of Chlothar II's reign was a period of relative peace and stability, detailed memories concerning which would probably have been rarer.[6] It may also be that the author, like the fifth-century chroniclers,[7] was himself more concerned to record events of immediately-perceived significance – of which there could be no better example than those culminating in Chlothar's re-unification of the *regnum Francorum* – than the affairs of peaceful civilian government. In other words, some of the unevenness of coverage may be, if not intentional, at least a product of the literary *genre* to which the *Chronicle* belongs. This is clear in the period after the mid 620s, when Fredegar seems to have been able to draw on official documents as well as his own memory.[8] In addition, despite his access to documents, the author does not seem to have been as closely associated with the court as Gregory of Tours had been. The result of this, combined with the form of the work, is that the normal workings of royal government can only be glimpsed incidentally, even for those parts of the Frankish kingdom – Austrasia and, more particularly, Burgundy[9] – with which its author was most familiar.

After its interruption in 642/3, Fredegar's work was continued to the accession of Charlemagne by two further authors. The earlier wrote *c.* 751, and was pro-Arnulfing, being in the pay of Charles Martel's half-brother, the *comes*, Childebrand: he adapted the *Liber historiae Francorum* (see below), transforming its Neustrian perspective to a pro-Austrasian and pro-Pippinid one.[10] The second continuator, who was active in *c.* 806, was much more ruthlessly pro-Carolingian.[11] Neither of the later writers was any more interested than Fredegar in the details of royal government, though their anti-Merovingian bias has to be taken into account when considering their depiction of the ways kings and their courtiers behaved, since they tend to enhance the role of members of their own faction, whether they held office at court or not.

The other narrative source for the seventh century – the one which was adapted by Fredegar's first continuator – is the *Liber historiae Francorum*, written in 727, probably at Soissons, possibly by a woman.[12] Although it has been treated as a second-rate document, the *Liber* has recently been rehabilitated, and has been shown to be a work of some sophistication, which glorifies the deeds of the Neustrians. The author's perspective is that of a Merovingian legitimist, and it is from this that much of the document's importance derives, since it means that its account of the late-Merovingian period is not the one of decay portrayed by the later Carolingian authors. Arnulfing power was only to be tolerated if it acted within the constraints of loyalty to the legitimate royal power of the Merovingian dynasty: hence Grimoald I's coup after Sigibert III's death was not to be condoned, but Charles Martel could be seen as the salvation of the Franks since he supported a Merovingian, Theuderic IV. For all the undoubted importance of the *Liber historiae Francorum* in terms of the general interpretation of the course of events from the 640s onwards, and for what it reveals concerning the attitudes of at least some of the Franks towards their kings in the late-Merovingian period, its concern is not with the details of royal administration, any more than was Fredegar's.

Both Fredegar's *Chronicle* and, to a greater extent, the *Liber historiae Francorum*, have a secular perspective. The largest body of non-governmental source material for the Merovingian period, however, is religious in nature, consisting of a *corpus* of hagiographical works larger than that for any other region in the post-Roman world. In the mid-seventh century, Jonas of Bobbio composed lives of Columbanus and his disciples, and a dozen further *uitae* were written in the late seventh century, mostly anonymously.

Works of this kind were primarily concerned with episcopal and monastic standards, and with the promotion of the cults of particular saints, but they often impinge on secular politics, at both local and national level.[13] Hence, for example, Jonas' account of the career of Columbanus presented events in a light favourable to Chlothar II, the ruler who gained most from the outburst of faction politics in the years around 600, rather than to Childebert II or Theuderic II who helped Columbanus to found Luxeuil, but who were representatives of the losing faction.[14] Similarly partisan is the body of hagiographical literature connected with the monastery of S.-Wandrille.[15] Thus the fact that a saint's life was produced within a few years of his death is not an absolute guarantee of the accuracy of the 'facts' it contains; nor, on the other hand, is a later *uita* necessarily fanciful.[16] For the present purpose, though, the politics are a subsidiary subject (though not one which can be ignored). In terms of administrative history, the kinds of activity in which secular officials engaged are unlikely to be wholly inaccurate, since the accounts of the contemporary hagiographers would have been based on an understanding of the ways in which the secular authorities would have handled the situations described: without this, the credulity of the contemporary audience would have been strained too far. Perhaps more limiting for the present enquiry is the fact that the primarily religious and political concerns of the *uitae* mean that the hagiographical material transmits only small fragments of information on the mechanics of secular government.

Even more fragmentary are the indications contained within another sizeable body of material produced by churchmen – the proceedings of the ecclesiastical councils. For the most part, such documents do not concern secular administration, but their prologues, which describe the circumstances in which individual councils were convoked, sometimes show royal involvement, thus providing evidence for one sphere of kingly activity. In at least one instance the prologue goes further, briefly commenting on the nature of royal power in such a way as to give an insight into the way in which churchmen thought about kingship. Material of this kind is a pale shadow of that which exists for the Visigothic kingdom, however, since the Frankish councils were not involved in the promotion of royal power in the same way as their Spanish counterparts, nor did they record the involvement of court officials in their proceedings to the same extent.[17]

The relations between churchmen and the royal court are in small measure illustrated by the one collection of letters – that of Bishop Desiderius of Cahors – which survives from the seventh century. In his early life, Desiderius was a member of Chlothar II's court, and he was *comes* in Marseilles under Dagobert I, but most of the thirty-six extant letters date from his tenure of the see of Cahors. They stand in the tradition of the great letter collections of late antiquity – exemplified by those of Symmachus and Sidonius Apollinaris – and represent an attempt by the Bishop to retain a range of contacts, many at the distant royal court, upon whose goodwill he could call should the need arise.[18] Desiderius is the only bishop known for certain to have engaged in this kind of activity, but the maintenance of correspondence is a reciprocal process, and a hint that other bishops behaved in a similar way comes from the fact that there are a few other, more miscellaneous, letters from seventh-century Frankia – though the light which they throw upon royal government is, on the whole, negligible.[19]

A document which has in the past been used to assist in understanding royal government is what appears to be a list of officials, often thought to have been produced during the reign of Dagobert I (623/9-638). It is now clear, however, that the text is not a working handlist of officials in a real court, but an educational text, or *aide mémoire*, produced in a church school and used to explain the names of officials not only in early medieval Europe, but probably also in the Bible. In addition, despite one piece of specifically Frankish material, the text cannot be proved to have originated in Frankia, Insular (and perhaps Anglo-Saxon) origin being more likely.[20]

One kind of educational document which did also have a function in secular administration is the formulary – a collection of model documents, concerning all types of legal process, compiled to assist those drafting written instruments. The dating of most of the Merovingian formularies is difficult, since their compilers – probably churchmen with access to well-stocked archives[21] – based their formulae upon documents of many dates. The result is that, while the models for some of the individual formulae may be readily dated, the period at which each compilation was made is considerably more difficult to assess, though it must be after the time at which the last document used as a model was produced. Hence, for example, although the *Formulae Aruernenses* contains documents dating from the early Merovingian period, the date of the collection as a whole cannot be determined.[22] More closely datable is the collection from Angers, which appears to have been drawn up in the late seventh century.[23] For the most part, such documents concern administrative and legal practices at local level, not involving the royal court.

The one major exception to this is the formulary of Marculf, which is arranged in two books, the first of which relates to royal documents. The date of the collection is not entirely certain, but both the main contenders – *c.* 650 and the early eighth century[24] – fall within the period covered by this study: the collection may, therefore, be seen as reflecting something of royal activity in the seventh century and earlier. The case of Marculf is particularly interesting in that the author states that he wrote his formulae, 'ad exercenda initia puerorum':[25] the work is dedicated to a bishop, perhaps indicating that Marculf worked at an episcopal school, but it has been suggested that his earlier career could have been spent at the royal palace.[26]

A formulary of the sort produced by Marculf would have been of direct assistance to those charged with drawing up the various *diplomata* (consisting of charters and *placita*) issued by Merovingian kings as part of the business of government. About eighty such documents can reasonably be thought to be genuine, of which some thirty-six survive as originals.[27] There is a group from the thirty years after 629, but numbers increase rapidly (though not consistently) from the late 670s onwards: this means that they are particularly helpful for the period after the relatively full narrative material provided by Fredegar comes to an end. Not only do the *diplomata* relate to a period of otherwise poor evidence, but they are also largely free from the propagandist purposes of such narrative material as does exist.

Documents of this kind provide a number of types of evidence. First, the very fact of their existence tells us something of the activities of kings (discussed in Chapter 2). Second, the *placita* contain lists of courtiers present at the royal tribunal, often with their titles, and some charters were signed by such men. In addition, the text of the documents sometimes indicates the roles of different officials in the palace's legal activities. Finally, many of the *diplomata* contain evidence concerning the way in which the royal writing office worked, and the officials who were responsible for it (discussed in Chapter 3). This last category of evidence is partly contained in tironian notes (an adapted form of Roman shorthand) at the end of the documents; the reading of such notes is extremely difficult, and has been the subject of some controversy, but the interpretations proposed by M. Jusselin in the early years of the twentieth century seem to have gained the widest acceptance, and are followed here.[28]

The main official collections of law produced during the period between the 590s and the early eighth century are the *Lex Ribuaria* and the *Pactus legis Alamannorum*, both of which probably date from the reign of Chlothar II (613-629);[29] the latter was revised by the *dux* Lantfrid in the early eighth century. The earliest recension of the laws of the Bavarians may also have been produced at a broadly similar time, but this is more controversial, the only certainty being that its present recension was made in the 740s.[30] Although all the codes provide evidence for the nature and practice of kingship (discussed in Chapter 2), their provisions are, like those of the earlier *Pactus legis Salicae*, mostly concerned with the establishment of scales of fines and compensation payments, and with what are essentially local procedures; they do not therefore provide a great deal of information concerning the operation of the royal court and its officials.

Despite the fact that there are relatively few documents other than the *diplomata* which contain much evidence for royal government, the *regnum Francorum* is better served than any of the other kingdoms discussed in this book. This is partly a mater of quantity, but it is the range of the documentation which is of real significance: the strength of one type of source is often the weakness of another, and the spread available for the seventh-century Frankish world may allow a more certain insight into some aspects of its administrative arrangements than is possible for any other part of Europe at that time.

2

Kings and Queens

Merovingian kings have traditionally been written off as 'rois fainéants' from as early as the second quarter of the seventh century. To a large extent, this is a picture deliberately created by their Carolingian successors, under whose influence the history of the seventh century was recast in order to glorify the achievements of the Arnulfings at the expense of the Merovingians. Interpretations of this kind at first seem to be reinforced by the earlier sources, but critical use of the documents discussed in the previous chapter enables a different picture to be painted – one in which kings certainly remained more important than the Carolingian authors allowed, and in which at least some of them were remarkably active, despite the efforts of the various aristocratic factions to dominate them and limit their spheres of activity.

Kings as war leaders

The fact that late Merovingian kings do not appear to have been very active is in some measure a function of the lack of a detailed narrative source; this is already a problem in the first half of the seventh century, but it is exacerbated once Fredegar's original work ends in the 640s. The main result of this is that it is rarely that any light is cast on the military activities of the later Merovingians: this presents a striking contrast with the sixth century, for which the main source – Gregory of Tours' *Decem libri historiarum* – is particularly informative concerning kings as warriors. The lack is, however, only relative: the first section of the fourth book of Fredegar's *Chronicle*, which extends to 613, illustrates the involvement of Theudebert II, Theuderic II and Chlothar II in civil war almost as clearly as Gregory would have done.[1] Parts of the story also appear in the *Uita Columbani* and the *Liber historiae Francorum*.[2] The ensuing section of the *Chronicle* is perhaps its weakest (see Chapter 1), but relates to a period in which there may genuinely have been relatively little military activity. For the period after the mid-620s, when the *Chronicle* again becomes fuller, there are records of Dagobert's Wendish campaigns of 630/1,[3] and of an expedition Sigibert III led to quell a Thuringian rebellion in 639.[4] In the period covered by Fredegar's continuators, though, such references become increasingly rare.

13

The decline in the reporting of kings' military exploits may have been caused by a number of factors. First, neither Fredegar nor his continuators was writing with Gregory's moralistic purpose, and war leadership may simply have been less important to them – indeed, Fredegar states, perhaps approvingly, that Chlothar II was noteworthy for 'pietas' and 'patientia'.[5] Second, there was a degree of genuine impotence in this sphere of activity because many of the later seventh-century kings were, for a time at least, minors, incapable of leading military expeditions. However, it may also be the case that those who continued Fredegar's work may deliberately have sought to create the impression that the Merovingians were ineffective. Such a suspicion may perhaps be heightened by the fact that on the only two occasions between the 640s and 721 when the continuators do mention the royal leadership of military campaigns – the battles of Tertry (687) and Vinchy (716) – the Merovingians were defeated by forces loyal to the Pippinids.[6]

Kings and the law

However important war leadership may have been among the qualities required by a king, it was not the only possible sphere in which kings were expected to act and, if the seventh century produced relatively little evidence for their military activities, it provides at least as much as the sixth century for royal involvement with the law. Again, most of the material for the revision of old law codes and the issuing of new ones appears to come from the first part of the century and, in particular, the reign of Chlothar II, but there are hints that such activity was also important later.

In the tradition of their sixth-century predecessors, Childebert II and Chlothar II issued modifications to, and extensions of, the *Pactus legis Salicae*, in the form of capitularies. Childebert's *Decree*[7] was in fact issued in three annual sections, and shows the king making legal enactments at successive Marchfield gatherings of the nobles of his Austrasian kingdom.[8] Each year saw the addition of amendments and new provisions to the existing body of law, clearly issued in response to changing circumstances or specific cases. In this, as in the earlier capitularies, there are parallels with earlier Roman practices concerning the issuing of edicts and rescripts.[9] Chlothar II continued in the same tradition, issuing a *praeceptio* and an edict (the *Edict of Paris*, 614).[10]

The same tradition can also be detected in *Lex Ribuaria*, issued under Chlothar II or Dagobert I. It is a much longer document than any of the capitularies, and takes the form of a complete revision and emendation of the *Pactus legis Salicae*, intended to replace the earlier code in Austrasia.[11] Much of *Lex Ribuaria* is based on the *Pactus legis Salicae*, but it also contains provisions which must have originated as individual royal edicts in response to specific circumstances.[12] Although the dates of such provi-

14

sions are not known, there is no reason to suppose that the practice of issuing them had ceased before Chlothar's reign; nor, despite the lack of later examples, is there any certainty that the tradition was not continued throughout the seventh century. Indeed, that legislative activity was important later is clear from the first *Passio Leudegarii*, which states that Bishop Leodegar, presumably on the orders of Childeric II, restored the law.[13]

The issuing of *Lex Ribuaria* may have marked a new stage in the development of law in the *regnum Francorum*, since it is the first occasion upon which law code was promulgated for a specific area. The context for this may have been Chlothar II's assumption of rule in Austrasia in 613, or the establishment of his son, Dagobert, as sub-king in the area ten years later. In either case, the promulgation of the code could have had the political purpose of trying to obtain support in newly acquired lands:[14] by recognising that Austrasia had an identity of its own, the king of a united *regnum Francorum* may have been indicating that the local aristocracy would retain the influence it had enjoyed in a smaller kingdom. Similar reasoning may be suggested by the issuing of the *Pactus legis Alamannorum*, which appears to have occurred at much the same time, and – though considerably less certainly – the first version of the *Lex Baiuuariorum*.[15]

The same concern may lie behind the *Edict of Paris*, which contains provisions – adapted from Roman imperial legislation – aimed at ensuring that the local aristocracy would retain power (cap. 12). It has been thought that this was a concession to the nobles, enhancing their position, but, when the clause is placed in the context of the entire *Edict*, it is clear that it is merely one of a set of measures concerning the power and duties of the king and of other officials within the kingdom. The clause may, therefore, have served a political purpose by reassuring the regions of the newly united *regnum Francorum* that unity would not lead to domination by officials from the centre.[16] Much of the *Edict*, issued very shortly after the downfall of Brunhild, could be read as an assurance that the new régime would behave reasonably and, perhaps, not seek vengeance for the events of the civil war. It may be significant in this context that the chapter guaranteeing the use of local officials is paraphrased in the hagiographical account of Leodegar's renovation of the laws, which was undertaken at another time of civil war and regional rivalry.[17]

In terms of content, the law which seventh-century Frankish kings administered was heavily influenced by late Roman law. This was as much the case as it ever had been with regard to the *Pactus legis Salicae*, which may have been based on Roman provincial law,[18] but is also true of some of the newer provisions in *Lex Ribuaria* which, it has been suggested, was drafted by Burgundian lawyers who had a knowledge of the laws of the Roman provinces.[19] It is also clear that Roman imperial law continued to be known and used during the seventh century, since it appears to have been employed as a source for some of the provisions in Childebert II's decree and Chlothar II's *praeceptio*.[20] Further, there is good evidence that bishops continued to learn, and sometimes to apply, Roman law, almost throughout the seventh century. Perhaps the relatively large number of sixth- to eighth-century manuscripts containing the Theodosian Code and *Lex Romana Uisigothorum* should be seen in this context, while the practical use to which imperial law was put may be illustrated by its preservation in the same manuscripts as some of the earliest copies of the *Pactus legis Salicae*, the *Pactus legis Alamannorum* and the formularies.[21]

Images of kingship

Another way in which Roman traditions – even though the Roman past was becoming ever more distant – continued to influence kings, concerns the ways in which they sought to portray themselves, in particular on gold coins. During the sixth century, almost all 'barbarian' rulers continued to issue imitations of imperial gold coins, without changing the emperors' names. This suggests that the kings, by respecting the imperial prerogative of minting gold coinage, were indicating that they were still in a sense part of the empire.[22]

The first Frank to break the tradition was Theodebert I (534-48),[23] but none of his successors followed suit until towards the end of the sixth century.[24] The form which the change took was not, any more than it had been under Theodebert, the development of entirely new types of coin. Instead, imperial types continued to be imitated, but with the important alteration that the king's name replaced that of the emperor. The nature of this declaration of greater independence shows that, although in the post-Justinianic age there was no longer any question of subordination to the empire, Frankish kings still saw themselves as operating in a Roman tradition: what they were doing was to claim a form of parity with the emperor, by adopting the only imperial style of which they had experience.

The evidence for this is smaller than that for the Visigothic kingdom (discussed in Chapter 7), because the Merovingians did not exercise a monopoly over the production of gold coins. In fact, royal coins appear to have been produced in a very *ad hoc* fashion even in the Neustrian heartland of the *regnum Francorum*; and the Provençal mints, from which the largest number of royal gold coins are known, were not even under direct royal control.[25] The reasons for this are not entirely clear, nor are the mechanics of coin production in the Merovingian world,[26] but it appears that – whether deliberately or not – Frankish kings did less to exploit the propaganda potential of gold coinage than did their Visigothic counterparts.

In a similar way, Merovingian kings did not exploit the image-building possibilities offered by having a proper capital city. Although Clovis had long since established Paris as the capital of the *regnum Francorum*, it was not the fixed seat of administration in the way that Visigothic Toledo or Lombard Pavia were, and the Merovingian royal court remained itinerant.[27] This may be partly due to a weaker Roman urban tradition in much of northern Gaul (the heartland of Merovingian power) than in Spain and northern Italy, and it may be pertinent that of fifteen places at which *diplomata* are known to have been produced between 594 and 721, only four appear to have been major urban centres, the remainder being royal villas.[28] The lack of a fixed centre may be underlined by the fact that the original charters never employ the word 'palatium' to refer to a place, but always in the sense of the 'government' or 'court'.[29]

A more positive way in which the Merovingians may have sought to express their power was by the adoption of a royal throne, hitherto an imperial prerogative.[30] The precise date at which this was first done is not clear. The first king reported to have a throne is Chlothar II:[31] while there is no reason to doubt the fact that Chlothar did have a throne (though the evidence comes from the eighth-century *Uita Eligii*), it is not possible to be certain that it was that king rather than one of his immediate predecessors who was responsible for the innovation. Unfortunately, the evidence of the *Uita Eligii* is not entirely without ambiguity, since the term it uses is 'sella' rather than *solium* or *thronus*: in the Roman world, the *sella* was a type of seat used by the holders of high magistracies, rather than the emperors. The significance of this may be demonstrated by the fact that Isidore of Seville recorded that Leovigild was the first Visigothic king to use a 'thronus' (the imperial throne), even though Sidonius Apollinaris had earlier painted a portrait of Theoderic II sitting on a 'sella'.[32] However, the fact that Chlothar's *sella* was a lavish piece of furniture, highly decorated with gold and gems, suggests that it was in reality a *thronus*, since a *sella* would have been much more mundane.[33]

Both the coinage and the adoption of the throne show that kings no longer sought legitimation from the emperor. They did not, however, feel so secure in their positions that they were no longer interested in claiming the support of some greater power, and it may be that it is partly in this light that the commencement of evidence for a theocratic interpretation of their position should be understood.[34] Sixth-century kings had been seen as having a religious role, and had been likened to King David.[35] This continued in the seventh century: for example, the proceedings of the ecclesiastical council held at Clichy in 626 or 627 liken Chlothar II to David,[36] and the author of the *Liber historiae Francorum* compares Dagobert I to Solomon 'rex pacificus';[37] further, a letter addressed to Clovis II (which stands in the tradition of Remigius' letter to Clovis I and Pope Gregory I's to Brunhild[38]) suggests that David and Solomon were appropriate models for him to follow.[39] What does not appear to have happened before the seventh century, however, is that the power of kings was deemed to be God-given, or that kings were God's agents. In some of Marculf's formulae the king is seen as God's representative on earth,[40] while the

17

Bobbio Missal contains a 'missa pro principe', probably of Merovingian origin, which accepts the divine institution of kingship;[41] this is also apparent in the 626/7 Coincil of Clichy referred to earlier. Perhaps more telling is a small number of *diplomata* in which, alongside the conventional religious invocations, the king signs in the form, 'Chlothacharius in Christi nomine rex' (or similar wording).[42]

Although these developments are, like the adoption of new styles of coinage, in some ways less striking than in the Visigothic and Lombard kingdoms, and in the later Carolingian era, they are still significant. The fact that there is less evidence for the new style of monarchy in the Merovingian kingdom than in Spain and Italy may be a reflection of the nature of the sources, but it may also be a geniune indication that the Merovingians felt less need to engage in certain types of promotional activity. This could result from a number of factors, including the fact that their territory (unlike that of the Visigoths and Lombards) was not directly challenged by Byzantine aspirations. In addition, their title to rule may have been more secure than that of many of their contemporaries elsewhere in Europe, because the Merovingian family had earlier managed to establish a potent dynastic image and principle, which did not exist in any of the other major kingdoms; it is significant that the first Frankish anointing ceremony was carried out at the beginning of the rule of the first non-Merovingian king, Pippin III.

That specifically Merovingian kings remained crucial to the kingdom, even at times of the greatest internal commotion, is clear from the fact that each faction always sought to promote a Merovingian or to fabricate a link with the dynasty. Hence, for example, a later tradition claims that when Grimoald I, in the 650s, had Dagobert II replaced by his own son, Childebert, he tried to claim that Childebert had been adopted by Sigibert III;[43] in the 670s, Ebroin, in response to his opponents' championing of Childeric II and, later, Theuderic III, backed an otherwise unknown son of Chlothar III (Clovis)[44] – and at the same time, the Austrasians recalled Dagobert II from exile.[45] Much later, even Charles Martel promoted the Merovingians, Chlothar IV,[46] and Theuderic IV.

Rois fainéants?

Even as late as the early years of the eighth century, though, Merovingian kings were often more than figure-heads. It was argued earlier that the fact that little is known of kings as war leaders after the 640s may be a function of the nature of the sources rather than an accurate reflection of reality – though there is no way of proving the case either way. There is also little in the way of major new legislative activity after what in some senses may have amounted to something of a restructuring of the monarchy for the conditions of the newly unified *regnum Francorum* under Chlothar II and, perhaps, Dagobert I. However, it is clear from the laws, formulae and *placita* that kings remained active in the administration of their kingdom. Hence, for example, *Lex Ribuaria* suggests that the king's was the court of last resort,[47] and that various types of civil process, such as the adoption of children, could take place at the king's court.[48] The royal formulae in Marculf's work, some of which certainly date from the end of the sixth century and later, indicate that the king could become involved in a host of legal and administrative affairs, including such matters as the granting of privileges to individuals or institutions,[49] the supervision of the transfer of property between parents and their children,[50] the hearing of trials and giving of judgements,[51] and the receipt of petitions concerning taxation.[52]

It is in activities of this type that the later Merovingian kings can really be seen in at work, owing to the survival of some of the *diplomata* which were produced as a result of their activity. The fact that the number of surviving documents of this kind increases from about 650 onwards (that is, at the time at which many of the other sources described in Chapter 1 begin to become less reliable) does not in itself mark a dramatic shift in the function of the king, but is a reflection of the fact that the earlier documents were largely written on papyrus, rather than the more durable parchment which superseded it.[53] What is perhaps more significant, though, is that such a large number of *diplomata* have survived. Such documents tended to be kept (either physically or in copies) by their beneficiaries, which were mainly monastic: on account of the very poor survival of monastic archives, it is almost certain that the extant documents represent only a small proportion of the total number produced.

The first kind of *diploma* is the charter making a grant of property or privilege to an individual or institution. Documents of this type indicate that kings were seen, like their sixth-century predecessors, as dispensers of patronage:[54] they thereby increased the well-being of the recipients, while at the same time creating loyal supporters. A second kind of charter is the royal confirmation of gifts made by other men, including earlier kings. As most of the gifts which were confirmed in this way would have been legally valid without the king's intervention,[55] the existence of confirmatory documents demonstrates that it must have been thought that royal authority made a real difference to the security of such transactions.

The *placita* are an even more direct attestation to the continuing importance of the king, and show him active in the administration of justice. These documents are the product of a process which started with a suitor presenting a petition to the king to intervene in his case,[56] and ended with the king, in the presence of his courtiers, sitting in judgement; the verdict was then written down and sometimes witnessed by those present. This kind of activity is also apparent earlier in the seventh century, since Fredegar describes an assembly of Burgundian nobles in 616, at which 'he listened to all their just petitions and confirmed his concessions in writing'.[57] The king can, therefore, be seen actively participating in the administration of justice throughout the seventh century, and even into the eighth, the last of the *placita* dating from 716.[58] This indicates that, quite late in the Merovingian period, individuals and communities were still prepared to take their affairs to the royal tribunal, which must, therefore, have been perceived as having power, presumably including that required to enforce its decisions.

Such enforcement demanded that the king should act with the consent of a significant body of courtiers and aristocrats, and the lengthy witness lists to some of the *placita* provide a measure of the extent to which this was achieved,[59] as does the frequent employment of words with the prefix *con-* (*coniurant homines*; *consacramentales*).[60] Such consensus was achieved through assemblies of magnates, some of which, like the annual Marchfield gathering which produced the provisions recorded in the *Decree* of Childebert II, were regular, while others were called to deal with extraordinary affairs.[61] Hence, for example, it was an assembly of the Burgundians which requested that the *maior domus* Warnachar II should not be replaced in 626,[62] and another, which in 643 appointed Floachad as *maior*.[63]

For the author of the *Liber historiae Francorum*, this characteristic of ruling with the *optimates* was one of the prime kingly virtues, and was exemplified by Childebert III.[64] In the faction-riven territory ruled by the Merovingians, the problem with this was that acting with the consensus of one group of nobles could all too easily mean acting without the consent of another. It is possible that an example of this may be seen in the restriction of the area in which Childebert III himself operated during the later part of his reign since, as he was seen gradually to favour the Austrasian Pippinids, the Neustrians seem to have withdrawn their support.[65] Before Childeric is written off as having weakly given in to the Pippinids, however, it should be noted that right at the end of his reign he made judgements against them, as he had done earlier:[66] it may be partly for this reason that the author of the *Liber historiae Francorum* could be so favourably disposed towards him. Later, after the death of Pippin II (in 714), the Neustrians reasserted themselves and established Chilperic II as their king. Five *diplomata* survive from his reign, and among the courtiers associated with them are a number who are also known to have been at court during Pippin's ascendancy:[67] this may be evidence not only for the tenacity of the Neustrian aristocracy, but also for the power of kings to retain their support, even with such a dominant figure as Pippin in the background. Chilperic II's own power may not have been noted by any of the narrative sources for his reign, which are all later and unfavourably disposed towards the Merovingians, but news of it had reached England, where it was commented upon by the author of the anonymous *Uita Ceolfrithi*.[68]

2. Kings and Queens

Queens

Kings were not the only members of the royal family who were powerful, particularly during periods of royal minority, when the king's mother was a potent force in the government. Very little – not even their names – is known of the wives of kings after Theuderic III (died 691). This cannot be taken to mean that they were unimportant, however, since the nature of the narrative sources after the end of Fredegar's *Chronicle* in the early 640s means that they cannot be expected to depict the actions of queens – as was seen earlier, their references to kings are sketchy enough. There are occasional glimpses of queens in hagiographical material, and one seventh-century queen, Balthild, wife of Clovis II, was herself the subject of a *uita*, which is the main source for her career.[69] During royal minorities, queen mothers, as regents, are rather more visible, partly becuase they signed *diplomata* in association with their sons. For the earlier seventh century – the period covered by Fredegar's *Chronicle* – some evidence is available, but it does not approach the scale of that provided by Gregory of Tours for the sixth century: this is again more likely to be a function of the different types of source than of a radical change in the position of royal women.

During their time as kings' wives, queens were largely responsible for the domestic administration of the royal palace. This is suggested by the *Uita Balthildis*, which depicts the court as revolving around the queen who looked after the king's *entourage* and the young aristocrats associated with it; she was also in charge of the domestic servants. In addition, she supervised royal acts of charity, to such an extent that Clovis II placed an almoner under her control.[70] The latter aspect of Balthild's work may be over-emphasised, since the only evidence for it comes from the *Uita*, which was produced to glorify the queen, but it is likely to have some basis in truth, particularly since it is a type of activity which would not be surprising in a sixth-century context.

The influence of queens, whether as king's wives or mothers, is suggested by a record of the presence of Theuderic III's wife, Chrodechild, at the funeral of Bishop Audoin of Rouen,[71] and by the fact that Childeric's wife, Bilichild, and her mother (Childeric's aunt), Chimnechild, signed a charter confirming a grant of land made by Sigibert II (husband of Chimnechild, and father of Bilichild – see Table I for the relationships).[72] More concrete evidence for the kind of power queens wielded comes from the fact that Brunhild used her position not only to promote a number of bishops,[73] but also to depose Desiderius from the see of Vienne.[74] Similarly, Balthild was influential in the appointments of Erembert to Toulouse and Leodegar to Autun.[75] Patronage was also exercised in the case of secular offices, with Brunhild elevating Protadius to the patriciate and, later, to the position of *maior domus*.[76] It was not only individuals who benefited from queenly generosity, but also institutions: Balthild was a patron of

Chelles, Corbie, Luxeuil, S.-Denis and S.-Wandrille, among other places.[77] There is very little evidence for this kind of activity at the end of the seventh century, but that may again be largely a consequence of the nature of the sources, rather than of a reduction in the importance of queenly patronage. Such an interpretation may perhaps derive some strength from the fact that a charter recording a donation to S.-Denis by Theuderic III in 688 notes that the grant was made 'at the suggestion' of his queen, Chrotechild.[78]

One of the main problems which faced all queens is that their positions were extremely insecure. One reason for Balthild's patronage of the nunnery at Chelles may have been to ensure that, when her power as queen, and then queen mother, came to an end – as she must have assumed it would when Chlothar III married – she had a safe retreat. Certainly, she was later obliged to retire there,[79] but probably counted herself fortunate not to have met the fate of Brunhild who, having run out of Merovingians to dominate, found herself on the losing side in a civil war and was cruelly executed.[80] The only exception to this appears to have been Chimnechild, wife of Sigibert II, who signed a charter issued jointly by her nephew, Childeric II, and his wife (her daughter), Bilichild.[81]

As long as their sons did not marry, queens could hope to retain their position – or even enhance it. Both Fredegar and Jonas were quite clear that Brunhild specifically tried to prevent Theuderic II from marrying in order that her own position would not be challenged,[82] and was even prepared to incur the wrath of so great a holy man as Columbanus himself in her quest to retain her place at court.[83] If a queen succeeded in this, and particularly if her son was a minor for whom she was permitted to act as regent, her position could be greatly enhanced. This was not only the case in the instance of Brunhild and Theuderic II,[84] but also of Nantechild and Clovis II,[85] and Balthild and Chlothar III.[86] Confirmation of this comes from the *diplomata*: for example Nantechild and Balthild signed such documents alongside their sons,[87] as did Chrotechild alongside Clovis III.[88] Chimnechild, mother of Bilichild and aunt of Bilichild's husband, Childeric II, was also active in suggesting a donation, and in making another jointly with Childeric II,[89] as well as in the case (mentioned above) where her signature appears alongside those of Childeric and Bilichild. Queens were not, however, the only contenders for power in times of royal minorities, and sometimes, as in the case of Clovis II's early years, had to share responsibility with a non-royal member of the household:[90] it is to such men that the next chapter is devoted.

3

The King's Household: *domestici* and *maiores domus*

In order to govern, kings required supporters and assistants: in reality, the two categories largely overlap, since the support of members of the aristocracy was often obtained by giving them a role (whether secular or spiritual) in the administration of the kingdom. The secular officials, with whom this book is primarily concerned, are here divided into two broad categories for the purpose of discussion – though the division is to some extent artificial. The first consists of members of the king's own household, or personal staff, many of whom, it will be argued, were of relatively junior status within the court, and were subordinate to the *maior domus* – the 'greater man of the household'. The second category – discussed in the next chapter – were of higher status than most household officials, many of them being 'companions' (*comites*) of the king; not all of their number were permanently resident in the court, some of them acting as the king's representatives and agents in the regions of the realm.

The largest single source of evidence for seventh-century courtiers (of both types) is the material found in the *diplomata*. Some of the evidence they contain allows the functions of the courtiers who were involved in their production, or in the processes they record, to be understood in some detail. The tironian notes, which record some of the internal procedures of the palace administration, provide vital clues to the varying roles of a number of officials. Many other men were present, either as participants in the making of donations or finding of judgements, or as witnesses to the proceedings: although they are listed, often with their titles, nothing is known of their roles in the administration. The same limitation is often also visible in the narrative and hagiographical sources: since their authors were not primarily interested in the workings of the court, such officials as feature in their narratives either do so incidentally, or appear more on account of their political or high-profile, than their routine administrative, activities.

This point may be illustrated by an examination of the evidence for the *cubicularius*, a figure about whom little is known even in the sixth century when the greater detail provided by the narrative of Gregory of Tours sometimes allows a little more of the workings of the court to be seen.[1]

Hence, on the only occasion on which an official of this kind is seen in action in the seventh century (which, incidentally, provides the last securely dated reference to the title), Fredegar recounts that Berthar, *cubicularius*, was instrumental in capturing Theudebert II on behalf of Theuderic II in 612.[2] Theuderic II also employed a Berthar to track down Columbanus who had escaped from exile at Besançon in 609, but both sources for the incident describe him as 'comes'.[3]

The references to Berthar are of significance for the present enquiry in three ways. First, there is no reason to doubt that the same person was involved in both incidents, or to assume that his 'office' had changed in the three years between them. Although the latter is feasible, it is not impossible that a *cubicularius* could be loosely described in more general terms as a courtier, or 'companion' (*comes*) of the king. This kind of use of official titles is known from a wide geographical area in both the fifth-century western Empire and the fifth- and sixth-century 'barbarian' kingdoms, including those of the Franks,[4] and there is nothing to suggest that the seventh century was any different, particularly since the authors of the documents concerned were not interested in Berthar's position save in so far as he was an agent of the king. Second, neither of Berthar's reported activities is likely to reflect his routine functions within the royal household. Instead, they reflect a situation in which the king could call upon any trusted courtier, no matter what his 'office', to carry out sensitive missions: both incidents required men of discretion, capable of exercising force, but also of unquestionable loyalty to Theuderic – qualities which would be expected of men who operated so close to the person of the king as did his personal attendants.

That it was exceptional events which were recorded is the third point to arise from the evidence concerning seventh-century *cubicularii*. Given the proximity of such men to the king, it is perhaps not surprising that there is little evidence for their routine activities which were largely related to the internal workings of the court: in view of the nature of the sources, the closer to the king an office was, the less information might be expected. This does not mean that such positions were unimportant – they may, indeed, have been highly influential – but there is little way of being certain of the precise functions of their holders.

The only other possibly significant piece of evidence concerning seventh-century *cubicularii* is in the eighth-century *Uita Eligii* which states that the '*praepositus* of the palace' is 'commonly called *maior domus*',[5] and also refers to Erchinoald, who is usually known as a *maior domus*, as '*praepositus palatii*'.[6] The importance of this is that the *praepositus* could be the successor to the Roman *praepositus sacri cubiculi*, the head of the *cubicularii*.[7] If this equation is correct, it would suggest that Frankish *cubicularii* were subject to the *maior domus* – one of the most influential men at court (see below).

A similar poverty of evidence affects the *seniscalc*. The only type of source which records the existence of *seniscalces* in the seventh-century *regnum Francorum* is the *placita*, which record their participation in the royal tribunal.[8] There is so little evidence concerning them that even the significance of the fact that they always appear in pairs cannot be assessed.[9]

Financial officials

An almost equal lack of information surrounds officials connected with the treasury and financial administration. This may at first sight seem rather more strange, since men who collected taxes came into direct contact with the world outside the court, and their activities might, therefore, be more visible than those of their counterparts whose sphere of competence lay primarily within the court. There can be no doubt that, however much the basis of taxation altered during the Merovingian period,[10] taxes of various kinds remained an important source of revenue,[11] and the possession of treasure – whether gained by taxation, confiscation or tribute – remained an important element in a king's ability to retain power.[12] This is a recurrent theme in the *Liber historiae Francorum*,[13] and is also clear from Fredegar's account of the establishment of a separate Austrasian court for the young Sigibert III, which records that the prince was given 'sufficient' treasure.[14]

The increasing number of grants of immunity meant that, as the seventh century advanced, there may have been less scope for royal tax collectors to come into direct contact with the population at large, and bishops, rather than courtiers, may have acted as collectors in at least some cases.[15] None of these developments, however, either singly or together, was enough to mean that the king no longer needed agents to collect taxes and administer the royal treasure, and the continued existence of such men is, in general terms, attested by *Lex Ribuaria*, which seeks to regulate the activities of financial officials; and, later in the century, by a charter confirming certain tax exemptions for the abbey of S.-Denis.[16] The lack of evidence concerning local treasury officials therefore again raises issues relating to the nature of the sources: the law codes only deal in generalities, rarely mentioning any specific type of governmental agent, and even the charters rarely have cause to be more specific. The concerns of the narrative sources are political – unless a tax aroused particular hostility, it would be unlikely to be mentioned, particularly given the extreme brevity of all the documents involved, and the same is largely true of the hagiographical literature.

No matter how it was raised, the substantial body of treasure owned by kings had to be managed. Here, although the existence of some officials can be demonstrated, few of their actual functions can be seen largely because, like the *cubicularii* and *seniscalces*, they probably operated largely within the court, near to the person of the king. Such men –

described as 'thesaurarii' – were sent by Dagobert I to seize Charibert of Aquitaine's treasure after his death.[17] There are a few other references to *thesaurarii*, but they are all uninformative as to their precise functions.[18] Desiderius, for example, was a *thesaurarius* of Dagobert I before he became bishop of Cahors, but all we know of his role is that, like any other courtier, he was able to provide petitioners with access to the king;[19] and the young Eligius (later bishop of Noyon) was put in the care of Chlothar II's *thesaurarius*, Bobo, who resided at court.[20]

In the sixth century, there is evidence for the existence of another type of treasury official, the *camerarius*, but the title is not attested after the end of the period covered by the *Decem libri historiarum* of Gregory of Tours.[21] It is not possible to be certain of the significance of this. For the sixth century, where the evidence for treasury officials is a little (though not much) greater, it has been possible to suggest that the *thesaurarii* were subordinate to the *camerarii*, either within the court or placed in the regions of the *regnum Francorum*; it has equally been possibly to envisage a situation in which the words *thesaurarius* and *camerarius* were synonymous, the former being a simple description, and the latter an official title.[22] The total absence of evidence for *camerarii* – even in the *diplomata*, where neither they nor *thesaurarii* feature in the lists of courtiers[23] – means that it is impossible to cast further light on the question. There is, in addition, no reason to assume that there may not have been a degree of evolution in the administration of the court during the seventh century.

Domestici

Another kind of official about whom relatively little is known – and for the same reasons – is the *domesticus*. There is evidence that sixth-century *domestici* were the personal attendants of members of the royal household, and that the term could be a generic description of such a position, rather than the designation of an 'office' with a specific set of functions.[24] In the seventh century there is a little more evidence, which, while generally confirming some of the trends observed in the earlier period, may cast additional light on some aspects of the position of *domestici*.

Perhaps the first point to be noted is that there could be more than one *domesticus* at court at the same time, as is demonstrated by Marculf's formula for a *placitum* and by several extant *placita*.[25] The same documents also indicate the prestige of *domestici*, since they formed part of the royal tribunal;[26] and their ability to act as judges is shown by a provision in *Lex Ribuaria*, in which they appear in a list of men who were not to accept bribes when sitting in judgement.[27] The importance of *domestici* is, finally, underlined by the fact that they could, on occasion, sign charters as witnesses.[28]

Valuable though the evidence of the *diplomata* is, it does not reflect anything of the specific functions of *domestici*. However, two of the formulae of Marculf suggest that the bearers of the title were in charge of the administration of royal palaces and villas,[29] and the same may be implied by the *Uita Eligii*, which describes the way in which *domestici* and *duces* were able to expropriate royal estates.[30] This would appear to be consistent with the later evidence from the Carolingian period, in which *domestici* were in charge of the royal fisc.[31]

Although the participation of *domestici* in the management of villas is clear, there are also indications that they could fulfil other duties, and it is again the *diplomata* which provide the evidence. In 688, Vulfoleac appears at the court of Theuderic III, involved in the production of a charter in a way usually associated with referendaries.[32] A few years later, in 692/3, he appears at the court of Clovis III, in a list of four referendaries,[33] and in 695, in Childebert III's court, he was again involved in the production of a charter in a way usually associated with a referendary.[34] In 697, though, he appears with the title of 'domesticus',[35] but later in the same year, he was once again involved in the production of a *diploma*.[36] It is possible that the position of Vulfoleac at court changed more than once, but it is perhaps improbable that such was in fact the case.[37] This may indicate that the term *domesticus* designated a general status within the court – perhaps simply that of a household official – rather than a specific office, and that referendaries were a special type of *domesticus*: in the same way, some *domestici*, could have been involved in estate administration. If this interpretation is correct, it is possible that *cubicularii*, *seniscalces*, and the financial officials discussed earlier could also have been *domestici* with more specific offices. It is also possible (perhaps even probable) that all such men were subject to the *maior domus* – the greater man of the palace.

Referendaries and documents

The importance of the royal writing office cannot be over estimated, particularly since the possession of a written document was the main means of proof in any legal case.[38] The point may be underlined by the fact that even so laconic a commentator as Fredegar mentioned on three separate occasions that kings had confirmed their actions in writing.[39] In such a culture, the possession of documents specifically emanating from the king's court is likely to have carried special weight.

The processes whereby royal documents were produced are revealed by a number of formulae within the *diplomata* themselves (sometimes in the tironian notes), and are relatively well understood. There are three main formulae: '*n*. recognouit', '*n*. optolit' and 'bene ualiat'. The *recognouit* and *optolit* formulae are alternatives, the former recording that the document was checked and verified by the person named,[40] the latter that the named official presented the document to the king for him to check and sign (*subscribere*).[41] Both these formulae have a variant in which the word *iussus* is incorporated, indicating that the courtier who carried out the actions described had been commanded to do so by a third party (who is sometimes named in the tironian notes[42]). The *bene ualiat* formula is an instruction that the document should be sealed, and was often covered by the seal since its significance was transient.[43]

The final sealing of documents was carried out by a referendary: the implication of this is that the 'bene ualiat' command was an instruction to the holder of that office, as also may be two more explicit commands that documents should be sealed.[44] The evidence for the involvement of referendaries in this sphere of activity is particularly impressive, a number of earlier, contemporary and later hagiographical sources stating that referendaries were in charge of the king's ring – which was a kind of symbol of their office – and used it for the sealing or confirmation of royal acts.[45]

Some of the hagiographical literature also indicates that referendaries were in some sense responsible for the actual compilation of the documents, and the *diplomata* suggest that the men who verified them or presented them to the king were usually referendaries.[46] The evidence for this is not as plentiful as might be anticipated, since the name which appears in the *recognouit* and *optolit* formulae is often not associated with a title. In fact, there are only two occasions on which it can be positively demonstrated that the official concerned was a referendary: in one case, Dado, identified as referendary in the text of a charter, presented the same document to the king;[47] and in another, Walderamn appears without a title in the *recognouit* formula, but is named as a referendary in the body of the document, this time a *placitum*.[48]

By analogy with earlier Roman practice, it would appear that the full sequence of events in the production of a *diploma* was that the king's wish was transmitted to the writing office by the referendary, who probably formulated the wording of the non-formulaic parts of the document. Once the *diploma* had been written, it was given to the referendary, who checked it to ensure that it accurately reflected the king's will, and/or presented it to the king for his subscription, after which the referendary sealed it and transmitted its contents to the relevant parties.[49]

From this, it has usually been concluded that the referendary was the head of the writing office, or royal chancellor.[50] Close examination of the evidence however, suggests that such was not the case, since it is clear that there could be more than one referendary in existence at a single king's court at the same time: one *placitum* lists no fewer than four such men.[51] This evidence is paralleled by that from the sixth-century eastern Empire, in which Justinian at one stage ordered a reduction in the number of referendaries from fifteen to eight.[52]

This is of some significance, since a small number of *diplomata* bear the phrase '*x* recognouit ad uicem *y*'.[53] Combined with the late date (697 and later) of the documents concerned, this has led to the suggestion that the position of the referendary was being undermined and that other men were taking over his function.[54] However, since more than one referendary could exist at the same time, it may be more likely that all that is being reflected is a situation in which the referendary who checked the final document was for some reason not the same as the one who had earlier conveyed the king's decision to the writing office. The fact that these instances only appear to occur late in the Merovingian period is not necessarily significant given the uneven chronological distribution of surviving examples; in addition, not all the post-697 *diplomata* bear the *ad uicem* formula, indicating that the normal procedures continued to be used. The only other piece of evidence which could support the idea of an undermining of the referendary's position is that in one case the person who verified the document was not a referendary, but was the future king, Dagobert III.[55] This is paralleled by an earlier instance in which Childeric II verified one of his own documents:[56] while such practices may have been unusual, it is not difficult to imagine circumstances which could occasionally have given rise to them, without envisaging a general diminution of the referendary's role.

The existence of more than one referendary at a time not only makes it almost impossible to see holders of the office as the chiefs of the writing office, but may also render it more likely that they were not of the highest rank within the court – which perhaps lends weight to the suggestion made earlier that they could have been *domestici*. This idea is further strengthened by the hagiographical evidence, which indicates that referendaries were often young men, near the beginning of their careers.[57] This does not mean that referendaries were unimportant: they were responsible for transmitting the king's will in unwritten form, which was necessarily more fluid, and could be altered (deliberately or otherwise) more easily, than completed documents.[58] By extension of this, referendaries could be used as confidential agents, as when Chlothar II sent his referendary Chadoind as an envoy to Brunhild.[59] A more unusual incident involving the same man saw him leading an army against the Gascons:[60] the explanation for this is likely to be that anyone who was a competent warrior might, no matter what his official position, find himself leading an army.

It is, however, probable that the referendary was chiefly involved with the transmission of the king's wishes to third parties, whether within the royal writing office or to other courtiers or agents. The closeness of the relationship with the writing office may be confirmed by the case of Aglybert, who signed a charter on 4 September 677 with the title of *notarius*, but, eleven days later, appears (with no title) in the *recognouit* formula of another document.[61] As the chances of two documents so neatly framing the date of an official's move from one office to another are remote, it is possible that a referendary was a special form of notary. This again has some parallels in the Roman world, where referendaries were drawn from the ranks of the *tribuni et notarii*, and are sometimes referred to as 'tribuni notarii et referendarii'.[62]

A final piece of imperial evidence which may be of significance is that newly created referendaries were informed of their appointment by the *praepositus sacri cubiculi*.[63] This may not only confirm the subordinate position of referendaries, but also cast light on their relationship with the *maior domus*, since, according to the eighth-century *Uita Eligii*,[64] the *praepositus* and the *maior* were one and the same. If this is correct, it suggests that the *maior domus* was in some sense the superior of the referendaries (as, probably, of all the other *domestici*). The implications of this are of the greatest importance, since they bear on a number of early eighth-century *diplomata* in which *maiores* appear to have performed some of the functions usually associated with referendaries. This has been understood to indicate that *maiores* were arrogating power to themselves and, by taking over aspects of document production, weakening the position not only of the writing office, but also of the king. Close examination of the evidence, however, may indicate that there are other possible interpretations.

In 717, it is recorded in the text of a charter in favour of S.- Denis that the *maior domus*, Ragamfred, requested the king to make the grant. At the end of the same document, he is recorded as having presented the document to the king to be subscribed and, in the tironian notes, appears to have subscribed the document himself.[65] Here, Ragamfred seems not only to have intervened in the referendary's sphere, but also to have interfered in the process of giving legal effect to the document, which was the king's prerogative. There is, however, a relatively innocent explanation for this: since the grant was being made at the request of Ragamfred, it is not altogether surprising that he should have taken a personal interest in the production of the document recording its provisions.

The case is not, however, entirely isolated, since there are two other documents from Chilperic II's reign (from which a total of ten survives) in whose production Ragamfred seems to have taken a hand. In one, the tironian notes are not fully legible, and his role is unclear, though it is possible that he was responsible for issuing some kind of instruction concerning one of the stages of its production.[66] In the other, the tironian notes contain the phrase 'per anolo Ragamfridi'.[67] That phrase is echoed in two other charters, one issued a mere eleven days later and the other from six years earlier: in the first, the name concerned may again be that of Ragamfred (though the reading is uncertain),[68] while in the latter it is that of the Pippinid *maior*, Grimoald II.[69] Before concluding that this is firm evidence for the undermining of the referendary's position by *maiores*,[70] another feature of the documents concerned may be observed – namely, that the same official (Actulius) was involved in the procedures for their authentication. This is intriguing, and, since Actulius is otherwise unattested, its significance cannot be ascertained. It may be, though, that the intervention of the *maior* in the sealing of the three documents could be related to some peculiarity in his position. In addition, if it is correct to see referendaries as the subordinates of *maiores*, there is perhaps less need to see the involvement of *maiores* in document production as suspicious – particularly if, as has been attempted here, the evidence is not seen against a pre-conditioned interpretation derived from later Arnulfing propaganda concerning the rise of *maiores*.

The final question relating to the production of royal documents concerns the actual writing of them. It is possible that in some cases this was performed by a referendary, but there is no certain evidence for it, and, given that, in the Empire, the positions of *magister scriniorum* (and, therefore, the notaries) and referendary were different,[71] it may be unlikely that it was a regular occurrence. In fact, the officials of the writing office proper are very rarely seen, and little can be deduced concerning them. In only two instances concerning whose authenticity there is little doubt are the writers named: one was written by Syggolen, and another by Fredebert, for neither of whom a title is given.[72] The only explicit reference to a notary in the royal *diplomata* comes when Aglybert signed a charter of Theuderic III as *notarius*.[73] It is possible that most royal documents were written by *notarii*, but, as in the Roman world, such men are almost invisible.[74] Another kind of official who could be involved in the writing of documents was the *cancellarius*, but there is very little contemporary evidence for such men within the royal court, and none which unequivocally points to a role in the production of *diplomata*[75] – though such evidence does exist for the Carolingian period.[76]

*

It has been argued above that the procedures by which royal documents were created had evolved from those adopted in the Roman period and in the contemporary eastern Empire. Such borrowings are also apparent in the forms of the documents themselves. The opening formulae of the *placita*, for example, are adapted from Roman models:[77] there are also similarities both between the opening of Chlothar II's edict and a Novel of Valentinian III,[78] and between other sections of the edict and further imperial documents.[79] In general, though, while the outward form of the *diplomata*, and many of the procedures for their production were borrowed from the central, imperial, administration, the main part of the text is more akin to Roman provincial documents.[80]

The script in which the original Frankish documents are written also bears witness to borrowings from the Roman world. The use of tironian notes is a clear indication not only of the survival of quite a high degree of education,[81] but also of the transmission to the Franks of what had always been specialist knowledge.[82] The cursive script in which the main section of each document is written is also Roman, but it is not the hand which

31

was used by the central, imperial, chancery. In 367, Valentinian I had issued a rescript insisting on a distinction between the script of the imperial chancery and that used by writers in the offices of imperial officials, whether in central or provincial administration.[83] It is not clear why it was the latter which the Merovingians imitated: it may be a reflection of the fact that the early Merovingians, who had presumably set the trend which their successors followed, did not see themselves as fully the equals of the emperors; but it could simply be that most of the documents which they found within the territories they controlled were not written in the imperial style.[84]

Maiores domus

It has already been suggested that the *maior domus* was in some sense in charge of the referendaries, and that he was the chief *domesticus* – in other words, head of the royal household and its officials. Any attempt to clarify the formal role of the *maiores* is complicated by the fact that many of the men who held the position of *maior* were extremely powerful in their own right, and used their position for their own advantage. The fact that, during the seventh century, there were attempts to make the office of *maior* hereditary, and, more especially, that it was one of the major dynasties of *maiores* (the Arnulfings) which eventually toppled the Merovingians from power, renders it all the more difficult to disentangle those elements of the authority wielded by *maiores* which derived from their office, and those which resulted from their power as members of the landed aristocracy. This distinction is of importance, since it affects understanding of the way in which the royal court worked, as well as having implications for the ways in which power was brokered within the kingdom. The politics of the late Merovingian period may form a background against which the *maiores* and, indeed, the entire royal government, operated; but it is important that the evidence concerning the actual administrative function of the *maiores* should be taken on its own terms, rather than as necessarily fitting the model of increasing dominance provided by the sources of the late eighth and ninth century. A further characteristic of the sources is that the extant *diplomata* – from which much of the detailed evidence for the functions of *maiores* within the palace is derived – almost all relate to Neustria rather than to Burgundy or Austrasia, thus rendering comparison between the three areas uncertain.

During the sixth century, while the kingdom was split between a number of rulers, each king had his own court and, therefore, his own *maior*, who acted as the head of the palatine administration.[85] It is clear that this continued to be the case, for the first *Passio* of Leodegar states that, when Ebroin was *maior*, he ruled the palace – a phrase identical to that used of Servilio by Fortunatus in the sixth century.[86] However, there was also a degree of change as the government adapted itself to the new circumstances imposed by a unified kingdom: the result was that there was sometimes more than one *maior* in existence at a time, each being responsible to the same king for a different one of the three main constituent parts of the kingdom – Burgundy, Austrasia and Neustria.

This change may be reflected in the fact that *maiores* feature to a greater extent in Fredegar's work than in that of Gregory of Tours, particularly since Fredegar seems to have been especially well informed concerning Burgundy, a *Teilreich* which no longer had its own king in the seventh century. According to Fredegar, when Chlothar II reunited the kingdom in 613, he made Warnachar II *maior* in Burgundy, and pledged that Warnachar would remain in that position for the rest of his life.[87] This has been interpreted as marking a significant increase in the power of the *maior*, and as giving him the authority to rule in the king's absence, leading to a weakening of specifically royal power in the area.[88] While the former suggestion may be correct, the latter does not necessarily follow: it would seem at least as likely that the appointment of a separate *maior* was intended to strengthen the authority of the king in the area by ensuring that there was a high-ranking official with both good local connections and immediate access to the king.[89] This suggestion may derive strength from the fact that, when Warnachar died, the Burgundian aristocrats requested that the king should not replace him, but should deal with them directly.[90] That request reveals that the *maior* stood between the king and the nobility, representing each side to the other.[91]

The crucial question was that of access to the king which, as probable successor to the imperial *praepositus sacri cubiculi*,[92] the *maior* controlled. What was required was a man of integrity, who was trusted by both sides. In itself, this was not new in the seventh century, for a little earlier Chrodoin is reputed to have declined the position of *maior* of Childebert II on the grounds that he was too closely related to members of the Austrasian aristocracy to deal with them impartially, and that they would not have had confidence in him.[93] What may be true, though, is that this aspect of the *maior*'s function became more important in periods when the kingdom was unified and the king was necessarily more distant from some of his subjects.[94]

The same development can be seen in the position of *maiores* in Austrasia. Although Austrasia came, under Chlothar II, to have its own sub-king in the person of Dagobert I, he was only a minor: the *maior* – Pippin I – appointed to his court therefore had almost as much freedom of action as his Burgundian counterpart.[95] This may not mean that royal authority was weakened – the *maior* may in fact have been largely responsible for keeping it ever-present at the centre of affairs during a period when the king was unable to govern on his own.[96] Once Dagobert came to rule the entire *regnum*, Pippin's influence was probably greatly diminished, and he may have ceased to be Austrasian *maior* for a time.[97]

Fredegar's account of the events surrounding Dagobert's accession to full power is difficult to understand in detail, and has occasioned debate, but, however it is interpreted, it is clear that Pippin was regarded as in some sense a representative of the Austrasian aristocracy as much as a royal servant.[98]

In Neustria, the situation was rather different since Chlothar II himself was based there. It is perhaps for that reason that little is known of *maiores domus* in the Neustrian *Teilreich* during his reign, and the same may be true of the period when Dagobert I was king there in his own right. On Dagobert's death, however, Aega was put in charge of the young Clovis II, and ruled the palace and kingdom with Nantechild, the queen mother.[99] The appointment of Aega as co-regent does not necessarily have to be solely related to the fact that he was *maior domus*, since he was earlier described as Dagobert's most trusted advisor.[100]

The three cases which have been examined above are all instances of the way in which *maiores* reacted to royal distance or minority: it may be the facts of distance and minority which account for the apparent increase in the strength of *maiores* in the early seventh century. There are here some parallels with the position of *praepositi sacri cubiculi* in the eastern Empire. Like *maiores* they controlled access to the ruler and, also like them, their power was enhanced by weak sovereigns: further, the gain in power was not permanent, for, on the arrival of a stronger emperor, their position was diminished again.[101]

At the end of his *Chronicle*, Fredegar provides accounts of two incidents concerning *maiores* which reflect aspects of their position during the 640s. First, on the death of Pippin I, his son, Grimoald I, tried to succeed him as *maior*.[102] He was not immediately successful, a certain Otto receiving the position instead. However, only about a year later Grimoald had Otto murdered and thereby managed to become *maior*.[103] This suggests that the position of *maior domus* was important enough to be worth fighting over, but that does not necessarily mean that its power had dramatically increased. It is also clear that Grimoald was a strong man in his own right, otherwise he could not have engineered Otto's downfall: this makes interpretation of Grimoald's later career as *maior* difficult since it is almost impossible to determine how much of his power derived from his family's position as leading aristocrats in Austrasia, and how much from his tenure of the office of *maior*.[104] Finally, the events surrounding Otto's tenure of the position demonstrate that the *maior* was not so powerful that he could operate without the consent of the king and/or the nobility: Otto cannot have acted alone, which means that there is likely to have been a sizeable faction opposed to Grimoald.

The same is also clear from the second case Fredegar reports from the early 640s, when Nantechild, as queen mother, appointed Floachad *maior domus* in Burgundy.[105] Fredegar's account is explicit on the fact that the appointment was made with the consent of the Burgundians. This cannot be taken as an indication of royal weakness, since it stands in the tradition of Chrodoin's suggested appointment in the sixth century, and of the events surrounding the lack of replacement for Warnachar II earlier in the seventh. What it does reflect is the desirability – from the king's point of view as much as from that of the aristocracy – that the courtier who had the easiest access to the king should be acceptable to both sides. It might even be possible to see the element of consensus as a strength – rulers who are in fear for their own position often become more autocratic rather than listening to the opinions of other great men.

Moving to the second half of the seventh century, *maiores* have an even higher profile. Attempts to understand the true import of this must, however, take into account the fact that there is a significant change in the nature of the sources at that point. Fredegar's own *Chronicle* – the source for almost all the preceding discussion – ends in 642: not only is it not succeeded by another narrative source of comparable detail, but such narratives as do exist were all written later and mainly from a pro-Arnulfing standpoint. The fact that the change in the sources coincides with a period during which royal minorities were relatively frequent may conspire to create an impression that *maiores* were routinely much more powerful than they had been earlier, while the inevitable weakness of child kings as individuals allowed greater freedom for factionalism (which attends most royal courts) to get out of hand. As powerful men, both in their own right and by virtue of their position, *maiores* were able to exploit such periods of relative power vacuum for their own ends. Even without bias, the sources – whether of narrative type or hagiographical – would be likely to give prominence both to such high-profile events, and to those who participated in them.

It may be significant that little is known of the activities of *maiores* during the late 640s and early 650s – that is, during the years when Clovis II and Sigibert III were at the peak of their power. This could be mere coincidence, but the fact that Grimoald I re-emerges as a dominant force in Austrasia after Sigibert's death may indicate that a powerful king was still able to keep his *maior* – even a forceful character like Grimoald – under control: had Grimoald's activities been unfettered during the period, they would perhaps not have been omitted by the pro-Arnulfing continuators of Fredegar's *Chronicle*.

However that may be, when Sigibert died and was succeeded by his young son, Dagobert II, Grimoald exploited the renewed relative weakness of the king in order to have him exiled and to set up his own son, Childebert, in his place.[106] Even this time, though, Grimoald's strength was not so great that he could not be challenged, for it was not long before he was executed[107] – though Childebert remained king until 662.

It is during the same period that Ebroin – one of the most disruptive forces in the *regnum Francorum* during the third quarter of the seventh century – first appears in the record, as *maior* at the court of the young

Neustrian king, Chlothar III. During Chlothar's minority, his mother, Balthild, was regent; once he came of age, she was forced into retirement. The reasons for this are not entirely clear, but one contemporary source indicates that it was Ebroin's work.[108] Despite this, Ebroin's precise function in the royal administration is not readily apparent during the ensuing years, his real rise to prominence not occurring until after Chlothar's death in 673. At that point his activities became of greater interest to the authors of the narrative and hagiographical sources which relate to the period, since he abused his position to promote the claims of Chlothar's brother, Theuderic III. The ensuing civil conflict which, for the first time, severely disrupted and weakened royal authority,[109] was not so much a result of the power of the *maior domus* as such, but a consequence of the fact that the holder of the office was the leader of a particular faction of aristocrats and, indeed, one which may have been split within itself.[110] (It is significant that even in this chaotic period every faction had its own pretender to the throne – Theuderic III, Clovis (III) and the restored Dagobert II.[111])

What is perhaps most striking about the events of the 670s is that they appear to have been in some measure transient: once Theuderic III was confirmed as Neustrian king, he seems to have been able to maintain a balance between the factions for much of the time, and even managed to gain control of Austrasia after the restored Dagobert II was murdered in 679 (an event which may suggest that Dagobert himself was powerful enough to excite opposition[112]). During this period, from which a number of royal *diplomata* survive, *maiores* appear much less prominently in the sources, perhaps indicating that their position as courtiers (as opposed to factional leaders) was not vastly more powerful than it had been earlier, at least when the king was old enough to rule in his own right. This does not mean that factional politics had come to an end – the Neustrian *maior*, Waratto, was displaced for a time by his son, Ghislemar[113] – but that they assumed less dramatic proportions when there was a strong king.

In 688 – often in the past seen as a turning point in the rise of the power of *maiores* and of the Arnulfings in particular – *maiores* again came to prominence when Pippin II, *maior* of Austrasia, defeated Waratto's successor in Neustria, Berchar, at the Battle of Tertry.[114] Once more, though, it is necessary to try to distinguish between Pippin's power as a landed magnate and that which he derived from his position as *maior*, as well as between the patchy evidence of the contemporary documents and the seductive narrative of the later pro-Carolingian sources. In fact, it seems that both before and after Tertry it was Pippin's position as land holder and leader of a faction, at least as much as that of a royal official, which gave him much of his authority[115] – hence, perhaps, the fact that after Tertry he preferred to establish other *maiores* in Neustria, while remaining near his own sectional power base in Austrasia.[116] The same point is also suggested by the fact that analysis of the signatories to royal charters in the period after 688 has shown that Pippin did not exploit his position of influence by packing the Neustrian court with his Austrasian followers, but by persuading individual Neustrian magnates to support his faction, and, at the same time, by dispensing patronage to monasteries and bishoprics in Neustria.[117] It is also clear that Pippin did not enjoy unlimited freedom of action, since two surviving documents of Childebert III's reign show the King making judgements against his family.[118]

When Pippin II died in 714, there was no obvious successor within the Arnulfing dynasty owing to the murder of Pippin's son, Grimoald II.[119] The Neustrian élite was not slow to exploit this dynastic weakness, refusing to accept the idea of having a child, Theudoald, as *maior*, invading Austrasia, and establishing their own choice, Ragamfred, as *maior*.[120] It was only three years later, when Charles Martel had secured his position as leader of the Pippinids, that the faction was again able to assert itself in Neustria, setting up Chlothar IV as a rival to Chilperic II. After the deaths of Chlothar and Chilperic, when Theuderic IV was made king, Charles, unlike Pippin II, ensured that the royal court was filled with his own supporters.[121] Hence, from the end of Chilperic II's reign, the Pippinids had a large degree of mastery over the court, and the period of effective rule by members of the Merovingian dynasty was over. It was, however, only with the advent of Charles Martel that Pippinid dominance of the office of *maior domus* was fully realised: this may be reflected by the fact that it was during Charles Martel's ascendancy, rather than earlier, that there was a single *maior* for the entire kingdom.

The narrative sources upon which much of the foregoing discussion is based are extremely laconic: only ten chapters of the continuation of Fredegar's *Chronicle* cover the eight decades from Clovis II to Chilperic II, and the *Liber historiae Francorum* treats the period in similarly small compass. Even leaving aside the fact that the authors of both texts had political reasons for writing, it would be scarcely surprising if a large proportion of their brief narratives were not devoted to the high-profile factional activities of the leading men of the kingdom; and it is unrealistic to expect that they should have been interested in recording administrative arrangements, which were routine and unremarkable to contemporaries. When the political aims of the authors are added, the emphasis placed on *maiores* becomes even more explicable, since Fredegar's continuators were anxious to demonstrate the rise to power of the Pippinids, and the author of the *Liber historiae Francorum* to present a pro-Neustrian account of the same events: for both, the activities of *maiores*, whether Pippinids or their opponents, were equally important. As a result of this, the narrative provided by both sources is restricted almost entirely to the years when faction-fighting was at its worst, and virtually nothing is seen either of periods of relative peace, or of the normal activities of *maiores* (or, for that matter, of other officials); similar problems beset the use of the hagiographical sources. It is vital not only to recognise the extreme selectivity of the picture presented by all these documents, but also to consider whether the impression it creates may be false. Only if this is done can the evidence of the *diplomata* be assessed on its own terms.

One aspect of the position of *maiores* which has already be touched upon – that of their importance during royal minorities – is confirmed by the *diplomata*. Some royal documents record that they were drawn up on the orders of the *maior domus*. This could be interpreted as evidence that *maiores* came to usurp the royal prerogative of document production (as Charles Martel may have done later in the eighth century), but closer examination may suggest that such is unlikely to have been the case. Of the six documents issued between 677 and 721 which contain (in the tironian notes) the phrase 'ordinante *n*. maiore domus', only one was certainly produced at a period when the king was not a minor.[122] It would not be unreasonable for a *maior*, as the man in charge of the palace – whether or not he was formally acting as regent – to authorise the production of documents at times when the king was unable to do so, particularly if, as suggested in the discussion of referendaries, he normally had some authority over the officials who were responsible for the content of royal documents. The circumstances surrounding the one document produced in this way while the king was old enough to rule in his own right are obscure, but a single document is perhaps not enough upon which to build a case for an extension of the power of *maiores*, particularly since there are other possible explanations, including the fact that donation being recorded was made partly at the suggestion of the *maior* concerned, Berchar.

The only other information concerning the functions of *maiores* which is given by the *diplomata* is the relatively obvious fact that they formed part of the royal tribunal.[123] From outside the *diplomata* there is little evidence, though what there is tends to confirm the generalisations made at the start of the discussion of *maiores*. Hence, for example, Desiderius of Cahors asked Grimoald I to present Abbot Lupus to Sigibert III,[124] Erchinoald received Fursey and his followers when they first arrived at the royal court,[125] and Wulfoald received Praeiectus when he attended court.[126] It was not only persons, but also petitions, which could be presented to the king *via* the *maior domus*: one of Marculf's formulae indicates that requests for the commutation of taxes should be sent to the king and the *maior*.[127] Further, *maiores* were clearly in a position to influence the king's decisions in such matters, for, when the Lombards sought a remission of tribute in 617 they sent presents to Warnachar, Gundeland and Chuc, respectively *maiores* of Burgundy, Austrasia and Neustria.[128] On yet other occasions, *maiores* can be seen acting on behalf of the king in ways which are less easy to classify, as when Pippin I supervised the division of Dagobert I's treasure after the king's death,[129] or when Waratto was sent to inspect a title deed at S.-Wandrille.[130]

3. The King's Household: domestici and maiores domus

Such commissions as the last two could probably have been entrusted to any senior and trusted courtier, irrespective of his precise office. It may, in fact, be possible to view many of the activities of courtiers in a similar light, and to suggest that the Merovingian palace was much less bureaucratic than it may at first appear. Many members of the royal household had specific titles which indicated particular areas of responsibility, but the tenure of an 'office' did not necessarily preclude activity in other spheres of government on occasion. Something of this has already been suggested in earlier sections of this chapter, particularly that concerning the relationship between the referendary and the *maior domus*. This kind of interpretation is also consistent what is known of Merovingian government in the sixth century – long before the rise of *maiores* to prominence.

For all the continuity from earlier in the Merovingian period, however, there was clearly a degree of change in the position of *maiores domus* as the number of kings diminished. Much of the evidence for the legitimate activities of *maiores* relates to Neustria, since it is drawn from the *diplomata*, which are almost exclusively of Neustrian origin. The lack of comparable evidence for the other two *Teilreiche* may be partly an accident of survival, but is also likely to be to some extent a reflection of the different circumstances in which Burgundian and Austrasian *maiores* operated.

The case of Burgundy is the simpler: as suggested at the beginning of the discussion of *maiores*, from the time of Chlothar II, Burgundian *maiores* represented the king and the local aristocracy to each other in a more independent way than when there had been a separate Burgundian king. The position was not, however, static during the seventh century: after Warnachar II's death there was a period without a *maior*, after which Floachad was Burgundian *maior*. It is not certain that Floachad was ever replaced, but there is some evidence that there was a Burgundian *maior* in the 650s and 660s.[131] However that may be, it is unlikely that the lack of evidence for any *maior* in Burgundy after the third quarter of the seventh century is a mere accident of survival: the logical result of the permanent merging of the Neustrian and Burgundian kingdoms was a single Neustro-Burgundian *maior*. Such a man is likely to have had more power in the kingdom than the separate *maiores* for the individual *Teilreiche* had enjoyed, but that does not necessarily mean that their position in relation to the king was any stronger.

It is possible that a similar broad development can be traced in Austrasia, though there the process occurred later than in Burgundy, largely owing to the continued existence of separate sub-kings or kings until the middle of the seventh century. Once Austrasia came to be more or less permanently ruled by the same king as Neustria and Burgundy, its separate *maior* became the kind of representative of the aristocracy and, indeed, of the king, as Warnachar II had been in Burgundy – the fact that things may in practice have been different is perhaps more likely to be a result of the different personalities involved than of a fundamental difference in the process. It may be partly on account of this evolution that new titles – especially that of *dux* – came to be applied to Austrasian *maiores* at the very end of the seventh century.[132] Although almost all the sources which reflect this change are products of the Pippinid circle, it is not necessarily relevant that it was to Pippin and his heirs that the titles were applied – it is possible that they would have been applied to non-Pippinid *maiores* in Austrasia had there been any, and that the Austrasian *maiores* were seen as occupying a position in some ways similar to that of the *duces* of areas such as Bavaria and Alamannia (see Chapter 4). If this interpretation of the new titles is correct, it may strengthen the suggestion that Pippin II's decision to remain in Austrasia after the Battle of Tertry is an indication of the fact that his real power base lay there rather than in the Neustrian court.

Charles Martel's rise to power was also dependent on his position within Austrasia, since he was unable to assert his influence in Neustria before he had secured his position as leader of the Arnulfing faction. His appropriation of the position of Neustrian, or sole, *maior*, was only possible on account of his ability to dominate the *regnum* militarily. Although the position of *maior* facilitated his becoming the leading actor in Neustro-Burgundian circles as well as in Austrasia, the actual office of *maior* need not, even at this late stage, have become vastly more powerful than it had been in the past: Charles' military strength was probably great enough for him to have been able to succeed in dominating the kingdom even without the position. The attraction of the office may have been that it lent an air of legitimacy and authority to Charles' position, rather than that it conferred a great deal of tangible extra power upon him. It may, therefore, be no accident that the Carolingian authors chose to dwell on this, the 'constitutional' basis of his power, rather than on his over-mightiness as a subject: their picture of the increasing power of the office of *maior* as such, rather than of the forcefulness of some of its occupants, should not be accepted at face value, nor should it be allowed to colour interpretations of the workings of the late-Merovingian royal household.

4

The Wider Court: *comites* and *duces*

In addition to the household officials discussed in the previous chapter, there were other secular members of the royal court – *comites*, or 'companions' of the king. Such men were probably of higher status than the *domestici*, and may be thought of as the members of the aristocracy who actively supported the king. Some of these men held specific offices in the court – those of *comes stabuli* and *comes palatii* – which will be discussed below. Other *comites* are not accorded any specific title by the contemporary documents, and may not, therefore, have held any 'office', but, as members of the court, could participate in any task the king might assign them as occasion demanded. A third, and final, category of *comes* was the governor of a particular area of the kingdom – usually a *ciuitas* – where he acted as the king's representative in many spheres of administration.[1] Many, if not all, *comites* of all kinds were powerful men in their own right, being members of the landed aristocracy, often with their own followers.[2]

Comites stabuli

Of the *comites* who operated within the palace, relatively little is known of the *comes stabuli*, such evidence as does exist coming from Fredegar's *Chronicle*. As with the officials of the household, the nature and brevity of the narrative sources is such that routine palatine activity does not feature: this will have included the administration of the stables, the sphere of competence implied by the title of *comes stabuli*. What is revealed, however, is that men of this kind could, as in the sixth century,[3] be used as envoys and ambassadors. Hence, two *comites stabuli*, Aeborin and Rocco, were sent by Theuderic II to ask the hand of the daughter of King Witteric of the Visigoths,[4] and Herpo was used as an envoy between Brunhild and Chlothar II.[5] The involvement of men such as these may in part have derived from the fact that it would have been desirable for embassies – especially those which crossed potentially hostile or unknown territory – to have been accompanied by men expert in horsemanship, but it is more likely that these particular courtiers were selected on account of their personal qualities and known trustworthiness: no king could afford to have incompetent or unreliable men in charge of his horses.

Given the importance of the position of *comes stabuli*, it is perhaps surprising that holders of the office do not ever appear to have witnessed charters or *placita*, or to have been part of the royal tribunal – they are not even mentioned in Marculf's formulae. This does not mean, however, that they did not in reality form part of the tribunal, since they could lie concealed in the lists of *comites* who feature in some of the *placita* without more specific title. Similarly, in Marculf's formula for a *placitum*,[6] where the only *comes* of any sort to be mentioned is the *comes palatii* (see below), *comites stabuli* may be subsumed under the phrase 'optimates nostri' or 'uel reliqui ... nostri fideles'.

Comites palatii

The only references to *comites palatii* in the non-administrative sources relate – as in the case of *comites stabuli* – to activities outside government. In one case, Fredegar records that Berthar was involved in the murder of the patrician, Willebad,[7] while the hagiographical sources reveal *comites palatii* involved in similar unsavoury enterprises.[8] What these references confirm is that *comites palatii*, in common with many other courtiers, could be powerful actors on the political stage. Owing to the fact that they were involved in the procedures of the royal tribunal, there are, however, also records (particularly in the *placita*) of the normal administrative activities of *comites palatii*.

What those documents,[9] and Marculf's formulae for them,[10] reveal, is that it was the responsibility of the *comes palatii* to testify as to the content of the law in relation to the particular point at issue: in other words, he was the chief legal adviser to the king and his tribunal;[11] the same role is attested by a document of the 720s.[12] Although there is no similar evidence from the sixth century, that is a function of the different nature of the sources for that period, and there is no doubt that *comites palatii* were in existence earlier, and may have developed from the Roman *comes et quaestor sacri palatii* – the legal adviser at the imperial court.[13]

On two occasions the *placita* record that the *comes palatii* was unable to perform his function, and that the law was stated by another official. On one of those occasions, the position of the substitute is not known – he is simply described as 'inluster uir'[14] – but on the other the second official was also a *comes palatii*.[15] The significance of this is not clear, since the need for two *comites palatii* is not obvious, particularly as there is no evidence to suggest that such officials (or, indeed, any court office holders) changed as kings moved from one villa or palace to another. One possible explanation might be that the regular *comes palatii* was for some reason unavailable, and that the king delegated the task of stating the law to another competent individual who assumed the role of *comes palatii* for

42

the specific occasion; the document produced at the end of the proceedings could have duplicated the title either as a record of the fact of what had occurred, or in an attempt to preempt any possible later suggestion of irregularity arising from the fact that the law had not been stated by the recognised authority.

However, it is not impossible that two officials bearing the same title could have existed at the same time. Although there is no positive evidence for this, two pieces of evidence could possibly be interpreted in such a way. First, in 692/3, Ghislemar appears with the title of 'comes', while in 703 he appears as a *comes palatii*;[16] similarly, Sigofred features in 692/3 as a *graphio*, and in 709/10 as 'comes palatii'.[17] Although neither case is conclusive, particularly since both men could have changed position at court during the ten or more years between the documents concerned, they may indicate a possibility: the fact that someone else – Audramn – was acting as *comes palatii* in the document of 692/3 would make it not unreasonable for Ghislemar and Sigofred to have appeared simply as *comites* – courtiers without special function – on that occasion. Such an interpretation must, however, remain extremely tentative.

Other *comites*

By far the largest number of references to *comites* (sometimes known by their Germanic title, *graphio*[18]) do not specify any precise office. Some of these men were, as in the sixth century, sent out from the court to govern parts of the kingdom, usually based on *ciuitates*. Hence, for example, Aenouales was *comes* in Saintonge,[19] Amalbert at Noyon,[20] Gaerin at Paris,[21] Garifred in Vermandois,[22] Herpin and Abbelin in the territory east of the Jura,[23] Ingomar at Thérouanne,[24] and Syagrius at Albi.[25] Few of the references to the men named indicate what were their functions within the administration of the kingdom: Herpin, Abbelin and Aenouales appear in Fredegar's *Chronicle* in the context of high-profile military activity (and, in the case of Herpin, of a rebellion he instigated), while the others appear as incidental characters in the events described by the hagiographers.

Perhaps the most significant point here is that, compared to the sixth century, there are relatively few references to men who can with certainty be located in specific *ciuitates*.[26] This, combined with the fact that, throughout the Merovingian period, *comites ciuitatum* feature less prominently than *duces* (see below), has led to the suggestion that such *comites* were less important than *duces* and, perhaps, that their position was in decline in the seventh century.[27] However, consideration of the nature of the sources may indicate that such an interpretation is open to question. The fact that Fredegar's *Chronicle* is so laconic by comparison with the *Decem libri historiarum* of Gregory of Tours, means that fewer officials of any kind will be mentioned during its course, and that those to whom reference is made will almost always have been engaged in high-profile activities – especially the military ones more associated with *duces* than with *comites* (see below). The same is also true of the one source which deals with the entire seventh century, the *Liber historiae Francorum*. After the early 640s, there is no real equivalent to Fredegar's narrative, since his continuators were only interested in highlighting the incidents in factional conflict which touched on the rise to power of the Pippinids – administrative activities cannot be expected to have found a place in the ten chapters which cover the seven decades following the end of Fredegar's own account, unless they played a leading role in the events described.

A further factor which may affect the overall picture is that a number – possibly even a large number – of *comites ciuitatum* may lie concealed in the administrative documents – the law codes, *diplomata* and formulae. To take the most extreme example, a *placitum* of 692/3 – the product of a royal tribunal held at Valenciennes – records the presence of no fewer than seventeen men described simply as 'comes' or 'graphio'.[28] Some of these men probably did not hold any specific office within the court; others may have done so, but yet others could have been *comites ciuitatum* who were present at court on that occasion. There was not necessarily any need for the precise details of offices to be recorded – unless the specific adminis- trative position held by an individual had direct relevance to the case, the important point may have been the rank of the people concerned. The possibility may derive added strength from the fact that in Marculf's formula for the opening of a *placitum*, *comites* do not feature at all: such men were probably subsumed under the general term 'optimates'.[29]

Other documents produced by the government may be subject to the same interpretation. For example, there are statements in *Lex Ribuaria* that unspecified *comites* could be involved in the administration of justice[30] and taxation:[31] these could apply equally well to *comites ciuitatum* or to *comites* who held no specific office, but were commanded by the king to act in particular cases. It is also not clear whether the *comites* who feature as the addressees of royal charters were based in the provinces.[32] That this was possible may be indicated by the fact that all but one of the same charters were also addressed to named *duces*, while another was ad- dressed to a *uicarius*[33] – the deputy of a *comes ciuitatis* – as well as to the *comes* himself;[34] similarly, a number of formulae for royal documents clearly state or imply that they were addressed to *comites* in charge of the administration of areas of the kingdom.[35] In other instances, however, the case is less clear cut, particularly as a large number of *diplomata* are addressed in the most general way either to a range of officials – unnamed *duces*, *patricii* and *comites* – or simply to unspecified royal agents.[36]

The uncertainty surrounding the identification of which references are specifically to *comites ciuitatum*, and which are to *comites* or high-ranking courtiers in a more general sense, makes it difficult define the precise activities in which members of either category normally engaged. *Lex Ribuaria* refers to the administration of justice and taxation, both of which are likely to have featured largely in the duties of *comites ciuitatum*; evidence for the latter is also provided by a *placitum* concerning the privileges of S.-Denis, in which the *comes* of Paris, Gaerin, is specifically mentioned.[37] Marculf's formulae confirm an involvement with the judicial system, but in addition concern a number of miscellaneous administrative matters (as does a provision in the formulary of Angers[38]), while the formula for the appointment of a regional *comes, dux* or *patricius* refers in general terms to what might be termed 'good government', with an emphasis on justice and ensuring the prompt payment of taxes.[39] It is likely that this reflects the true situation – *comites ciuitatum* could be expected to act in any administrative capacity, being general agents of the king in the area entrusted to them. Military leadership is not mentioned in the formula, but it is clear from the activities of Herpin, Abbelin and Aenouales that *comites ciuitatum* could lead armies on occasion,[40] though, as in the sixth century, this was perhaps not their primary function.[41]

It has in the past sometimes been suggested that the seventh century saw a growth in the involvement of bishops in the administration at the expense of *comites ciuitatum*: this could either reflect a usurpation of comital powers by the bishops, or may have been encouraged by the king to facilitate local administration, or to provide a counter-balance to the local power of the *comites*.[42] Examples of this kind of episcopal activity include Desiderius of Cahors' laying water pipes in his city, and receiving a letter from Gallus II of Clermont concerning the closing of roads to prevent the spread of plague;[43] while Leodegar of Autun was involved with the repair of the city's walls.[44] In addition, the first *Passio* of Leodegar refers to Desideratus of Chalon-sur-Saône as exercising 'principatus' over his city, and to Bobo of Valence as having 'dominium' in his.[45] While these indications may reflect a genuine increase in the involvement of bishops in civil government in the seventh century, its significance is difficult to assess. Bishops had long been involved in various kinds of governmental activity, particularly those relating to the administration of justice, and had engaged in various kinds of charitable undertaking, of which the activities of men such as Desiderius of Cahors could be seen as an extension.[46] In addition, while the fact that a number of seventh-century bishops had been members of the royal household prior to assuming episcopal office may have been part of a royal policy of placing men of proven loyalty and competence in the provinces, perhaps partly as a means of watching members of the secular aristocracy (including the *comites ciuitatum*), this was also a practice of long standing.[47]

It is possible that the impression of an increase in governmental activity on the part of bishops at the expense of local *comites* may be to some extent created by a change in the nature of the sources between the sixth and seventh centuries. There is no real sixth-century equivalent of the letters of Desiderius of Cahors, and the seventh-century saints' lives treat individual subjects at greater length than do those of the sixth – although the hagiographical *œuvre* of Gregory of Tours is substantial, individual bishops and abbots of his own time rarely receive extended attention. On the other hand, Gregory's *Decem libri historiarum*, by presenting a more detailed account of its age than do the seventh- and early eighth-century narrative works, may include more information concerning local *comites*.

Other *comites*, not attached to specific regions, might be involved in any sphere of activity from time to time, carrying out the king's commands as occasion demanded. A few of those activities were significant enough – either in their own right, or in terms of the precise subject of an individual author – for them to be recorded in the narrative and hagiographical material, but most were not, because they were unspectacular. It is, for example, clear that Chlothar II's use of Ingobod, *graphio*, to look after Theuderic's son, Merovech, was a highly exceptional task:[48] Ingobod and his office are incidentals in an event which was deemed worthy of inclusion in Fredegar's *Chronicle* on its own merits. A slightly different example is that of Theudoald, *comes*, who was jointly responsible with Saffronius, bishop of Nantes, for escorting Columbanus on his way into exile:[49] here, the incident is only recorded because of its importance in relation to Jonas' subject – the life of Columbanus. On other occasions, unspecified *comites* appear to have been acting on their own behalf – often illegitimately, as when Dotto and Erichius attacked religious foundations connected with the holy men in whose lives they feature.[50]

Duces

Like *comites*, *duces* could also be royal agents based in the provinces, usually in charge of larger areas than single *ciuitates*. It is not, however, clear that all references to *duces* in the seventh-century sources are to men of this kind – though the evidence is not of a quality to permit of certain interpretation. That *dux* could have a non-technical meaning (as in the sixth century[51]) is suggested by Fredegar's account of events after Dagobert I's death, when Pippin I and the Austrasian 'duces' supported Sigibert III's claim to inherit his father's position.[52] While this could refer to regional officials, there is nothing to suggest that it relates to anything other than the leading men of the Austrasians – that is, not necessarily office-holders at all.

It is possible that other references to *duces* can be read in the same way. Hence, for example, Fredegar records that Radulf of Thuringia provoked Adalgisel, 'dux', and rebelled against Sigibert III in the late 630s.[53] While it is possible that Adalgisel held an 'office' of *dux*, the term need not signify more than that he was a leading man in the area. In the more detailed account of Sigibert's reaction to the rebellion, Adalgisel is again described as 'dux', as is Grimoald:[54] the latter is the later disruptive *maior domus*, and there is no other suggestion that he ever held any kind of formal office of *dux* – all that the context here requires is that the two men were leaders in Sigibert's resistance. In the case of Adalgisel, the case may be strengthened by the fact that his name appears in three *diplomata* without a title, possibly implying that he held no specific office. The same may be as true of the 'duces exercitus' of Sigibert who were in league with Radulf during his rebellion, and this logic could even be applied to Bobo, 'dux Aruernus': he may have been a 'leader from Auvergne', rather than '*dux* of Auvergne'.[55]

Some men described as *duces*, however, clearly did hold a specific office, because it is recorded that they were made *duces* at a particular time. Hence, for example, Genialis was made *dux* over the Gascons after Theudebert II and Theuderic II had defeated them in 602,[56] and Radulf was made *dux* of Thuringia by Dagobert I.[57] The same is also indicated by a number of references to *ducatus* – both in relation to territory[58] and to the tenure of the office by an individual[59] – including in the formula for the appointment of a *dux*.[60] Such territorial *duces* had existed in the sixth century, when their responsibilities were primarily military and the territories they controlled were usually frontier areas or other regions liable to periodic unrest.[61] The military involvement of such men in the seventh century is amply attested: Chrodobert of the Alamans led a force against the Slavs,[62] and Radulf of Thuringia campaigned against the Wends,[63] while other *duces* – not all of whom were necessarily territorial – also engaged in military leadership.[64]

Some of the *ducatus* consisted of the territories of non-Frankish peoples who had been subjected to Frankish hegemony (*imperium* – though not stated in these terms): Alamannia[65] and Thuringia;[66] probably also Bavaria, though it seems to have enjoyed a greater degree of independence.[67] Other *ducatus* were in frontier areas, either internal or external – the area east of the Jura,[68] Champagne (between Austrasia and Neustria),[69] Dentelin (disputed between Austrasia and Neustria).[70] Aquitaine may fall between the two, having at one stage been subject to division between the kings of the three main Frankish *regna*, and, under Dagobert I, a sub-kingdom for Charibert.[71] The military significance of these *ducatus* may be underlined by the case of Champagne, the area subject to which varied during the seventh century as control changed hands between Neustrian and Austrasian partisans, and as the location of the threat it was supposed to counter shifted. Hence, in the time of Pippin II and his son, Grimoald II, its centre moved south as it became a means of pacifying Burgundy, but after Grimoald's death it was extended north again by Chilperic II to act as a buffer between Neustria and Austrasia.[72]

There are, however, other references to *duces* with some kind of regional power, though the areas with which they are associated may have been rather smaller and/or militarily less significant: such men as Waldelen, who was succeeded by his son Chrameln in the area near Besançon,[73] Rabiac in the Els-Gau,[74] or Theotchar in the Mosel region.[75] The precise position of such people is not clear: some may have been no more than the leading magnates of the area, who probably had their own bands of retainers;[76] others may have had a more formal position as local military leaders. Both possibilities could account for the fact that *duces* and *comites* were sometimes jointly addressed in the *diplomata*.[77] In addition, although there is no specific reference to a major *ducatus* in the Paris region, two charters (separated by a decade) concerning S.-Denis were jointly addressed to Wandalbert,[78] who is otherwise only known (described as 'dux') for his involvement in the murder of the patrician Willebad.[79] That not all the *regnum Francorum* was divided up into such *ducatus*, however, may be suggested by Fredegar's account of Dagobert I's campaign against the Gascons, which, after a list of the *duces* who participated, goes on to say that several *comites* above whom there was no *dux*, were also involved.[80] Certainty on this point is unattainable on account of the fragmentary nature of the source material.

Similar difficulties surround a suggestion that some *duces* had no territorial jurisdiction, but remained in the king's household.[81] Such a situation may have prevailed in the Visigothic kingdom where some army leaders may have been resident at court and have formed an *ordo* of *duces* (see Chapter 8), but there is so evidence to support such a hypothesis in the Frankish kingdom.

The fact that the narrative and hagiographical sources most often depict *duces* when they are involved in war leadership is not surprising, given that their nature is such as to highlight events which were of immediately-perceived significance, or were germane to the particular purposes of their authors. It is perhaps for a related reason that most of the *duces* to whom reference is made by Fredegar and his continuators, and the author of the *Liber historiae Francorum*, are either those of the large peripheral *ducatus* or, more especially, those of the great interior *ducatus* which were important in the internal politics of the kingdom. Both the great *duces* and the lesser ones (within the three main *regna*) were also engaged (perhaps by extension of their main duties) in a degree of civil administration. That this was expected is clear from Marculf's formula for the appointment of a *dux*, patrician or *comes*, which does not mention military leadership, but exhorts the office holder to provide 'good government' in general terms, specifically mentioning the administration of justice and taxation.[82]

Something nearer to the realities of the involvement of *duces* in civil government can be seen in the documents produced by the administration itself. *Lex Ribuaria*, for example, includes provisions which show that *duces* could preside over judicial proceedings,[83] and a number of charters were addressed to named or unnamed *duces*, often jointly with other officials.[84] In addition, *duces* were sometimes present at the royal court, and could both advise the king and sign his acts.[85] That *duces* could form part of the royal tribunal is clear from Marculf's formula for a *placitum*,[86] though they are never specifically mentioned in the extant documents of this kind, where, like many of the *comites*, they may be hidden amongst men described as 'optimates'.[87] There is, however, rather less evidence of this kind than there is for *comites* – fewer of Marculf's formulae, and fewer sections of the *Lex Ribuaria* – which may indicate that the military aspect of the power of *duces* was primary. As powerful men in the provinces, *duces* might act in a civil capacity on occasion, and could, like *comites ciuitatum*, be treated non-bureaucratically, as general agents of the king – as, for example, when Arnebert was ordered by Chlothar II to murder Warnachar's son, Godin, and by Dagobert I to assassinate Charibert's uncle, Brodulf;[88] or when Dagobert commanded Barontius to convey Charibert's treasure to him;[89] or when Venerandus and Amalgar were sent as envoys to the Visigothic king, Sisenand.[90]

The evidence for *duces* of all types during the second half of the seventh century is not plentiful, but what there is suggests that the leaders of the great *ducatus* on the frontiers of the Merovingian kingdom gained a greater degree of autonomy.[91] One of the most significant indices of this is a change in the terminology used for these *duces*: they begin to be referred to as 'duces Francorum' and as 'principes (Francorum)'. Until *c.* 700, both the claim to be a ruler of the Franks and the concept of *principatus* were the preserve of kings.[92] To an extent the origins of this may, like the changing role of *maiores domus* in Burgundy and Austrasia (see Chapter 3), be a reflection of the realities of power in a *regnum Francorum* in which there were fewer contemporaneous kings than in the sixth century: the larger a king's territory (the greater his *imperium*), the more considerable the physical distance between the king and some of his subordinates and therefore, perhaps, the greater the power of those subordinates. The issuing of a separate law code for the Alamans by Chlothar II may mark an implicit recognition of the new circumstances, while its re-issue in the early eighth century by the then *dux*, Lantfrid, illustrates a further stage in the process.[93]

Another, and perhaps more important, aspect of the power of the *duces* of the non-Frankish subject peoples was that they acted as a counterbalance to the attempts of the Austrasian aristocracy and, in particular, the Pippinids, to dominate the *regnum Francorum*. This is clear from Fredegar's account of the creation of the first Thuringian *dux*, Radulf, who was, he says, appointed specifically in order to strengthen Dagobert I's position against the Austrasians, to whom Thuringia had been subject in the sixth century.[94] The military importance of Radulf's position is also shown by the fact that he defended the Frankish kingdom from attacks by the Wends, which the Austrasians declined to do.[95] Flushed with this success, Radulf appears to have declared himself king[96] – long before the use of new titles for other *duces* (see above) – but the full implications of this are not known, nor is the length of time for which it lasted.[97] It is not necessarily the case that the Thuringian *duces* were anti-Frankish or

anti-Merovingian – it is possible that they were seeking to escape dominance by their Austrasian neighbours led by the Arnulfings.

Similar problems – though of greater extent – surround the position of
the Bavarian *duces* in the seventh century. As in Alamannia, Frankish
influence in the area is suggested by the issuing of the *Lex Bauuiariorum*.
Later in the century, however, it appears that Bavaria became disengaged
from the Frankish world, and more closely aligned with that of the
Lombards.[98] Again, this need not be taken as evidence for specifically
anti-Frankish sentiment, especially since the Agilolfings were opponents
of the Pippinids and harboured fugitives from them.[99]

If this kind of interpretation is correct, it may assist in explaining the
timing of the grant of new titles to the *duces*, since it occurred during the
period at which Pippinid influence began to weigh heavily on the Merovingian kingdom – that is, during the ascendancy of Pippin II.[100] What the
duces may have sought could have been not so much independence, as a
balance of power within the kingdom, in which the Austrasians would have
had a part, but not a dominant one.[101] In a sense, therefore, the increase
in their independence could, paradoxically, in part be seen as a measure of
their loyalty to, and defence of, the Merovingian kings who had created
their power. It might even be possible to interpret Lantfrid's re-issuing of
the *Lex Alamannorum* in this way, since it was Frankish law, originally
promulgated by a Merovingian king: as will be seen in Chapter 12, the
Lombard *dux* Arichis II did something similar in the late eighth century.

The patrician

Marculf's formula for the appointment of regional *comites* and *duces* was
also applicable to patricians,[102] indicating that the latter were also, at least
sometimes, made responsible for the administration of specific provincial
areas. In the sixth century, there is evidence which suggests that Provence
may usually have been governed by a man of this title, but that the word
'patrician' usually denoted an honour rather than an office, as it had done
in the western Empire of the fifth century.[103] This situation probably
survived into the seventh century almost unchanged. There was at least
one patrician of Provence, Hector,[104] and it is possible that Ricomer, and
before him, Wulf, held a similar position, especially since Ricomer was
described as a 'Roman', which would have been appropriate for what had
been the most heavily Romanised part of the kingdom.[105] Less certain is
the case of Willebad, who is described by Fredegar as 'patricius genere
Burgundionum':[106] he could have held office in Provence, which was closely
associated with Burgundy, or he could simply have been a Burgundian
who, on account of the high esteem in which he was held, had been
accorded the honorary rank of patrician. The second interpretation may
more certainly be applied to the case of Protadius, highly regarded by
Brunhild, who made him patrician of the area to the east of the Jura.[107]

4. The Wider Court: comites and duces

Such a title is otherwise unknown, and what it may signify is that he was made *dux* in the area, but with the additional distinction of the patrician rank:[108] authors from outside the kingdom certainly seem to have used the title in this way, for Bede refers to the *maior domus* Erchinoald as 'patrician' as do the *Uita* and the *Uirtutes Fursei*.[109]

The evidence for the activities of patricians hardly clarifies their position, since it is extremely limited. Marculf's formula does little more than exhort territorially-based patricians to be equitable in the administration of justice and taxation, and to practise good government:[110] it does not assist in determining whether the office of patrician was found outside Provence. Other sources also demonstrate involvement with justice[111] and the exaction of money for the fisc,[112] as well as showing that patricians, like almost all other courtiers, could be involved in military leadership.[113] It is therefore clear that patricians could, at least on occasion, find themselves acting in all the spheres also associated with *comites* and *duces*, an impression further strengthened by their appearance as addressees of *diplomata* (both in Marculf's formulae and in actual documents).[114] This reinforces the impression that, while some courtiers held specific offices either in the central court or in the regions, government was not bureaucratically arranged: all courtiers, no matter what their office, could be expected to intervene on the king's behalf in a wide range of activities.

5

Conclusion

The preceding chapters have sought to assess the evidence for the nature of Merovingian kingship and the structure of the royal court in the period from the end of the *Decem libri historiarum* of Gregory of Tours (594) to the rise of Charles Martel, who all but destroyed independent Merovingian power. Although hindsight enables us – as it enabled the Carolingians – to know that the Merovingians were ultimately to be overcome, the knowledge of what came later should not be used to colour interpretations of the earlier period. It is legitimate to seek to trace the origins of the Pippinid ascendancy, but there has for too long been a tradition of seeing its seeds in all aspects of the seventh century without considering alternative interpretations of events. Such a historiographical model has been encouraged – if not caused – by the fact that much of the narrative of the seventh century was supplied by Pippinid sympathisers and later Carolingian writers whose specific purpose was to make people believe it.[1] What has been attempted here, by contrast, is to comprehend in its own terms the period from shortly before Chlothar II's re-unification of the *regnum Francorum* to the end of Chilperic II's reign.

An adequate understanding of the nature of the sources is a vital precondition for this. The very fact that the narrative histories covering the second half of the seventh century are so brief means that – even leaving aside the tendentious nature of the continuations of Fredegar's *Chronicle* – the period can appear to have suffered from a power vacuum when compared to the earlier seventh century, for which Fredegar's own work is slightly fuller, and, more especially, in comparison with the relative wealth of detail supplied by Gregory's great work. Moreover, the very brevity of the seventh-century narratives means that only some of the most sensational events were recorded in them; in the same way, the secular events which were recorded in the substantial saints' lives were often only those which disrupted the normal pace of life, leading to an impression of greater instability and chaos than may in reality have existed.

This does not mean that the period was untroubled for the Merovingians – as has been seen, there were frequent struggles with over-mighty subjects who, because they were inherently powerful, not unnaturally came to occupy some of the leading positions in the government – but to a large extent it may have been no more so than the sixth century with its periods of civil war so lamented by Gregory of Tours.[2] What traditional interpretations have tended to miss is that the chronology of the decline of Merovingian authority does not have to be the same as the decline in the quality of the coherent narrative accounts of the period.

Another reason – not connected with the character of the evidence – for an impression of royal powerlessness by comparison with the sixth century is that the nature of the kingdom had altered, largely owing to its more permanent unification. The greater an area ruled by a single king, the less visible his authority is likely to be, at least in some regions, and the more he has to rely on agents who operate at a distance from the court. It may be mainly on account of this that *duces* and regional patricians feature more largely in the seventh century than earlier, both in the core areas of Neustria, Burgundy and Austrasia, and in the territories of peoples subject to Merovingian *imperium*. Such men were likely to become – if they were not already – the leading aristocrats of their regions, with large bodies of retainers; although they or their forebears were probably established for primarily military reasons, they became, by a natural progression, agents of the king, who could intervene in all aspects of administration. This was not symptomatic of the breakdown of order, but represents a new form of order, appropriate to the new circumstances of the seventh century.[3]

While the holders of some titles may have had specific spheres of administrative competence, they were not precluded from acting as the king's agents in other matters, at least on occasion. This is clear from the way in which many charters are addressed to all the king's agents or to a number of types of officials – *duces*, *comites*, patricians and others. The same is true of some provisions in the law codes, notably *Lex Ribuaria*:[4] the lists of titles of officials there need not even be taken as definitive. What the laws and charters were intended to do was to cover any eventuality, which meant listing many of the officials who could sometimes be involved: there is nothing peculiarly Merovingian about this (as will be seen, in particular, with regard to the Visigothic kingdom) and the imprecision involved is not a sign of administrative chaos, but of a degree of flexibility.

The same logic can be applied to the *maior domus*. Holders of this position may have fulfilled some specific functions but, as heads of the royal household, could intervene in any sphere in which household officials operated. If it is correct to see the referendaries and notaries as members of the household staff (as discussed in Chapter 3), this interpretation of the more general, non-bureaucratic, structure of 'office' means that it is no longer necessary to see the intervention of *maiores* in aspects of document production as marking an increase in their powers. The fact that such evidence comes from the last third of the seventh century and later is not surprising, given that most of the surviving documents were produced in that period. What is true, though, is that *maiores* were at times more powerful than they had been earlier, partly on account of the number of royal minorities, and partly as their position, like that of some of the *duces*, changed as a result of the unification of the kingdom.

Given the size of the unified kingdom, it may not be surprising that those in charge of some of the large regions sought power for themselves, whether as *maiores domus* or as *duces*: this theme recurs in both the Visigothic and Lombard kingdoms. Rather than concentrating on how weak Merovingian kings were in the seventh century, it may be better to consider how remarkable was their survival: in both Visigothic Spain and Lombard Italy, the ruling house changed on more than one occasion as *duces* and other regional leaders sought to dominate the kingdom by becoming kings themselves. The unique Merovingian achievement was to retain authority for so long – a factor which alone deserves a more positive reputation than the rulers of seventh-century Frankia have often been accorded.

PART II

Visigothic Spain

Seventh-century Visigothic kings have a reputation almost as poor as that of their Frankish contemporaries: they were unsuccessful and weak, and in order to overcome this they resorted to brutality. To some extent, judgement has been coloured by the fact that the kingdom did not survive attack by the Arabs in the eighth century but, according to traditional historiography, collapsed almost immediately.[1] A second factor is the failure of any one dynasty to establish a monopoly of power, leading to an insecure succession. In recent years, however, it has been shown that both elements of this picture are in need of revision: the kingdom was not completely destroyed in a single Arab campaign, nor was the Visigothic succession (although not strictly dynastic) any more vexed than that in other seventh-century kingdoms, including that of the Franks where, as seen in Chapter 2, the dynastic principle did not by any means always ensure a smooth transfer of power from father to son.[2]

In order to overcome the problems posed by the succession, and to weld their large and diverse kingdom into a coherent entity, kings and their supporters sought to create a 'national consciousness' which was fostered by many of the surviving documents of the period, and has led to an interpretation of the Visigothic kingdom as more centralised than its Frankish and Lombard contemporaries.[3] Further, kings used – among other devices – specifically imperial imagery to bolster their position and to set themselves apart from, and above, potential rivals, thereby giving some commentators the impression that they were more sophisticated, more 'Roman' and better organised than their contemporaries elsewhere.[4] Other historians, on the other hand, have suggested that many of the imperial trappings are hollow – that they are only imagery and have little relation to reality.[5]

That such divergent opinions are tenable is largely due to the nature of the source material for, while it is strong on legal enactments (both secular and spiritual), there is very little that is narrative or hagiographical, and there are almost no royal *diplomata*. The result is that it is very rare that anything other than a schematic or theoretical picture of royal government can be obtained. Compensating for this is particularly difficult on account of an almost complete lack of source material for the first two-thirds of the sixth century, making rare the opportunity for comparison

55

between the seventh-century rulers and their sixth-century predecessors. Despite this, the Visigoths of the late sixth century and after did not emerge from a vacuum, and their responses to the situations they faced were as likely to be conditioned by their earlier experiences in the Roman world as were those of the Franks. While continuities are difficult to demonstrate in these circumstances, and caution must be exercised in suggesting them, discontinuities can often only be posited on the basis of arguments from silence. That the conversion of the monarchy to Catholicism marked a major point in the history of the kingdom, and in relations between monarchs and the churchmen who were the writers of their time, is indisputable, but neither it, nor the change in the character of the sources which it fostered marked a complete break with the past.

6

The Sources

After an almost total lack of contemporary source material for the history of the Visigoths and of Spain in the period between the defeat of Alaric by the Franks at the Battle of Vouillé in 507, the last third of the sixth century saw the production of a relatively plentiful (by early medieval standards) body of evidence. A degree of the impetus for this was provided by the threat posed to the integrity of Spain by the Byzantine Empire which had, since the early 550s, established a foothold in the south-east of the peninsula, based on Cartagena. Byzantine interest was partly prompted by the Justinianic aspirations for the reconquest of the west, and partly by a desire to protect north Africa, but it is important also to note that the occasion of their arrival in Spain was an invitation by a local noble, Athanagild, who was resisting the imposition of central royal control under kings Theodisclus (548-549) and Agila (549-554).[1] This emphasises the fact that there were many regional loyalties in an area of the size and geographical diversity of Spain, and that it was the task – and, in large measure, the achievement – of the Visigothic kings to create a sense of internal cohesion, or 'national consciousness', which would weld their realm – an *imperium* – together in the face of external threats. Many of the sources used in this study of royal administration, if not produced as part of that process, share its concerns. Without the conversion of the Visigoths to Catholicism under Reccared, however, it is unlikely that such a large body of material would have been produced, since it was almost entirely the work of Catholic churchmen. While the Visigoths were still Arian, they lay outside the literary and historical traditions of the Catholic Roman world.[2]

The points made above are well illustrated by the first of the narrative histories produced in the late sixth century, the *Chronicle* of John of Biclaro. That work, which was begun almost immediately after the conversion, at the Third Council of Toledo in 589, takes the form of a continuation of Victor of Tunnuna's revision of Prosper Tiro's *Chronicle*, which was itself a continuation of Jerome's great world chronicle. This enabled the Visigoths to be portrayed as standing within the Roman tradition: Reccared is depicted as a 'new Constantine', thereby opening the way for a suggestion that the Visigoths were at least the equals of the Byzantines. That is achieved by a gradual change of emphasis during the course of the *Chronicle*: the early part is dominated by Constantinople, while later sections give greater prominence to Spain as it came of age as a Catholic power in its own right with the conversion of Reccared – the event which provides the work's climax.[3]

For all that it was propagandist, John's *Chronicle* shares many of the limitations of other works of the same form when it comes to understanding the mechanics of royal government. Its entries, although fuller than those of some of its predecessors, tend to be laconic, and concentrate on religious affairs and high-profile secular events, such as changes of ruler and military campaigns. While such events have undoubted importance, and the structure of the document reveals something of contemporary thought concerning the nature and position of the Visigothic monarchy, the *Chronicle* is not concerned with the details of royal administration, which hardly feature in its pages.

Similar restrictions are also characteristic of the historical works of Isidore of Seville, whose own *Chronicle* drew on the same tradition as John's: it sought to proclaim Spain's theological independence from Constantinople (partly by claiming that Justinian was a heretic), while the same author's *Historia Gothorum* declared its political independence.[4] The aim of the *History* was to show how Spain and the Goths were destined for each other from a time before the Roman invasion of Spain,[5] thus creating a long history to counter that of the Empire, and at the same time bolstering the monarchy's at times tenuous hold over the Iberian peninsula.[6] It is important to see the *History of the Goths* in association with Isidore's histories of the Sueves and Alans, who had also settled in Spain, but whose power had come to and end.[7] The *History of the Goths* begins with the *Laus Spaniae*[8] (drawing on traditions established by Prudentius and Orosius[9]) which is essentially an anti-Byzantine manifesto,[10] and ends with the accession to the throne of Suinthila (621-631) who secured the final victory against the Byzantines and had notable military success against the Basques.[11] Between those two points, the work takes the form of a 'gallery of kings', showing how the individual character of each ruler shaped the destiny of the Goths and of Spain.[12]

The *Historia Gothorum* presents a tendentious interpretation of history not only in relation to the Empire, but also with regard to the Visigothic monarchs themselves. It is likely that Isidore began to compile the work at the instigation of King Sisebut, but the account of Suinthila's final victory at Cartagena seems to have been added a few years later, when Suinthila was himself king; at that time, Isidore appears to have recast some of the earlier material to transfer credit from Sisebut to Suinthila. Although the *History* was not subsequently modified to take account of Suinthila's forced abdication in 631, it is possible that Isidore would have carried out further modifications had he not died in 636, since some manuscripts contain a preface dedicating the work to Sisenand. It has been suggested that these features indicate that the work was not only inspired by the monarchy, but may have been of an 'official' nature.[13]

Whether that is the case or not, the *History* is the nearest to a narrative source which exists for the seventh century: after its conclusion, there is very little literature of an unequivocally historical nature. The form of the work is not, however, such as to provide a great deal of information concerning the ways in which the monarchy worked or the royal court was organised. What it does is to provide a picture of what kings and their associates liked to think was their position, and, in more general terms, to give an insight into the claims which were made by and on behalf of the rulers. As will be seen, this is characteristic of some of the other kinds of document found in the Visigothic kingdom.

One piece of later literature which was specifically compiled in order to strengthen the position of the monarchy is the *Historia excellentissimi Wambae regis de expeditione et uictoria quae reuellantem contra se prouinciam Galliae celebri triumpho perdomuit*, written in the 670s by Julian of Toledo. Like John of Biclaro and Isidore, Julian drew on Roman traditions,[14] but he also used Biblical models.[15] The work is an account of the origins of Wamba's rule, and of his crushing of a revolt in Visigothic Gaul in 672. The overt purpose of the *Historia Wambae* is to exhort the young to virtuous deeds, by means of recounting the glorious events of the past:[16] in this, it has much in common with hagiography. Beneath that veneer, however, there is another aim – to illustrate the ways in which a new king could establish his legitimacy;[17] like the works of Isidore, Julian's *History* is not concerned with the function of the king or his courtiers so much as with the symbols of his power.

The seventh century saw the production of a number of hagiographical works, though they are few by comparison with the wealth of such material which exists for Frankish Gaul. The *Uita Desiderii* is unique in being written by a king – Sisebut (612-621) – and, while hagiographical in form, it was treated as an official document, preserved alongside diplomatic letters. Its purpose was to improve relations between the Visigoths and the Franks after the strains caused by the activities of the Visigothic princess, Brunhild, who had married Sigibert I of Austrasia: the cruelty of Brunhild's execution by Chlothar II was overlooked, as were her Visigothic origins, while the martyrdom of Desiderius by Brunhild and by her grandson, Theuderic II, was vilified.[18]

Of a rather different propagandist purpose is Braulio's *Uita Aemiliani*, which was written to be read during mass on the Saint's feast day.[19] The *Life* appears to have been produced in order to present its subject as the national saint of Visigothic Spain:[20] it has even been suggested that Braulio wrote the document in the aftermath of Chindasuinth's seizure of power in 642 as a way of supporting the position of the new king.[21] One other hagiographical work deserves special mention – the *Uitas Patrum Emeritensium*, which was an anti-Arian work. Its author followed John of

Biclaro and Isidore in depicting Reccared as a holy king or new Constantine, and the work was written largely for the glorification of the church at Mérida. Whatever their individual purposes, saints' lives record little of direct relevance to the study of royal administration: kings and more especially courtiers usually only feature as incidentals, in the same way as they do in Frankish hagiography (see Chapter 1).

Two of the writers of saints' lives – Braulio and King Sisebut – also composed a number of letters which survive. The contents of Braulio's correspondence fall into three broad categories, the largest of which is concerned with ecclesiastical affairs, as might be expected given his position as bishop of Saragossa. The second group consists of documents addressed to members of the author's family, mostly at times of personal crisis. Finally, a number of letters were either addressed to, or received from, kings: while these documents provide valuable insights into the ways in which bishops participated in the guidance of government, they tend to be allusive, as is often the case with personal correspondence, and do not provide details of royal administration. The letters of Sisebut are much fewer in number,[22] but are unique in apparently having been written by a king himself. For the most part, this correspondence again concerns ecclesiastical affairs, though a small number of letters are of a diplomatic nature.

Despite the small volume of the evidence supplied by the hagiographical material and the letter collections, those kinds of source are of importance, for they illustrate the spheres of activity in which officials of the royal court actually operated, rather than the theory of how they should behave: that is the strength of the legal materials discussed in the remainder of this chapter. Even if some of the actual events presented in the hagiographical sources are of questionable authenticity, the types of activity in which kings and their officials are shown to have participated are likely to reflect the assumptions of both author and reader concerning their behaviour and, accordingly, to be based in reality.

The largest single source for Visigothic Spain, though, is the law code, successively amended and re-edited by Leovigild, Reccesuinth, Chindasuinth, Ervig and Egica.[23] The purpose of the law was to assist judges to settle cases brought before them – a point made by the fact that the official name of the collection is *Forum iudicum* or *Liber iudiciorum*.[24] In addition, the code itself contains a statement as to what the price of a manuscript was to be, suggesting that it may have been fixed at a level which most judges would have been able to afford.[25]

One of the consequences of this almost 'didactic'[26] character is that the laws were written in such a form as to ensure that they had the widest possible application. Hence many contain lists of officials who might be involved in resolving cases of the kind envisaged: one law, for example, refers to the '*duces* or *comites*, *tiufadi* and *uicarii* or whatever other persons' had knowledge of the matter.[27] A further result of the nature of the law is that it rarely refers to the officers of the royal court, since the king himself was responsible for finding judgement in any case which reached the royal court after failing to be resolved at a lower level (see Chapter 7):[28] the fact that he might consult his leading men did not require a statement to that effect in every title in the code. Most of the judges or royal agents mentioned in the laws are, therefore, those who were likely to find themselves involved in various forms of provincial administration. This does not mean that courtiers were never involved, since, as will be seen in Chapter 8, many high-ranking members of the provincial administration (the *duces prouinciarum* and *comites ciuitatum*) were also members of the court, while the term 'comes' has a wide application to refer to anyone who formed part of the royal entourage.

It clear that the laws were not the only royal enactments which were written down – land grants, individual judgements and many other matters must have formed the subject of written instruments. The importance of such royal documents is underlined by the fact that the laws prescribed heavy penalties for those found guilty of any kind of alteration to them,[29] and judges were commanded not to let original documents out of their hands.[30] In addition, a large number of private documents survive,[31] and there is a set of models or formulae for such documents, probably initially drawn up between about 615 and 620 in Córdoba, but perhaps added to later in the seventh century.[32] In contrast to the evidence for Merovingian Gaul, however, almost no royal *diplomata* have survived, even in later copies, only one apparently genuine charter having a detailed witness list.[33]

By contrast, the proceedings of some of the national councils of the Visigothic church, held at Toledo, usually in the presence of the king or his representatives, and often with members of the royal court in attendance, do contain witness lists which record courtiers' titles. The conciliar proceedings are officially inspired documents which were primarily propagandist in purpose, aiming to show – in a way similar to the writings of John of Biclaro and Isidore of Seville – how the king and the Catholic Church worked together: the king lent his support to ecclesiastical and moral legislation, while the Church often added its sanction to royal measures which were sometimes promulgated in the proceedings.[34] In addition, the Church, as seen through the councils, was able to offer legitimation of the king's position, so that the monarch could claim that his power derived ultimately from God. More than that, the very form of the councils was modelled upon the ecclesiastical gatherings of fourth-century Gaul and of the eastern Empire, suggesting that the Visigothic kings were to be considered the equals of the emperors.[35] The propagandist nature of the councils means that their main evidence concerns the way in which royal government was perceived, rather than its administration. The detailed lists of signatories may bear a greater relationship to the organisation of the royal household but, as will be seen in Chapter 8, it has sometimes even been argued that the official titles recorded are more related to image building (particularly in relation to the Empire) than with Visigothic reality: while that suggestion will be contested, the propagandist nature of the councils is not in question.

7

Kings: warriors and lawyers

One of the most debated features of the Visigothic monarchy concerns the principles of succession to the throne, with some seeing it as fundamentally elective, and others as hereditary.[1] While it is true that a number of kings were deposed during the early seventh century, it would appear that the principle remained hereditary, succession outside the family being exceptional.[2] After Chindasuinth's accession the picture is more clear-cut, partly owing to his ruthless elimination of almost all potential rivals:[3] apart from the rebellion of the *dux*, Paul, against Wamba, the later succession was remarkably smooth, though there was competition between the families of Chindasuinth and Wamba (see Table II on p. 184).[4] Despite this, it is clear that kings' hold on power was somewhat less secure than in Frankia, where there was a much stronger dynastic principle: as a result, they were concerned to a greater extent than the Merovingians to find means of enhancing their title to rule.

One of the ways in which Visigothic kings sought to ease the process of succession was by designating their heirs and/or making them *consortes regni* during their own lifetime.[5] This was probably a borrowing from late Roman traditions,[6] but in other respects the Visigoths were prone to be more innovative, and to imitate contemporary Byzantine imperial practices. Part of the background to this was the requirement to create the image of a united and powerful Visigothic monarchy in order to assist in the successful opposition to Byzantine incursions into Spain. While John of Biclaro could still describe Leovigild's kingdom as a 'prouincia',[7] and a law of Reccared might refer to all the 'provinces' belonging to the kingdom,[8] perhaps suggesting that an earlier tradition of seeing the kingdom as still part of the Roman Empire was still alive,[9] there are also signs of a different kind of borrowing from the Empire, aimed at proclaiming equality with it, rather than subordination.

The evidence for the newer kind of monarchy begins with the reign of Leovigild (569-586), but it is impossible to be certain that his predecessors, Athanagild (who invited the Byzantines into Spain, but later unsuccessfully opposed them) and Liuva I, did not take the first steps, since both John of Biclaro and Isidore were anxious to discuss the events leading up to the establishment of the Catholic monarchy, which began under Leovigild's son, Reccared, rather than those which took place under earlier,

Arian, kings. However that may be, Isidore explicitly states that Leovigild was the first king to use a throne – a symbol of imperial authority not previously overtly claimed by the Visigoths:[10] the only 'barbarian' kings to have used a throne at an earlier date were the Vandals, who were also in conflict with the Empire.[11] By the second half of the seventh century, the throne was such an important symbol of power that the *dux*, Paul, is said to have had a portable *thronus* when he tried to have himself set up as king in place of Wamba.[12]

A similar kind of adoption of imperial prerogatives is witnessed by Leovigild's foundation of a city, Reccopolis, which bore the name of the heir-apparent, Reccared.[13] The King may, however, have been making a different kind of point when he selected Toledo as his capital. Unlike the former Visigothic capital of Toulouse, or the other main centre of the Aquitanian kingdom, Bordeaux, Toledo did not have a distinguished Roman past. What Leovigild may have sought to do, therefore, was to build a kind of Constantinople – a new creation, which he could adorn with monuments redolent of his own, Visigothic, power.[14] In other words, while he may have been declaring his own independence, he was doing so in a 'Roman' way – and one which the eastern Empire would clearly understand. Despite the adoption of a ceremonial capital, it is unlikely that kings ceased to move around their kingdom – indeed, one of Egica's laws was issued at Córdoba[15] – or that earlier royal centres (such as Mérida[16]) completely ceased to be used. The lack of a narrative source for much of the seventh century makes the extent of kings' mobility impossible to assess: care must, therefore, be exercised, before seeing the Visigothic kings as differing radically from their more obviously mobile Frankish counterparts. That there were royal residences outside Toledo is clear from the fact that Reccesuinth died at a villa at *Gerticos*, 120 miles from the *urbs regia*,[17] while there is a suggestion that Chindasuinth was elected king at *Pamlica*, near Burgos.[18]

A different kind of imitation of imperial traditions can be seen in the way in which seventh-century kings celebrated victory over rebels. Under Reccared, for example, the rebel *comes*, Argimund, had his head shaved and his right hand amputated, and was humiliated by being conducted round Toledo seated upon an ass.[19] Nearly a century later, Paul, the *dux* who rebelled against Wamba, was treated in an almost identical fashion, again at Toledo.[20] Both incidents are redolent of imperial triumphal processions, especially in relation to the ritual humiliation of the victim by association with shameful animals.[21]

A point closer to the establishment of Toledo as a 'capital' was made by the gold coinage of Leovigild and his successors. Before Leovigild's reign, the *solidi* were of pseudo-imperial type, retaining the names of the Byzantine emperors; thereafter, coins were issued in the names of the kings themselves.[22] This did not mean that there was no imperial influence on the designs. Leovigild copied the coins of Tiberius II Constantius but, instead of the obverse bearing the emperor's portrait and the reverse the king's monogram or portrait, it was the reverse type – the cross on four steps – which was copied, the obverse being non-imperial:[23] this was precisely the method used earlier in the sixth century by the Merovingian Theodebert I when he sought to claim independence from the Empire.[24] Not only this, but the coins of Leovigild and his successors attribute the imperial qualities of *pietas, iustitia* and *uictoria* to the kings,[25] while the laws make similar claims, referring to royal *misericordia* and *pietas*,[26] and the Toledan councils describe the king as 'diuus',[27] and his treasury as 'sacratissimus'.[28]

This kind of declaration of parity with, and independence from, the Empire raised the problem of how to create a monarch who would be recognised by all his subjects – not only the Goths, but also by the Romans and by the other Germanic peoples (including the Sueves) who formed part of the kings' *imperium*. In the past, it had been possible to claim – whether truthfully or not – that the Empire had in a sense validated a monarch's claim to power, but that was clearly no longer possible. The answer to this was supplied by the Church, and first appears in the form of kings or their rivals claiming divine sanction. The earliest claim of this kind appears, significantly, to have been made by a rebel against a legitimate ruler, when Hermenegild, in revolt against his father, Leovigild, minted coins which bore the words 'regi a Deo uita'.[29] This move was quickly followed by Leovigild himself, who, in the course of his military campaigns, began to issue coins claiming divine assistance in obtaining victory.[30] These and similar assertions were made by successive kings,[31] and, by the end of the seventh century they were probably in advance of the emperors in this respect, since Ervig may have issued coins bearing the head of Christ (rather than his own bust) before the earliest imperial types of this kind, which appeared in 692 under Justinian II.[32] Nor was it only on coins that such claims were made, for as early as the reign of Reccared I (586-601) legal enactments were claiming God's support for royal power.[33]

If kings asserted that they enjoyed the support of the Almighty in this way, the Church does not seem to have been reticent in supporting them, at least once the monarchy had converted to Catholicism. In fact, the Church went further, and ultimately acted as the mediator of divine aid for kings. One of the first stages in this development is marked by the resolution of the Fifth Council of Toledo (636) that anyone aspiring to the throne other than by popular election or the choice of the nobility was to be excommunicated.[34] The Church was not here arrogating to itself (or being given) a positive role in the king-making process, but was becoming involved in the creation and maintenance of stability once a new king had been come to power. Such measures did not, however, prove adequate, for there were always those willing to run the risk of excommunication: if they were successful there was, in reality, not much which could be done about their usurpation.[35]

A later stage in the evolution of the king-making procedure is witnessed by the willingness of the Church for the king to be anointed – a custom with clear Biblical overtones first referred to when Wamba was made king in 672.[36] Again, though, this was only possible after the king had been selected by nomination, election or acclamation:[37] in other words, traditional methods of selection, as practised in the late Roman world, were still fundamental in the actual creation of a ruler, the religious element providing an additional sanction after the event.[38] As such, anointing was not necessarily a guarantee of legitimacy, as may be illustrated by the case of Paul, the *dux* who rebelled against Wamba, who, in a letter to the legitimate king, claimed that he had himself been anointed.[39] In other words, all that a rebel had to do was to convince a bishop (perhaps with threats) that he had undergone some form of legitimate election (which Paul claimed[40]) and, as a result, should be anointed. What anointing could do, though, was to overawe many potential rebels since, as many Biblical examples showed, attempts to overthrow the Lord's anointed could have dire consequences, which were underlined by the triumphal character of kings' celebrations of victories over internal opponents.[41]

Once a king had established his position and secured his title to divine support, the way was open for him to assert that, like the emperor, he was *minister* or *uicarius Dei* or *Christi*[42] – a position accepted by Isidore in his comments on *uicarii Dei* in his *Etymologies*.[43] Equally significant is the fact that the Spanish liturgy often compares the king to Moses or David,[44] a theme echoed in a letter Bishop Braulio sent to Chindasuinth concerning the royal succession, in which the King is likened to David and his son, Reccesuinth, to Solomon.[45]

For the most part, the mutual interest of the monarchs and the Church in stability seems to have allowed harmonious co-operation, but there was a danger for the Church in depicting the king as God's agent, as Braulio found out when Chindasuinth made his deacon, Eugenius, Bishop of Toledo against his will: Chindasuinth was able to make the irrefutable claim that he was the executor of God's will.[46] Eugenius himself seems to have faced a similar problem when the king commanded him to ordain an unsuitable candidate to the priesthood.[47]

To a great extent, kings from Leovigild onwards were successful in welding the Iberian peninsula into a single political entity, for, as E.A. Thompson once noted, while the rebellions against Leovigild were aimed at gaining or preserving independence from the central control exercised by the monarchy, most of the seventh-century revolts were aimed at replacing one king with another, the unity of the monarchy rarely being questioned.[48] The claims made by kings for their own power, and by the Church on their behalf, are likely to be linked to their success and, therefore, to have had some practical effect, both within the kingdom and with regard to the perception of the monarchy's position in relation to the Empire. However effective the propaganda, though, the actions of kings must have been at least as important. According to Sisebut, who wrote a metrical letter to Isidore concerning the nature of kingship, the main functions of the king were those of a war leader and a law giver:[49] this may be taken as a starting-point for an investigation of the practicalities of royal power.

Kings as warriors

Although it is clear that Visigothic kings, like their counterparts elsewhere in Europe, had to be competent military leaders,[50] they can only relatively rarely be seen in this capacity, and such evidence as does exist almost all relates to the period before the 630s.[51] The best-documented war leader is Leovigild, whose campaigns are recounted in John of Biclaro's *Chronicle*.[52] This is probably partly a reflection of John's concern to show Leovigild as the 'John the Baptist' of the Catholic monarchy, but may also be a reflection of the form of his work which, as a chronicle, was likely to concentrate on events of immediately-perceived importance, such as military campaigns.

In his account of the reigns of the kings from Leovigild to Suintila, Isidore also lays stress on military prowess, but it is by no means always certain that the rulers themselves took the field. Hence, although Isidore states that Reccared waged war against hostile peoples, his comments on the campaign against the Franks indicate that it was the *dux* Claudius, rather than the king himself, who led the army; this raises the possibility that Reccared may also not have been directly involved in the campaigns against the Byzantine enclave.[53] It may be that Isidore's presentation is coloured by the fact that he sought to depict Reccared, the first Catholic monarch, as a man of peace. By contrast, he states that Witteric, of whom he disapproved, was bellicose – though his campaigns were not attended with success: the only victory Isidore records during his reign was, he pointedly notes, gained when his *duces* (not the king) took prisoners at Saguntum.[54] Here, while it is clear that a successful king should be a (victorious) war leader, not all campaigns were led by the king in person. This is confirmed by Isidore's account of Sisebut's reign: the king was famous for his military example and victories, and certainly fought the Byzantines in person, but he brought Asturia under his control 'having sent an army', and overcame the Ruccones 'through his *duces*'.[55] Suintila also had a reputation for military glory, and may have taken the field himself, but this is uncertain, even though his competence is unlikely to be in question since he was a *dux* before becoming king.[56]

Isidore's *Chronicle* provides no supplementary evidence, largely because it is so laconic. After Isidore's death, there is no narrative source, and the military aspects of kingship are almost lost from sight. It seems clear from the *Historia Wambae* that military leadership continued to be of some importance throughout the seventh century, and Egica was a *dux* before becoming king in 687, perhaps implying that he had some military competence. That the lack of evidence for war leadership is likely to be a function of the nature of the sources for the last three-quarters of the seventh century must be stressed in view of the defeat of the Visigoths in the early eighth century. There is nothing to suggest that the last kings were any less competent than their predecessors, and any attempt to see the defeat as a result of a lack of effective royal leadership would rely on an argument from silence.

Kings and the law

The second element of kingship as illustrated by Sisebut's letter concerns the administration of justice, and was in some ways nearer to Isidore's heart, as it was a kind of activity in which emperors engaged. According to Isidore, *iustitia* was one of the main kingly virtues,[57] and his interest in kings as law-makers is underlined by the fact that his *History of the Goths* explicitly mentions that kings (both Euric and Leovigild) made written law.[58] That this activity was genuinely of the greatest importance may be judged from the size of the extant *corpus* of legal material from the reign of Leovigild and later: laws survive in the names of Leovigild himself, Reccared, Sisebut, Chindasuinth, Reccesuinth, Wamba, Ervig, Egica and Wittiza – that is, half the kings who ruled from 569 to 711 – while some of their number revised and reissued the entire code.

It is interesting that all the kings in whose names laws survive ruled for at least seven years, while of the nine kings in whose names there are no surviving laws, only two (Witteric and Suintila) reigned for more than six years. This could be coincidence, but might indicate that, important though legislative activity was, it was only after a ruler had secured his position that he was able to participate fully in the law-making process. It may be significant that legislation concerning the royal succession, which tended to be made at times of weakness and uncertainty, was not included in the general body of law, but was given the additional sanction of ecclesiastical approval, finding its place in the enactments of the Toledan councils of the 630s and 680s.[59]

The process by which law was produced is illustrated by Isidore's record of the legislative activity of Leovigild: the King corrected the fifth-century code of Euric, adding new measures and removing those which were superfluous.[60] What Leovigild was doing, therefore, was ensuring that the law was kept in a form which was appropriate to his day, in the same way as had his predecessor, Theudis, whose legal enactment of 546 is one of the very few documents to survive (albeit in fragmentary form) from earlier in the sixth century.[61] Some later kings, like Reccesuinth and Ervig, also felt the need, having added new laws of their own, to reissue the code as a whole, while others were content to promulgate Novels concerning types of case not previously encountered.[62] There was nothing radical or new in this, since it was exactly what the fifth-century western emperors had done, and what earlier 'barbarian' kings had imitated.[63] What may be significant, though, is the that the new laws are referred to as 'nouellae' – a word with specifically imperial overtones – while Leovigild's legislative activity can be seen as an imitation of Justinian's 'restoration' of the law.[64] Similarly, the promulgation of *leges in confirmatione* of the Toledan councils, which commenced with Reccared's conversion at III Toledo, is likely to be a conscious imitation of the imperial tradition of issuing laws to sanction the decrees and canons of the major councils.[65]

The process whereby new law was made also stands in the tradition of emperors (east and west), and of earlier 'barbarian' kings. All cases were to be judged according to the law[66] – in one case, specifically according to the law as written or received by royal notaries.[67] Any case which was not covered by existing law was to be referred to the king so that it could be speedily terminated and, if desirable, a new measure inserted into the *corpus*.[68] (This is almost identical to the statement by the earlier Burgundian king, Sigismund, that the details of specific cases should be published so that they could have a 'general application'.[69]) On other occasions, the king might legislate on his own initiative, in response to events other than individual judicial cases: Wamba, for example, promulgated a law in response to the defection of various provincial officials to the rebel *dux*, Paul, requiring that all functionaries in an area where there was an attack on the 'gens uel patria' should organise resistance.[70] Even in those instances, however, the new law tried to apply the lessons from a specific case to wider conditions, and it may well be for this reason that many of the laws contain lists of officials of varying types and ranks who might be involved in their application.

It is not only in relation to the law-making process that there is continuity with earlier periods, since the new law which was created built upon earlier precedents. Isidore is explicit in referring to Leovigild's legislative activity as a revision of Euric's code, which was essentially Roman provincial (as opposed to imperial, or rescript) law.[71] The implication of this is that such fundamentally 'Roman' law continued to be practised throughout the seventh century – and beyond – albeit adapted and supplemented as new situations arose.[72] That Roman law was still known in seventh-century Spain seems clear from the fact that the *Formulae Wisigothicae* is not only of Roman form,[73] but its contents refer to various Roman legal compilations, such as the *Lex Romana Uisigothorum*,[74] the *Lex Papia Popea*,[75] the Aquileian laws,[76] and the *ius praetorium et urbanum*.[77] The last is perhaps of the greatest significance. If the Visigothic code was not essentially Roman provincial law, it would be unexpected to find reference to the praetorian law, which was never written down in one place: after a century of Visigothic rule in Spain, it would hardly have been remembered. An alternative explanation might be that the Formulary was an antiquarian document of no practical value;

but, if that were the case, it would be unlikely for so many such documents to have been produced in the early middle ages, including a number in Frankia (see Chapter 1).

In addition to their general duty to ensure that the law was up to date and was fairly administered, kings were also open to be petitioned to alter laws or otherwise provide favours for their subjects. Given the lack of a narrative source for much of the seventh century, and, more particularly, of a large volume of hagiographical material, the dispensation of patronage is not easy to discern, but the poverty of the evidence should not in itself lead to the assumption that it was not a function of great importance. One of the few occasions on which the process can be demonstrated to have operated is revealed by the *Uita Fructuosi*, which describes how a royal *gardingus* petitioned the king to intervene on his behalf when the woman to whom he was betrothed decided to become a nun rather than marry him.[78] Less direct, but suggestive, is evidence that the revisions of the law undertaken by Reccesuinth and Ervig may have been commenced after criticisms of their predecessors' tenure of the monarchy.[79] That such criticisms were made is not in doubt,[80] and they may, at least in part, have taken the form of representations to the kings, perhaps of the kind made by Braulio when he requested Chindasuinth to associate Reccesuinth with him in his power and to designate him as his successor.[81]

Queens

The person most directly able to influence the king was the queen, who was clearly of importance in relation to the succession, and is likely to have been so with regard to the dispensation of patronage. Despite this, almost nothing is known of individual queens (not even their names, in many cases), or of queenly activity.[82] In more general terms, the proceedings of the thirteenth council of Toledo illustrate the importance of queens in issues surrounding the succession, for they contain legislation forbidding widowed queens to marry again or to commit adultery:[83] in other words, a queen could legitimise a new ruler by marrying him, or produce further children who would have a claim to the throne. One way round this, as the Franks knew, was to send lone royal women to nunneries, but, while the third council of Saragossa suggested this, XVII Toledo made it clear that this should only be done with the consent of the woman concerned.[84]

Almost the only occasion on which a Visigothic queen is seen in action is in the proceedings of III Toledo, when Baddo, wife of Reccared I, signed a statement affirming the Catholic faith.[85] Even such signatures of queens are a rarity in the absence of a *corpus* of diplomatic material, though one of the very few surviving royal charters was witnessed by Reciberga, Chindasuinth's queen.[86] This lack of evidence is highly unlikely to be a reflection of the importance of queens in the functioning of royal government, but is, like the paucity of evidence concerning petitions to the king, a function of the nature of the sources: neither the proceedings of the church councils, nor the secular laws, are of a nature to record routine queenly activity in the administration of the palace and the distribution of patronage. The lack of a detailed narrative source or of much hagiographical material further conspires to silence concerning royal women, but this should not be taken to suggest that they were any less active than, or behaved in a radically different way from, their contemporaries elsewhere in Europe.

8

The Royal Court

Although the king was ultimately responsible for the administration of the kingdom, he could not act alone, either in terms of war leadership, or in relation to civil administration: not only was he physically unable to do everything himself, but he had to consult and involve members of the aristocracy in order to retain their support.[1] The process is illustrated by the fact that a number of laws record the assistance of members of the *officium palatinum*, or of the *seniores palatii* in their composition.[2] That the same principle operated in relation to at least some military activities is clear from Wamba's consultation with the *primates palatii* before raising his army against the rebel *dux*, Paul.[3] After the rebellion had been put down, the king again sought consensus, for Paul was judged in the presence of the 'seniores palatii', the 'gardingi' and all the palace officials.[4] Wamba was not here being 'democratic' for its own sake, but was bound by the principle, enunciated in the thirteenth council of Toledo, that all palace officials were to be tried before their peers.[5]

The importance of the court as a mechanism for arriving at, and displaying, support for the king is underlined by the fact that courtiers were often present at the great national Church councils the proceedings of which they witnessed. The form of the signatures in the witness lists is variable: sometimes courtiers are simply described as 'uiri illustres' or 'uiri illustres officii palatini',[6] but on three occasions the more specific titles held by members of the *officium palatinum* are recorded.[7] These lists are of the greatest importance, since they record titles not attested in any other type of source, including the main part of the conciliar proceedings: the significance of this will be discussed below, after some of the titles themselves have been examined.

Comites with specific titles

The workings of the royal court are largely obscure, owing to the absence of sources of a nature to reflect them. The laws are generally directed at provincial officials and, even then, are cast in general terms, often referring to categories of office rather than to individual positions. Hagiographical material is scarce and in any case only seldom refers to courtiers; the lack of a narrative source is a further handicap.

8. The Royal Court

The problems are well illustrated by the evidence surrounding some of the courtiers most closely associated with the king – the *cubicularii*. According to VIII Toledo, there were two *comites cubiculariorum*, Odoagrus and Offila; IX Toledo contains reference to a single holder of the office (Eterius); while the thirteenth council was signed by Ataulf, 'comes cubiculariorum', and Argemir, 'comes cubiculi'. Of these men, Odoagrus may appear as 'Odoarus', *comes cubiculariorum* in a charter of Chindasuinth,[8] and Ataulf features in the witness list of XII Toledo, where all court officials are described simply as 'uiri illustres'. Two features of the evidence are problematic. First, in neither the Empire nor any of the other 'barbarian' kingdoms is there a precedent for the existence of more than one *comes cubiculariorum* at a time. It is possible that it is only the eighth council which records this situation, since Argemir (in XIII Toledo) could have been a *comes* within the *cubiculum*, rather than having been in charge of it, but that does little to clarify the position, for which no satisfactory explanation has ever been adduced. Second, Odoagrus, Offilo and Argemir are styled 'dux' as well as being described as *comites cubiculariorum*: the significance of this will be discussed below.

A similar case is that of Argimund who, according to John of Biclaro, was a *dux prouinciae* but was also 'quidem ex cubiculo' of Reccared.[9] The interpretation of these two positions is problematic, since 'dux prouinciae' implies a permanent posting away from the court as the highest-ranking representative of the king in one of the provinces. What may be signified here, therefore, is that Argimund had been based at court as a member of the royal bedchamber before being sent into the provinces. It is possible that such a progression was not unusual (there are similarities in the fifth-century western Empire[10]), since it was a means of trying to ensure that powerful provincial administrators were of proven loyalty: if this was the intention, however, it failed in the case of Argimund, for the incident John recorded was an abortive rebellion against the king.

In the late Roman Empire, the imperial bodyguards (*spatarii*) formed part of the *cubiculum*, and such may also have been the case in seventh-century Spain, though the evidence is not of a kind to permit of certainty. There are several references to *spatarii*, who appear with differing forms of title: in XIII Toledo there are four 'comites et spatarii' (one of whom also appears, simply as 'comes', in XVI Toledo), one 'comes spatarius'; one 'comes spatarius et dux', and one 'comes spatariorum';[11] the last title also appears at VIII Toledo, and in a charter of Chindasuinth, in both of which it is similarly applied to a single official.[12] The *comes spatariorum* was probably the man in charge of the bodyguards – hence the presence of only one at a time – but his subordinates were nevertheless of high enough rank to have been *comites* in their own right. While this is not the same as the kind of usage found in Merovingian Gaul, it may represent no more than a different evolution from a similar origin. Indeed, such a development could already have been prefigured in the fifth century, when Sidonius

Apollinaris' description of Theoderic I's court includes reference to a 'comes armiger'.[13] That *spatarii* did enjoy high standing is confirmed by the case of Theudemund. The proceedings of the sixteenth Toledan council record that Bishop Festus of Mérida obliged the *spatarius* to perform the duties of a *numerarius* in his city, 'contra generis uel ordinis sui usum'. King Egica decreed that the Bishop had acted wrongly, and that Theudemund and his descendants were to be free from such burdens in perpetuity. In the list of signatories, Theudemund appears with the titles of *comes* and *procer*.[14]

Another title with parallels in the Empire and in the earlier and contemporary 'barbarian' kingdoms is that of *comes stabuli*, but although it may be reasonably assumed that the functions this official fulfilled were broadly similar to those of his counterparts elsewhere, nothing save the existence of the position is known in seventh-century Spain, there being a single reference to the title in a conciliar witness list.[15]

Financial officials

Slightly more evidence is available for the courtiers in charge of the financial administration of the kingdom, among whom was the *comes patrimonii* or *comes patrimoniorum*. Officials of this kind were clearly of the greatest importance to the king,[16] and signed the proceedings of the eighth, ninth, thirteenth and sixteenth councils of Toledo, as well as a royal charter. At the eighth council (in 653) two men are recorded with this title, but it is possible that this results from scribal error, since their names, Reccila and Requira, are similar; while this cannot be proved, the fact that Reccila appears (as Richila) alone both earlier (in a charter of 646[17]), and later, at IX Toledo (655), may lend added weight to the suggestion.[18] Vitulus, who appears in XIII Toledo as 'comes patrimonii', bears the same title in the witness list to the sixteenth council, ten years later (693), though there he is also described as 'dux'.

In addition to the material from the conciliar witness lists, there is a small amount of evidence concerning *comites patrimonii* in other sources. A document drawn up in 592 and inserted into the proceedings of the first Council of Barcelona (540), the *de fisco Barcinonensi*, refers to the appointment of *numerarii*[19] of the fisc in the provincial towns, and indicates that this was carried out by the *comes patrimonii* (in this instance, Scipio),[20] though his role may have been limited to that of confirming the choice of the bishops and people.[21] There is also a reference to a *comes patrimonii* in the laws, as Reccared admonished a range of officials, including *comites patrimonii*, that they should not impose excessive financial burdens on the provincials.[22] It is not unexpected that it is the *comites patrimonii* (clearly involved in financial administration) who are the first of the officials so far discussed to feature outside the witness lists, since their sphere of juris-

74

diction, unlike those of the other courtiers, extended outside the palace itself and could impinge directly on the provincials.

The administration of the royal finances was not, however, the responsibility only of the *comes patrimonii*, since the signature list of XIII Toledo contains reference not only to an official of that kind, but also to Isidore, 'comes thesaurorum et dux', while the second council of Seville, held much earlier, in 619, records the existence of a 'rector rerum fiscalium', and of a 'rector rerum publicarum'. Since the *comes patrimonii* was in charge of the fisc, it is likely that he was the 'rector rerum fiscalium'.[23] If this is correct, the *comes thesaurorum* is likely to have been the 'rector rerum publicarum', and could be seen as an equivalent of the imperial *comes sacrarum largitionum*, who had earlier been in charge of the provincial treasuries.[24]

That there were provincial treasuries in the Visigothic kingdom is not in doubt,[25] and it is possible that they were the direct successors of the Roman provincial treasuries, particularly since the boundaries of the Roman provinces may have remained largely unchanged.[26] Furthermore, there is some evidence to suggest that the principle of *adaeratio* continued in force for at least some taxes, since the *de fisco Barcinonensi* shows taxes rendered in kind being translated into gold.[27] What is perhaps unexpected, though, is that, apart from the reference in II Seville (in 619), the *comes thesaurorum* only features in one of the conciliar witness lists. It is not possible to explain this satisfactorily, but it may not be coincidental that it is the thirteenth council at which the *comes* features, since Ervig used the occasion to promulgate a law concerning the remission of taxes[28] – a matter in which the *comes thesaurorum* would have been intimately involved.

The precise relationship between the *comes patrimonii* and the *comes thesaurorum* equally cannot be understood fully, especially since, as seen above, it was the *comes patrimonii*, rather than the *comes thesaurorum*, who appears to have been involved in the appointment of *numerarii* – that is, officials concerned with the collection of taxes. It may be that it is wrong to seek a fully bureaucratic solution, especially since there was – at least on occasion – some overlap between the spheres of competence of the fifth-century imperial *comites rerum priuatarum* and *sacrarum largitionum*, the predecessors of the two offices concerned.[29] It is also possible that the relationship evolved during the course of the seventh century, since in 653, at the eighth Toledan council, a distinction was drawn between the wealth of the monarchy as an institution and that of the king as an individual. This could have necessitated the reorganisation of the court's financial administration, but the evidence is simply too sketchy to permit of more than speculation.

The writing office

Of equal importance to the king as his financial officials, was the writing office, through which all written royal *acta* passed. As most of the work of the writing office was conducted internally within the court, it is predictable that there is little evidence concerning its administration, particularly given the lack of a body of royal *diplomata* of the kind which has survived from Merovingian Frankia. The only type of official connected with the writing office to feature in the Toledan councils is the *comes notariorum*, whose title implies that he was in charge of the notaries and may, therefore, have been the head of the writing office. Although only two such men – Paul and Cixilla – are known by name, this should not lead one to underestimate their importance to the government, since between them they feature in the witness lists of all three Toledan councils at which the detailed titles of the signatories were recorded.[30] Paul also witnessed a charter of Chindasuinth,[31] while Cixilla's name appears amongst those of the *comites* and *uiri illustres* who signed XV Toledo in 688.

The precise functions of *comites notariorum* are not known, but notaries of unspecified type were active in the transmission of royal pronouncements to the Toledan councils,[32] and public notaries had a monopoly over pronouncing, writing and confirming the law.[33] Although it is not clear whether the *comes notariorum* had formal jurisdiction over public notaries in the provinces, the last point is of some significance, for the *comes* was presumably ultimately responsible for seeing that the law was written down and transmitted accurately. This may imply that the *comes* was also answerable for the pronouncement of the law, in much the same way as was the Ostrogothic quaestor[34] or the Merovingian *comes palatii* (see Chapter 4).[35] This suggestion may derive added strength from the absence of quaestors or *comites palatii* from the conciliar proceedings, since men of such high rank are very unlikely to have been omitted. It may be, therefore, that, as with the adoption of the title *comes thesaurorum* rather than that of *comes sacrarum largitionum*, the Visigoths created a new title, albeit one of a 'Roman' type.

More direct evidence for continuing Roman traditions may be adduced from the form of the documents themselves. As with Frankish royal *diplomata*, Visigothic documents were written in a script derived from the Roman administration – but in the cursive provincial script, rather than that of the central imperial court.[36] That royal *acta* were sealed during the sixth century, in a manner similar to their Frankish counterparts, is clear from the law of Theudis, which was confirmed by this means, and which also contains the *recognouit* formula (see Chapter 3).[37] Although there is no similar evidence from the seventh century, that is likely to be a function of the poverty of evidence rather than of a fundamental change of practice. Documents produced in court cases were certainly authenticated by means of seals, and (non-royal) seals have been found archaeologically:[38]

it is therefore highly improbable that kings adopted radically different methods.

Comites scanciarum

The court office most frequently attested in the detailed conciliar witness lists is that of *comes scanciarum*. Twelve holders of this office are known, five from VIII Toledo, and seven from XIII.[39] The only other source to mention a *comes scanciarum* is a charter of Chindasuinth, which Evantius, known from VIII Toledo, signed.[40] Two of the *comites* in XII Toledo also appear in the twelfth council, but, like all the other courtiers there attested, simply as 'uiri illustres'.[41] Otherwise, with one possible exception, none of these men appears elsewhere, nor is the title known from any other source.[42] Eight of the *comites scanciarum* were also *duces*.

Given the nature of the evidence, it is impossible to arrive at any understanding of the functions of these officials except through their title, which is derived from the Gothic *scanc*, meaning 'trestle', 'table' or (perhaps) 'tableware'.[43] This implies that they were involved in the domestic administration of the palace, and it has been suggested that they were the equivalents of the Byzantine *comites pincernarum*.[44] While this is possible, it must remain uncertain, since it is not clear whether the *scanciae* were men (domestic servants) or objects ('tables' – in which case the title would be akin to that of *comes thesaurorum*.) The latter may be suggested by the multiplicity of *comites scanciarum* in existence at one time: if *scanciae* were men, the *comes* would presumably have been in charge of them, and there would be no need for more than one such chief *scancia*. If, on the other hand, *scanciae* were 'tables' or 'cups' or some such, it would be possible to envisage the involvement of several courtiers in domestic administration: in the same way as some *spatarii* were also *comites*, many household officials could have been *comites*.

Honorary titles?

Many of the titles discussed so far share one or more of the following characteristics: precise spheres of jurisdiction cannot be ascribed to them; few are attested outside the witness lists; none is known to have existed before Leovigild's reign, either in the kingdom of Toulouse or in Spain; all have direct parallels with titles found in the imperial court, or are of similar nature; at least two (the *comites cubiculariorum* and *scanciarum*) could be held by more than one man at a time. The combination of all these features has led more than one modern commentator to suggest that some, if not all, of the titles were purely honorary.[45]

If this is accepted, it is not difficult to produce an explanation for the adoption of such titles, particularly given the image kings sought to create that they were the equals of the eastern emperors. Part of their propaganda could have included the creation of an 'imperial' court: the proceedings of the Toledan councils, which were partly held in order to boost the kings' image, would have been the ideal place to present such an image. This appearance need have been no more than superficial, and would not necessarily have borne much resemblance to the practicalities of royal government.[46]

Although this kind of argument fits all the evidence, and could therefore be correct, it has one major weakness: at its core lies a series of arguments from silence. First, the absence, in the period from before Leovigild's reign, of references to courtiers of the kinds which appear in the conciliar material is not surprising, for the earlier part of the sixth century is a period about which almost nothing is known of Visigothic history. Even if some of the precise titles found in and after Leovigild's reign are new, and the product of an 'imperialising' policy, they could be no more than new titles for old appointments: the *comes spatarius*, for example, could be a new title for the *comes armiger* of Sidonius Apollinaris' description of Theoderic I's court.[47]

Second, given the nature of the sources for the seventh century, it is not surprising that a proper impression of the functions of court officials cannot be gained, for there is no type of document which would reveal such men in action. The dangers inherent in ignoring this are clear from the case of the *comes patrimonii*, who does appear outside the signature lists (in the laws), and would appear to have had some form of genuine involvement in the financial administration of the kingdom – even if his role cannot be closely defined. As noted above, it is predictable that it is this official, rather than one involved solely in the internal administration of the palace, who is attested in such a way.

The extent of the similarity between the Visigothic titles and those found in the imperial court (either of the fifth-century western Empire, or the sixth- and seventh-century Byzantine one) is questionable. Some of the titles – those of *comes cubiculariorum, comes patrimonii* and *comes stabuli* – are directly paralleled in the imperial court, but others – *comes notariorum* and *comes thesaurorum* – are not. It may be that the last two titles are in fact derived from the traditions of provincial administration which the Visigoths found in Spain. Each Roman province had public notaries and *thesauri*, and the Visigoths could well have placed courtiers in charge of them: such courtiers were given simple descriptive titles, rather than ones such as quaestor (or referendary) or *comes sacrarum largitionum*, derived from the imperial court. If this is accepted, the suggestion that such titles were not all invented in or after Leovigild's day may gain added strength.

The final argument in favour of the honorary nature of the titles derives from the ability of more than one man to hold the same title simultaneously. As suggested above, the precise form of the title *comes spatarius* makes it possible to see how this could be the case, while yet allowing its holders an active role in the court. It is possible – though less certain – that the same type of explanation can be advanced for the *comites scanciarum*. Allowing that the last case is at least debatable, that only leaves the fact that on a single occasion (VIII Toledo) there were apparently two *comites cubiculariorum*: while this cannot readily be explained, it does not provide enough evidence upon which to build a general hypothesis concerning the significance of the duplication of offices.

Duces

Some of the issues raised in the discussion of *comites* with specific titles – and particularly the contemporaneous use of duplicate titles – can be explored further by an examination of the position of *duces* in the Visigothic kingdom. The evidence for *duces* is greater in volume and more diverse in nature than that for the *comites*, being drawn not only from the conciliar witness lists but, to a significant extent, from the laws, as well as from narrative literature, which is the only kind of material likely to show *duces* in action.

In his account of the attack on Narbonensis made by the Frankish King Guntram, *c.* 589, John of Biclaro describes Boso, leader of the Frankish force, as 'dux'.[48] As so often in the chronicles, this may simply mean 'leader', in a non-technical sense (whether or not he held an office of *dux*). By contrast, the Gothic force was jointly led by Claudius, 'dux Lusitaniae': this implies that he held a permanent office in the province of Lusitania. In other words, Claudius' position was heir of that of the late Roman *dux limitis prouinciarum*, a position known to have been adopted by the Visigoths in the fifth century, when *Duces* Victorius and Vincentius were permanently based in newly conquered frontier provinces.[49] The other Gothic leader of the Frankish campaign, Gedeon, is described simply as 'dux', and it is impossible to determine whether he was a *dux prouinciae* or simply the leader of an army. Similar uncertainty surrounds the significance of John's earlier references to the *duces* of Reccared who had defeated a previous Frankish campaign, led by Desiderius, and the *duces* of Leovigild who put down the rebellion of Malaric in Galicia.[50] Such problems of interpretation are not confined to John's work, for it is not certain that Isidore always used *dux* in the technical sense of a *dux prouinciae*: that the latter is possible is clear from his account of Claudius' anti-Frankish campaign, where, unlike John, he describes Claudius simply as 'dux',[51] but on other occasions, such as his comments on the activities of Witteric's army, the case is debatable.[52]

The evidence of the other main source of narrative type – Julian of Toledo's *Historia Wambae* – which contains material of relevance to this question, permits slightly more certainty in at least some cases. One of the supporters of Paul's rebellion against Wamba, Ranosind, is specifically described as 'dux Tarraconensis',[53] but the case of his fellow rebel, Wittimir, as of Paul himself, is less clear, since both men are only described as 'dux':[54] given that Julian was careful to give Ranosind's proper title, however, it may be unlikely that Paul and Wittimir were *duces prouinciarum*. This seems to be ruled out for at least some of the *duces* involved in suppressing the rebellion, by virtue of the fact that they were chosen or elected by the army.[55] It would seem very unlikely that Wamba – or any other king – would have allowed soldiers to select *duces prouinciarum* who might have become permanent, but he might have allowed them some say as to who their leaders for the campaign should be.

That *duces prouinciarum* were permanent is implied by a law of Egica which refers to Gallia Narbonensis as a *ducatus*,[56] and there is little reason to doubt that their position was broadly similar to that of the great Frankish *duces*. Their power certainly seems to have been primarily military, at least in origin, and their position may be best described by the *Uita Fructuosi*, which refers to a 'dux exercitus prouinciae'.[57] As observed earlier, Claudius, *dux* of Lusitania, was commissioned to oppose Frankish incursions into Narbonensis.[58] Military power may also account for the fact that Claudius was responsible for putting down the rebellion by the Arian bishop, Sunna, in Mérida.[59] (The fact that the source for this event describes him as 'dux Emeritensis ciuitatis' is not significant, since Mérida was the administrative centre of Lusitania.)

The laws also refer to *duces*, though the significance of the term is not always entirely clear. As in the narrative and hagiographical material, *duces* might be involved in military affairs,[60] but whether this means that they were army leaders or *duces prouinciarum* is not known: perhaps either was possible. The position is further complicated by the fact that the laws also record involvement in other types of activity, such as the administration of taxation;[61] judicial affairs (notably those concerning adultery);[62] the despoliation of churches;[63] capital cases;[64] the enforcement of proper court procedure, and crimes committed by other judges.[65] In the last two instances, it is clear that the *duces* concerned were envisaged as being of very high status, since the powers involved set them above other judges. It is highly unlikely that such men were army leaders, and they were probably *duces prouinciarum*.

If this is correct, it is possible that, as in the Frankish world, the functions of *duces prouinciarum* evolved during the seventh century, when the extent of the kingdom was greater than it had been previously. As the king was less able frequently to be present in each of the provinces, more power – including civilian jurisdiction – had to be delegated to the *duces*, who may thereby have come to enjoy enhanced autonomy.[66] It is conceivable that such an evolution is reflected in the fact that, with one possible exception, the earliest of the laws which refer to *duces* date from the reign of Chindasuinth.[67] While this may indicate a change in the power of *duces*, caution must be exercised in using this piece of evidence to date the change precisely, since it was only in the seventh century that laws came to be of a nature to record the existence of such officials. Euric's *Code*, and Leo-vigild's amendment of it were essentially derived from Roman provincial law of a kind which rarely mentioned procedural matters. It was only later that kings came to issue novels which included procedures, and that the law noted officials of any kind: the first king from whom a large body of such legislation survives is Chindasuinth.[68] This means that, if there was indeed an extension of the power of *duces prouinciarum*, it could have occurred rather earlier, perhaps following the unification of Spain during the late sixth century.

Duces feature in the detailed signature lists of the eighth and thirteenth (and, to a more limited extent, the ninth and sixteenth) Toledan councils, where the title is combined with those of the *comites* of the court-based administration. It is possible that all these men – and, indeed, all *duces* from during or after the reign of Chindasuinth – were *duces prouinciarum*, a figure of eight provinces being feasible (though six is more likely – see Map II).[69] While such a hypothesis is attractive, particularly since one might expect *duces prouinciarum*, who are otherwise unattested in the proceedings, to have been present at the national church councils, it cannot be proved.

If, despite what was argued above, the *comes*-titles are purely honorary, the likelihood that the *duces* are *duces prouinciarum* may be increased;[70] if, on the other hand, the other titles genuinely reflect court administration, the suggestion becomes more difficult to sustain, partly on account of the duplication of some titles, and partly because it would seem unlikely that the king would have countenanced a situation in which some of those who worked most closely with him and were responsible for his security – his *cubicularii* and *spatarii* – were under the control of powerful men with territorial power bases who might be his rivals. Allowing that the other titles are substantive, an alternative seems to be called for. As was observed earlier, the army was on occasion allowed to choose its leaders (*duces*) for specific campaigns. It is no more likely that the choice was completely free than that kings entrusted their personal security to *comites prouinciarum*, and it may be that the soldiers chose their leaders from men whom the king deemed suitable – whether for reasons of birth, merit or loyalty. Such men are likely to have been courtiers (whether permanently based at the court or provincial administrators), and could have borne the title *dux* in addition to their other titles. That men like Isidore, *comes thesaurorum*, whose court-based functions had nothing to do with military affairs, could also be *duces* does not present difficulties, for as was seen in Chapter 3, a Frankish courtier such as the referendary, Chadoind, was expected to lead armies on occasion.[71] Such men, together with the *duces prouinciarum*, could have formed the 'ordo' of *duces* referred to in an edict promulgated by Ervig at the twelfth Council of Toledo, and the 'officium ducum' which apparently made Wamba king.[72] It is possible that these men could also be described as *duces exercitus Hispaniae*,[73] though, given that the phrase occurs in a hagiographical source, it is not clear whether it has any technical significance.[74]

Other *comites*

Within the provinces which were administered by the *duces prouinciarum* there were local royal representatives – the *comites ciuitatum* – whose main role seems to have been primarily civilian, at least in origin. The scarcity of narrative sources once again means that such men are not seen in action, almost the only reference to one of their number in a work of that kind being that to Ilderic, *comes* of Nîmes, whose involvement in the rebellion against Wamba was recorded in Julian's account of Paul's rising.[75] From the laws, however, it may be learnt that *comites ciuitatum* were responsible (among other things[76]) for administering justice according to the law,[77] and punishing persistent adulterers,[78] and could intervene in cases of divorce;[79] they were also to ensure that rivers were not dammed or diverted.[80] The proceedings of the Council of Narbonne (589) record that they were to exact fines for Sabbath-breaking, and to punish fortune-tellers.[81] There are also, however, laws which indicate that *comites ciuitatum* could become involved in military affairs, for they were to exact penalties from those who were unwilling to join the local muster, while yet protecting clergy from demands for military service;[82] they were also to distribute supplies to the army,[83] as well as to prevent soldiers from devastating the countryside.[84] The sum of this evidence suggests that, as in sixth-century Gaul,[85] the *comes ciuitatis* was the main royal representative in his city, and could intervene in almost any sphere of local administration.[86]

The laws which refer to the civil jurisdiction of *comites ciuitatum* make it clear that theirs was not the court of first instance in the provinces, but that cases only reached them after other *iudices* had failed to act or in order to have their decisions enforced.[87] This is underlined by a law which reserves cases of persistently adulterous servants to the court of the king, *dux* or *comes ciuitatis*.[88] The reason for this must be that *duces* and *comites ciuitatum* had a higher status than that of other kinds of judge, possibly derived from the fact that they were members of the king's entourage. This may be confirmed by another law which states that the king, *dux* or *comes* (not *comes ciuitatis*) should hear cases concerning unnecessary delays in the administration of justice.[89]

Similar unspecific references to *comites* are found elsewhere in the laws,[90] and there is no reason to suppose that what is meant is always *comes ciuitatis* rather than simply 'companions of the king' (though it may sometimes be[91]): *comites* of the king, no matter what (if any) their specific office, could almost certainly act as the king's representatives in any matter, as occasion demanded.[92] Concrete examples of this kind of activity are very hard to find, but that is likely to be a function of the lack of narrative and hagiographical sources. Even on the rare occasions when named *comites* do appear outside the conciliar signature lists, the references do not always illuminate the functions of such men: one, for example, is simply known as the recipient of a letter from Pope Leo II,[93] while another benefited from the powers of St Aemilianus.[94] Perhaps the only exception to this is the case of Angelas, *comes*, who was sent by the king to mediate between an unnamed royal *gardingus* and his fiancée, Benedicta: after her betrothal, Benedicta had decided to enter a nunnery instead of marrying, and the *gardingus* appealed to the king to force her to honour her vows to him.[95]

In the conciliar signature lists, some *comites* appear without more specific titles; some of their number are *proceres* in addition to being *comites*.[96] This term is never applied to *comites* who held an individual office, nor to men described as *duces*, and does not itself seem to denote such an office. Instead, the word may apply to a particular category of senior courtier and either be an honour (perhaps similar to the patriciate) or, as C. Sánchez Albornoz y Menduiña has suggested, a member of the king's inner advisory council which may have had certain similarities with the imperial *consistorium*.[97]

Gardingi

The *gardingus* in the story concerning Benedicta clearly had a direct relationship with the king, since he is described as 'gardingus regis'. The only other occasion on which such a man is referred to outside the legal material is in Julian's *Historia Wambae*, which states that one of the rebels was Hildigisus, 'sub gardingatus adhuc consistentes'.[98] This may imply that the title was applied to someone relatively junior, who might expect some kind of promotion, and, coupled with the Benedicta story, could be interpreted to show that *gardingi* were relatively young. Equally, the account of Wamba's trial of the rebel Paul distinguishes the *gardingi* who were present from the *seniores palatii* and members of the *officium palatinum*:[99] this accounts for their absence from the lists of *uiri illustres* who signed the Toledan councils. Such men were clearly not of low status, however, for they did participate in the trial of Paul, suggesting that they were in some sense his peers,[100] and are on more than one occasion numbered (with *duces* and *comites*) among people of the 'maior locus':[101] they were also accorded the same privileges at law as bishops and *optimates palatii*.[102]

The actual functions of *gardingi* are very poorly documented, since such men only appear in a very small number of laws. From one such law it is clear that *gardingi* held or administered land, since, in common with landowners, they were obliged to supply soldiers;[103] another law places them in a list of officials who might be responsible for opposing rebellions and invasions, and does little to differentiate their position from that of other officials.[104] From this, it has been suggested that *gardingi* were primarily military officers, perhaps in charge of the cavalry or of specialist units.[105] Such an interpretation is, however, too narrowly based upon the laws, and does not take adequate account of the meaning of the term *gardingus* itself, or of the effect the nature of the sources may have on the understanding of the position of men described by it. *Gardingus* is clearly related to the Gothic *gards*, meaning 'house', 'family' or 'court',[106] and is an adequate translation of the Latin *domesticus*.[107] To see *gardingi* as equivalent to late Roman and Frankish *domestici* may help to explain some of the features of the Visigothic evidence. First, since it was seen in Chapter 3 that Frankish *domestici* were often young men, it is possible that the suggestion that Visigothic *gardingi* were also young may be strengthened. Second, as in both the Frankish kingdom and the earlier Roman world, *gardingus* may have designated a rank, rather than a specific office – in other words, it may have been analogous to the non-specific use of the term *comes*.

Finally, if *gardingi* were *domestici*, the poverty of the legal evidence becomes explicable since most of them would have been based in the royal court, sometimes engaged in low-level palace administration, and would rarely have come in contact with the provincials in such a way as to necessitate reference to them in laws intended to be applied outside the king's court. The exception to this would have been any *gardingi* who, like some of the Frankish *domestici*, were responsible for the administration of individual royal estates: it may be to this category of men that the laws are addressed. If this is the case, it is perhaps not surprising that the laws concern the raising of armies, for that was a sphere in which the activities of those *gardingi* who were estate administrators would have impinged directly on the provincials.

Lesser officials

As was seen above, although *gardingi* were not classed as *optimates* or *seniores palatii*, they were among the men of the 'maior locus', who included bishops, *duces* and *comites*; the other officials who feature in the law codes are designated 'inferiores' or even 'uiliores'.[108] This raises the question as to who were the lesser men, and what was it was which distinguished them from the greater men.

One of the officials who appears to be designated in this way is the *uicarius*. When this title appears in the laws it always immediately follows that of *comes*:[109] this suggests that the *uicarius* was the deputy of some kind of *comes* – an interpretation which derives added credibility from the fact that on one occasion there is specific reference to a *uicarius comitis*,[110] while one of the Visigothic *Formulae* mentions *comites* or their 'uices agens'.[111] None of these references relates to any specific type of *comes*, but the *comes* most likely to have had a permanent deputy is the *comes ciuitatis*, and it is clear that *uicarii*, like *comites*, could intervene in almost any sphere of government, including the administration of justice, taxation and of the army.

A similar range of activity is attributed to another official – the *tiufadus* – whose title often appears in the laws either immediately before or after that of *uicarius*. It is clear from these documents that *tiufadi* might be involved in the administration of justice,[112] in that of the army,[113] and in that of taxation;[114] two further laws concern the involvement of *tiufadi* in preventing bishops from alienating Church property,[115] and in the apprehension of fugitive slaves.[116] On other occasions, the *tiufadus* appears without the accompaniment of the *uicarius*, in relation to military and judicial affairs.[117]

The precise nature of the office of *tiufadus* is obscure, partly on account of the character of the sources, which – yet again – precludes seeing such a man in action. The picture is rendered more murky by a disagreement as to the meaning of the word. One school of thought holds that *tiufadus* is a Latinisation of *thusundi-faths* (leader of a thousand men) and, therefore, an equivalent of the pure Latin *millenarius*.[118] Such a proposition has derived strength from the fact that Euric's fifth-century law code records the involvement of the *millenarius* in certain inheritance disputes, whereas in Leovigild's revision of the law such cases were to be dealt with by the *tiufadus*.[119] However, the equation of *tiufadus* and *millenarius* has been demonstrated on more than one occasion to be linguistically unlikely.[120] That *faths* means 'lord' or 'superior' is not in question,[121] but the first half of the word may be related either to *thius* ('slave'),[122] or to *thiuda* ('people' or 'group of people').[123] It is not possible to come to a firm conclusion between the two possibilities. Most recently, H. Wolfram has concluded that *tiufadus*, while originally meaning 'lord of slaves', later came to designate simply the leader of a unit of the army, perhaps made up of young soldiers.[124] Whether the last part of the suggestion is correct or not, it is perhaps unlikely that an association with slaves persisted in the seventh century, since it would seem strange that a 'leader of slaves' should appear in the laws in close association with men of the rank of the *comes* and the *uicarius*:[125] it may, therefore, be better to see the *tiufadus* simply as a 'leader of men'. It is not even possible to be certain that the *tiufadus* was primarily a military official: civilian duties are not apparent before the reign of Chindasuinth, but, as in the case of *duces*, the changing nature of the law makes it difficult to draw conclusions from this.[126]

In addition to *uicarii* and *tiufadi*, the laws often refer to *iudices*,[127] who are sometimes described as 'iudices locorum',[128] 'iudices territorium',[129] 'iudices ciuitatum',[130] or even 'iudices prouinciarum':[131] the phrase *iudex ciuitatis* may on occasion be synonymous with *comes ciuitatis*,[132] and it may be that *iudex prouinciae* is equivalent to *dux prouinciae*, though that is no more than speculation. On occasions when the *comes ciuitatis* and the *iudex* both feature in a single law, the *iudex* is always lower down the list of officials who might be involved in the type of case being discussed, and the *comes* heard appeals from his court.[133] In those instances, *iudex* must refer to a lesser official, and may be a generic term for such men rather than an specific office.[134] Where the *iudex* is referred to as being attached to a *locus* or *territorium*, what may be meant is simply a local official, such as a *uilicus*; as such, the term may also have embraced *uicarii* and, possibly, *tiufadi*, who were presumably locally based.

The main distinction between the position of the *comes* and the *dux* who heard appeals from the courts of the other *iudices*, and that of those other *iudices* themselves, was that the *comes* and *dux* were members of the king's entourage, even if they were in charge of the administration of a city or province. This seems to be the distinction between officials who occupied the *maior locus* and the *inferiores*. Given the way in which officials of many types, from *duces* to *tiufadi*, could, on occasion, intervene in many spheres of the administration – military, judicial and financial – the factor which determined the precise nature of their involvement may have been their status rather than the formal office they held. This cannot, however, be taken to indicate that the offices as such were honorary, even if specific spheres of jurisdiction are difficult to find: given the nature of the sources, that would be an argument from silence. The title of an official – of whatever rank – is as likely to have reflected his main function as it did in the Frankish kingdom: it did not, however, preclude him from acting in other capacities if occasion demanded and if he was of appropriate rank.

9

Conclusion

Any attempt to understand the workings of the seventh-century Visigothic royal court and provincial government is, to an even greater extent than in the Frankish kingdom, beset by problems posed by the nature of the sources. For the court, the signature lists of the great Toledan church councils provide many titles, and more names, of officials, while the laws furnish evidence of positions within the provincial administration. Few of the offices attested in the councils feature in the laws, and it is rare for a functionary of any kind to be seen in action. Further, almost none of the titles found in either type of document can be demonstrated to have existed before Leovigild's time.

The combination of these features has led to suggestions that Leovigild undertook a far-reaching re-organisation of his court in conscious imitation of the Byzantine empire.[1] It is clear that Visigothic kings from Leovigild onwards set themselves up as in some sense equal to the emperors, rather than as subordinate to them (as in the fifth century), and claimed legitimation from God rather than from the East; but it does not follow that they deliberately created a palatine administration which mirrored that of the emperors. The absence of evidence for the organisation of the royal court in the first two-thirds of the sixth century makes it impossible to demonstrate the extent of any reshaping undertaken towards the end of the century; and a suggestion that Leovigild instituted radical change is in danger of being based largely on silence. Further, detailed examination of the courtiers' titles has suggested that by no means all of them have direct parallels in the Byzantine court, but that they represent adaptations from provincial administrative positions such as the Visigoths would have found when they occupied Gaul in the fifth century, and Spain in the sixth.[2]

Although the Visigothic court appears differently organised from its Frankish counterpart, the divergence may be partly (though not entirely) due to the different nature of the sources for the two kingdoms. Both courts contained officials with titles derived from, or imitating, the imperial court – the Frankish referendary, and the Visigothic *comes cubiculariorum*, for example. Perhaps the most significant difference is the apparent duplication of titles in the Visigothic court, which has led to the suggestion that the 'offices' they represent were no more than honorary. Close examination of the duplicate titles, however, makes it possible to interpret them in a different way, and as representing variant forms of adaptation from Roman organisation, in which a greater number of men (such as bodyguards) were ranked as *comites* ('companions') of the king. This does not necessarily reflect significantly greater 'Germanic' influence, but may be no more than a variation in the evolution from the mixture of tribal, imperial and provincial traditions which were the common inheritance of both the Franks and the Visigoths in Gaul in the fifth and earlier sixth centuries.

The fact that very few court-based officials are mentioned in the sources other than the conciliar witness lists has in the past been adduced in support of the case for the honorary nature of court office. It has here been demonstrated, however, that if the nature of the sources is fully taken into account, other interpretations are again possible, since the laws – by far the largest body of source material – cannot be expected to refer to court-based officials as they are addressed to functionaries who operated at a distance from the court, in the provinces. To some extent, the converse is also true, since relatively few of the provincial officials would have attended the court regularly, even for the great church councils. Neither the conciliar proceedings nor the laws are therefore likely to reflect both the central and the provincial administration.

Within the provinces, as in the court, there was a large degree of continuity from the fifth century, when the Visigoths who settled in Gaul adapted some of the institutions of Roman provincial administration to the new circumstances of the settlement – though evolution continued throughout the sixth and seventh centuries. *Duces prouinciarum*, for example, may originally have had primarily military jurisdiction, while *comites ciuitatum* may have been mainly civilian; even in the fifth century, there were occasions when the distinction between the two spheres was blurred, and this may have become more widespread in the seventh century, gradually giving rise to the situation in which *duces* were superior to the *comites*, whose territories were smaller. In this there are parallels with Frankia, and it is possible that, also as in the Merovingian kingdom, the great provincial leaders were able to retain, and even enhance, their freedom of action following the enlargement of the kingdom by Leovigild.

For all the theocratic statements concerning the nature of their power, the realities faced by Visigothic kings were probably little different from those of their Merovingian contemporaries, particularly in the second half of the seventh century, when the succession was restricted to two families. Aristocrats and powerful officials had to be accommodated, and on occasion they rebelled. After Leovigild's time, however, such rebellions were directed against individual kings, and represent the attempts of over-mighty subjects to acquire or dominate the crown; the fact of kingship and the unity of the kingdom were seldom seriously challenged. The degree of cohesion seems to have been greater in the seventh century than earlier, but the extent of centralisation (and its practical implications) is considerably more difficult to assess. In the sixth century the major *ciuitates* appear to have been in large measure autonomous: apart from occasions when kings were present in them, royal authority was sometimes little more than nominal.[3] The more kings stayed in or near their ceremonial capital at Toledo during the seventh century, the greater the likelihood that the local officials and magnates could act semi-autonomously. The character of the sources does not, however, allow a proper assessment of the extent to which this occurred: the lack of a narrative source, of a large body of hagiographical material, or of a *corpus* of royal *diplomata* – all of which might show kings in action in different parts of the kingdom – is a major handicap, and makes the secular politics and the realities of power in Visigothic Spain almost impenetrable.

PART III

Lombard Italy

Although the Lombards had been settled within the territory of the former Empire, in Pannonia, since the 520s, little is known of their sojourn there (at least in strictly historical terms). By contrast with the Franks and Visigoths, the Lombards therefore only emerge fully into history with their conquest of Italy at the beginning of the period covered by this book. By that time, the Franks and Visigoths had become well established in their respective territories, and, although there were frontier and internal disputes, warfare was not so prominent a feature of their seventh-century history as it had been during some of the earlier phases of their settlement within the Empire, nor as it was to the Lombards as they sought to establish themselves in the Italian peninsula (see Map III on p. 180).

Military arrangements were also rendered peculiarly important to the Lombards by the tenacity of the Byzantines, which denied the Lombards the opportunity to rule the entire Italian peninsula. Not only was there a land frontier in the south, but the territory subject to the Lombards was itself divided into two blocks by Rome, the Exarchate of Ravenna, and the corridor between them. The inhabitants of that corridor were as anxious to defend their freedom from Lombard rule as the Lombards were to take it: the reasons for the attitude of both parties were not only practical, but also symbolic, since the corridor contained the two greatest former imperial centres.

A consequence of these circumstances was that there were a large number of powerful military leaders – the *duces* – who engaged in high-profile activities, against both external enemies and internal rivals. The major narrative source for the history of the Lombards – Paul the Deacon's *Historia Langobardorum* – therefore devotes a great deal of space to such leaders and to warfare of all kinds, as do the almost entirely hostile references to the Lombards in the Papal sources. In the absence of a large body of other coherent evidence, modern historians have often tended to follow Paul's lead, and to see the Lombards as more warlike – and therefore more 'barbaric' – than the Franks and Visigoths. This has been particularly unfortunate for the reputation of the Lombards on account of the fact that the major source for their Ostrogothic predecessors in Italy – the *Uariae* of Cassiodorus – deliberately sought to stress precisely opposed qualities.[1]

91

What has often been missed is that Paul was not an objective historian, but deliberately selected his material to illustrate a particular theme. The recognition of this means not only that the impact of the biases within his own account has to be appreciated, but that other kinds of evidence – particularly those which reveal aspects of government other than the military – have to be given due weight. Only when those factors are taken into account can an understanding of the true nature of the Lombard state be approached.

10

The Sources

Unlike the Frankish and Visigothic kingdoms, the history of the Italian kingdom of the Lombards forms the subject of a single large-scale narrative source, Paul the Deacon's *Historia Langobardorum*. The only major lacuna in its coverage is the period between the death of King Liutprand in 744 and the Frankish conquest of the kingdom thirty years later. The gap exists despite the fact that Paul lived through the period following Liutprand's death, probably writing his *History* in the 780s: either he deliberately chose not to write of the decline of Lombard power after Liutprand's reign, or, particularly given that the work lacks an introduction or dedication, it is possible that it was incomplete at the time of Paul's own death.[1]

The *History* is very much a the story of a *gens* or *natio*, tracing the history of the Lombard people from its origins to the point at which it began to lose its individual identity: much of the anecdotal material contained within the work reveals characteristics which distinguished the Lombards from other peoples, whether Franks or Romans.[2] The bulk of the narrative concerns the Lombards in Italy: a similar focus is found in Paul's other historical work, the *Historia Romanorum*, and it is likely that the author sought to show that Alboin's occupation of the peninsula was no less legitimate than that of Odoacer and Theoderic had been in the fifth century.[3] In line with this there is an element within the *History of the Lombards* which stresses the Christian nature of Lombard rule, or at any rate does not draw attention to pagan and Arian elements.[4]

The propagandist element in the work may be largely accounted for by the circumstances in which it was written. Late in his life, Paul was closely associated with the ducal court of Benevento at a time when the *dux* was Arichis II, whose wife, Adelperga, was daughter of the last Lombard king, Desiderius, at whose court Paul had lived for a time.[5] Not only did Arichis represent the continuance of the Lombard dynasty after the Carolingian conquest of the northern heartland of the kingdom, but he also had associations with Friuli, Paul's own homeland. It is likely that, in writing the *History*, Paul sought to strengthen the legitimacy of Beneventan independence from the Carolingians under Arichis and his son, Grimoald III.[6] As part of that process, it was necessary to provide a more general depiction of the legitimacy of Lombard rule in Italy.

Within this overall framework, Paul's narrative is selective and uneven. The period of Lombard settlement in Italy is treated at some length, as is its aftermath, to the accession of Agilulf in 591. The ensuing seventy years are covered in much more cursory fashion, while the reign of Grimoald I occupies almost the whole of Book V; the last book carries the story forward to the death of Liutprand in 744.[7] The emphasis is therefore on the establishment of Lombard rule, and on the reign of Grimoald I, whose namesake, Arichis II's son, Grimoald III, may have been the intended recipient of the *History*.[8] Paul's geographical coverage is equally unbalanced, with very little space devoted to Tuscany and areas such as the territories of Genoa and Parma; the north east, by contrast, is well represented, as are Pavia (the centre of the kingdom) and Benevento.[9] The last is not surprising given Paul's association with Arichis, and the north-eastern bias may be accounted for by the Paul's Friulian origins, which perhaps gave him access to detailed information concerning the area.

The narrative Paul constructed has been described as 'primarily a record of deeds, or acts, of the magnates and kings' of the Lombards,[10] and elements of it have more in common with epic than with history in a narrow sense.[11] This, combined with other characteristics of the work (including its regional bias), has suggested to one modern historian that the *History* may have drawn on oral tradition for much of its material.[12] While there is merit in that case, the concentration on kings and other leaders (particularly those involved in military events which are high-profile and of immediately perceived importance) is inevitable in a work consisting of no more than six short books, and which seeks to provide an explanation for the legitimacy of Lombard rule: there are parallels between this and the type of evidence supplied by chronicles, whether concise ones like that of Marius of Avenches, or longer documents of the kind written by Fredegar. The peaceful, administrative actions of both kings and war leaders are more seldom depicted in the *History*, and very little can be gleaned from Paul's work concerning officials resident at the central royal court, or those of lesser status.

In addition to oral evidence, Paul used earlier written sources when he compiled his *History*. Perhaps one of the most important of those documents was a chronicle written by Secundus of Trent, which provided a contemporary account of the events of the late sixth and early seventh centuries.[13] Secundus' work is now lost, but other sources available to Paul survive and retain independent value as evidence. One such document is the *Origo gentis Langobardorum* which was probably written around 670, and provides an account of the early history of the Lombard people – largely before their entry into Italy, and so of little assistance for the present enquiry.[14] Another source was formed by the letters[15] and *Dialogues* of Pope Gregory the Great, the latter being intended for moral instruction with some similarities of content and purpose (though not of form) with the hagiographical works of Gregory of Tours.[16]

10. The Sources

The final major source which would have been available to Paul is the *Liber Pontificalis*, the biographies of which were, in the period between 530 and 816, written during or immediately after the lives of the popes who form their subject.[17] The independent value of the *Liber* is particularly important for the period after Paul's *History* ends in 744, but it is reduced both by the purpose of the document and by its hostility to the Lombards – something which it shares with other sources for the last years of the kingdom.[18] The individual lives contained within the *Liber* were written according to a predetermined schema and were designed to show how opposition to the papacy (and, therefore, God) ultimately ended in disaster – whether it was by the Franks, the Goths, the Lombards or the Byzantines; a second purpose was to serve as some kind of guide to the papal archives:[19] both characteristics render it largely unhelpful for this enquiry.

As in Visigothic Spain, relatively little hagiographical material has survived from Lombard Italy, and it is not clear how much was produced. Although Jonas of Bobbio wrote lives of saints, his main work, the *Uita Columbani*, relates to Frankia rather than to Italy. The only other hagiographer of note is Ambrose Autpert, abbot of S. Vincent at Volturno from 777 to 784, who wrote an account of the life of Paldo, the founder of his monastery, and of his nephews.[20] Like the small quantity of other ecclesiastical material – a few poems, and most of the letters collected in the *Epistolae Langobardicae* – Autpert's work contains little of relevance to the study of kingship and the organisation of government.

It is in another monastic document – the *Regestum Farfense* compiled in the eleventh century by Gregory of Catino – that are preserved many of the *diplomata* which have survived from the Lombard kingdom. Of 540 known documents produced by kings, by *duces* in Spoleto and Benevento, and by private individuals throughout the kingdom, something over a quarter are preserved in this one source, including almost all those drafted within the duchy of Spoleto:[21] the *Regestum* is even more remarkable in that it appears to contain only genuine documents.[22] The same cannot be said of much of the diplomatic material purporting to be from the Beneventan duchy which is found in the *Chronicon Uulternese* and the *Chronicon s. Sophiae*, both written in the early twelfth century.[23] The sources for the *diplomata* produced in the northern parts of the Lombard kingdom are more diverse: over two-thirds of the large number of eighth-century private documents which are known survive as originals, but none of the royal *diplomata* remains as more than a copy.[24]

Although the Lombard *diplomata* lack detailed witness lists such as are occasionally found in the Frankish material, they – whether private, ducal or royal – contain valuable evidence for the way in which they were produced. This allows the activities of certain officials to be seen, particularly in relation to the drafting of the documents themselves: this (in contrast to the Frankish material) is as true of some of the private as of the royal documents. The ducal *diplomata* are without parallel in the Frankish and Visigothic kingdoms, and the reasons for their production will be discussed in Chapter 12: in terms of their character, the only difference between them and royal documents was the issuing authority.

In addition to the *diplomata*, an impressive quantity of royal legislation has survived – almost as large a *corpus* as for the Visigothic kingdom. This law, which will be discussed more fully in the next chapter, has often been seen as being 'Germanic': in other words, despite some influence from Roman imperial law, it is often seen as essentially a written version of Lombard custom.[25] Given that most 'barbarian' law of the fifth and sixth centuries is now thought to consist largely of Roman provincial law,[26] it is likely that the first Lombard code – that of Rothari – is of a similar nature. This may be reflected in its title – it is an *edictum*, which was the term used by the Romans for the pronouncements of the praetorian prefects to apply imperial law and modify it for use within the areas subject to their jurisdiction.[27] As in the case of the Visigoths, the law was not monolithic, but was amended and re-issued by some of Rothari's successors in response to new circumstances. There is, however, no parallel to the lists of officials found in the individual provisions of Visigothic law, the general character of Lombard legislation being nearer to that of the Franks: accordingly, while the law can make a significant contribution to the understanding of royal functions, it reveals relatively little concerning the activities of provincial officials, and even less of those of courtiers.

Taken collectively, the sources for the Lombard kingdom – at least in so far as the present study is concerned – are more varied than those for its Visigothic counterpart, and may allow a fuller understanding of politics and of at least the provincial aspects of royal administration. The largest part of the evidence was produced relatively late in the kingdom's existence (or after its end) – apart from the laws of Rothari and Grimoald, most of the sources (including by far the majority of the *diplomata*) are products of the eighth century. Although the circumstances surrounding the Lombard invasion of Italy are relatively well documented thanks to the comments of foreign chroniclers and the writings of Gregory the Great, much of the seventh century is poorly represented, especially given the unevenness in Paul the Deacon's coverage (see above). While it may, therefore, be relatively easy to discuss aspects of the administrative structures of the Lombards in their mature form, it is considerably less so to trace their evolution during the preceding century and a quarter. This means that there may be a danger (which is unavoidable) of presenting too static a picture: in addition, because the chronological weighting of the evidence differs from that relating to the Merovingian and, more especially, Visigothic worlds, some direct comparisons are difficult to make.

Kings and Queens

Lombard kingship is often seen as a weak institution and kings as insecure, real power in the realm being wielded by the *duces*, who were only
gradually brought under full royal control.[1] There is certainly some merit
in the proposition that the institution of monarchy was relatively weak in
the early days of the Italian kingdom, since in the ten years following
Cleph's death (574) there was no king, the *regnum* being in the hands of
the *duces*.[2] The significance of this is difficult to estimate, but, unless the
period is interpreted as a regency for Cleph's son, Authari,[3] it is hard to
provide an explanation consistent with strong kingship.[4] After the restoration of the monarchy, however, while *duces* staged many *coups d'état* (of
which ten or eleven were successful), what was being sought was not a
revolutionary destruction of the monarchy: rather, it represents a series of
rebellions against individual kings by men who aspired to possess royal
authority themselves.[5] This is testimony to the power both of the institution of monarchy (since it is unlikely that so many magnates would have
thought empty titles worth fighting over) and of at least some individual
kings (since some weak kings could have been dominated more easily than
overthrown): in this there are some parallels with the position of the
Merovingians.

The restoration of the monarchy after the interregnum was occasioned
by the threat of Frankish invasion in 584.[6] Already the *duces* had conceded
an annual tribute of 12,000 *solidi* to the Franks, a fact which Fredegar
(though not the propagandist Paul the Deacon) notes immediately before
a statement that they placed themselves under Frankish overlordship.[7]
The implication of this is that a king was necessary for the defence of the
kingdom and that war leadership may have been his most important
function. As will be seen, although leading armies was certainly an important element of the king's role, it was not the only one.

Images of kingship

The Lombards occupied Italy by right of conquest and, although the
Byzantines may have made use of them from time to time,[8] the Empire
was never fully reconciled to the existence of their kingdom. This meant
that legitimation could not be sought from the Empire (as earlier 'barbar-

ian' rulers – including the Ostrogoths – had attempted), and, combined with the internal opposition experienced by individual rulers, created a climate in which alternative forms of authority were required. One way in which a ruler could hope to secure his position was by election,[9] but more was needed and, as with the Visigoths, a theocratic doctrine was developed. One of the earliest examples of this dates from the reign of Agilulf: a votive crown deposited at the church of St John at Monza by the king and his queen, Theodelinda, bears an inscription claiming that Agilulf ruled 'by the grace of God'.[10] Similarly, the Prologue to Rothari's *Edict* states that the king was under the Lord's special protection, while the laws issued by his successors consistently claim that they were issued with divine inspiration by kings who ruled with the aid of God or Christ: laws were made according to the law of God, and their provisions were necessary to the salvation of the Lombard people.[11] This kind of concept enabled kings to project an image of themselves as agents of God and, therefore, both to claim legitimacy and to enhance the perception of their position in relation to other magnates and their more humble subjects. The most developed form of this doctrine is to be found in the Prologue to the first laws issued by Liutprand, where it is stated that, as Solomon said, the king's heart is in God's hand.[12] (The convenience of this concept from the king's own standpoint is clear, but its benefits could also be felt by his officials, for anyone who committed murder on the king's orders was held blameless since the king's relationship with God meant that it was inconceivable that anyone whose death he ordered should be entirely free from guilt.[13])

It was not only in the law codes that such ideas were articulated, for they appear in three seventh- and eighth-century poems. One expresses the hope that Cunincpert (679-700) should be protected in life by Christ and, in death, should receive eternal life;[14] the second, written in 739, describes the then king, Liutprand, as 'pius' and refers to his Christ-given holiness.[15] Similarly, verses erected in the church of St Anastasius which Liutprand built at Corteolona – and presumably written with the king's consent – return to an Old Testament theme, referring to the position of the king as mediator between God and the mass of the Lombard people.[16]

For all that Lombard kings were not recognised by Byzantine emperors, and were often in conflict with them, they, like other 'barbarian' leaders, were influenced by Roman traditions. Hence, for example, from as early as the re-establishment of the monarchy after the interregnum, kings used the imperial 'Flavius' title.[17] It may not be coincidental that this occurred at much the same time as the Visigoths began to use it,[18] but it is not clear whether it should be interpreted as an expression of parity with the emperors themselves, or whether it indicated a form of subservience, since the exarchs of Ravenna used the same title: the latter possibility may be strengthened by the fact that the royal charters refer to the king as 'uir excellentissimus', also used of the exarchs.[19] It may be significant that such Roman-style titles only appear in the *diplomata* – that is in documents of a kind also issued in Ravenna – rather than in the laws, where kings are referred to as *reges Langobardorum*.[20]

A similar ambivalence is shown by the coinage issued by the Lombard kings. Under the Empire, the issuing of gold coins was an imperial prerogative: this finds an echo at least from the time of Rothari (636-652), who legislated to the effect that anyone who struck gold coin without the king's permission should have his hand cut off.[21] Despite that, kings did not mint silver or gold coins in their own name until the time of Perctarit, and their own busts did not appear on gold coins until later in the seventh century.[22] Before then, gold coins were pseudo-imperial, using types copied from those of Maurice (with Victory on the reverse) and Heraclius and Constans II (with a cross).[23] As noted in relation to the Visigoths, the introduction of a fully royal coinage is associated with an expression of autonomy – of independence from, and equality with, the Empire. The last third of the seventh century is very late for such a move, but it may reflect increased confidence and assertiveness after the failure of Constans II's invasion (673),[24] which had left the Lombards the largest and most powerful force in Italy. Alternatively – or additionally – it may indicate a realisation that, after the invasion, it was no longer possible to hope that the Empire would ever accept the legitimacy of the Lombards.

The coins copied from Maurice associate the Emperor with victory: this, in common with other elements of Roman ceremonial, was adopted by Lombard kings from the reign of Agilulf onwards. On his votive crown, for example, the king appears flanked by Victories holding standards bearing their name.[25] Not only that, but, later, Cunincpert seems to have staged a triumphal *aduentus* at Pavia after his victory over *Dux* Alahis *c.* 688,[26] perhaps using as a backdrop a ceremonial gateway next to the palace which Perctarit had reconstructed.[27] A further imitation of imperial practices may be seen in Agilulf's elevation of his infant son to the position of *consors regni* (itself perhaps an idea borrowed from the Empire[28]), which took place in the circus at Milan, echoing the ceremonial use of the hippodrome at Constantinople.[29]

The power of this kind of ceremonial depended as much upon the place at which it was conducted as on the ritual itself. Although the centre of Lombard power lay in the north of the Italian peninsula, and did not encompass either Rome (the imperial city itself) or Ravenna (home of the last western emperors) kings deliberately associated themselves with cities which had long-standing traditions as centres of power in the Roman and post-Roman periods – Verona, Milan and Pavia.

The first Lombard capital was at Verona,[30] and there are probably several reasons – both strategic and symbolic – for the choice. When Alboin entered Italy in 568, he did so from the north-east; one of the main centres of resistance to his advance was Ravenna. Verona was well placed with regard to any threat from that direction, and was protected, both naturally and by the remnants of Roman fortifications; it also lay at the centre of the

99

web of roads which formed the main means of communication in the region. It is not clear whether Alboin intended Verona to form the permanent centre of the kingdom, since he may have been hoping to install himself in Ravenna, which had been both an imperial residence and the home of the Ostrogothic rulers (especially Theoderic the Great, with whom the Empire had established a *modus vivendi*).[31] However that may be, and no matter how strategically placed was Verona, it is unlikely that its own position as one of Theoderic's favoured residences was overlooked by the Lombard king, or that he was unaware that it had been the last stronghold of Ostrogothic resistance to the imperial re-conquest. Alboin's choice may, therefore, have been at least partly governed by a desire to be seen as the legitimate successor to the (legitimate) Ostrogothic presence in Italy.[32]

Although Verona is the sole place at which Alboin is known to have resided, there is only one reference to it in the sources, and, as the kingdom expanded, other royal centres were established further west. One such was the former imperial city of Milan, from the capture of which Alboin dated his reign[33] – though he does not seem to have made it a principal residence. Of equal importance was Alboin's taking of Pavia, in his account of which Paul the Deacon notes that the palace built there by Theoderic was still in use.[34] Alboin's successor, Cleph, was elected king at Pavia,[35] probably as another conscious act of association with the rule of Theoderic. The site of Cleph's main residence is, however, uncertain, and it is possible that Pavia was at this stage no more than a ceremonial, rather than a residential, capital.

After the interregnum, Verona was certainly again used as a royal centre by Authari,[36] though he was at Pavia when he died.[37] It is not necessarily significant that Authari took refuge in Pavia during the Frankish invasion of 590,[38] since his choice was probably dictated by military necessity. A more secure indication of the importance of Pavia is that Authari's successor, Agilulf, took thence the large treasure he recovered from the island of Comacina.[39] Since the location of royal treasure was often an indication as to where the centre of power in an early medieval kingdom lay, this incident should probably be interpreted as indicating that Pavia was, by the early seventh century, firmly established as at least the symbolic capital of the Lombard kingdom.[40]

Despite that, Agilulf's main residence was at Milan, near which, at Monza, his queen, Theodelinda, built a royal palace and church: this was designed to be a summer residence in the hills a short distance from Milan, which lay in the hot and unhealthy Po valley.[41] Further, Agilulf was made king at Milan rather than Pavia, and it was at Milan that he made his son, Adaloald, *consors regni* (see above); in addition, the one royal document to have survived (in a later copy) from Agilulf's reign was written in the palace there.[42] Agilulf seems to have been the only king to have favoured Milan in this way, and it may represent part of a policy of demonstrating that he was heir to imperial, as well as to Ostrogothic, traditions: while

100

Theoderic seems to have established a palace at Monza,[43] Milan, unlike Verona and Pavia, was also a former imperial residence, as well as the seat of the last *uicarius Italiae* of the imperial administration. The quality of the evidence is not such as to permit of absolute certainty on the point, but it may be possible to link Agilulf's preference for Milan with the association of the king with victory, and his claims to rule with God's grace, as depicted on his votive crown, as well as with the adoption of the 'Flavius' title which appears to have occurred at much the same time.[44]

After the early years of the seventh century, Pavia became the dominant centre for both ceremonial and residential purposes – other than at times of joint rulership (notably the division of the kingdom between Godepert and Perctarit in 661), when Milan was of equal significance.[45] The church of St Saviour at Pavia was a royal foundation and acted as the mausoleum of the dynasty of kings descended from Garibald of Bavaria (Aripert I, Perctarit, Cunincpert and Aripert II were all buried there), while Ansprand and Liutprand were buried in the church of Our Lady, founded by Perctarit's wife, Rodelinda.[46] Liutprand also built a new palace (adorned with marble and columns from Rome) at the nearby Corteolona.[47]

The significance of Pavia is clear from the events surrounding a new king's assumption of the throne, particularly if he was a rebel, as Pavia seems to have been the recognised place for the election of kings.[48] Hence, for example, Grimoald, who seized the kingdom from Perctarit in 662,[49] was made king at Pavia, as was Perctarit himself when he was restored after Grimoald's death.[50] Similarly, when *Dux* Alahis of Brescia tried to replace Cunincpert in 688, he made the attempt while the latter was absent from Pavia, and rapidly established himself in the royal palace;[51] as with Perctarit, Cunincpert's restoration took place in the same city.[52]

It was not only for such constitutional purposes that Pavia had significance, however, for approximately half of the known royal documents dating from between 613 and 773 were produced in the palace there,[53] including (explicitly) the law codes issued by Rothari in 643 and Aistulf in 750.[54] This is important because it provides testimony independent of Paul the Deacon of the importance of Pavia, which appears to have been an administrative capital of a kind unknown in contemporary Frankia and not fully visible in Visigothic Spain.[55] This does not mean that kings were immobile, or that they could not fulfil administrative functions elsewhere: kings were active war leaders (see below) and documents were issued by Liutprand in Spoleto and by Aistulf in Ravenna in the wake of campaigns against those cities.[56] Even in times of peace, it is likely that kings travelled around their kingdom, partly because their authority would have been enhanced by their periodic presence in each of the main regions. Hence, although little is heard of Verona or Milan after the early seventh century, kings and their consorts are likely to have resided there from time to time. There were certainly royal estates in the territories of almost all cities, the royal *placita* alone suggesting major centres at Arezzo, Brescia,

101

Chiusi, Lucca, Parma, Piacenza and Siena,[57] and there were others. It is likely that kings associated themselves with earlier power structures even in some of those lesser cities, by taking over surviving *praetoria* which had once housed Roman provincial governors.[58]

Kings as warriors

Turning from the ways in which kings sought to portray their authority and claim legitimacy for their rule to what they actually did with their power, the restoration of the monarchy in 584 provides a convenient point of departure, since the reason for the creation of a new king might be expected to provide a clue as to his function. As noted earlier, that reason was connected with the threat of invasion by the Franks, suggesting that military leadership was, if not the over-riding function of a king, at least of considerable importance. Such an impression may be reinforced by Paul the Deacon's explicit comment that Agilulf was active and warlike, and that his suitability for the kingship derived as much from his physique as from his mind.[59]

The importance of this aspect of royal office is borne out by other aspects of Paul's account of the history of the kingdom. It was, of course, Alboin himself who led the Lombards into Italy in 568;[60] in 590/1, Authari led a campaign to the south of Italy,[61] and the same king took the field against Droctulf, a rebel *dux*;[62] Agilulf led an army which regained cities taken by the Byzantines,[63] and another to recover his daughter who had been captured by the Exarch of Ravenna;[64] Grimoald fought against Constans II in 663;[65] Liutprand also led armies against the Romans and the Byzantines.[66]

Stress on war leadership – even, if successful, as conferring legitimacy on a king[67] – may not be surprising in a work such as the *History of the Lombards*. Paul was concerned to show the way in which the Lombards fitted into Italian destiny, and also sought to glorify their achievements (see Chapter 10). In a work of this kind, particularly given its brevity, it is conspicuous events such as military campaigns which take centre stage. Equally, few other sources are of a character to support the picture painted by Paul, though a passage in the late seventh-century *Carmen de synodo Ticinensi* suggests that Cunincpert's title to rule derived not only from his selection by God, but also from the fact that he had crushed a rebellion by the *dux*, Alahis.[68]

The only other body of evidence which reveals anything of kings' military function is the large corpus of their law. Although the nature of this material is very different from that of Paul's writings, some provisions underline the association between kings and warriors. Hence, for example, cases concerning thefts committed by soldiers were, ultimately, the king's concern,[69] as were instances of *duces* abusing the rights of men in their charge.[70] Anyone who, although eligible for military service, refused to join the local muster or to perform guard duty, was to compensate the king as well as the appropriate *dux*;[71] so too was the man who did not assist his *dux* in the pursuit of justice,[72] or who declined to apply to his *dux* for justice.[73]

Kings and justice

It is with the administration of justice and the provision of legal documents that kings are most frequently associated outside the pages of Paul's *History*. Although that work itself nowhere depicts a judgement scene, it does refer to the fact that both Rothari and Grimoald drew up law codes.[74] Involvement in the actual administration of justice is attested by the laws themselves, which show that certain types of legal case, such as those involving female fornicators,[75] and those which could not be heard by the usual judge within twelve days of his being notified, were reserved to the king's court.[76] The survival (in later copies) of several royal *placita*[77] provides further testimony to kings' active involvement in judicial affairs.

The nature of the law administered by Lombard kings has been (and still is) the subject of much debate. Rothari's *Edict* is usually seen as essentially Germanic – perhaps more so than Visigothic law – though with some Roman influence in specific provisions; the supplementary legislation of later kings is seen as having greater (though still not widespread) affinity with Roman law.[78] Part of the reason for the emphasis on the 'Germanic' nature of Rothari's code is that its Epilogue states that it is a revision of the old laws 'of our fathers',[79] while Paul the Deacon states that Rothari wrote down the laws of the Lombards which continued to exist only in memory and through use.[80] The association of the law with the Lombard past is further emphasised by the inclusion of a king list in the Prologue.

Given that it is likely that even so 'un-Roman' a law code as that drawn up by Euric for the fifth-century Visigoths was largely based upon Roman provincial law,[81] and that the same argument can be applied to most of the 'barbarian' law codes (apart from the *Leges Romanae Visigothorum* and *Burgundionum*) of the fifth and sixth centuries,[82] it is worth considering whether Lombard law is radically different. As noted in Chapter 10, Rothari's compilation is an *edictum* – it is not *lex*: this suggests that it stands in the tradition of the edicts of praetorian prefects, and could contain large quantities of Roman provincial law. At all events many provisions of the code, such as that concerning forged charters,[83] cannot have formed part of Lombard custom from time immemorial. The presence of the king list is clearly intended to indicate the association of the ensuing law with previous generations of Lombard rulers. While that association could be genuine, however, it is also possible that it is largely fictional, and could have been made for propagandist purposes: the king list and Epilogue may have been included in an attempt to claim what was essentially

Roman provincial law for the Lombard people by marking it with a specifically Lombard identity. It is, indeed, questionable as to the extent to which the law associated with the Lombards in 643, when Rothari codified it, could have been 'Germanic', since by then the people had been established in Italy for seventy-five years and, taking into account their previous settlement in Pannonia, had been in the former Empire for a century and a quarter. Unless they had lived in complete isolation during that period, it is likely that Lombard institutions and law would have been heavily influenced by those they found in the provinces they came to occupy.

The suggestion that Rothari's *Edict* was largely Roman means that it would have applied to all the king's subjects (Lombard and Roman), as implied in the Epilogue, where they are charged with preserving it.[84] If the law was Germanic, it could only have applied to the Lombards, and the Romans would have continued to live according to their own, different, legal provisions, as some historians have suggested.[85] However, if such a situation had really pertained in Lombard Italy, it is strange that one of the provisions of Rothari's code should have stated that foreign immigrants were to be subject to his laws:[86] this might be understandable for other Germanic peoples, but Romans from other kingdoms would almost certainly have expected to live under Roman law, had that been an option.[87]

Whatever the 'national' character of Rothari's law, the occasion of producing a written code was used to correct, renew and amend provisions which were already in force, to add such new clauses as were deemed necessary, and to remove any superfluous material from earlier enactments.[88] This places Rothari not only firmly in a tradition associated with other post-Roman rulers, but also in that established by emperors Theodosius II and Justinian.[89] Moreover, the process of amending and adding to the law did not come to an end with Rothari's work, any more than did legislative activity in the Visigothic kingdom with the issuing of Leovigild's *Codex reuisus*: rather, Rothari's *Edict* was seen as the foundation on which later kings could build, adding new laws and amendments as occasion demanded. Such later changes were often specifically made in response to particular cases: the clearest expression of this is in the Prologue to Liutprand's laws of 725, which refers to the new law being made because cases had been presented to the king which could not be resolved either in accordance with custom or with laws issued earlier.[90] So important was this process, which, in the words of the early sixth-century Burgundian *Liber constitutionum*, gave a 'general application' to 'specific cases',[91] that new laws were added with great frequency under Liutprand, and more than once during the relatively short reigns of Ratchis and Aistulf.[92] There are similarities between this and the imperial practice of issuing rescripts in response to individual requests for guidance from judges, and it has been noted that the Prologues and Epilogues to the Lombard laws are stylistically related to the *proemia* of imperial novels.[93]

Since, in making new law, the king was responding to legal cases which required the clarification or expansion of existing provisions, he was not acting unilaterally: judges had to refer such cases to him for consideration. Further, it is clear from the law collections themselves that decisions were not taken by the king alone: he acted with the assistance, or even the consent, of the people (as represented by the judges, nobility and royal *fideles*).[94] The kind of national assembly implied by this process has parallels in the Frankish world, especially since the laws of Liutprand, Ratchis and Aistulf were almost all promulgated on 1 March,[95] suggesting the same kind of arrangement as is reflected in the *Decree* of Childebert (see Chapter 2). Such assemblies demonstrate the fact that kings could only rule if they commanded a certain degree of consensus within the kingdom,[96] and there are hints that the approbation of the people (at least as represented by the nobility) was a necessary part of the process whereby a new king was chosen,[97] though the precise nature and powers of the assembly are not clear.[98]

Queens

It was not only by being chosen by the people, or by God, that kings could claim legitimacy for their rule, but also by their relationship to the previous ruler. When son succeeded father, the case was relatively simple, but, on the numerous occasions when that was not the case, one of the main means by which legitimacy was sought was through the new king's association with his predecessor's wife, since she could not only transmit a claim to the throne to her children, but also to a second husband (see Table III on p. 185). Queens are, therefore, of great significance in the history of the Lombard kingdom and, thanks to Paul the Deacon's concern with the legitimacy of Lombard rule in Italy, this aspect of their position is well documented – though, as will be seen, his account is not always unproblematic.

According to Paul, when Authari died in 590, his widow, Theodelinda, married Agilulf, *dux* of Turin, who became king.[99] There is no reason to doubt this testimony, but the details of the case are less likely to bear a direct relationship to the truth, for Paul says that, when Authari died, the Lombard people were so enamoured of Queen Theodelinda that they allowed her to continue to reign as queen, giving her free choice of second husband, promising to accept her choice as the new king. Elegant though the tale is, it has more in common with the world of epic than with that of reality, and it is more likely that Authari simply seized the throne (thereby setting in motion the series of rebellions which occurred during the 590s[100]) and forced Theodelinda to marry him in order to provide an appearance of legitimacy. Despite its lack of verisimilitude, Paul's account does enunciate the principle that queens could transmit claims to the throne.

That same principle is demonstrated by two further stories concerning the succession. In the first, both Paul and the Frankish chronicler, Fredegar, state that when Arioald died (636), his queen, Gundiperga, sent for Rothari, then *dux* in Brescia, made him abandon his wife, marry her, and become king.[101] The sequence of events is as unlikely as that surrounding Theodelinda, and suspicion is heightened both by the fact that Gundiperga was Theodelinda's daughter (suggesting that the story may be a doublet of the earlier account), and by the fact that Rothari later had Gundiperga incarcerated, only releasing her after diplomatic pressure from the Merovingian Clovis II, to whom she was related.[102] The idea that royal women – whether acting freely or under duress – could confer legitimacy on new rulers is, however, reinforced.

The second case is more involved and less clear cut, though it is still informative. After Alboin's wife, Rosamund, had murdered her husband, she married her accomplice, Helmechis, who tried to usurp the throne, perhaps on the assumption that his union with Rosamund was proof of his legitimacy. On this occasion, however, the usurpation was unsuccessful and the couple fled to Ravenna. There, Rosamund continued to pursue her ambitions, trying to rid herself of Helmechis in order to marry the prefect of Ravenna, Longius. According to Paul she did this so that she might increase her power.[103] It is not entirely clear what this implies, since it is perhaps unlikely that Rosamund thought she would be more powerful as wife of the governor of Ravenna than as queen of Lombard Italy, though the Exarchate would have been some compensation for the loss of the kingdom. Is it possible that she aspired to transmit a claim to Longius, regain the kingdom with Byzantine assistance, and become wife of the ruler of all (northern) Italy?

Royal women (and not only queens who married twice) were important in this way throughout the history of the Lombard kingdom. Later in the seventh century, Grimoald married the daughter of King Aripert when he overthrew her brothers, Perctarit and Godepert in 662, and established himself as king.[104] Although Grimoald was an indirect relation of Alboin, the king who led the Lombards into Italy, marriage to a member of his immediate predecessor's dynasty was clearly seen as advantageous. More tenuous is the case of Liutprand, who was linked to the main dynasty though the marriage of his niece, Gumperga, and the *dux* of Benevento, Romoald II, who was also the great-grandson of Grimoald: it may be significant that the marriage took place after Liutprand became king.[105] Finally, at least in the eyes of Paul the Deacon, the marriage of Desiderius' daughter, Adelperga, to Arichis II of Benevento, meant that Arichis was the true heir to the Lombard kingdom after its conquest by Charlemagne.

The marriages of royal women were of importance not only with regard to the succession, but also for diplomatic purposes. Hence the marriage of

Authari to Theodelinda, daughter of Garibald of Bavaria, may have been designed to secure the northern frontier of the kingdom against the Franks,[106] while an earlier agreement that Authari should become betrothed to Chlodosuinda, sister of the Merovingian king, Childebert II, was similarly part of a cessation of hostilities between the Frankish and Lombard kingdoms, and even persuaded Childebert to use his influence with the emperor to discontinue his war with the Lombards.[107] In addition, although the marriage never seems to have taken place, Agilulf's son (Adaloald) was betrothed to a daughter of Theudebert II.[108] These dynastic relations with the Franks may gain added significance when seen in the light of the fact that, during the interregnum which preceded Authari's reign, the *duces* had agreed to pay an annual tribute to the Franks, suggesting some kind of subordination to them: could Childebert's eagerness for a marriage agreement have been designed to further Merovingian claims in Italy?[109]

That the importance of kings' daughters was not lost on enemies of the Lombard state, may be illustrated by two incidents. In the first, the imperial patrician, Gallicinus, managed to capture Agilulf's daughter and son-in-law, Godescalc, who were taken to Ravenna, no doubt to be used as useful counters in diplomatic relations between the Exarchate and the kingdom.[110] The second case concerns Grimoald's daughter, Gisa, who was taken hostage as surety of a treaty between her brother, Romoald, *dux* of Benevento, and Emperor Constans II.[111]

Once they were married and installed as queens, royal women could be important in a more active way. Rosamund, for example, was clearly a force to be reckoned with inside the court, for she persuaded two courtiers to murder Alboin – even though one of them was far from enthusiastic.[112] More telling is Theodelinda's persuasion of Agilulf, an Arian, to patronise the Church and to make a peace treaty with Gregory the Great: her power was clearly appreciated by the Pope for he engaged in correspondence with her,[113] sending her a copy of his *Dialogues*.[114] The Pope may have hoped to use the Queen to assist in the conversion of the Agilulf to Catholicism, in the same way as he used Bertha to assist in the conversion of the Anglo-Saxons,[115] and it is clear that Nicetius of Trier had similar aspirations.[116]

If queens could expect to influence their husbands in this way, and could transmit power to second husbands, it is probable that their position could be even more important if, after the death of their husbands, they did not re-marry, but, rather, became regents for sons who were minors. Owing to the lack of a fully dynastic principle in the Lombard kingdom, this eventuality was considerably rarer than in Merovingian Gaul, since rivals could claim the throne. The situation did, however, arise on one documented occasion when, after the death of her second husband, Agilulf, Theodelinda became regent for her young son, Adaloald.[117]

The nature of the sources is not such as to reveal a great deal concerning routine queenly functions, either during minorities or at other times, but such women were clearly important as dispensers of patronage, both in their own right and in association with their husbands. Theodelinda not only made a donation to Bobbio during Adaloald's minority,[118] but had earlier built the palace and endowed the church at Monza.[119] Similarly, Gundiperga, wife of Arioald, built a church at Pavia dedicated to St John the Baptist,[120] and Perctarit's wife, Rodelinda, built a cemetery church outside the same city.[121] Sometimes, such donations were made jointly with the king, as is illustrated by Theodore's privilege for Bobbio, which shows Gundiperga and Rothari (her second husband) acting in this way,[122] and by a charter of Aistulf in favour of the episcopal church of S. Gemini-ano at Modena, which was made with Queen Giseltrude;[123] other instances are known from the reign of Desiderius, who made joint donations with, or donations at the suggestion of, his wife, Ansa, to the monastery of SS. Michael and Paul (later St Saviour) at Brescia.[124] This kind of distribution of patronage, though relatively poorly documented for much of the Lombard period on account of the scarcity of surviving diplomatic material,[125] was probably one of the most important aspects of kingly, as well as of queenly, activity, allowing individuals or institutions to gain land and wealth, while at the same time building up a body of support for the donor.

12

Provincial Administration:
duces and gastalds

The leading men in Lombard provincial government were *duces* and gastalds. These two kinds of official have often been seen as opposing each other, the *duces* (whose authority was primarily military) tending to wish to maintain a large degree of autonomy and often acting against the kings' interests; and the latter (whose power developed from that of administrators of royal estates) being royal representatives who acted as a counterbalance to the activities of *duces*, whom they sometimes replaced as kings came to gain authority in a given area. Such a view may owe much to a historiographical tradition which sees the development of Italy in terms of a constant struggle between local and national power. While interpretations of that kind are valid for some periods of the peninsula's development, it is important not to assume that it holds for every age. The paucity of sources for the Lombard kingdom makes it difficult to provide coherent interpretations which are not in part theoretical, and the account presented here is unlikely totally to succeed in avoiding that fate. What is attempted, though, is an approach to the subject built upon a greater awareness of the impact of the nature of the sources than has sometimes been achieved in the past.

Duces

Apart from kings, the Lombards who feature most prominently in Paul the Deacon's *Historia Langobardorum* are the *duces* – the most powerful of the regional aristocrats and office holders, in charge of armed followings and responsible for the defence of the territories (almost always based on cities) where they were stationed. It was these men who controlled the kingdom during the interregnum which followed Cleph's death in 574, and, after the restoration of the monarchy, there were many occasions on which *duces* rebelled against the king. In the south of the kingdom, the holders of the *ducatus* based at Spoleto and Benevento appear to have been largely independent of the kings for much of the seventh century, issuing their own *diplomata*; in the late seventh century, Beneventan *duces* even issued their own coinage.

The combination of these circumstances has often led to a perception that Lombard *duces* were more powerful than many of their counterparts elsewhere in Europe, and that the history of the Lombard kingdom was one of constant struggle between the monarchy and *duces*, with the final victory of the centralising monarchy not occurring until the eighth century, when the southern *duces* were for the first time subjected to consistent royal control. Although elements of this interpretation are undoubtedly true, some aspects of the question merit re-examination. It cannot, for example, be demonstrated that *duces* lacked interest in some kind of kingship, for, although individual *duces* rebelled against particular kings, there was no attempt, after the interregnum, to dispense with the monarchy: indeed, it was the *duces* themselves who re-established it, and surrendered half their lands as an endowment for the crown.[1] The later rebellions can themselves be interpreted as a sign of the power of the institution of monarchy, since *duces* are unlikely to have thought it worth their while to try to acquire or dominate a weak kingship.

The precise reasons for some of the rebellions are not clear, but revolts may often have been responses to a king's failure to satisfy the ambitions or aspirations of particular individuals: there may be some similarities between this and the problems the Merovingians faced in maintaining equality of treatment for all aristocratic factions. When, for example, Droctulf rebelled against Authari,[2] or Maurisio against Agilulf,[3] and joined the Byzantine cause, the individual *duces* concerned may have been venting their frustration at their own failure to occupy the throne: Authari's kingship was a new creation after the interregnum, and did not necessarily have to be given to the son of the king who immediately preceded it; Agilulf was either genuinely the choice of the widowed Theodelinda, or had staged a successful coup (See Chapter 11). Alternatively, Droctulf and Marausio had something to fear from the kings, and may have been seeking better prospects with new overlords. Other rebellions can also be seen as those of disappointed pretenders to the crown, or of their supporters – for example, shortly after Agilulf's succession (590), in 591, Gaidulf, Mimulf, Ulfari and Zangrolf rose against the king,[4] while there was certainly tension between that king and the *duces* of Trent and Cividale until *c.* 602;[5] similarly, when Arioald succeeded in 626, he faced a rising by Taso.[6] Such problems tended to occur at times of instability immediately after the death of a king, accession of a new ruler, and imposition of a new settlement (whether by direct descent or other means), such as the establishment of the partnership between Perctarit and Cunincpert in 680, against which *dux* Alahis of Trent rebelled – he was unsuccessful, but survived, as *dux* at Brescia, only to rise against Cunincpert for a second time (also ultimately without success) when Perctarit died, *c.* 688.[7]

Not all bids for power on the part of *duces* were unsuccessful. As noted in Chapter 11, the *duces* Agilulf and Arioald gained the throne by more or less legitimate means though they also appear to have waited until their predecessors (Authari and Adaloald) had died before making their moves, as did Rothari.[8] Grimoald, on the other hand intervened at a time of dispute between Godepert and his brother Perctarit, initially (apparently) acting on behalf of Godepert: having deposed Godepert's brother (as requested), he proceeded to outstay his welcome, and acquired the crown for himself.[9] This incident also provides evidence that not all the reasons for the instability of the succession can be traced to rebellious *duces*, but could result from the lack of a clear strategy for the descent of the crown within the ruling house. A problem of this kind also lies behind the rising of Raginpert against Liutpert, son of Cunincpert, in 700, for Raginpert, although *dux* of Turin, was also son of an earlier king – Godepert – whose credentials were at least as good as those of Cunincpert.[10]

To see the rebellions – and, therefore, *duces* – as forces working against the monarchy is too simple, for it not only fails to take account of the fact that the object of many of the rebels was to acquire the crown for themselves, but it also takes inadequate cognizance of the fact that a fair proportion of those who sought the kingship were part of the royal dynasty as well as being *duces*. The problem was perhaps more one of a lack of a coherent system of inheritance within the dynasty than one of over-powerful *duces*: a similar situation existed in early seventh-century Spain (see Chapter 7), though there is no evidence that the *duces* involved at that stage in the Visigothic succession were part of the royal dynasty. It is also possible to over-emphasise the destabilising impact of *duces* in other ways. Only on relatively few occasions was more than one *dux* involved in a rebellion; when a group was involved, the numbers were small – there seem to have been few instances of *concerted* attempts to remove an individual king, let alone (after the interregnum) to dispense with the monarchy again: *duces* were looking after their individual needs and ambitions, not expressing a collective desire for greater 'freedom'.

In addition, there are few instances in which it is possible to trace more than the beginnings of a ducal dynasty in any region – Cividale was possessed of one until the 630s, and only Benevento retained one into the eighth century.[11] Many *duces*, even in the relatively independent Spoleto (see below) were royal appointees, whose loyalty to the king who created them was largely guaranteed.[12] Some such men were relations of the kings (Table III on p. 185 shows some of the relationships): Gisulf I of Cividale, for example, was Alboin's nephew,[13] while Gundoald of Asti was appointed by his brother-in-law, Agilulf;[14] rather later, Grimoald made his son *dux* in Benevento before departing to the north of the kingdom in his bid for the crown,[15] while a later Beneventan *dux*, Gregory, was Liutprand's nephew.[16] Other royal appointees do not appear to have formed part of the royal dynasty – men such as Arichis I of Benevento, who was made *dux* by Agilulf, and, later, Gisulf II of Benevento, who was placed in power by Liutprand.[17] Liutprand also deposed Pemmo of Cividale, and elevated

111

Ratchis (Pemmo's son) in his place.[18] In many cases, there is no evidence as to whether the succession was hereditary or not, since Paul's *History* does not mention the fact:[19] it would be wrong to conclude either that it was in all instances, or that royal approval was not given.[20]

In order to elucidate the relationship of the *duces* and the crown more fully, it is necessary to define the function of *duces* as royal appointees and agents. Since the history of – and evidence for – the southern parts of the kingdom is rather different from that of its northern heartland, the *ducatus* of Spoleto and Benevento will be discussed separately, after their northern counterparts.

Northern duces

The largest body of evidence concerning the legitimate activities of *duces* relates to their role as military leaders – a function known to have existed throughout the Lombard kingdom's history, from the period of the interregnum, when Amo, Zaban and Rodanus invaded Gaul,[21] to Liutprand's reign, when the *dux* of Vicenza captured Ravenna,[22] and beyond. The enemies against whom *duces* operated range from the Franks, to Avars, Bavarians, Slavs, the Exarchate of Ravenna, and the peoples of southern Italy.[23] In almost all these cases, the *duces* concerned were acting on behalf of, or in concert with, the king of the day in repelling an attack from outside the kingdom, or in attempting to expand its area.

The creation of the first Lombard *ducatus* – at Cividale (see Map IV on p. 181) – makes the military association, as well as the position of the *dux* as a royal agent, clear, for Gisulf I (Alboin's nephew) was left to defend the newly conquered area as the king and the main body of the Lombard army pushed west on the path of conquest in 569.[24] The site was of immediate strategic importance because it secured Alboin's rear, but it remained significant throughout the history of the kingdom as the centre for the defence of the eastern frontier against possible incursions from the Avars and Slavs who lay beyond.

Other cities also became the centres of *ducatus* which can reasonably be argued to have lasted almost continuously throughout the Lombard period. Perhaps the greatest of them in the north was Trent, known to have existed from 574 until 603, and again in Cunincpert's reign (679-700), and strategically placed to defend the heartland of the kingdom from attack from the Bavarians to the north.[25] The frontier was a constant feature, and some kind of defensive arrangement would have been desirable even at periods when the Bavarians did not pose a direct threat, so that it is unlikely that the lack of continuous evidence for *duces* is connected with anything more significant than the internal structure (and bias) of Paul the Deacon's narrative. A similar case may be made concerning Turin, which, though much closer to the heart of the kingdom, defends the Frankish march.[26] Brescia[27] and Bergamo[28] both stand on the edge of the northern plain, and would have been well placed to prevent any attack from outside, as well as any resurgence of native opposition in the mountains and passes to the north and, though less fully documented, are also likely to have been more or less permanent ducal seats.

There are further cities in the north of the kingdom which were associated with *duces*,[29] but the evidence only relates to a single period. The significance of this is impossible to assess – it could imply that *duces* were only based in some areas on a temporary basis, to meet specific offensive or defensive requirements; or it might indicate that the sources only refer to the existence of *duces* at times when they were particularly important – either in absolute terms, or in relation to the purpose of the source. Hence, for example, the fact that only one *dux*, Gundoald, is known to have been based at Asti (in the north-west of the kingdom), under King Agilulf, could suggest that the town was temporarily the seat of a *dux* during a period of hostilities with the Franks, since it is well placed to counter attack from that direction. On the other hand, it may be that the only *dux* of Asti who did anything significant in terms of Paul the Deacon's narrative was Gundoald, who was important on account of the fact that he was the brother of Queen Theodelinda, and the father of the later king, Aripert.[30] Similar problems surround the case of Verona, where the only known *dux*, Zangrulf, rebelled against Agilulf and was executed: was he the only *dux* to have done anything the author of the *Origo gentis Langobardorum* and Paul the Deacon found significant, or was he the sole *dux* of Verona?[31]

Even more difficult to interpret are cases such as those of the *duces* at Modena, Parma, Piacenza and Reggio nell'Emilia mentioned in two letters from the Exarch of Ravenna to Childebert II of the Franks:[32] were these *ducatus* permanent, or were they a temporary response to an immediate military situation? The second letter was written at a time when three of the cities were under siege, and clearly had armies stationed within them: is it even possible to be certain that the term 'dux' here signifies a formal office, rather than simply the leader of the Lombard force?

Problems of a different nature are presented by the evidence for central Italy, especially Tuscany. A private charter of Liutprand's reign records the presence of a *dux*, Walpert, at Lucca,[33] and the *Liber Pontificalis* noted that Desiderius was 'dux in Tusciae' before becoming king.[34] It has often been concluded that, even if there was a *dux* permanently at Lucca or elsewhere in the region,[35] most Tuscan cities never had *duces*.[36] This may well be true, but it might be no more than a reflection of the fact that the area was not one of those concerning which Paul the Deacon seems to have been well informed, or, at any rate, in which he chose to take a specific interest (see Chapter 10).

Whether they were permanently sited in a town or not, the evidence for *duces* in northern and central Italy clearly points to their military function, both in terms of the activities in which they can be seen to have engaged, and in terms of the places at which they were based. The same is true of the vast majority of references to *duces* in the law codes. Provisions in Rothari's *Edict*, for example, indicate that soldiers were subordinate to *duces*, since it is stipulated that those who rebelled against such men (or other superiors) were to be subject to capital punishment;[37] on the other hand, *duces* were not to treat their soldiers unjustly or unreasonably,[38] and were to uphold discipline within the ranks.[39] Similarly, one of Rothari's laws states that *duces* could rely upon their soldiers for aid in pursuing justice,[40] while other provisions demonstrate that they were responsible for the administration of justice in relation to their subordinates,[41] both in general, and specifically in relation to any unreasonable demands made of them by gastalds.[42]

None of the legal provisions relating to *duces* implies any jurisdiction other than over soldiers; even in the last case cited, the *dux* was primarily to defend his own interests, and those of his subordinates: it does not indicate that he was the superior of the gastald. There are only a very few instances in which *duces* (other than those in the south of the kingdom – see below) can be positively demonstrated to have acted outside the military sphere. On at least three occasions, *duces* were involved in diplomatic activity, as, for example, when (according to Paul the Deacon's *History*) *Dux* Euin, who was based at Trent, was sent by King Agilulf to negotiate a peace treaty with the Franks;[43] the *Liber Pontificalis* similarly refers to the use of *duces* in negotiations with the Papacy on more than one occasion during the eighth century.[44] This kind of activity is only slightly removed from the military, and there is clear evidence that *duces* were employed as ambassadors elsewhere in the fifth- to eighth-century west: they were men of status and power, as was appropriate to diplomatic activity, and, as military leaders, must have been trusted by the king.

On a few occasions, *duces* are known to have been involved in administrative tasks much further removed from war leadership. King Aistulf, for example, charged *Dux* Alpert with overseeing an exchange of lands with the bishopric of Lucca in 754;[45] on another occasion, *Dux* Walpert, in conjunction with a number of other officials, was responsible for an investigation into a dispute between the bishops of Lucca and Pistoia in 716,[46] while *Dux* Adaloald was one of a number of judges at an enquiry concerning a long-running jurisdictional dispute between the sees of Siena and Arezzo.[47] It is no coincidence that all the evidence for this kind of activity comes from the *diplomata*, since the recording of such essentially administrative events would have been inappropriate to Paul the Deacon's purpose, and it is probable that, were the diplomatic *corpus* to be larger, other instances would be known. However, at least two of the cases cited are not routine, and caution should be exercised before ascribing large specifically civilian spheres of jurisdiction to the northern *duces*: it is at least as likely that, as high-ranking officials based in the regions of the

114

kingdom, they could, on occasion, be called upon to carry out particularly important or sensitive tasks in any branch of the administration.

It is possible that during the interregnum *duces* were indeed responsible for the civil administration of their cities. The case cannot, however, be made with certainty, as there is no firm evidence concerning the means by which the kingdom was governed at that period. Paul the Deacon reports that there were thirty-five *duces*, but most historians have doubted that so many cities were the centres of *ducatus*.[48] It is possible that the term here has no more specific meaning than 'leader', and implies that the Lombards were led by some form of council of thirty-five men, or it is possible that Paul was simply mistaken. Whichever interpretation is correct, the means by which the cities – whether those with *duces* or those without – were ruled during the interregnum is not clear: all that is certain is that there is no positive evidence that *duces* fulfilled such a function after the interregnum (this is discussed further, below, in relation to gastalds).

Spoletan and Beneventan duces

Many elements of the foregoing discussion of the northern *duces* can be applied to their southern counterparts, but there are also significant differences, and the origins of the *ducatus* of Spoleto[49] and Benevento[50] are obscure.[51] According to G.P. Bognetti, the two *ducatus* were founded by Lombard leaders (Faroald and Zotto) who were mercenaries in the pay of the Byzantines, as a bulwark against the expansion of the Lombard kingdom into the southern half of the Italian peninsula.[52] Faroald was certainly at one stage a mercenary commander, as was his successor, Ariulf, who led imperial forces against the Persians in 582, but whether either remained in imperial service after reaching Spoleto is unclear; even more uncertain is whether their establishment in that city was due to Byzantine intervention. The first *dux* of Benevento, Zotto, was denounced by Gregory the Great for having betrayed the Byzantines,[53] implying that he had been in their pay, but, as in the case of Faroald and Ariulf, there is no positive evidence that he had not already left imperial service when he established himself at Benevento.[54] An alternative explanation would be that the two *ducatus* were established – possibly during the interregnum – as part of the Lombard conquest of Italy and were in origin military outposts, perhaps designed as much with an eye to attack in the south as to defence against the Byzantine forces of Rome, Ravenna and the deep south.

However they were founded, the southern *ducatus* seem to have enjoyed a greater degree of autonomy than their northern counterparts for much of the Lombard period but, as will be seen, that does not necessarily mean that their leaders saw themselves as anything other than part of the kingdom. As noted earlier, when Zotto of Benevento died, his successor,

115

Arichis I was appointed by the king, as were Transamund I[55] and, almost certainly, Agiprand,[56] of Spoleto. Most seventh-century *duces* are only known from Paul the Deacon's narrative, and feature solely in relation to the succession, making it impossible to be certain how they defined their relationship with the kings. Although more is known of eighth-century *duces*, much of the evidence also relates to the succession, more details being recorded because there was a series of conflicts with the crown.

It is sometimes contended that the reason for the eighth-century hostilities was that Liutprand and his successors, as part of their drive to enlarge the Lombard kingdom, sought to end the autonomy of the southern *duces* and to integrate the kingdom for only the second time (the first occasion having been achieved by Grimoald I after he had left Benevento and become king).[57] It is certainly true that the territorial gains made by Liutprand in central Italy brought royal power closer to the ducal seats, and probable that *duces* may have wished to retain the autonomy which distance from the centres of royal power had brought to their predecessors. However, not all the *duces* reacted in the same way: Faroald II of Spoleto, for example, obeyed Liutprand's command that his conquest of Classis be handed back to the Exarch.[58] It seems likely that Faroald's action caused his son, Transamund II, to depose his father, and to usurp the *ducatus*: thereafter, Transamund's career was one of constant opposition to Liutprand, by whom he was only finally defeated after nearly fifteen years.[59] While this could have been an expression of a desire for Spoletan independence, it is at least as likely that Transamund's action was born out of frustration at the fact that Liutprand had obtained the crown, for Transamund himself, as a descendant of Grimoald I, had a claim to the throne: rather than rebelling against the monarchy (or royal power) as such, he may, therefore, like so many of the northern *duces*, have been opposing a particular king from another branch of the royal dynasty. Later, after the death of *Dux* Lupus in 751, King Aistulf may have dispensed with a *dux* in Spoleto altogether for a time:[60] the reasons for this are not altogether clear but, whatever the significance of those events, when Aistulf himself died in 756, there was already a new *dux*, Alboin, who refused to co-operate with the new king, Desiderius.[61] Nothing is known of the circumstances of Alboin's appointment, but it would appear likely that he was made *dux* by Aistulf (particularly if there was an interregnum in Spoleto), and it may be that he was unhappy with Desiderius' usurpation of the throne, rather than with the monarchy itself.

The situation in Benevento is more complex, but a similar interpretation for the rebellions of the Beneventan *duces* and people may be possible. Like Transamund II of Spoleto, Romoald II, as great-grandson of Grimoald I, had a claim to the throne which was at least as good as, if not better than, Liutprand's, and it may have been partly this which drove him into conflict with the king.[62] It is also possible that the other Beneventan leaders were equally unhappy about the elevation to the kingship of

Liutprand, whose dynastic claim appears (on the available evidence) to have been very weak. It is possible that there was a desire for complete independence from the Lombard kingdom; but it may be equally likely that, when Romoald died in 731/2 leaving only a minor (Gisulf II),[63] the Beneventans were propelled to select their own *dux*, Adalahis, by a view that Liutprand was an illegitimate ruler, since the king seized the opportunity afforded by Gisulf's youth to impose as *dux* his nephew, Gregory. Not only that, but Liutprand then proceeded to 'adopt' the young Gisulf, and later dictated whom he should marry. The reasoning behind this may have been to ensure that Gisulf (whom the Beneventans would be likely to accept as the legitimate heir to Romoald) would not follow his father's opposition to the king. If that was the calculation, it appears ultimately to have met with some success: after Gregory's death, the Beneventans again elevated their own *dux*, Godescalc, who refused to co-operate with Liutprand; after three years, the king managed to remove him and restored Gisulf to the *ducatus*.[64] Later, Gisulf's son and successor, *Dux* Liutprand, like the Spoletan Alboin, rebelled against the usurper, Desiderius: he was defeated and replaced by the king's son-in-law, Arichis II.[65]

The changes in royal dynasty in the eighth century make it almost impossible to be certain of the extent to which the rebellions in the southern *ducatus* were occasioned by discontent with new kings, or by a more general desire for autonomy. The case for the latter interpretation may be strengthened by the fact that, in the late seventh century, Beneventan *duces* began to mint their own coins, the earliest known being issued by Gisulf I (689-706). This coinage was derived from imperial types, but with the initials of the *dux* on the reverse; the leaders of Spoleto, however, do not seem to have followed suit.[66] The significance of this, and particularly of its timing, is not entirely clear, particularly since Tuscany also had a coinage which was not fully integrated with the royal issues of the north of the kingdom,[67] but it is likely to be an expression of a degree of autonomy greater than that enjoyed by the northern *duces*. Similar conclusions may be drawn from the issuing of charters by the *duces* of both Benevento and Spoleto: this appears to have started during the reign of Liutprand, though whether it represents a manifestation of the discontent of the *duces* with Liutprand is unclear, since it is possible that southern *duces* could have begun issuing charters earlier, with the first examples (like all but a handful of seventh-century royal documents) having been lost.

It is obvious that many of the eighth-century *duces* of Spoleto and Benevento enjoyed a degree of autonomy not shared by their northern counterparts, and it is likely – particularly in view of the evidence of the coinage – that such a situation had prevailed for at least part of the seventh century. None of this necessarily means, however, that the southern *duces* saw themselves as anything other than a part of the kingdom:

in the 660s, Grimoald I had become actively involved in northern politics, acquiring the crown for himself.[68]

The use of almost vice-regal powers by southern *duces* does not have to be seen as representing a desire to withdraw from the kingdom. On the one hand it may reflect the fact that Spoleto and Benevento were situated at a distance from the heartland of the kingdom, and were physically separated from it by the corridor linking Rome and Ravenna: in such circumstances, the *duces* may have had to assume a greater degree of autonomy on account of the king's inaccessibility. On the other hand, some of the desire for autonomy, as manifested by the refusal to co-operate with Liutprand and his successors (particularly Desiderius) may have been occasioned less by a specific desire for independence from the kingdom, than by a refusal to recognise the legitimacy of the changes of dynasty which the eighth century witnessed: in this there may be some parallels with the great *ducatus* on the frontiers of the Frankish world, the rulers of which declined to support the Carolingians. That this could have been the case may be further suggested by the fact that the southern *duces* did not use titles which claimed that they were the equals of the kings: whereas kings were *uiri excellentissimi*, the *duces* used the title of *uir gloriosissimus*, which was a subordinate style, derived ultimately from the titles of Roman military leaders.[69] Only after the takeover of the kingdom by Charlemagne did a *dux* – Arichis II of Benevento – claim to be a *princeps*, and begin to use a crown and sceptre and issue laws.[70] All of these were symbols of autonomy and refusal to accept Carolingian rule, the last perhaps similar to the Alaman Lantrid's re-issuing of his people's Merovingian laws in the early eighth century.

Gastalds

Apart from the *dux*, the most prominent official in the provincial administration was the gastald – a royal appointee who administered royal *curtes*.[71] It is frequently assumed that men of this kind, who were often based in cities, were installed as counterbalances to the independent *duces*,[72] or as replacements for them as they rebelled or were removed from office for other reasons during the seventh century.[73] Part of the reason for this suggestion lies in the perception of *duces* as semi-autonomous opponents of royal power who were effectively the governors of the cities in which they were based. In view of the paucity of evidence for their civil authority, and of the possibility that *duces* were not necessarily *permanently* based in every city in which their presence is attested at one time or another (see above), the question of the relationship of the gastalds and *duces* merits re-examination. If, for example, the *dux* at Brescia was primarily a military official, the gastald of the same city[74] does not have to be seen as acting in opposition to him, but could simply have fulfilled a different function. Similarly, if Parma, Piacenza and Reggio nell'Emilia were only temporarily the seats of *duces*, the fact that gastalds are later found there[75] might be of less significance than is sometimes supposed.

A second part of the argument concerning gastalds is that the number of known holders of the office increases during the seventh and eighth centuries.[76] This is almost certainly no more than a reflection of the nature of the sources.[77] Paul the Deacon's concern was with prominent (largely military) subjects, and since, as will be seen, gastalds were primarily administrators, they could not be expected to feature largely in his *History of the Lombards* either during the early years of the kingdom or later: in fact, only one gastald is mentioned in the work, in highly exceptional circumstances.[78] Administrative documents – whether law codes or *diplomata* – are more likely to record the presence and activities of officials of this kind, but they only begin to survive from the seventh century, and gradually increase in number in and during the eighth century.

In order to arrive at an understanding of the position of gastalds in the administration of the Lombard kingdom, it may be as well to start with an exploration of the activities in which the holders of the office can with some certainty be seen to have engaged. As indicated above, the law codes state in general terms that gastalds were responsible for the administration of royal estates:[79] more specific provisions relate to their duty to return fugitive slaves from royal estates to their masters upon request, and otherwise to assist lords to recover their runaway slaves.[80] They were also involved in making royal slaves of certain free women who married slaves,[81] were to take fornicators before the king for judgement,[82] and were to collect fines for such crimes as the despoliation of graves.[83] The law codes similarly provide that gastalds were to ensure that *duces* did not unreasonably impose on their soldiers, while *duces* were to ensure that gastalds acted equally justly.[84] In addition, royal (and Spoletan and Beneventan) charters frequently state that gastalds, among other officials, were not to interfere with the land which was the subject of the grant.[85] Apart from the legal provision that gastalds should ensure that the *duces* did not impose unreasonably on soldiers, there is only one piece of evidence suggestive of their involvement in military affairs – when an unnamed gastald was among those defeated at Cumae by the Byzantine *dux*, John, of Naples, in 746 or 747.[86] The involvement of the gastald in a military campaign need imply no more than that anyone capable of fighting or leading troops could become involved in such activity: it does not necessarily mean that such was a regular feature of gastalds' activities. On some of the further occasions on which gastalds can be seen in action in an official capacity, their role is likewise other than routine: two gastalds were sent by Liutprand as envoys to Pope Zacharias to confirm a territorial settlement in 740/1;[87] and King Desiderius commanded Assiulf, gastald of Pavia, to form part of a judicial tribunal to deal with a specific case which had been taken to the royal court.[88] Perhaps less unusual was the involvement of gastalds in the royal (or, in the south, ducal) tribunal.[89]

119

On one occasion, a gastald of Rieti in the Spoletan *ducatus* was involved in the drafting of a private charter,[90] and in many other instances they were sought as witnesses to such documents throughout the kingdom,[91] while the importance of their position, at least in Spoleto, is attested by the fact that their names often appear in the date clauses of *diplomata*, both private and ducal.[92]

The sum of these activities – both official and private – suggests that gastalds were of greater importance in provincial government than a role in estate administration alone would suggest. Despite this, and although the references in the laws to the duties of gastalds in relation to royal estates do not necessarily indicate that such was their exclusive function, it has been thought that estate administration (perhaps, in view of their collection of fines, allied to financial competence) was their primary purpose, with other, more wide-ranging powers slowly being added until they became general royal agents.[93] (This cannot, however, be taken to suggest that gastalds eventually became little different from the *duces* (whom they allegedly replaced),[94] since there is almost no evidence that they regularly had military competence.)

The association of gastalds with royal estates, or *curtes*, is not in doubt but neither is the fact that they also tended to be based in cities,[95] the *curtis* probably often being co-terminous with the *ciuitas*.[96] Taken together with the sum of their powers, the evidence relating to their siting may render it possible to see gastalds as the main royal representatives in the provinces of the kingdom, perhaps enjoying a jurisdiction in some ways similar to that of the *comites ciuitatum* in the other early medieval kingdoms.[97]

If that is the case, it may be possible, by using a combination of philological evidence and comparative material from elsewhere (particularly the Ostrogothic kingdom), to elucidate something of the origins of the power of gastalds. Historians who have seen gastalds as being primarily estate administrators have suggested that they were first created when the monarchy was endowed with half the estates of the *duces* at the end of the interregnum.[98] Etymologically, however, the word *gastaldius* has no direct relationship with the idea of the estate or *curtis*.[99] One possibility for its original meaning is that it was derived from the verb *gastaldan*, meaning to administer[100] – in which case the subject of the administration could as well be a city as an estate, or even a body of people. An alternative is that the word is composed of two elements: *gast* (or *gasts*), meaning 'guest', and *waldan*, 'to rule'.[101]

Assuming the latter to be the correct derivation, the title could originally have been applied to the governors (as opposed to war leaders, or *duces*) of groups of Lombard settlers, since according to two passages in Paul's *History*, the latter were *hospites* (guests).[102] Before the interregnum, such men would probably have been royal appointees, as were the *duces*, but there is no reason to suppose that they would have ceased to exist during the ten years during which there was no king. On the restoration of the monarchy, they could again have acted as royal representatives, but with the additional task of administering the newly created royal estates. As royal agents, gastalds might gradually have come to exercise authority over the native population of the *ciuitates* in which they were based, and so have become more like *comites ciuitatum*: the processes could be similar to (though not identical with) those by which the Ostrogothic *comites Gothorum* may have been transformed into *comites ciuitatum* with power over Romans as well as Goths.[103] (The same processes may be envisaged for the southern *ducatus*, where gastalds were the representatives of the more autonomous *duces*.)

Although it is clear from the *diplomata* that gastalds continued to be an important feature of city administration throughout the Lombard period, they only feature in two laws issued by Liutprand, and in none of the enactments of Ratchis or Aistulf. The reason for this seems to be that they were instead referred to by the more general term of 'iudex': the equation is strongly suggested by the fact that almost all the laws concerned make it clear (if not explicit) that the *iudex* was associated with a particular city.[104] This cannot be combined with a similar reduction in the number of references in the laws to *duces* to suggest that the later laws were framed more generally so as to be applicable to both *duces* and gastalds in a period when the former were being replaced in many cities by the latter:[105] not only, as argued above, is there little evidence for such a change, but such a situation would already have existed in Rothari's time; in addition, almost all the laws in which *iudices* are implicated relate to civil jurisdiction of a kind which it cannot be demonstrated was ever exercised by *duces* (see above). The reason for the decline in references to *duces* may be that the rules of military leadership were adequately set by the time of Rothari, while civil affairs – particularly those relating to procedures – were subject to more continuous evolution. The replacement of the term 'gastald' by '*iudex*' may be of equally little significance, being more a matter of style than of substance, particularly since Visigothic *comites ciuitatum* could be referred to as *iudices ciuitatum*.[106]

Other provincial officials

Some of the same laws which refer to gastalds as *iudices* also reveal that such officials had subordinates – *sculdahis*,[107] of whom more than one might be answerable to a single *iudex*.[108] These men, who may be the same as *centenarii*[109] were involved in a wide range of civil affairs, similar to that within the purview of the gastald/*iudex*, including dealing with debtors,[110] fugitives,[111] trials,[112] witches and sorcerers, and those who caused disturbances in graveyards[113] (including the despoliation of graves[114]), as well as with those who became involved in marital irregularities.[115] They were also expected to participate in military campaigns:[116] it is, predictably, in

121

relation to this that Paul the Deacon made his only reference to a *sculda-his*, when he recounted how Argait, who was based in the territory of Cividale, was actively involved in defeating an invasion of the Slavs which allegedly took place at the invitation of the local *dux*.[117] *Sculdahis* are also found in the *diplomata* which reveal that they could be involved as judges at royal and ducal tribunals and inquisitions,[118] and, in the case of two Spoletan charters, that they could have a role in the drafting of documents.[119] Finally, *sculdahis* witnessed more private charters than any other kind of secular official,[120] perhaps underlining their importance in the local community, and their status as members of the hierarchy of provincial officials.[121] However, these men were of relatively low status in that hierarchy, as may be attested by the fact that the immunity clauses of charters do not mention them alongside *duces*, *comites*, and gastalds: instead, they are probably subsumed under the more general term *action-arii*.

A second title encountered with some frequency in the *diplomata* is that of *scario*. Men of this kind occasionally signed private charters;[122] Pictus, an 'old *scario* of the king', gave evidence at a hearing into a dispute between the Bishops of Arezzo and Siena,[123] and another *scario* was one of the judges who had to resolve a boundary dispute between Parma and Piacenza.[124] Similarly, when King Aistulf and Bishop Walprand of Lucca performed an exchange of land, the charter recording the transaction stated that it was administered for the Church by (among others) an archpresbyter, an archdeacon and a *scario*, and, for the King, by a range of officials including a *dux* and a *scario*.[125]

All these references do is to confirm that *scariones* were in some sense royal agents: they do not reveal anything of their specific, routine, functions. One suggestion is that they were 'manorial bailiffs', the evidence being that Pictus (see above) was described as being attached to a royal estate.[126] It is, however, impossible to be certain that there is any implication that Pictus did more than live on the estate, and an alternative may be that they were leaders of some kind of war band,[127] perhaps related to the *escaritos* referred to in a Frankish context by Fredegar, and who survived into the later middle ages as *scarii* (members of a *scara*).[128]

The position is, however, complicated by the fact that there may have been more than one kind, or rank, of *scario*: a private charter was signed by Saxo, 'maiescarius',[129] and a law enacted by Aistulf mentions an 'ovescario'.[130] The latter is of particular significance, since the law stipulates that oaths in court were to be administered by the *ovescario* (= 'court-scario'[131]), unless the case was relatively trivial, in which case an 'actor' could perform the task. This suggests that *ovescariones* had some kind of legal competence,[132] though how his position related to that of the ordinary *scariones* is entirely unclear.

Conclusion

Despite the fact that the Lombards were the second generation of 'barbarians' to settle in Italy, and arrived after the tremendously disruptive Gothic wars, there was a degree of continuity from earlier arrangements for the administration of the provinces. Although the overall settlement pattern suffered great dislocation,[133] both before and during the Lombard conquest, the *ciuitates* remained the basic administrative units of the kingdom, becoming the seats of local representatives of the king, who bore some similarities to the *comites ciuitatum* of the Ostrogoths and of the peoples who settled in Gaul and Spain. It is likely that either the *duces* – who were also based in cities – or the gastalds took over the former Roman *praetoria* where they survived (the Beneventan *duces* certainly did[134]), thus associating themselves with earlier administrative traditions. It is also likely that the territories of the *ciuitates* survived largely intact,[135] and that even a *ducatus* like that of Cividale, which covered a number of such units, may have respected their boundaries.[136]

There are parallels between this continuity of administrative units and the situation in contemporary Frankia and Spain,[137] and there may also be greater similarities between the officials of Lombard Italy and their Frankish and Visigothic counterparts than can be appreciated from an uncritical reading of Paul's *History*. Throughout the kingdom, it is likely that the *ciuitates* were administered by gastalds who were possessed of primarily civil power, and who also controlled such royal estates as lay within the territories for which they were responsible: although not necessarily identical with the *comites ciuitatum* of the other kingdoms, the similarities between them may be greater than the differences.

Military leadership was provided by *duces* who were permanently based in some cities or larger territories, particularly on the frontiers, but some of whom may have been associated with other centres on a more *ad hoc* basis, as circumstances dictated. In those areas which were furthest from the seat of royal power, such *duces* were more autonomous, as in the Frankish world, having a greater degree of civil authority than their northern counterparts. This does not necessarily mean, however, that they were opposed to kingship – though they certainly were not enamoured of certain kings – but it may mark the same evolution from the *dux* as military leader to the *dux* as superior of the *comes* which can be traced in other seventh-century polities.

13

The Royal Court

Unlike *duces*, members of the royal court rarely feature in Paul the Deacon's *History*, largely because they, like gastalds, were involved in administrative functions, rather than in high-profile events – particularly those relating to the succession. Similarly, as in other early medieval kingdoms, courtiers seldom find mention in the law codes which were largely concerned with the application of justice in provincial courts of a type with which royal courtiers were relatively infrequently involved. The *diplomata*, on the other hand, provide more plentiful information, though it is not on the scale of that of the witness lists to the Visigothic councils. In addition, with the exception of the officials of the writing office who were involved in the production of the documents themselves, the evidence of the *diplomata* often only indicates the existence of certain types of official, yielding little concerning their spheres of operation.

Comites

The most common general term for a courtier in the early medieval world is *comes*,[1] but in the Lombard sources it is rarely found outside the charters, where the title often appears in the lists of officials who were to respect the grants, between the *duces* and the gastalds.[2] Part of the explanation for the paucity of references to *comites* in the law codes lies in the fact that *comites ciuitatum*, often subsumed under the general term *comes* in documents such as the Visigothic laws, bore the separate title of gastald, which is extensively used in Rothari's *Edict* (see Chapter 12). A second reason for the silence of the laws is that *comites* who were not *comites ciuitatum* were also known as *gasind(i)i*[3] – a term which is occasionally used in the legal material, as well as in the *diplomata*. From such sources it is learnt that *gasindii* were accorded special protection,[4] and had a higher wergeld than other men;[5] could be attached to the queen,[6] as well as to the king;[7] could participate in court judgements;[8] could witness private (and, presumably, royal) charters.[9] Members of the retinues of high-ranking officials could also be referred to as *gasindii*, in the more general sense of 'companion'.[10]

Paul the Deacon uses the term *comes* on only three occasions, once to refer to a 'comes Langobardorum de Lagare' (near Trent) who was defeated by the Franks,[11] and twice in relation to Transamund, *comes* of Capua, who helped Grimoald of Benevento to become king before, in turn, becoming *Dux* Transamund I of Spoleto.[12] The precise position of neither man is clear, especially since Paul's reference to the *comes de Lagare* relates to the interregnum, when the royal court did not exist. While such men could be seen as descendants of the late Roman *comites rei militaris*,[13] it is possible that all Paul meant to convey was that both were powerful men:[14] such may also be the meaning of the term in a phrase in which Gregory the Great claimed that under Agilulf (in 594) the Lombards had 'neither king, nor *duces* nor *comites*'.[15]

The royal household

Some *comites* / *gasindii* will have held more specific offices within the court – like the Frankish *comites palatii*, or the Visigothic *comites et spatarii*. However, although the titles of many such positions are known from the Lombard evidence, it is almost impossible to determine which of them were associated with the status of *comes*. Moreover, there is no evidence of a rank similar to that of *domesticus* – though that does not mean that such a status did not exist, nor that the holders of some of the specific offices were not of that grade. A further problem is that despite references to quite a large number of offices, it is impossible to determine (in other than the most general of terms) the spheres of activity in which their holders were involved: this is partly due to the fact that some of the titles are Germanic terms which are linguistically obscure, and partly to the lack of a detailed narrative source of the kind provided for sixth-century Frankia by Gregory of Tours.

The difficulties may be illustrated by a number of titles connected with the domestic administration of the palace. In 730, a man described as a royal *canauarius* bought some land and had the transaction recorded in writing:[16] he is likely to have been some kind of butler[17] but, beyond that, his position and status within the court are unknown. Similarly little is known of men such as the *diliciosi* and *hostiarii* who were able to pass secrets out of the court,[18] and less of the queen's *antepor* who signed a private charter in 769.[19] Sometimes, differing interpretations are possible, as in the case of the queen's *scaffard* who signed another private document in 771: according to one interpretation, holders of this title were butlers, but it is has also been suggested that they could be *uesterarii* (or *uestiarii*).[20] The existence of *uestiarii* is not in doubt, but details of their precise functions are themselves unclear: although they have been seen as treasurers,[21] the only occasion on which a functionary of this kind is seen in action (other than witnessing documents[22]) is when one Prandulus, together with two *duces*, was sent by Desiderius to negotiate with Pope Hadrian I.[23]

One official concerning whom it is possible to be more certain is the *spatharius*, two of whose number sat on a royal tribunal to determine the boundaries of the estates of Parma and Piacenza.[24] There is no evidence as to whether they were *comites* as in the Visigothic court, or of lesser rank, but, although participation in proceedings of this kind is unlikely to have been a routine sphere for bodyguards, they were clearly trusted royal agents. Related to the *spatharius* was the *scilpor*, which, Paul the Deacon helpfully notes, was the *armiger*,[25] and which is likely to have been the same as the *scildepor* – one of whom was also a judge in the enquiry mentioned above. Unusually, Paul refers to men of this kind on two occasions:[26] predictably, both involve plots (one successful, the other not) to assassinate kings – that is, events relevant to Paul's interest in tracing the succession and demonstrating the legitimacy of Lombard rule.

Paul also explains, on two occasions, that *strator* and *marpahis* are synonyms:[27] the *maripassus* of a *diploma* is likely to be the same,[28] and both terms are related to *mar(i)scalc*, indicating that they refer to men involved in the care of the royal horses – similar to the *comites stabuli* of the Franks.[29] It is not, however, in relation to their main role that men bearing these titles are ever seen: one of Paul the Deacon's references is a passing account of the fact that the first *dux* of Cividale, who was King Alboin's nephew, had earlier been a *strator*, and the other relates how Cunincpert, wishing to carry out an assassination, consulted his *strator*. Neither does anything more than underline the status and position of trust of men of this kind; similar evidence is furnished by the fact that *stratores* could sit on royal tribunals.[30] Two of the documents concerned reveal that several such men could hold office at one time: the significance of this is unclear, though it might mean that *stratores* were not of the highest rank, perhaps being subject to an official of higher status, as in the fifth-century Roman Empire, in which *stratores* were subordinates of the *comes stabuli*.[31]

Almost nothing is known of financial administration within the court. Some officials bore the title of *stolesaz*, glossed in the *Liber Papiensis* as 'infertor',[32] which may relate to the treasurer of the royal court, since his counterpart in the ninth-century ducal court at Benevento was described in this way.[33] The only evidence from sources contemporary with the Lombard kingdom comes in one of Rothari's provisions, which states that there were circumstances in which a *iudex* could be compelled by one of the *stolesaz* to pay a fine to the fisc.[34] Understanding of the position of the *stolesaz* has been confused by a tradition of seeing the holder of the office as being a *seniscalc* who, further, may have been identical to the *maior domus*.[35] While the first equation could be correct, the latter perhaps less likely, particularly in view of Frankish evidence which suggests that the *seniscalc* was differentiated from the *maior*.[36]

In contrast to his Frankish counterpart, the Lombard *maior domus* is a shadowy figure, virtually nothing being known of his activities, legitimate or otherwise. In fact, the evidence is almost entirely restricted to judicial

126

matters: on two occasions, *maiores* formed part of tribunals;[37] and, on another, a *maior* was sent by King Liutprand to take charge of an investigation into a dispute between the Bishops of Siena and Arezzo.[38] The last case is particularly important, since the *maior*, Ambrose, is referred to as *maior domus* in Tuscany, perhaps suggesting that such officials could, as in the Frankish kingdom, be connected with specific regions: did the Lombard regions of Austrasia and Neustria also have *maiores*? If, so, did they perform functions similar to those (legitimately) undertaken by their counterparts in the *regnum Francorum*?

The writing office

Compared to the rest of the court, the royal chancery[39] is relatively well documented on account of the fact that its officials were themselves involved in the production of some of the sources of evidence and, as part of the procedures whereby the authenticity of such documents was ensured, recorded some aspects of their own activities. The main evidence comes from formulae found at the end of *diplomata* which record some of the stages by which the documents reached their final written form. There are several such formulae, all of which represent variations on a theme rather than fundamentally different procedures. In all cases the documents were finally written by notaries[40] or by officials whose title is not recorded:[41] whether this inconsistency is significant, or is stylistic, is not clear.

Notaries not only wrote documents, but were responsible for their authentication. Although the processes are not as clearly recorded as they are in the Merovingian *diplomata* (see Chapters 3 and 4), the Epilogue to Rothari's *Edict* states that the notary, Ansoald, was responsible for the verification (*recognitum*) and sealing (*requisitum*) of the only copies of the laws which were deemed to be valid.[42] The precise form of verification is uncertain, but it probably involved the imprint of a ring, as in the Merovingian world, for one of the royal *placita* states that the king had ordered it to be marked with his seal, though it is not explicitly stated that it was the notary (as opposed to a referendary) who was responsible.[43]

Notaries were also involved in the procedures by means of which the king's command that a document should be drafted was transmitted to the man who produced the final written version; those procedures (unlike the writing) could also involve referendaries. The stages through which a document passed are recorded in a number of different formulae. The simplest states that the king's command was notified to the writer through ('per') a single intermediary who might bear no title, or might be a notary or a referendary.[44] Alternatively, it was sometimes stated that the writer produced the document following the dictation of an intermediary, who was acting on the king's orders.[45] That these two procedures could in reality be identical is suggested by the existence of a third formula recording a document's production: it states that the king's command was transmitted and dictated by the same person, and was particularly popular in the last years of the kingdom.[46] On two occasions, however, the transmitter and the dictator were not the same person. The reason for the existence of two formulae recording the involvement of a different number of people is not known – it may have been related to the precise circumstances in which individual documents were drafted – but it is unlikely that the procedures envisaged were fundamentally different.

Given that the roles of transmitter of the king's order, and of dictator – who drafted the actual text of the document[47] – could be carried out by both notaries and referendaries, it is difficult to understand the distinction between the two types of official. Since Rothari's instructions concerning the verification of copies of his *Edict* referred to a notary, it is unlikely that referendaries had any more of a monopoly over those procedures than over other aspects of document production, and the distinction may be less one of function than of rank. It is not, however, possible to see the referendary as being the head of the writing office, for there is evidence that more than one such official could be in existence at the same time.[48] That the difference was nevertheless one of rank may be suggested by the fact that at least one royal notary, Andreacus, later became a referendary.[49] While it is possible that there was a difference in the function of the bearers of the titles which is not apparent simply because of the small volume of source material, it is not inconceivable that the title of referendary was little more than an honour: although this would have been different from Frankish and imperial usage (see Chapter 3), it could represent a variant adaptation from the imperial court in which referendaries were drawn from the ranks of the notaries.

The precise status of the notaries themselves has also occasioned some debate. There can be little doubt that the notaries who feature in royal documents were members of the king's court, though they are never described as such in the royal *diplomata*: the only reference to a specifically royal notary in a document issued in the king's name is in the Epilogue to the laws Liutprand promulgated in 713. By contrast, a number of private documents, usually written by men simply described as notaries, do specifically refer to *notarii regis*[50] or *notarii regiae potestatis*,[51] which are probably synonymous.[52] It has been suggested that these titles relate to a different kind of notary from that found in the royal documents, the latter being an official in the chancery, and the *notarius regis* being the king's private notary.[53] That, however, implies a greater degree of complexity and bureaucracy than seems warranted at this period, and the significance of the different titles may be no more than that royal notaries drew attention to their status when they were involved in drafting documents outside the court, in a way which was unnecessary when producing documents in the king's name.[54]

Notaries and referendaries did not only act outside their specific court roles in a private capacity: like other royal officials, they are sometimes found carrying out a variety of less routine tasks on behalf of the king. Hence, for example, Ultanus, a notary of Liutprand, was send by the king to chair an enquiry into a dispute between the bishops of Lucca and Pisa;[55] it may be that Guntheram, who was involved in the adjudication of a dispute between Siena and Arezzo, was similarly a royal notary, but the fact is not specifically mentioned in any of the surviving documents connected with the case,[56] any more than it is in relation to the notary Teodorus who was amongst the judges at the inquest into a boundary dispute between the *curtes* of Parma and Piacenza.[57] More certainly royal is the only notary to be mentioned by Paul the Deacon, when he recounts how, in *c.* 606, Agilulf sent his notary, Stabilicianus, to negotiate a treaty with Emperor Phocas;[58] similar is the case of Andrew, referendary (and former notary), who was sent by Desiderius to negotiate with Pope Hadrian I in 772 and 773.[59]

It is entirely predictable that it is in relation to this kind of event, rather than to routine or administrative functions, that Paul the Deacon and the author(s) of the *Liber Pontificalis* each make their rare reference to the officials of the writing office. It is also predictable that such functionaries only rarely appear in the law codes, and at that largely in relation to the provision of authentic copies of the documents rather than in specific enactments. If the *diplomata* did not exist, or did not contain formulae relating to the way in which they were produced, the Lombard writing office would be as shadowy as the rest of the court: the fact that they do exist, and were drafted in such a way as to reveal some of the procedures involved in their production should caution against the temptation to think of the other, less well-documented, court offices as any less important than in the Visigothic and Frankish kingdoms.

14

Conclusion

There can be no doubt that the arrival of the Lombards in Italy in 568 was destructive and caused major disruption to the inhabitants, for such are the inevitable consequences of war.[1] According to Gregory the Great, for example,

> Soon there followed terrible signs in the sky, as burning spears and armies were seen in the north. The race of the Lombards, brought forth from the scabbard of its homeland, smote our necks; and the species of man which, by its great destiny, had risen in that land was cut and mown down like a field of corn. Towns were depopulated; fortifications overthrown; churches burnt; monasteries – both of men and of women – destroyed. As farms were devoid of men and destitute of all cultivation, the land was left in solitude. Animals occupied the places which had formerly sustained many men. And I do not know what was happening in other parts of the world: for in this land, where I live, the end of the world was not merely proclaimed, but was made manifest.[2]

No such cataclysmic account of life in seventh-century Spain or Frankia exists, and the image of violence and disorder is only heightened by Paul the Deacon's account not only of the Lombard settlement, but of the entire history of the kingdom.

Before concluding, however, that the Lombards were more savage than the other peoples of early medieval Europe, a number of factors must be considered. First, at the time when Gregory the Great wrote, the Lombards were engaged in the conquest of Italy: the Franks and Visigoths, by contrast, had long been established in their respective territories, and while warfare was not uncommon, they were not perceived as a new threat. Second, the very fact that most of the West was relatively settled at the end of the sixth century probably heightened the impression of Lombard violence. Third, and perhaps most importantly, Gregory – like the fifth-century chroniclers, and like earlier theologians (such as Salvian) – had a moral and eschatalogical purpose: he was not seeking to be objective, and the Lombards served to illustrate the evils against which he was struggling.

With regard to Paul the Deacon, his emphasis on war leaders is partly a reflection of the fact that his relatively short history almost inevitably accords sensational events (such as those in which military leaders engaged) an important place – even the account of sixth-century Frankia provided by the much longer history of Gregory of Tours shares this bias. What Paul lacks, though, is Gregory's moral dimension, which led him to include more detail concerning specific incidents and, especially, characters. Instead, Paul's aim was political: it was to show, in broad terms, the destiny of the Lombard people and the legitimacy of their rule in Italy. It was this which led him to concentrate on the vicissitudes of the succession, and one of the most significant features of his account is that many (though not all) of the rebellions against specific kings can be seen as contests between rivals many of whom had some dynastic claim to the throne.

There is no doubt that the *duces* – the main military leaders – were of the greatest importance during the conquest, and their significance may be underlined by the fact of the interregnum (almost whatever interpretation is placed on that occurrence). Equally, given that the Lombards never conquered the entire Italian peninsula, and that their kingdom remained divided by hostile territory, the role of military leaders almost certainly remained of greater significance than it did in the interior of Merovingian Gaul or Visigothic Spain. Despite that, detailed examination of the evidence for the activities of *duces* suggests that the differences between them and their Frankish and Visigothic counterparts can be overestimated.

Similarly, Lombard kingship shares many features with that of the Visigoths and Franks. This is true not only in terms of aspects of kingship – such as the choice of places of residence – revealed by Paul in his quest to demonstrate the legitimacy of the Lombard claim to Italy, but also of aspects of royal power upon which he did not choose to dwell, but which are revealed by other types of evidence. The early gold coinage, for example, suggests that the Lombards had some respect for imperial traditions, and, even when the kings began to issue coins in their own name, their models were derived from the Empire. Equally, as elsewhere in the West, the ways in which kings chose to administer the law were greatly influenced by Roman traditions. It would, indeed, be surprising if this were not the case since the Lombards had been settled on former Roman territory for a generation before their arrival in Italy, and during that time, if not earlier, had been in contact with the Byzantines in a variety of ways, ranging from commercial transactions to the service of some of their number as imperial mercenaries. At the least, therefore, their leaders were familiar with Roman ways of doing things, and, even though very little is known of their Pannonian period, it is questionable to what extent they entered Italy with a 'Germanic' as opposed to 'Roman' *weltanschauung*.[3]

While kings and *duces* feature large in Paul the Deacon's *History*, members of the civil administration – whether the gastalds and their subordinates in the provinces, or members of the royal household – do not:

almost the only court officials to feature in his account were associated with military affairs. This does not mean, however, that the royal court was any more 'barbarian' than its Frankish and Visigothic counterparts: it was simply not germane to Paul's purpose to depict the life of the court, either for its own sake, or in order to illustrate the virtues and vices of particular men; the only reason military courtiers feature in his narrative is that it was they, rather than administrators, were likely to be involved in events (such as assassinations) which were of interest to him. That other kinds of courtier existed is clear from the presence of a large number of titles describing them; and that they were not mere ciphers is suggested by the evidence of the *diplomata* concerning the writing office, which – although not fully understandable – was clearly capable of producing documents of some sophistication by means which were as much derived from Roman models as were those employed by the Franks. It is not impossible that many other aspects of the royal government – whether of the gastalds in the cities, or in spheres such as financial administration – were at least as important and as well organised as the writing office: the main difference between the chancery and other sections of the administration is that there is no source capable of revealing the workings of the latter.

PART IV

Anglo-Saxon England

The history of early Anglo-Saxon England has rarely been treated in the context of the development of the post-Roman kingdoms on the continent. Until recently, most historians who have sought comparative material have looked for parallels and influences in the Celtic world and in those Germanic areas which were not influenced by the Roman Empire. This is in large measure the reason why there has been little perception of the possibility of continuity from the Roman period into the British, still less the Anglo-Saxon, era. To some extent that is a function of the nature of the written sources for post-Roman Britain: the British have left remarkably little other than Gildas' work, and the Anglo-Saxon sources do not dwell on the period before the very end of the sixth century. The scraps of information which do exist appear to show the British and Anglo-Saxons in such conflict as to preclude the possibility that the latter learnt anything of the former when they acquired control of an area. In addition, unlike the Franks, Visigoths and Lombards, the Anglo-Saxons did not enjoy a sustained period of direct contact with the Roman world before their arrival within its frontiers, thus reducing the possibilities for direct Roman influence upon them.

Advances in the understanding of texts, together with the evidence which has accrued from archaeological research, have, however, begun to modify traditional assumptions. There is a growing perception that there may have been continuity from the Roman to the British periods, and that the Anglo-Saxons may have been more open to influence than a previous generation would have considered. In turn, this may yield the potential for more fruitful comparison with developments in the continental kingdoms than has hitherto been widely considered likely. If it can be demonstrated that there were similarities between England and the continent in the seventh century, fresh questions may be posed concerning the ways in which they arose.

This is not the place in which to try to evaluate the evidence for the transition from Roman Britain to Anglo-Saxon England – not even of all those aspects susceptible to historical, as opposed to archaeological, analysis. What is attempted is an appreciation of the evidence for royal government as it emerges into the historical record: many of the suggestions made, or conclusions reached – particularly in Chapter 18 – are acknowledged to be tentative (even if, in order to avoid being cumbersome, some are presented in more concrete form). It is hoped that, by treating the evidence for Anglo-Saxon England in exactly the same way as that for the continental kingdoms, new insights will be gained, and that the relationship between the development of England and of the continental kingdoms (in the seventh century, if not before) may be better comprehended. Such an understanding also has implications for both the earlier and the later development of England itself. J. Campbell has suggested that the roots of late Anglo-Saxon England's sophistication cannot have lain in 'mere chaos' in the fifth and sixth centuries[1] – still less, by implication, in the seventh and eighth: the following contribution seeks to bring some order to at least the second half of the period – that is, to an age which an earlier generation saw as having witnessed the first clumsy steps of the proud savages who were the early Anglo-Saxons towards civilisation.

15

The Sources

The evidence for the history of early Anglo-Saxon England is dominated by Bede's *Historia ecclesiastica gentis Anglorum*, written at Jarrow in the 730s.[1] Until relatively recently, Bede's account was treated as being 'objective' in a way unparalleled in the early middle ages; in recent years, however, it has been demonstrated that such is not the case, and it has become possible to see that his version of events was created for as much of a purpose as, for example, was Paul the Deacon's account of the Lombards.[2] Precisely what that purpose was is the subject of some debate, but it clearly centred on the development of the Roman version of Christianity in the British Isles: the Irish – though profoundly mistaken in some of their practices – are given a modicum of credit for missionary activity, while the British are condemned for their failure to convert the Anglo-Saxons. Bede's story of the development of the Roman church itself is not entirely free from bias, since he presents Bishop Wilfrid in a much less favourable light than Stephen's pro-Wilfridian *Life* of the Saint – though whether the prime object of the *Ecclesiastical History* was to discredit Wilfrid is more debatable.[3]

However its precise purpose is viewed, one of the main themes of the *Ecclesiastical History* is the salvation of the English people,[4] the presentation of which is depicted in terms which owe much to the historical books of the Old Testament, particularly I Samuel.[5] A large element of the work is, therefore, theological and didactic: the prosperity of the English was assured by their adherence to the one true (Roman) faith. This message was illustrated by examples of good men – particularly kings, bishops and monks – being attended with success, and (though to a lesser extent) of the fate of the evil:[6] this gives the work a moral dimension, and lends it something of the character of hagiography[7] – a *genre* in which Bede was also expert (see below).

Given its nature and preoccupations, it will be apparent that the *Ecclesiastical History* is an imperfect source of evidence concerning forms of secular government. Although kings feature large in the work, and Bede's narratives concerning their actions are likely to be accurate, much of his interpretation of, and comment upon, the events may be influenced at least as much by Biblical models as by seventh- and eighth-century reality. Secular officials – whether collectively or individually – tend to

135

appear as supporting characters but, as in hagiographical literature, the ways in which they behaved are unlikely to be greatly distorted; as in so many narrative sources, however, it is likely to be those engaged in dramatic events (often of a military, rather than an administrative character) who feature prominently, and members of the king's household may often be described in general terms, reflecting their rank, rather than by more specific titles.

Even in relation to the Anglo-Saxon areas of Britain, coverage of events is not uniform either in terms of time or of geography. Although Book I opens with a description of Britain and an account of its Roman and post-Roman history, this does little more than set the stage for the ensuing action, and much of the account is derived from the earlier work of Gildas (see below). Bede was not fundamentally interested in the period of British domination, nor in the history of the English until their conversion to the Roman faith during and after Augustine's mission to Kent in 597. Had he been concerned with the pagan period, it lay so far in the past that any account he offered would have been at least secondary and might not, therefore, have been unimpeachable. Within the period which did interest him there is also a chronological imbalance, a more factual account being presented of the years before the 690s than of the period of Bede's own adulthood; the nearer Bede approached the time of writing, the more hagiographical (and overtly didactic) his account becomes, with greater concentration on wonders and visions.[8] It has been suggested that the explanation for this lies partly in the politics of Northumbria during the quarter century of dynastic rivalry which followed the death of King Aldfrith in 705:[9] Bede was clearly unhappy about the events, and may have preferred to seek out examples of good conduct during such a period rather than to hold up the wicked as examples; he may also have felt it prudent to appear to be neutral. There may, however, be another reason for the chronological imbalance, more directly connected with Bede's spiritual purpose. The early seventh century was the period during which the leaders of the main kingdoms were converted; once that had been achieved, the nature of Bede's narrative may have changed as he was obliged to seek other kinds of manifestation of divine providence. Whatever its precise cause, the changing character of the *Ecclesiastical History* means that the period for which one might expect the greatest detail (for the purposes of the present enquiry) is less well served than an earlier age for which Bede is not a fully primary authority.

Geographical coverage is no more even than chronological, the Northumbrian element of the *gens Anglorum* receiving such disproportionate attention that the *Ecclesiastical History* has been described as a history of the Northumbrian church in the context of the English.[10] Leaving aside the question of Bede's precise purpose, such a bias is not unexpected in a work composed in a Northumbrian monastery and dedicated to a Northumbrian king. This does not mean that information on other parts of the country is lacking, or that it is of poor quality – the Preface reveals that Bede had informants in Kent (Albinus), London (Nothhelm – who also supplied material from Rome), and the lands of the South and West Saxons (Daniel) – but it does mean that rather more is seen of Northumbrian kings and courtiers than of most of those elsewhere in England.

The *Ecclesiastical History* is not the only work of Bede's which provides evidence relevant to the subject of royal government, there being small amounts of such material in his *Historia abbatum* (*Life of Ceolfrith*) – an account of the foundation and subsequent development of the double monastery of Monkwearmouth-Jarrow – and in his prose *Life of St Cuthbert*, written in the 720s. Both of those works were based on earlier writings, the anonymous *Life of Ceolfrith* (also known as the anonymous *Historia abbatum*), written shortly after 716 at Wearmouth,[11] and an equally anonymous *Life of St Cuthbert* written *c*. 700 at Cuthbert's own house of Lindisfarne.[12] Nor do those anonymous works exhaust the hagiographical sources for early Anglo-Saxon England, the other such documents being the *Life of Gregory the Great* (again, anonymous) produced at Whitby between 710 and 720, the *Life of St Guthlac* (of Crowland), written by Felix at Wearmouth, after *c*. 721, and, above all, Stephen's *Life of St Wilfrid*, produced shortly after 710 at Ripon.[13]

These saints' lives all share the general limitations of hagiography. They were all written in approximately the first two decades of the eighth century[14] – that is, during the same period as that in which Bede was active; of similar date is the only non-English hagiographical work to contain significant material relevant to the present enquiry, Adomnán's *Uita Columbae*.[15] Although the concentration of hagiographical output at one time means that the period before the late seventh century is hardly documented outside the *Ecclesiastical History*, it does enable some of Bede's other biases to be seen, as parts of the *Life of Wilfrid* and the *Life of Columba* cover the same events as Bede's *Ecclesiastical History*, while giving rather different interpretations.[16] Further, although all the English *Lives* were written in Northumbria, Felix's work concerns Mercia and the Fenland of eastern England, and Stephen's version of Wilfrid's life contains a large amount of Mercian material,[17] thereby extending the geographical area from which evidence can be drawn.

For the period before the mid-seventh century, almost no such checks on Bede's narrative exist, while the era between the departure of the Romans in the early fifth century and the arrival of Augustine at the end of the sixth is almost a blank. Into that period fall the *Life* of Germanus of Auxerre, written by Constantius of Lyons probably in the 470s, though it contains almost nothing of relevance for the present purpose, and Bede's main source for the sub-Roman period, the *De excidio et conquestu Britanniae* by Gildas. The latter, the date of which (traditionally thought to lie in the mid-sixth century) is debated,[18] is a work of prophecy, or of moral history, providing kings and clergy with admonition and advice in the manner of the Old Testament.[19] On the whole (although, as will be suggested in Chapter 18, the work may contain some valuable clues concerning post-Roman Britain), Gildas treats his subject in such a general way as to provide remarkably few concrete facts concerning the fifth and sixth centuries either in relation to his own people – the British – or to the Anglo-Saxons.[20]

Other sources, of more narrative type, contain information claiming to be relevant to the history of the sub-Roman period. The greatest of them is the *Anglo-Saxon Chronicle*, written in the late ninth century as a work of propaganda for the West Saxon royal house.[21] Although parts of its early sections may be based on reliable sources, there is no way of demonstrating the fact, nor is it always possible to determine the extent to which the presentation of the early material results from manipulation in order to provide the necessary background for those portions of the work relating to the time of Alfred. It might, nevertheless, be possible that both the depiction of kings, and the technical language used to describe them and their supporters, survived intact, for there might have been little need for the compiler of the *Chronicle* to have altered them; however, it is at least as likely that such aspects of the document would have been written in terms familiar to the ninth-century audience for whom the past was being reinterpreted. The same caveats are, in general, applicable to a work compiled earlier in the ninth century – the *Historia Brittonum* (written *c.* 829-30, and incorporating material relating to the north of Britain which was probably compiled at the end of the previous century).[22]

Of broadly similar date to the *Historia Brittonum* are the royal genealogies, drawn up to illustrate (or create) the title to rule of the dynasties in existence at the time of their compilation. While they may be accurate for the eighth century, their usefulness for earlier periods is limited to where they can be checked against other sources. For much of the fifth and sixth centuries there is no way of verifying the material they contain, and it is clear (both from internal evidence and from the comparison of different genealogies) that there was some standardisation of generations, and some creative writing.[23]

None of the sources considered so far was of an administrative nature, but such documents did exist, in the form of charters and law codes. The earliest royal charters to have survived date from the 670s[24] – about the same time as extant *diplomata* in the Frankish and Lombard kingdoms become plentiful. While the existence of the charters attests to a degree of sophistication of administrative structures, the documents contain relatively little evidence beyond the titles of certain officials for the way in which the administration functioned. Even in relation to the latter, Anglo-Saxon diplomatic material is less helpful than its continental counterparts since the documents never bear any outward marks of authenticity, such as seals, and contain almost no evidence concerning the mechanisms by which they were drawn up.[25] The reason for this is that, in contrast to continental practice, they were written in the greater churches, by the recipients of the grants they record, rather than in the royal court itself.[26] This does not mean that Anglo-Saxon charters owe nothing to Roman traditions,[27] but those traditions were largely mediated by the Church, rather than being directly derived from imperial practice or from the contents of Roman municipal archives.

The first law code to be produced in Anglo-Saxon England – that associated with Æthelberht of Kent – may also have been drawn up under ecclesiastical influence, possibly following models brought to England by Augustine and his followers[28] (the issues surrounding this will be more fully discussed in the next Chapter). Its form is largely that of a list of compensations for different kinds of injury (physical or otherwise), some of the sanctions varying according to the rank of the victim or perpetrator. There is little of a procedural nature either in that code or in the enactments of Whitræd a century later (in 695); slightly more material of that nature is found in the code of Hlothhere and Eadric (673x685), and a more significant quantity in that of Ine (688x694).

The law codes help to redress the uneven geographical coverage of both Bede and the hagiographers, the first three all having been produced in Kent and the last in Wessex. The charters are likewise southern or western rather than northern or eastern in origin: this is more likely to reflect the disruption of monastic foundations in the north and east by Viking raids in later centuries, rather than that charters were unknown in Northumbria and East Anglia. The administrative documents do not, though, assist in redressing the chronological imbalance apparent in sources of other kinds, as almost all of them relate to the last third of the seventh century or later. The overall pattern of the evidence means that it is impossible to discuss the governmental structures in the fifth and sixth centuries in anything other than the most partial and tentative of terms, and that for the first two-thirds of the seventh century such discussion is almost wholly dependent on what can be gleaned from Bede's *Ecclesiastical History*.

16

Kings and Queens

In his *Ecclesiastical History*, Bede dwells on the pious works of kings –
especially of rulers such as Oswald and Oswine of Northumbria, and the
Sigeberhts of the East Angles and East Saxons. This suited his concern
with edification, and also had parallels with Biblical kingship: in his
description of the peace which accompanied the reign of the good King
Edwin, for example, there has been found a parallel with the description
of Solomon's rule in I Kings.[1] Important though the Biblical model was,
however, it is unlikely to have been the only source for Bede's account,
since there is a strikingly similar narrative in a Scandinavian legend
concerning Frothi, reported by Saxo Grammaticus. According to Bede,
Edwin commanded drinking vessels to be hung at wayside springs in order
that travellers might refresh themselves, and esteem for him was so great
that no one removed them; Saxo recounts that Frothi had gold rings placed
at the roadside, and, similarly, no one touched them until he was old and
weak.[2] The parallel seems too close to be coincidental: assuming that Bede
knew the legend, what he appears to have done is to Christianise the
heroic saga, transforming the rings into cups from which 'living water'
might be drunk, thus emphasising Edwin's holiness and, perhaps, mirror-
ing the king's conversion. This may tell us much about Bede and his ideals,
but probably says little about Edwin's power.

Obtaining royal power

The use of Biblical terms to describe a king's role as a war leader[3] may also
reflect Bede's ideas concerning what kings should do, but there is little
reason to doubt that, as on the continent, war leadership was a vital royal
function: indeed, the establishment and maintenance of peace required a
powerful and successful king. Accordingly, many kings are depicted as
having participated in battle against external foes – Æthelfrith,[4] Ecgfrith,[5]
Edwin,[6] Oswald[7] and Oswiu[8] of the Northumbrians; Cædwalla[9] and Cenwahl[10] of the West Saxons; Æthelred[11] and Penda[12] of the Mercians; and
Sigeberht and Ecgric of the East Angles (for the approximate location of
the main kingdoms, see Map V on p. 182).[13] Further, the fact that there
was no system of primogeniture meant that it was often only thanks to a
man's prowess as a warrior that he was able to become king, as he had to

fight off the rival claims not only of brothers, but also of more distant relations. Hence, for example, when Oswald of the Northumbrians died, his brother, Oswiu, became king in Bernicia, but his second cousin, Oswine, ruled in Deira (see Table IV on p. 186 for some of the inter-relationships between rulers); Oswiu felt cheated out of part of his inheritance, and had to defeat (and kill) Oswine in battle before gaining what he thought was rightfully his.[14] In such circumstances, it was possible for both claimants to lose control, as when Egbert of Kent's son, Eadric, rebelled (with South Saxon assistance) against his uncle, Hlothhere, who had succeeded his father in 673: the result was that men termed by Bede as 'reges dubii uel externi' (one of whom may have belonged to another branch of the ruling dynasty[15]) gained control of Kent for a time, before the 'legitimate king', Wihtræd, was able to establish himself.[16]

Pretenders who lost in battle, or chose not to contest the issue by force of arms, often lost everything, and had little alternative but to go into exile for, had they remained at home, their rivals would almost certainly have disposed of them. This accounts, for example, for the Pictish exile of Oswald and Eanfrith, sons of King Æthelfrith of the Northumbrians, during the rule of their father's successor and brother-in-law, Edwin;[17] Edwin's own sons were later removed from Northumbria and sent to Gaul in order to escape the threat posed by Oswald,[18] who also caused Edwin's nephew, Hereric, to live in exile with the British king, Cerdic.[19] Similar circumstances surround the exile in Frankia of Sigeberht, later king of the East Angles, while his brother, Eorpwald, was ruling.[20] Some pretenders did not go so far, or so peacefully: Cædwalla of the West Saxons[21] and Æthelbald of the Mercians[22] 'seem to have been driven into brigandage', for a time – the lesson was not lost on the former who, after gaining power, was almost as ruthless as the Merovingians Clovis I and Chlothar II in exterminating potential rivals.[23]

Sometimes, relations of the reigning king could be given authority over part of the kingdom, perhaps as consolation for failing to gain the throne, or as a way of preparing them for the assumption of full power later. When Sigeberht of the East Angles abdicated in order to become a monk, he left the kingdom to his kinsman, Ecgric, who had 'formerly held part of the same kingdom':[24] it is not clear whether Ecgric's earlier power was 'legitimate', nor whether Sigeberht's departure was voluntary. A similar case is that of Æthelred I of the Mercians, who appears to have made his nephew, Cenred, king and, like Sigeberht, retired to a monastery; Cenred later himself gave up the throne to go on pilgrimage to Rome.[25] Also in the Mercian kingdom, Peada was made ruler ('princeps') of the Middle Angles during the reign of his father, Penda.[26] After Oswiu of the Northumbrians had defeated and killed Penda, he allowed Peada to retain control of the 'south Mercians'. Bede explained this by reference to the fact that Peada was Oswiu's kinsman (son-in-law), suggesting that Oswiu's action was one of Christian virtue; it is at least as likely that the explanation should be sought in terms of *realpolitik*: Oswiu may not have been powerful enough to destroy Peada and his supporters, or to have extended direct control over the furthest parts of Mercia.

It seems likely that similar forms of co-rulership existed in Kent.[27] Although, as noted earlier, Eadric rebelled against his uncle, Hlothhere, the fact that the two men jointly issued a law code may indicate that they had earlier shared power.[28] In addition, there is a legend that Eorconberht, grandson of the great Æthelberht, shared his kingship with a brother, Eormenred.[29] Not in all instances, however, can it be shown that the two kings were blood relations: in 690, after Eadric's rebellion, Swæfheard confirmed grants made by king Oswine of Kent,[30] while another charter of the same years describes Swæfheard (son of Sæbbi, king of the East Saxons), as king of Kent;[31] Swæfheard seems also to have ruled alongside Wihtræd for a time.[32]

Some of those who ruled parts of larger kingdoms may have been described on occasion as *subreguli*, though the term is rare in those early documents which can reasonably be thought to be genuine. Bede, for example, only uses the term once in the *Ecclesiastical History*, when he says that on the death of Cenwahl of the West Saxons, *subreguli* took over the government for a period of ten years, after which they were defeated by Cædwalla, who established himself as king.[33] It is not clear who the sub-kings were, but Bede's use of the term implies that they were not fully kings: could they have been rulers of parts of the kingdom? If so, there might (on a smaller scale) be some parallels with the Lombard inter-regnum; alternatively, the sub-kings may have been fully royal but have acknowledged the overlordship of Cenwahl.[34]

In a charter recording the donation of land to the minster at Chertsey, the donor, Frithuwold, is described as 'subregulus prouinciae Surri-anorum'; some of the witnesses are also described as *subreguli*, but it is not stated with what areas they were associated.[35] The king beneath whom these men were placed was Wulfhere of Mercia, as is revealed by the fact that he confirmed the donation. It is again not clear what the exact status of the *subreguli* was, the possibilities being the same as in the case of Wessex.[36] Similar uncertainty surrounds the precise position of Beorn-hæth, *subregulus*, who, according to Stephen's *Life of Wilfrid*, helped King Ecgfrith in a campaign against the Picts.[37]

There is probably no reason to assume that the term *subregulus* neces-sarily has precisely the same meaning in all contexts, but in some instances greater certainty may be possible. Oshere of the Hwicce, for example, is described as 'king' in a charter of 693,[38] but an eighth-century document refers to him as 'subregulus' and 'comes' of Æthelred I of Mercia:[39] this may imply that he was the recognised royal authority within his own territory, but was subject to the overlordship of Æthelred – as more certainly appears to have been the case later in the eighth century.[40] The same kind of arrangement may be envisaged for the East Saxons, of whom

Bede noted that Kings Sigehere and Sæbbi succeeded Swithhelm in 664, even though they were subject to Wulfhere of Mercia.[41] Within Mercia proper there may also have been room for this kind of ambiguity, as one Berhtwald was described as a king in a charter recording a donation of land he made to the monastery at Malmesbury, but as a prefect in Stephen's *Life of Wilfrid*:[42] this instance is, however, more problematic, both because Berhtwald was a nephew of the Mercian king, Æthelred I, and because the charter is of questionable authenticity. What does seem likely, though, is that whereas once independent kings who were subjected to others may have tried to retain as much of their royal status as possible within their own territories, their overlords would have sought to ensure that they knew their place, and may accordingly have described them by lesser titles than that of 'king'.[43]

Similar issues are raised by the terms used to describe the overlords themselves: although they are never described as more than kings, they are sometimes said to have exercised *imperium*. The latter is a term which has been much discussed by historians,[44] especially in relation to a passage on the *Ecclesiastical History* in which Bede lists seven rulers possessed of such authority.[45] That text is particularly problematic since it refers to no rulers of this kind later than Oswiu of the Northumbrians – though elsewhere in the work the rule of more recent kings is described as an *imperium*, as is that of some Mercians,[46] whose power the *Ecclesiastical History* as a whole does not adequately recognise.

What seems to be implied – and not only in Bede's writings – by the term *imperium*, is simply 'overlordship'.[47] In the same way as men described in some contexts (especially within their own territories) as kings might also be designated as *subreguli* in relation to more powerful rulers with whom they were associated in a subordinate position, so those more powerful rulers might be referred to either simply as kings wielding royal power, or as rulers with greater authority – that is, *imperium*. The special quality of such *imperium* was that it involved the exercise of authority over a larger area than a ruler's own kingdom.[48] While all kings ruled a *regnum*, only some had *imperium*: it was therefore possible for *regnum* and *imperium* to be used to some extent interchangeably in relation to kings who possessed the latter, but the two terms were not synonymous. *Imperium* was not fixed, nor was it heritable or associated with particular territories:[49] it was personal, having to be built up afresh by every ruler who aspired to it, and it implied no more than that its holder might expect those over whom he exercised it to obey his commands:[50] there are some parallels between this and the kinds of overlordship enjoyed by some sixth-century Frankish kings – notably Theodebert I.[51]

Given that kings other than the seven named in Bede's famous selection are described by the same author as having possessed *imperium*, the list is clearly artificial. One possibility is that it was compiled from some kind of earlier list of great kings,[52] but it is perhaps more likely that it was constructed by Bede himself for reasons which are no longer apparent.[53] The most salient point concerning the text is that it does not include any of the rulers of Mercia[54] – and it may be no coincidence that the only place within the *Ecclesiastical History* in which Bede refers to such men as having exercised *imperium* is not in the main text, but in the recapitulation contained in the last chapter of Book V: he may have been simply uninterested in portraying Mercian power or, more likely, deliberately trying to suppress material relating to Mercia, the rulers of which were often engaged in hostilities with Northumbria.

Leaving aside Bede's bias, it is clear that there was no 'constitutional' position of overlord: *imperium* was fluid and complex, as may be illustrated by the case of Æthelberht of Kent. According to Bede, Æthelberht was one of those who held *imperium*, in this case apparently extending over all of England south of the Humber.[55] Redwald of the East Anglians was possessed of similar authority, even while Æthelberht was still alive.[56] This may mean one of several things: that Bede's claim that Æthelberht was overlord of the entire area south of the Humber was grandiloquent; or that Æthelberht lost *imperium* during his lifetime; or that the area over which he had authority was reduced – presumably following some kind of rebellion; or that there could be hierarchies of overlordship, with Redwald exercising authority over a number of other rulers while at the same time recognising the greater power of Æthelberht. The last possibility would make Bede's claims for the extent of Æthelberht's *imperium* more plausible, and that the situation envisaged is not impossible may be suggested by the fact that Æthelberht himself was almost certainly a dependant of the Merovingians from at least the time of his marriage to Bertha.[57]

Whatever the extent of Æthelberht's overlordship, no powers can be demonstrated to have been specifically associated with *imperium* in his case or any other. It is indeed possible that the nature of the authority wielded by overlords was not the same in all cases. While being highly significant in terms of the politics of the early and mid-Saxon periods, *imperium* reveals little concerning the nature of kingship, except that some kings were successful enough to be able to impose a degree of temporary authority over others.

Kings in power

Once they had gained power – often by warfare – kings frequently still had to fight to maintain their position (see above), but, however important war leadership was, it was not their sole activity. Neither the *Ecclesiastical History* nor the hagiographical sources reveal a great deal of the administrative functions of kings, but it is clear from the law codes that, as in the continental kingdoms, the administration of justice was one of their main concerns, as Bede himself implied when he recalled that Æthelberht of Kent issued decrees.[58]

The source of early Anglo-Saxon law has, however, occasioned much debate, largely on account of Bede's statement that Æthelberht's edicts were produced 'iuxta exempla Romanorum'. Given that the laws are in Old English, rather than Latin, and that they bear little relation to Roman imperial law, a number of hypotheses have been put forward as to what Bede meant. One solution to the problem is that it was the fact that the laws were *written* that gave them their Roman character:[59] an objection – though not necessarily a fatal one – to this might be that *exempla* is in the plural. Perhaps in order to answer this, J.M. Wallace-Hadrill suggested that Bede was indicating that Æthelberht had available to him copies of continental 'barbarian' codes brought by the members of Augustine's mission from the Roman church. This is an elegant solution to the problem posed by Bede's phrase, particularly as it accounts for similarities between certain of the provisions of Æthelberht's laws and those found in a range of continental edicts, from Leovigild's *Codex reuisus* to the Burgundian, Lombard and Frankish compilations.[60] The fact that there is a larger degree of similarity with the *Pactus legis Salicae*[61] than with any of the other codes is explicable in terms of Æthelberht's relationship with the Franks (see above), while the spur to enact legislation could have come from a perception that it was the correct thing for a Christian king to do.

In view of more recent interpretations of the continental laws as being re-enactments and modifications of Roman provincial law, the questions raised by Bede's statement may be worth re-examining. It may not, for example, be so important as was formerly thought that Æthelberht's compilation bears so little relation to Roman law books, since the latter were almost all concerned with imperial legislation. In addition, the fact that Anglo-Saxon law is written in the vernacular does not completely distinguish it from its continental counterparts, some of which (such as the *Pactus legis Salicae* and the Lombard laws) contain vernacular vocabulary and/or glosses.

The last point may be underlined by the fact that at least one of the vernacular terms in Æthelberht's code has a direct equivalent in the Roman world, though attention has not previously been drawn to it. The term in question is 'hlafæta', which is only attested in the law code,[62] but which clearly refers to a man of dependent (though not fully unfree) status. The word, which literally means 'loaf eater', can be seen as a neat translation of the Latin *bucellarius* (found not only in the Roman world, but also in Euric's Visigothic laws[63]), which refers to a category of private soldier used not only to defend the interests of his patron but also as part of the imperial army, *bucella* being a special kind of biscuit distributed to such men as rations.[64]

A second term which only appears in an Old English form in Æthelberht's compilation is *læt*. Like *hlafæta*, it refers to a category of semi-free man, though members of the group were divided into three classes, each with a different wergild.[65] *Lætas* have been explained in a variety of ways, ranging from their being members of a 'British peasantry surviving under Jutish rule';[66] to their being representatives of a Germanic institution with parallels in the *liti* of the Frankish law codes and the *aldiones* of the Lombard laws;[67] to the term designating the descendants of Roman *laeti* (concerning whose existence in Britain there has been much debate).[68] A final term which may be of significance in this context is *leode*, which is an Old English rendering of the *leudes* found in a Frankish context and, on one occasion, in the Visigothic laws.[69]

The fact that *hlafæta* and *læt*, if not *leode*, appear to be translations of terms found in continental codes not only underlines the relationship between Æthelberht's laws and those of other 'barbarian' kings, but also suggests that the institutions referred to existed in England in the years around 600, for, no matter what Æthelberht's source(s), it is perhaps unlikely that the king would have included reference (still less in translated form) to classes of men who did not exist amongst his subjects. That raises interesting possibilities concerning the earlier development of sub-Roman Britain, but it does not answer the question of Æthelberht's source, any more than does the fact that, in more general terms, Roman vulgar law seems to have influenced Anglo-Saxon land law.[70] What it may do, though, is to strengthen the possibility that there was indeed some kind of copy of Roman provincial law available to the king: while Wallace-Hadrill's suggestion can by no means be disproved, a neater solution might be to take Bede more literally, and to explain the parallels between Æthelberht's code and those of a *number* of continental ones in terms of a single common ancestor (the body of Roman provincial law, which varied between dioceses) rather than of a cobbling together of provisions from disparate codes brought by the Augustinian mission.

Whatever the origins of the material he used, Æthelberht's legislative activity clearly stands in the same tradition as that of continental kings: so do the laws enacted by other early Anglo-Saxon monarchs, both in Kent and elsewhere. Hence, for example, it is stated in the Prologue to the laws issued by Hlothhere and Eadric that the kings were adding to the laws of their forefathers, while the Prologues to the laws of Wihtræd and Ine reveal that the codes were made after consultation with the leading men of Kent.[71] In all three cases there is an implication that earlier enactments had been found wanting, and it may be that, as on the continent, new laws were sometimes made in response to particular cases. This interpretation derives added strength from the recent work of P. Wormald, which has suggested that Ine's code may not be the the result of a single legislative act, but may consist of a series of such acts similar to those exemplified by the Frankish capitularies or the almost annual decrees of the Lombards.[72]

16. Kings and Queens

Symbols of power

It was not only in terms of the ways in which they acted that Anglo-Saxon kings displayed similarities with their continental counterparts, but also in the ways in which they chose to portray their power. By comparison with the Visigothic and Lombard kingdoms, there is relatively little direct evidence for a theocratic interpretation of kingship, though Bede clearly thought in such terms.[73] Apart from that, the Prologue to his laws states that Ine claimed to rule by God's grace, and a few charters make the same affirmation on behalf of the kings who issued them.[74]

Of a more Roman nature is part of Bede's account of Edwin of Northumbria's reign in the same section of the *Ecclesiastical History* which contains the account of that king discussed at the beginning of this chapter. After describing the great peace wrought by the king, the passage goes on to describe how Edwin progressed around his kingdom behind a standard of a type which Bede says the Romans called a *tufa* (rendered in Old English as *thuuf*).[75] It has been suggested that Bede may have obtained the idea from Vegetius' *Epitoma rei militaris*, where it occurs in a list of different types of standard.[76] That standards of some kind were known to the Anglo-Saxons is clear from poetic references to such symbols, one of which, belonging to Emperor Constantine, was, significantly, described as *thuf* or *segn*,[77] and some such device – along with other Roman-influenced ceremonial equipment – was found in Sutton Hoo Mound One.[78] The origins of the use of standards in an Anglo-Saxon context are not clear, but Bede's description evokes something of the flavour of a late-Roman *aduentus*,[79] and could have implicatons similar to those of Einhard's description of the last of the Merovingians traversing his kingdom in an ox-cart in a way reminiscent of the progresses of late Roman provincial governors.[80]

The idea of a Northumbrian *aduentus* can be taken a stage further, since, after making a ceremonial arrival in his capital, a late Roman emperor might hold games and participate in other public ceremonies[81] of a kind for which the wedge-shaped amphitheatre at Yeavering could have been built.[82] Although the Yeavering building is unique in having been constructed after the Roman period, it is clear that other theatres and similar structures remained standing long after the Romans had left, notably at Canterbury, and could have been used for similar ceremonial purposes.[83] There are also parallels between Yeavering, at which there was also a temple, and St Albans where, in the Roman period, the temple and theatre were placed in close proximity, as was common in Roman Gaul: there, the theatres were used for public gatherings (particularly at religious festivals) at least as much as for simple entertainment.[84] That the Yeavering building was indeed modelled upon some Roman structure may recently have become more likely with the apparent discovery of an amphitheatre at Catterick, which was also a significant (probably royal) centre, and the scene of a mass baptism of the Deirans.[85]

147

The use of amphitheatres and of Roman-type ceremonial in seventh-century England would not be surprising. It was seen in Chapter 11 that Lombard rulers adopted such customs, and that the young Adaloald was elevated to a share in the kingdom at the circus of Milan (in 604).[86] Furthermore, the Yeavering 'amphitheatre' was constructed only a generation after the Frankish king, Chilperic I, had built amphitheatres at his capitals of Soissons and Paris.[87] Chilperic's actions would almost certainly have been known to Edwin, whose wife, Æthelburga, was the daughter of Æthelberht of Kent and the Merovingian Bertha. It is less certain that the kind of ceremonial involved would have been adopted anywhere in England before the arrival of the Augustinian mission, as its associations may have been as much Christian as Roman, but the possibility of earlier adaptations of some Roman practices cannot be entirely dismissed.

A further similarity between Northumbria – or, more specifically, Bernicia – and the continental kingdoms concerns the 'capital' of the kingdom. When King Ecgfrith was defeated at Nechtansmere, Cuthbert advised queen Iurminburg, who was with him at Carlisle, to flee to the *ciuitas regia* – that is, Bamburgh.[88] This could suggest that Bamburgh was the main fortress of the kingdom, and the place at which any attack on the queen could best be warded off; but it may also be that it was precisely at Bamburgh that such an attack was expected, and that it was vital for any pretender to the Bernician throne to gain possession of the place in the same way as it was important for Lombard pretenders to control Pavia: in other words, Bamburgh may have been the capital of Bernicia.[89]

The fact that Bamburgh – not a town, and not a Roman site – may have had a significance similar to that of such a Roman and urban centre as Pavia highlights one of the most significant contrasts between England and much of the remainder of the former western Empire in the early middle ages – the marked differences in urbanisation. Kings are most often seen at non-urban centres, such as the *uillae regiae* or *vici regii*[90] at *Ad Murum*,[91] *Campodunum*,[92] Millfield,[93] and Yeavering[94] in the Northumbrian kingdom, and Rendlesham[95] in the East Anglian. Bamburgh is not alone in being described in urban terms (as *urbs* or *ciuitas*) even though it was clearly not a town such as we might recognise, since Stephen described Dunbar as 'urbs'.[96]

Roman towns did, however, continue to have some secular administrative significance. The clearest case is that of York, where Edwin had a palace,[97] but at least some other Roman centres were the seats of royal officials, such as the *praepositus*, Waga, at Carlisle,[98] the *praefectus*, Blæcca, at Lincoln,[99] and the *wicgerefa* of London recorded in the laws of Hlothhere and Eadric.[100] Similar officials may have existed at other towns, but the coverage of the sources is so patchy as to make certainty impossible. Archaeological evidence can be interpreted to suggest that at least some such centres may have continued to fulfil some kind of administrative function (though not a properly urban one) for at least part of the sub-Roman and early Anglo-Saxon period, and it is possible that there may be less of a contrast with some aspects of the administrative geography on the continent than has been thought.

In three Roman towns – Wroxeter, Leicester and Lincoln, small parts of the forum or *basilica* complexes still survive, in the form of the Old Work, the Jewry Wall and the Mint Wall, respectively. The fact of survival suggests either that the administrative centres themselves continued in use or that later buildings on the same site made use of sections of their fabric. It is clear that some kind of occupation continued at Wroxeter into the sixth century,[101] though its nature is not known: P.A. Barker suggests that it became a complex of 'religious or public buildings, or, more probably, the private demesne of a great man'.[102] There is no direct evidence for the religious option, and it might be difficult to distinguish between 'public buildings' (which could include the residence of some kind of governor) and those associated with a 'great man'. Although Wroxeter seems finally to have been abandoned in the late fifth century, the model of continued use of Roman sites may be applicable elsewhere.[103]

At Leicester, Kathleen Kenyon suggested that the Jewry Wall was incorporated into a post-Roman structure which could have been an early predecessor of the church of St Nicholas which lies only a few feet to its east.[104] There was a bishop at Leicester from 675, but it is possible that the church was built next to (rather than attached to) an early administrative building which incorporated the Wall: the fact that there are no signs of sub-Roman occupation in the vicinity[105] is not conclusive evidence against this hypothesis, since the excavation techniques of the 1940s would not have recovered settlement of the kind found at Wroxeter.

The fact that the conversion of the kingdom of Lindsey took place at Lincoln indicates that the town was of some significance, and it has been suggested that it fulfilled a role similar to that of York in Deira. It has also been thought that the seventh-century church of St Paul-in-the-Bail, which lies within the former Roman forum (of which the extant Mint Wall formed a part) was a palace church.[106] The combination of these circumstances suggests that, even if true urban occupation did not continue into or through the fifth century, the administrative centre of Lincoln retained significance well into the Anglo-Saxon period.[107]

Similar survival of at least some Roman administrative buildings into the post-Roman period can be suggested for a number of other towns in which the Roman fabric no longer survives. One general indicator of the continued existence and, perhaps, significance, of earlier structures may be the number of churches which were built on former forum sites.[108] Given that the churches were not built until the seventh century or later, some other agency may have been responsible for the survival of Roman sites, and it may be that at least some such sites continued to have administrative functions for a time – perhaps until the arrival of the Church with its 'Roman' and urban connotations.[109] The association of the forum and minster at Winchester, for example, is well-documented,[110] and it may be significant that the first bishop of Dorchester, Birinus, was buried at Winchester rather than his episcopal centre,[111] for this could suggest that Winchester, rather than Dorchester, was at that date the main West Saxon royal centre.[112] More tentative is the case of Exeter, where the *basilica* and forum were demolished and the area given over to burials, which respect the alignment of the old curia, in the fifth century. By *c.* 680, there was a monastery near by which used the old administrative site as its burial ground. This has given rise to speculation that the earlier burials were bounded by surviving Roman buildings which could have been adapted for use as a church or shrine:[113] it may, however, be equally possible that such buildings (perhaps still associated with a religious site) formed part of a post-Roman administrative centre which only later gave way to the monastic cemetery. A similar kind of development could even be envisaged for London, where St Peter's-upon-Cornhill stands within the site of the Roman *basilica*[114] – though there is no positive evidence for early Anglo-Saxon activity on the site.[115] Elsewhere, it has been suggested, in differing contexts, that there may have been some continuity, at least into the sub-Roman period (and sometimes beyond), in towns such as Bath, Cirencester, Gloucester, Kentchester, Silchester, and Worcester.[116]

Although the evidence is tentative and circumstantial, it may be possible to suggest that some Roman towns retained a position in the administrative and, perhaps, ceremonial geography of England.[117] There are parallels for the adaptation of Roman governmental buildings in many other 'barbarian' kingdoms – notably at Geneva in fifth- and sixth-century Burgundy, at Carthage in the Vandal kingdom, and in both Ostrogothic and Lombard Italy.[118] The difference in England was that no Roman town retained fully urban functions – particularly social and economic ones. The shift away from towns was not, however, a specifically post-Roman feature, since it had already begun in the last third of the fourth century;[119] nor was the move unique to Britain: there are similar instances in at least some parts of Gaul.[120] In fact, there are other similarities with the Frankish world since, although the main centre of each Merovingian kingdom was a Roman town, the kings – both in the sixth century and later – are most frequently seen on rural estates (see Chapter 2).[121] As in other aspects of kingship, there may, therefore, be greater likenesses between the Anglo-Saxons and their continental contemporaries than has often been assumed.

Queens

As kings travelled around their territories, they were often accompanied by their wives – Stephen, for example, depicts Ecgfrith and Iurminburg jointly making their way around Northumbria with worldly pomp and ceremonial.[122] As in the other kingdoms discussed in this book, the choice of queen was often (perhaps usually) made for political purposes (see Table IV on p. 186). This is clear in the case of the wife of Edwin of Northumbria, Æthelburh, who was the daughter of Æthelberht of Kent, and was sent to Northumbria in order to cement an alliance between the two rulers.[123] An agreement between the Mercian and Northumbrian leaders was similarly sealed by the marriage of Oswald's niece, Osthryth, to Æthelred of the Mercians;[124] while the marriage of Oswiu to his cousin, Edwin's daughter, Eanflæd, must be seen in the context of an attempt to stabilise the Northumbrian dynasty and, possibly, of an establishment of good relations with Eorconberht of Kent, who was also a cousin of Eanflæd.[125] Although less explicit, it is probable that the marriages of Æthelthryth, daughter of Anna of the East Angles, should be seen in the same light: her first husband was Tondberht, *princeps* of the south Gyrwe, over whom Anna may have been extending his authority; after Tondberht's death, Æthelthryth became queen of the Northumbrians as the first wife of Ecgfrith.[126]

Æthelthryth's later career is also of significance, since, after some years, she abandoned Ecgfrith in order to become a nun at Coldingham. The motivation for this is obscure, as is the source of the initiative: Bede characteristically presents an interpretation in terms of the queen's sanctity, recording that Æthelthryth had remained a virgin throughout her two marriages. It is, however, at least as likely that Ecgfrith was the prime mover, whether from political or personal reasons (that the latter is possible may be demonstrated by the careers of some members of the Merovingian dynasty, such as Dagobert I[127]). However that may be, the selection of Coldingham as a place of retreat was clearly dictated by the fact that the abbess was Æbbe, Ecgfrith's aunt – a person who could be expected to prevent Æthelthryth from engaging in 'inappropriate' activities. That Æthelthryth did not lose all her political power is, nevertheless, suggested by the fact that she later became abbess of Ely – that is, in the territory associated with her first husband and, therefore, with her father. The importance of Ely to the East Anglian royal house is further demonstrated by Æthelthryth's succession there by her sister, Sæxburh, who also returned thence after being married to a king – in her case, Eorconberht of Kent.[128]

Many other royal women entered nunneries at various times during their lives. Eorcongota, daughter of Eorconberht of Kent, became a nun at Brie in Gaul, as did a third daughter of Anna of the East Angles, Æthelburh, and the same king's step-daughter, Sæthryth.[129] Ecgburh, daughter of another East Anglian king, Aldwulf, was an abbess,[130] as was Ælfflæd, sister of Ecgfrith of the Northumbrians;[131] the same ruler's second wife, Iurminburg, entered her sister's nunnery at Carlisle after Ecgfrith's death at the Battle of Nechtansmere.[132] Part of the reason that there is such a large body of evidence concerning the association of royal women with religious institutions is that it was a topic of concern to the authors of saints' lives and, especially, to Bede. There is, however, no reason to doubt the fact of the associations, since they prevented the women concerned from transmitting claims to the throne to husbands or children: this applies as much to princesses as to royal widows. Further, there are clear parallels with the English situation in the Frankish world, where, for example, Clovis II's queen, Balthild, entered the nunnery of Chelles when her son, Chlothar III, became king in his own right,[133] while Basina (daughter of Chilperic I), and her cousin, Chlotild (daughter of Charibert), were sent to Holy Cross at Poitiers.[134]

The delicate position of widowed queens is highlighted by the fate of Æthelburh, wife of Edwin of the Northumbrians, and daughter of Æthelberht and Bertha of Kent. After the death of her husband at Hatfield, Æthelburh fled to her home – Kent – accompanied both by her own children and by Yffi, a grandson of Edwin by his former marriage to Cwenburh. The reason for flight was that the children (and Æthelburh herself) were potential rivals to the new king, their cousin, Oswald. However, Æthelburh's problems were not at an end once she reached Kent, since her own children could have represented a threat to her brother, Eadbald, who was by then king there, or to his children. In order to secure the future of the children, Æthelburh therefore had to send them still further afield, to the court of Dagobert I, to whom she was related through her mother, Bertha.[135] That the dangers were not imaginary may be illustrated by the fate of Osthryth, a member of the Northumbrian royal house who married Æthelred of the Mercians: even before her husband's death, she was murdered by the leading Mercians.[136]

The role of queens in early Anglo-Saxon politics was not only passive: the wives of kings could be highly influential, if only because they were often close to the person of the king. It was, for example, allegedly Iurminburg who turned King Ecgfrith against Bishop Wilfrid and had him deprived of his see,[137] and Redwald's queen is credited with having dissuaded her husband from murdering the exiled Edwin.[138] Even if the details of those precise incidents are incorrect, such activity was clearly expected and well understood by contemporary authors. Similarly, it is significant that Popes Gregory I and Boniface V tried to use Queens Bertha and Æthelburh to assist in the conversion of their husbands[139] – attempts with direct parallels in the Lombard kingdom (see Chapter 11).

Another aspect of queenly power is illustrated by the early career of Wilfrid who, having decided that he wished to live a religious life, sought assistance, advice and patronage not from King Oswiu, but from his wife, Eanflæd. Not only did the Queen provide advice – that Wilfrid should go to Lindisfarne – but she was also able to nominate someone to take care of him. Later, when Wilfrid resolved to go on pilgrimage to Rome, he again appealed to Eanflæd, who sent him to her cousin, King Eorconberht of Kent, with a request to find him a suitable guide.[140] Later still, another queen, Æthelthryth, donated the land at Hexham upon which Wilfrid built his church.[141]

The importance of queens – and not solely in relation to patronage – is also demonstrated by the charters. Three queens – Æthilberga[142] and Kynigitha[143] (wives of Wihtræd of Kent), and an Æthelthryth[144] – feature as witnesses in such documents. In two instances, the queen was not only a signatory, but also consented to the donation which was being made,[145] while on another occasion, Æthilberga is described as one of the donors.[146] That the co-operation of royal women was of importance in at least some cases is suggested by a grant of King Nunna of the South Saxons to the abbot of Selsey, which is signed by an otherwise unknown King Æthelstan and Queen Æthelthryth.[147] Presumably Æthelthryth was Æthelstan's wife rather than Nunna's, as Nunna himself did not sign the charter: in that case, Nunna appears to have sought the consent not only of a co-ruler, overlord or friend in another kingdom, but also of the latter's wife.

Although, as noted earlier, the king and queen often travelled round the kingdom together, this was not always the case, particularly when the king was away at war. Hence, for example, Iurminburg stayed at Carlisle while her husband, Ecgfrith, went to fight the Picts in the campaign in which he lost his life.[148] Similarly, when Edwin died, Æthelburh was not with him and was already in charge of the children, for whose upbringing she was presumably (like her Frankish counterparts) responsible.[149] Such a role may also be indicated by the fact that when Oswiu's son, Ecgfrith, was a hostage in Mercia, he was in the care of the queen, Cynuise, rather than of her husband.[150]

In order to be effective as consorts, and to live independently on occasion, queens required some kind of staff or household and, although this is not well documented, there are hints of the existence of such an organisation. For example, when Æthelburh was sent from Kent to marry Edwin of the Northumbrians, it was envisaged that she would take a retinue of men, women, priests and retainers – an incident which conjures up a scene reminiscent of that surrounding the Merovingian princess Rigunth when she was on her way to Spain to marry the Visigothic prince, Reccared.[151] Similarly, when Queen Æthelthryth went to the Mercian kingdom from that of the East Angles, she took with her Owine, 'primus ministrorum et princeps domus eius';[152] while it is on another occasion recorded that she had a *minister*, Imma.[153] Discussion of the structure of the court – both of the queen and of the king – and the significance of the titles of its officials, however, forms the subject of the next chapter.

Courtiers and Noblemen

It is often assumed that the highest-ranking officials in an early Anglo-Saxon kingdom were the *principes*. Hence, for example, J. Campbell, while acknowledging that the term was 'not easy to define', thought that it could be used of kings as well as of some of their subordinates – perhaps those who retained a degree of independence.[1] Others have attempted slightly greater precision, suggesting that, at least in a Mercian context, most *principes* were *subreguli*, and that they were usually of royal birth.[2] In one instance – that of Peada, son of Penda – *princeps* probably means 'prince',[3] but it is less possible to be certain of the royal credentials of some of the other men who are described in this way.

Despite the quest to define a specific office which is designated by the term *princeps*, there are many instances in which it is clear from the context that something more vague is meant. For example, in Stephen's account of Wilfrid's return to Northumbria with a papal judgement that he should be reinstated to the bishopric at York, it is recorded that the bishop presented his documents to a synod constituted of 'serui Dei' and all the 'principes';[4] later, in 706, *principes* were involved in a further synod concerning Wilfrid's future.[5] All that is implied here is that the 'principes' were the leading men of the kingdom. A similar interpretation is possible for the *principes* whom Bede records as having been established in Mercia by Oswiu, and whom three Mercian *duces* drove out when Wulfhere was established as king.[6] It is possible that Oswiu divided Mercia into three territorial units, each with a *princeps* or sub-king at its head, but it may be at least as likely that Bede, who was not primarily concerned with the details of secular administration, was simply recording the establishment of three local leaders, without giving them a precise title. This kind of interpretation can be extended to the diplomatic material, in which it is sometimes recorded that the donations which the charters record were made with the consent of all the *principes*,[7] or 'cum omnibus prouincialibus principibus':[8] even the latter need indicate no more than that the senior courtiers or officials were involved – the reference to the 'provinces' may refer to leading men who were not members of the royal household, or may do no more than designate the kingdom (a usage not uncommon on the continent).

Such leading men clearly stood at the apex of the social system, since one of their number, Tondberht, *princeps* of the South Gyrwe, married Æthelthryth, daughter of King Anna of the East Angles.[9] Even here, though, it is not possible to demonstrate conclusively that Tondberht was *the* leader of the South Gyrwe, rather than that he was one of a (small) number of that people's leading men: even if the former is the case, it is still not necessary to see the term as referring to a specific 'office'. More complex is the case of Berhtfred, who, according to Stephen, was among the *principes* at the 706 synod convened to decide Wilfrid's fate; later in the same passage Berhtfred is referred to as 'secundus a rege princeps'.[10] Even here, though, it is not clear that *princeps* refers to a specific office: all that the context demands is that he was the most powerful man in the kingdom after the king – a fair description for a man who was regent for the young Osred. This suggestion may derive added strength from the fact that Bede, referring to the 711 campaign against the Picts, called Berhtfred a *praefectus*[11] – a title which, as will be seen below, almost certainly denoted his specific function within the administration.

The evidence of the law codes poses different problems, largely because they were written in Old English, rather than Latin. The term which most nearly matches *princeps* is *ealdorman*,[12] the commonest translation employed by the author of the ninth-century *Old English Bede*[13] – though he also used *ealdorman* for a large number of other Latin titles,[14] indicating that it may have designated a general status rather than a specific office. In the Prologue to Ine's laws, it is recorded that *ealdormen* were present at the code's promulgation,[15] and the term should probably be interpreted (before the mid-eighth century[16]) in the same way as was *princeps* in the case of the synods and charters. The high standing of *ealdormen* is confirmed by the fact that they received greater compensation for forced entry to their property than ordinary courtiers (*gesithas* – see below),[17] and were empowered to hear legal cases concerning the households of the latter.[18]

The only other significant evidence concerning *ealdormen* in the early period again comes from Ine's laws, in a clause concerning those who concealed thefts or let captured thieves escape: in general, men guilty of these offences were to pay compensation equal to their wergild, but *ealdormen* were to forfeit their *scir*.[19] This does not mean that *ealdormen* were necessarily in charge of a territorial unit known as a *scir*[20] – although that was the case from the late eighth century – since *scir* can have a more general meaning, referring to any administrative 'office'.[21] The distinction Ine may have been drawing was one between men in general and high-ranking men or office-holders – particularly as it would be strange for only one kind of official to have been singled out for an especially harsh penalty. Even here, therefore, *ealdorman* may have a very general meaning: there may be some similarities between this and some of the usages found in the Visigothic laws (see Chapter 8).

A term more rarely found in the early sources than *princeps/ealdorman* is *patricius*. In the *Ecclesiastical History*, Bede only uses the term in relation to Romans (such as Aetius[22]) and Franks (such as Erchinoald[23]). A charter of 688x690, however, records that Ine made a grant of land to Hean, *patricius*, and to Ceolswyth, in order that they might found a monastery;[24] at a similar date, Aldhelm tried to recover land bought from the monastery at Malmesbury by the *patricius*, Baldred.[25] Finally, a charter of Eadric states that a grant to St Peter's, Canterbury, was made 'with the consent of my *patricii*'.[26] These references do not denote a specific administrative position, any more than do those to *principes*: either *patricius* is another general term for men of high rank, as the last example suggests, or, when applied to individuals, it may, have been an honorary title – though even then there is no firm evidence that its usage was as formal as that in the Frankish kingdom (see Chapter 4).

Words other than *patricius* and *princeps*[27] are used in the charters for the men who were consulted by kings in making land grants, and have similarly general significance. Two charters record the consent of the king's 'primi';[28] another that of his 'sapientes'.[29] According to Bede, when Edwin was considering becoming a Christian, he consulted with those of his 'primates' whom he considered to be 'more wise', and later asked the opinion of each of his 'amici principes' and 'consiliarii' ('main friends' and 'advisers') – who are later collectively referred to as 'maiores natu ac consiliarii',[30] one of whom is described individually as 'optimas regis'.[31] Similarly, Kings Aldfrith and Oswiu consulted the 'wise men' of their people about who should be bishop after the departure of Colmán following the Synod of Whitby.[32] There is nothing formal about any of these 'titles' – any more than there is about Adomnán's rhetorical reference to the royal tribunal[33] as 'senatus':[34] the only significance of any of them is that of 'leading men'.

Duces

A further term which has sometimes been thought to have a similarly general significance is *dux*.[35] The high standing of men of this description is attested by the fact that when King Æthelwalh of the South Saxons was baptised, he was in the company of his *duces* and *milites*,[36] while Oswald interpreted Aidan's preaching to his *duces* and *ministri*[37] and Edwin is on one occasion depicted as feasting in the company of his *duces*.[38] On all these occasions, a general interpretation of the term is reasonable, as it may also be in a passage in Bede's *Chronica maiora*, which contrasts *duces* with 'priuati'.[39] The evidence of the charters is, however, less clear cut, since it is possible that named men who are described as *duces* held some specific kind of office, of which *dux* was the title. This could apply, for example, to Wilfrid and Æthelward, *duces*, who signed a charter of King Æthelbald of the Mercians,[40] and to Bruny, *dux* in the land of the South Saxons, who granted land to a monastery.[41]

On almost all occasions on which *duces* are seen in action, they feature as war leaders. The South Saxon *duces regis*, Bercthuno and Andhuno, for example, repelled the invasion of the West Saxon king, Cædwalla, even after their own, king, Æthelwalh, had been killed;[42] *duces* of Penda were involved in the Battle of Winwæd, where thirty of them lost their lives;[43] Berht, a *dux* of Ecgfrith of the Northumbrians, invaded 'Hibernia' in 684;[44] fourteen years later, Berctfred, *dux* (possibly the same as Berht), was killed by the Picts.[45] It is likely that the three Mercian *duces*, Immin, Eafa and Eadberht, who rebelled against Oswiu's rule in Mercia and established Wulfhere as their own king,[46] were also involved in war leadership. Outside the strictly military sphere, *duces* were responsible for taking Wilfrid to his imprisonment at *Broninis*[47] – though it is not difficult to see why high-ranking soldiers might be used for such a mission.

In all the incidents referred to in the last paragraph, *dux* could have a general sense, being used to designate high-ranking men – perhaps those who would elsewhere be described as *principes* – when they were involved in military leadership. Possible – though very tentative – evidence against such an interpretation is that such men are specifically referred to as *duces regis*, which could imply that they held a specific position in the military hierarchy of their kingdoms, as elsewhere in the early medieval west. The fact that *duces* do not appear to have been specifically associated with subdivisions of the kingdoms, as some of their continental counterparts were, is not of significance partly because there were similarly non-territorial *duces* in both Frankia and Spain, and partly because the small size of the Anglo-Saxon kingdoms may have meant that military administration could be more centralised. There is, however, not enough evidence to determine the exact significance of the term *dux* in the early Anglo-Saxon period: all that may be said with any degree of certainty is that on at least some occasions it appears to have a general meaning; but that does not necessarily preclude a more formal significance in other contexts.

Praefecti

One of the titles which appears most frequently in the Latin sources is one rarely found on the continent – that of prefect. Men described in this way were not only associated with the king, but could also, like a certain Hocca, belong to the entourages of other great men, such as Wilfrid.[48] The reference to Hocca is only made in passing, and does little to elucidate his function. The same is true of some of the evidence concerning royal prefects: in the anonymous *Life of St Cuthbert*, for example, it is recorded that Cuthbert saw the soul of a deceased prefect being carried up to the sky;[49] on another occasion, the same saint is reported (in Bede's *Life*) to have cured the wife of Hildimir, 'prefect of King Ecgfrith';[50] while, in his

Ecclesiastical History, Bede recounted that Oswine and one of his *milites* were assassinated by Æthelwine, a prefect of Oswiu.[51]

Other passages are of slightly greater assistance, and make it clear not only that royal prefects were men of consequence,[52] but also that they could be used to perform a variety of administrative and governmental tasks. Hence, for example, when King Ecgfrith released Wilfrid from prison, the Bishop was assisted by the prefect Berhtwald, nephew of King Æthelred of the Mercians.[53] On another occasion, Egbert of Kent sent his prefect, Rædfrith, to greet Archbishop Theodore in Gaul;[54] while another prefect, the Northumbrian, Berhtfred (the same man as was on one occasion described as 'secundus a rege princeps'[55]), was involved in a campaign against the Picts.[56] Much of this material relates to exceptional events – the release of Wilfrid, and the delegation to Theodore – and does little more than indicate, in the most general terms, that prefects were royal agents who could be entrusted with delicate and important missions: there is little hint in this material of their precise, or routine, position in royal administration.

Other evidence, however, shows that at least some prefects did hold a more specific office, associated with centres of royal power. Only one such man is explicitly mentioned in Bede's *Ecclesiastical History* – Blæcca, at Lincoln – but merely in relation to the conversion of the kingdom in which he was based, and not in such a way as to elucidate his function.[57] Other prefects of this kind are found in Stephen's *Life of Wilfrid*: the prefect at Dunbar, Tydlin, was commanded to look after Wilfrid while he was a prisoner in that place,[58] as Osfrith, the prefect who governed *Broninis* had earlier been when the bishop was held at his seat of power.[59] The wife of the same Osfrith was later the subject of a cure performed through Wilfrid: on that occasion, Osfrith is described as 'praefectus urbis';[60] he also features as 'comes autem … regis'.[61]

The last point may be of more than passing significance, since a prefect based at a specific place who was also a *comes* might not be very different from a Frankish or Visigothic *comes ciuitatis*. There is nothing in the kinds of activity associated with *praefecti urbium* to invalidate such an equation. While there was a lesser degree of strictly urban continuity in England than in the continental kingdoms, it was seen in Chapter 16 that at least some Roman towns retained administrative and ceremonial functions and that other non-Roman centres (such as Bamburgh) seem to have fulfilled a similar role, and have been given a specifically 'urban' designation (though *urbs*, rather than *ciuitas*):[62] the prefects could, therefore, have been the king's main provincial agents. If this is correct, it may be that all prefects were based in such centres, 'prefect' being a specific title for *comes ciuitatis*, in much the same way as 'gastald' may have come to be in the Lombard kingdom (see Chapter 12): the evidence is not, however, such as to permit of certainty, and it remains possible that some prefects formed a more permanent part of the royal court.[63] What seems more clear, though, is that prefects – at least when described as such – were usually engaged in civil administration, rather than military leadership.[64]

One other title is specifically associated with a *civitas* in the Latin sources – though only on one occasion, when the author of the anonymous *Uita Cuthberti* describes Waga as 'praepositus ciuitatis' at Carlisle.[65] This man would almost certainly have fulfilled the same functions as a prefect, and it is possible that the two titles are synonymous, particularly since Bede and Stephen only use 'prefect' in relation to men based in *ciuitates* or *urbes*, while the anonymous author only used 'praepositus' in that context.

The suggestion that there was a relationship between at least some prefects and *comites ciuitatum* is further strengthened by the fact that there are eighth-century Frankish documents (written in Germany by Anglo-Saxons) in which *graphio* is translated into Latin as *praefectus*, rather than as the more normal *comes*.[66] This is also significant because in the Old English of the law codes, the term *gerefa* (which may possibly be related to *graphio*[67]) features; while in later vernacular documents this is the translation for both *praefectus*[68] and *praepositus*.[69] Furthermore, in one instance, the Laws of Hlothhere and Eadric make mention of a 'cyninges wicgerefa', based in London,[70] indicating that some reeves could, like prefects, be associated with towns.

The range of activities performed by *gerefan*, as recorded by the small body of legal material, is quite wide. Wihtræd's laws reveal that *gerefan* were responsible for dealing with accusations that servants of the king or bishop had been unjust,[71] while Ine stipulated that those who captured thieves and them let them escape again had to make their peace with the king or with his *gerefa*.[72] The *gerefa* of London was to supervise commercial activities in the town on the king's behalf. These references strengthen the impression that prefects/*gerefan* were the main provincial agents of the king, and that their position was broadly similar to that of *comites ciuitatum*.

Comites

Other *comites* are often mentioned in the early sources, though without an indication as to whether they held any specific office. Many of the references are as unhelpful in terms of elucidating their position as some of those to prefects, as such laymen are frequently only mentioned in relation to the virtuous deeds of holy men. That *comites* were of considerable status is revealed by two such accounts: in one, the wife of the *comes* Puch was healed by Bishop John of York at her husband's *uilla*,[73] while in another, Cuthbert healed the servant of Sibba, *comes*, at the latter's *uicus*.[74] Other references of this kind confirm than *comites* held land[75] and employed various kinds of servant,[76] while the two *comites* who murdered King Sigeberht of the East Saxons were apparently the king's brothers.[77] Even on occasions on which *comites* are depicted in a king's presence, however, very little is forthcoming concerning their actual functions: *comites* of Æthelberht of Kent listened to Augustine's preaching with the King;[78] *comites* of Peada were baptised with their ruler at *Ad Murum*;[79] Cuthbert, *comes* of King Oshere of the Hwicce, signed a charter recording a donation by the king to Abbess Cutsuitha;[80] *comites* could fight on behalf of their kings.[81]

The vernacular equivalent for *comes* is *gesith* (related to the Lombard *gasindius*) – a word meaning, like its Latin equivalent, 'companion'.[82] This term does not, of itself, appear in the early laws, but only the compound *gesithcund* man. Men of this kind were clearly of high status: they could own or administer land;[83] they could have servants, including *gerefan*, smiths and nurses for their children;[84] and infringements of marital law by them, as well as forced entry by others to their property, attracted relatively high compensation.[85] It is not, however, clear that such men were necessarily courtiers, and the implication of *gesithcund* may be that they were members of the nobility from which royal officials, or courtiers, were drawn.[86]

However that may be, there is little to suggest that *comites* were anything other than the 'companions' or courtiers of the king:[87] the term denoted a condition or status, rather than a specific office.[88] It is perhaps a consequence of this – combined with the lack of procedural material in the early laws – that *gesithas* (as such) do not appear in the law codes: like the Lombard *gasindii*, they were normally resident with the king, rarely operating independently outside the court; they were probably subsumed within the terms *eorl*[89] or *ealdorman*, unless they held specific office as prefects/*gerefan*.

Ministri

Alongside *principes* and *comites* are men described in the Latin sources as *ministri*: they were clearly part of the court,[90] and could sign royal charters as witnesses.[91] However, they were not the same as the *comites* and *duces*, since they are sometimes mentioned alongside the latter in a way suggesting that they were differentiated from them.[92] The distinction is probably to be elucidated by Bede's *Uita Ceolfrithi*, for it recounts that Eosertwine, acting Abbot of Wearmouth, had formerly been a 'minister regis';[93] elsewhere in the same work, Benedict Biscop is stated to have been a *minister* before entering the Church: when about twenty-five years of age, he was given land suitable to his rank ('gradus suus').[94] These references imply that the men concerned were relatively young when they were at court, which, in turn, suggests that they were junior members of the king's entourage, perhaps such as might later in life have become *comites*.[95] If this is correct, it is possible to see them as broadly the equivalent of the Visigothic *gardingi* or Frankish *domestici*: it is perhaps significant that the only occasion on which Bede uses the term *domesticus* is in a description of King Oswine warming himself in his hall surrounded by *ministri*[96] – a passage in which *domesticus* may have been used to avoid repetition of *minister*. The suggested equation is strengthened by the fact that the East Anglian princess, Æthelthryth, had an official, Owine, described as 'primus ministrorum et princeps domus eius'[97] – a phrase which suggests he occupied a position similar to that of the Frankish *maior domus*, who was in charge of *domestici* (see Chapter 3).

If this is correct, *minister*, like *comes*, denotes a status, rather than a specific office, and it is possible that men described in this way could hold more definite positions in royal administration, though there is no positive evidence for this. One possibility is that some *ministri* were bodyguards, for one of their number, Lilla, is described simultaneously as *minister* and as *miles*.[98] However, it is at least as likely that *miles* simply denotes a retainer,[99] and may have been largely synonymous with *minister*.[100]

The vernacular equivalent of *minister (regis)* is *(cyninges) thegn*. The word *thegn* is often considered to be directly related to the concept of service, meaning a servant, or a member of a retinue;[101] but it has also been suggested that such a meaning is only derived, the root of the word being connected to the Gothic *theihan*, meaning 'to thrive' (modern German 'gedeihen'), and hence conveying the idea of a young man occupying a humble position.[102] As members of the court, *thegnas* only rarely feature in the law codes, but such non-philological evidence as exists has occasioned as much debate as the etymology of the term, largely owing to a provision in Ine's law code.

According to Ine's laws, the penalty for breaking into the *burh* of an *ealdorman* was 80 shillings, while infringement of the rights of a *cyninges thegn* led to the forfeiture of 60 shillings, and that of a *gesithcund* man of 35.[103] This has been understood to set the *thegn* above the *gesith*, and led H.M. Chadwick to suggest that, while *thegn* was the equivalent of *minister* in the Northumbrian kingdom, it denoted a higher rank in the south of England.[104] H.R. Loyn, on the other hand, thought that the reason for Ine's apparently preferential treatment of the *thegn* was that the term was used only of men – including *gesithcund* men – who were absent from home on the king's business.[105]

It is possible, however, that there is another way of viewing Ine's provision, particularly if, as suggested earlier, there is a distinction between the *comes/gesith* and the *gesithcund* man. If the former were subsumed in 'ealdorman', it could be that the law does not relate solely to courtiers: 'ealdorman' might here include *gesithas* as the senior members of the court. 'Thegn' would then represent the younger members of the king's entourage,[106] and 'gesithcund' man other members of the nobility, who would be accorded a lower level of protection because they did not stand in such a direct relationship to the king.

The division of the court into two broad classes with *principes, ealdor-*

men and *duces* on the one hand, and *ministri* or *thegnas* on the other,[107] is far from being a uniquely English phenomenon, but is paralleled in the Frankish kingdom and, more particularly, in Visigothic Spain, where a different, but similarly varied, range of terminology is used to distinguish between the categories (see Chapter 8). That few titles can be related to specific offices with discrete spheres of jurisdiction is not necessarily an indication that 'the Latin terms for the various dignitaries of the English state were not yet definitely fixed' in Bede's day.[108] It will be suggested in the next chapter that there are other possible interpretations of the situation, which largely centre upon a deeper understanding of the impact of the character of the sources for the period.

18

England and the Continent

In the preceding chapter it was argued that most of the titles by which secular officials are designated are general – even in some instances, non-technical – ones, indicating the rank of the men concerned. Almost the only title which appears to have designated a specific office is that of 'praefectus' denoting a position similar to that of the continental *comes ciuitatis*. This cannot, however, be taken to imply that the Anglo-Saxon royal administration was less well organised (or, to use the terminology of a previous generation, 'advanced') than its continental counterparts, for much early English practice can be paralleled on the continent. Further, it was seen in Chapter 16 that the evidence concerning the kings and queens who stood at the apex of the governmental system stands comparison with that for their contemporaries on the continent in both general and specific terms, and in relation to the rulers' actions as well as to the imagery of power.

None of this should occasion surprise, for despite the 'hiatus' of the sub-Roman period in the history of England, and the possibilities which that, combined with the proximity of the Celtic peoples, offered for a greater loss of 'Roman' practices, the Anglo-Saxons formed part of a continental world: contacts with the Frankish territories, in particular, were legion.[1] So great, indeed, are the similarities between some aspects of Kentish material culture and those of their Frankish neighbours that it has even been suggested that the 'Jutes' Bede records as having been responsible for settling Kent were in reality Franks, or that Kent was subject to a secondary settlement from Frankia.[2]

Even if that is not correct – and it is still debated – there is clear evidence of sustained political contact at more than one level, and spreading well beyond Kent. The best-known example is the marriage of Æthelberht of Kent to the Frankish princess, Bertha,[3] but there are other instances:[4] Sigeberht of the East Angles, for example, was an exile in Gaul during the reign of his step-father Redwald and, on his return, is reported as having sought to imitate many things which he saw as being well arranged in Gaul, including establishing a Frankish-type school in his kingdom.[5] Knowledge of the Frankish world – if not Frankish influence – reached Northumbria with the marriage of Æthelberht and Bertha's daughter, Æthelburh, to Edwin: that the Frankish association was kept alive may be confirmed by Æthelburh's sending of her children to Dagobert I's court for safety after Edwin's death (see Chapter 16). The Frankish connections of Kentish rulers were maintained by the marriage of Eadbald, Æthelberht's son, to Ymme, daughter of the Frankish *maior domus*, Erchinoald.[6] Other kinds of contact involving the royal houses of England are also attested, notably in relation to the number of royal women who entered Frankish religious houses,[7] and the presence of Frankish bishops in Anglo-Saxon kingdoms.[8]

Inter-marriage between the Anglo-Saxon and Frankish royal houses did not necessarily mean that the two sets of rulers saw themselves as equals. Bertha, for example, may have been a princess, but she was of only secondary importance, and her marriage to Æthelberht can be interpreted to imply that Kent was in some way subject to Frankish hegemony.[9] As I. Wood has demonstrated, there is other evidence which suggests the same thing – most notably letters written by Gregory the Great in relation to Augustine's mission;[10] and a similar case can be made in relation to the East Anglian kingdom.[11] That much of the evidence for this kind of relationship originated outside England is not surprising: Anglo-Saxon rulers would probably not have sought to emphasise any relationship in which they were subordinate, while Bede – the only author who might have hinted at it – would have been more concerned to stress the 'Roman' and Papal credentials of the ecclesiastical connections than the Frankish ones.

Even if it is not correct to see at least some of the early Anglo-Saxons as subject to the Franks, there were clearly political (and economic) links which spanned the Channel. Against this background it is impossible to conceive that the rulers of England were not informed concerning the institutions of monarchy on the continent – and not only in Frankia, for the Lombard Perctarit spent time in England as an exile,[12] and Cunincpert married an Anglo-Saxon, Hermelinda[13] (though it is not known if she was royal). In view of this range of contacts, and the many similarities between aspects of kings' and queens' power in England and on the continent (Chapter 16), the apparent lack of specific court offices seems to require further investigation.

It is difficult to see how royal government of the sophistication implied by the evidence for kings and queens themselves (including their foreign contacts) could have been conducted – even in the relatively small geographical areas presupposed by the multiplicity of kingdoms in England – without at least some officials whose functions were better defined than is usually considered to have been probable in England.[14] As was suggested in the last chapter, there are in fact hints that some members of the royal entourages did hold specific offices – there are the prefects of *ciuitates*, and there was a possible equivalent for the *maior domus*. At a much lower level, Æthelberht's laws refer to the existence of a royal smith and of the king's messenger – the latter being echoed in a provision of Ine's code which accords such a man enhanced protection.[15]

The charters of Æthelberht

There exists a further potential source of information concerning the constituent members of the royal court, at least in early seventh-century Kent – a series of charters which purport to record grants made by King Æthelberht to the religious institutions of Rochester and Canterbury.[16] Of the three documents relating to Canterbury all have a witness list derived from a common exemplar, which contains mention of a referendary and a *graphio*. Despite an attempt by Margaret Deanesly in the 1940s to argue that the documents are genuine – or, at worst, are based on genuine traditions[17] – they have been generally dismissed ever since, largely owing to a harsh polemical attack made on her arguments almost immediately by W. Levison who believed them to be the products of the twelfth-century forger, Guerno of Soissons.[18] There is little doubt that Deanesly did not present her case to best advantage, but, as one of the recently-published papers of the late J. Morris has demonstrated, there are also significant flaws in Levison's case, which is altogether too hasty and convoluted.[19]

The most important manuscript source for the Canterbury grants is provided by Thomas Elmham, who, in the fifteenth century, inserted two transcriptions of them into his *History of St Augustine's Abbey*, one made in as good an imitation of the original hand as he could manage, and the other in the script of his own day.[20] Despite Thomas' efforts, palaeographical arguments are likely to be weak, but both Levison and (ultimately) Deanesly thought that at least two of the documents Thomas was copying were probably written in an Anglo-Saxon hand of *c*. 800.[21]

One of the reasons for dismissing all the documents in the past has been that, until relatively recently, it was widely held that charters were unknown in England until the arrival of Theodore of Tarsus as archbishop of Canterbury in 669: part of the case rested on the fact that no surviving charters of unimpeachable authenticity could be demonstrated to have existed before then. In reality, the case is considerably more complex than that, and all that may be said with certainty is that the date at which charters began to be used in England is not known: there is a case for seeing their introduction as being related to the Augustinian mission, but the firm evidence is lacking.[22] Accordingly, while it cannot be demonstrated that Æthelberht or the churchmen to whom his grant was made could have had the donation recorded in writing, it is not impossible that such written instruments were known – Bertha, her Frankish bishop, Liudhard, and the Augustinian missionaries would all have been familiar with such documents.

There is, therefore, little by way of conclusive external criteria by which to judge the charters – even Bede's account that Æthelberht made a grant to St Augustine[23] cannot be taken to indicate their authenticity, since it could have provided the point from which a forger started. It is therefore necessary to turn to the contents of the documents and, in particular (for the present purpose), to the witness list, which exists in three versions. Deanesly believed that the longest of the lists, found in S 3,[24] was used as the exemplar for the abbreviated versions found in the other two, though it is, on its own terms, the most objectionable of the three: it refers to Æthelberht as 'rex Anglorum', rather than 'rex Canciae' or 'rex Cancuariorum' which would have been normal before 724;[25] each of the signatories signs with a different formula in a way unprecedented in the early period;[26] there is reference to an official named Graphio, who is styled 'comes' – yet *graphio* is not a proper name, but the Latinised version of the Frankish word for *comes*.[27] The second point is unique to S 3, but the first and third are shared by one of the other charters (S 4). None of these objections can, however, be raised to the remaining version of the list (S 2):

> Ego Æthilberhtus rex Canciae sana mente integroque
>   consilio donacionem meam signo sanctae crucis
>   propria manu roboraui confirmauique.
> Ego Ægustinus gratia Dei Archiepiscopus testis
>   consentiens libenter subscripsi.

Eadbald	Thangil
Hamigil	Pinca[28]
Angemund referendarius	Geddi
Hocca graphio	

Here, Æthelberht is 'rex Canciae'; the detailed formulae are absent; the only reference to *graphio* is as the title of one of the signatories, Hocca – there is no mention of a *comes*. According to Levison, the document to which this version of the list is sometimes attached (it is missing in some manuscripts) was probably compiled using a Kentish model of the mid-eighth century or later[29] – that is, approximately the date of the script in which it may have been written. Is it possible that, despite both Levison and Deanesly, the shorter list was the source for the longer, and represents an elaboration of the earlier list, made when royal styles and witness formulae had assumed their later form?[30] If that were the case, the list might begin to look less suspicious.

The provision of a tentative eighth-century context for the document does not, of itself, however, provide a solution to the question of the origins of the list, for it still contains two features – the titles of referendary and *graphio*, which are not positively attested in England before the twelfth century.[31] The solution to this could be that the eighth-century forgery did not have a witness list until the twelfth century, or that it had by then lost its original list: while that is possible, some reasoning other than Levison's elaborate hypothesis is required. An alternative is that the list was concocted at the same time as the earliest document, in the eighth century. For that to be likely, either a context has to be found for the invention of otherwise unattested titles for two of Æthelberht's courtiers, or such titles would have had to be current at the time of the forgery – something for which there is as little other positive, and less circumstantial, evidence as for the period around 600. It is conceivable that a forger might have known of Æthelberht's Frankish connections, and have adapted a Frankish model, but it is perhaps more likely that within the Canterbury archives he found some kind of document which incorporated a list of Æthelberht's courtiers including the referendary and *graphio*.[32]

Levison objected to the idea that there might have been a referendary at an English court on the grounds that Anglo-Saxon charters were written by their recipients – usually churchmen – rather than by lay officials of the royal court such as the referendary.[33] Such a view, however, requires acceptance only if the referendary was the head of the chancery. As was seen in Chapter 3, however, that was not in reality the case in the Frankish (or the imperial) court, and it is unlikely to have been in the Lombard (see Chapter 13): the referendary was a subordinate, responsible for transmission of the king's will to the writer, and for checking the final document or presenting it to the king for verification. Similar procedures may have been required when the documents were produced by churchmen: the king's will had to be accurately transmitted to them, and it could have been all the more important that the content be checked by a royal agent,[34] since beneficiaries could easily have used the opportunities afforded by drafting charters to claim more than that to which they were entitled.[35]

Another reason why the evidence of the witness list has been dismissed is that there is no other evidence for either a referendary or a *graphio* in Kent or in any of the other early kingdoms. It is true that none of the early charters produced after 670 contains a witness list giving the specific offices of the signatories, but neither do Lombard charters, nor the majority of Frankish ones (the *placita*, which are unparalleled in England, are a different case); and it is not impossible that the style of charters might have changed in the sixty years between Æthelberht's death and the survival of the first unquestionably genuine charter.[36] There is, however, another possible explanation for the slightly unusual form of the witness list – that is, that it was not originally the witness list at all, but a list (or part of a list) of Æthelberht's courtiers made for some other purpose and only made to serve as a witness list by the eighth-century forger.

While it is acknowledged that the authenticity of the short version of the witness list cannot be proved, there is far from being enough evidence to condemn it completely, and it should be treated with an open mind. Given the small amount of source material for the early period, the most significant evidence against the existence of specific offices would be a demonstration that another source, of more obviously reliable character, failed to mention them when it could reasonably be expected to have done so. Against this background, I propose to return briefly to the sources discussed in Chapter 15.

The other sources

The documents produced by the government itself – the charters and law codes – present a relatively simple case. Nothing can be read into the absence of detailed witness lists from the charters for, as stated above, charters of donation produced on the continent rarely contain such lists: more details of courtiers are found in continental *placita*, and in clauses connected with the way in which the documents were drawn up, but, as discussed earlier, such material does not exist for England.

Equally, almost nothing can be deduced from the law codes, the provisions of which were, like their continental counterparts, framed in general terms so as to be applicable in a variety of circumstances which could involve different types of official. Neither the Lombard nor the Frankish laws reveal much concerning specific offices; and even the Visigothic code, with its lists of officials who might become involved, is almost entirely silent concerning members of the court resident with the king: such men would rarely have dealt with legal cases other than as part of the royal tribunal, and may, in any case, have been subsumed under the general term 'comes'. Although, as was seen in Chapters 8 and 9, the silence of the law codes concerning courtiers has been interpreted as indicating that the titles used to describe such men in the conciliar witness lists are purely honorary, a full appreciation of the character of the evidence shows that there is no reason to doubt that the court was organised in the way suggested by the lists of signatories.

Turning to the more narrative sources, the poverty of the evidence furnished by the hagiographical documents needs little comment in the light of the small amount supplied by the much larger body of Frankish material. Hagiographers were not primarily concerned with individual members of the laity save when they were essential to a narrative, or could be used as a foil against which the sanctity of a holy man could be revealed. On the whole, all that mattered to the author of a saint's life was to show the rank (either elevated or very humble) of the people involved. The royal agents with whom holy men most often came into contact were the king's representatives outside the court – the *praefecti ciuitatum* – who did hold a more specific office, and are referred to, at least in Stephen's *Life of Wilfrid*, in such a way as to make that clear.

The last point is of particular significance in relation to Bede's *Ecclesiastical History* for, although several prefects are mentioned, only on a single occasion is one of their number explicitly linked to a place, when Blæcca is described as 'praefectus Lindocolinae ciuitatis'.[37] This may reflect two (not mutually exclusive) things concerning Bede's evidence.

First, much of Bede's narrative concerns a period well before his own adult lifetime, and it is possible that in some (perhaps many) instances, the specific positions of the men to whom he refers were no longer remembered in his day, though their general status might have been. Second, Bede may simply not have been interested, any more than were the hagiographers (with whom his work has much in common), with the precise details of the offices held by the king's officials. It was not Bede's concern to record details of secular administration – he was writing an *ecclesiastical* history – and in any case the example of Paul the Deacon shows that not all authors with secular interests can be expected to reveal the workings of the royal court.

Conclusion

Bede's lack of interest in the details of secular administration is not the only feature of his work which is relevant to the present enquiry, for his bias against the British church has often (at least until very recently) led to a conclusion that the Anglo-Saxons in general owed little to the British. Such may not be the only interpretation which the evidence permits: while it is possible that the Anglo-Saxons imposed their own institutions on the areas they came to rule (whether by conquest or more peaceful means), it is at least as likely that they – like their continental counterparts – adapted what they found, and that what they found owed something to Roman traditions.[38]

That aspects of Roman administration could have continued into the British period is no longer a matter of great controversy,[39] and some of the ways in which the Anglo-Saxons were initially accommodated in England may even have been related to the kinds of federate agreement known from the fifth-century continent: it has, for example, more than once been argued that such is the implication of Gildas' use of such terms as *annona*, *foederatus* and *hospes*, as well of words describing various kinds of ruler.[40] While the latter is not a convincing argument in what is essentially a literary work, especially as Gildas' descriptions of secular officials could as well have been derived from the Bible as from the Roman past (or the British reality of his own day), it is less easy to dismiss the terminology relating to the arrangements for the support of the Anglo-Saxons. Further, the fact that the names of the Northumbrian kingdoms – Deira and Bernicia – are Celtic,[41] suggests that there, at least, the Anglo-Saxons took over pre-existing political units, as they probably did elsewhere in the north. While the new overlords no doubt introduced features of their own into the administration, it is *prima facie* unlikely that there was a complete discontinuity of such arrangements. Elsewhere, the possibility that West Saxon kings may have been at least partly of British descent makes complete discontinuity in the south equally questionable.[42]

Unlike the situation on much of the continent in the fifth century, the urban institutions by means of which many aspects of administrative literacy were transmitted to the 'barbarian' rulers decayed almost completely; neither the remaining native aristocracy nor the leaders of the British church appear to have co-operated with their new masters in ways familiar from the continent. In part, that may be attributable to the paganism of the early Anglo-Saxon rulers: the British Christians may have been unwilling to lend assistance, while the pagan incomers may not have been enthusiastic recipients, particularly given that many forms of literacy (administrative and otherwise) were associated with Christianity. It is also possible that documents which were produced during the pagan or British period may not have been preserved by later generations simply because they were associated with ideologies which were at best no longer current or, at worst, abhorred. There may here be some similarities with the position in Spain: there is almost no evidence for the first two-thirds of the sixth century, when the kings were still Arian, but, after the conversion, sources – many of which, whether administrative or not, were produced by churchmen – become more plentiful.

The Visigothic parallel may be carried further, for the fact that documents (of whatever kind) begin to survive from the time of Reccared's conversion, combined with the first appearance of many court offices at the same period, has led to the suggestion that the organisation of the court was radically altered at or shortly after the time of the conversion. As was seen in Part II, however, that may not have been the case, particularly since such an interpretation largely rests on the argument from silence engendered by the lack of earlier evidence. In the same way, the fact that Anglo-Saxon documents begin to survive from the period of the Augustinian mission could lead to a suggestion that all forms of government related to those of the Roman period or similar to continental practices were introduced at that time, the 'Roman' religion bringing with it a desire for association with 'Roman' governmental institutions. Such an impression might be strengthened by Bede's account of Anglo-Saxon history.

Given Bede's precise interests, however, it may be pertinent to ask whether this kind of interpretation is the only one. In the same way as his legitimate focus on the history of the Church may mean that he was not interested to record precise details of courtiers' positions, even though the latter may have existed, so his concern with the 'Roman' Church, combined with his hostility to British religion, may create the impression that Æthelberht's reign marked a break with the past over a wider range of activity. That was no doubt a view Bede sought to encourage. Even though his interpretation may have been coloured by the availability of evidence for the period before his own lifetime – which is itself likely to have been affected by the adoption of the 'Roman' religion – it is no coincidence that the earliest period for which Bede supplies a narrative of any coherence is that of the Augustinian mission. Baptism is a form of re-birth, the first step

170

on the road from the darkness of ignorance to the light of salvation. The spiritual logic is inescapable, but caution must be exercised before accepting Bede's silences, even subconsciously, as a pre-condition for the understanding of early Anglo-Saxon England as a whole: they do not necessarily have a significance beyond the religious framework of his *Ecclesiastical History*.

Conclusion

One of the paradoxes of the study of early medieval kingship is that the seventh century is sometimes implicitly presented as showing the beginnings of the 'civilisation' of Anglo-Saxon government – that is, of the rulers of the most un-Roman of the 'barbarians' – at the same time as that of the Visigoths and, more particularly, the Franks, entered a period of decline. The analysis of the preceding chapters has demonstrated that traditional judgements of many aspects of seventh-century royal government stand in need of revision, as they have often been reached without taking adequate cognizance of the character and limitations of the sources: this not only affects comprehension of the internal history of each of the kingdoms concerned, but has made comparisons between them, and a wider appreciation of the evolution of governmental institutions in western Europe, peculiarly difficult.

By following the approach adopted here, of analysing the impact of the character of the differing sources for each kingdom, it has been possible to construct a different picture – one in which seventh-century continental rulers appear less decadent than has often been supposed, and in which some (but not all) of the distinctions between the kingdoms seem more apparent than real. One of the chief factors which determines modern reactions to kings and their courtiers may be the existence of a detailed narrative source. The case of the Merovingians is particularly unfortunate in that the main narrative is not only extremely brief, but is provided by authors opposed to their rule: the combination of the two means that the material recorded is highly selective and was chosen in order to provide a coherent tendential account – though in truth its very coherence renders it suspect. The Visigoths were not subject to the same kind of opposition, but the complete lack of a narrative makes their rulers appear hardly more sophisticated than the Merovingians, especially since they lost their kingdom to an external foe in the early eighth century. The Lombards have also suffered from being defeated, but not to the same extent, perhaps largely because, for all Paul the Deacon's concentration on the activities of *duces*, there is a narrative framework for the kingdom, and one in which kings – or the institution of monarchy – occupy a near-central place. That is all the more the case for the Anglo-Saxons, since Bede made kings some of the main agents in his history of salvation: not only do they feature in a coherent narrative, but they are presented as having been effective, and they form part of an essentially optimistic story.

Only if the purpose of each individual author is analysed is it possible to provide the evidence for each kingdom with its correct internal context; from that, it becomes possible to make meaningful comparisons concerning the varying depictions of royal government. Perhaps the best example relates to the evidence of the Frankish *diplomata*, which has in the past been used to reinforce the view (based on an uncritical acceptance of the narratives for the period) that the power of the *maiores domus* (whether Pippinid or not) rose throughout the late seventh and early eighth centuries at the expense of that of the Merovingians. Approached in its own terms, however, the testimony of the royal documents is considerably less compelling, seeming less coherent (as befits its small volume and disjointed nature) and subject to other interpretations. In turn, that realisation raises questions concerning the accuracy of the depiction of kings in the narrative sources.

Similar issues are raised by the character of Paul the Deacon's *History of the Lombards* which, although not opposed to kings in the same way as the Frankish narratives, does not show anything of the workings of the royal court: so great is the gap that it can lead to the questioning of the reality (as opposed to the imagery) of Lombard royal power.[1] It is again the *diplomata* which enable aspects of the court-based administration to be seen – a fact which challenges modern historians to account for Paul's silence. This is particularly instructive, for the fact that such documents exist shows that, had they not survived, any suggestion that the palace administration was unimportant would be tantamount to demonstrating a negative from silence.

A proposition that the court-based administration was unsophisticated has found favour among some historians of seventh-century Spain, for which much of the evidence is particularly exiguous, amounting to little more than confusing lists of official titles. Even viewed on their own, however, the sources for Visigothic administration are capable of sustaining other interpretations, as was argued in Part II. Seen in the light of the problems posed by the Lombard evidence the caution urged against arguments derived from the lack of particular kinds of source material (narratives and *diplomata*) may gain added force.

One of the most striking points of comparison in relation to this theme is the apparent significance of rank in both the Visigothic and Anglo-Saxon kingdoms, the Visigothic *seniores palatii* appearing to be not altogether different from the Anglo-Saxon *ealdormen/principes*, and the *gardingi* being broadly similar to the *thegnas/ministri*. That this, together with the rough equivalence of *comites ciuitatum* and *gerefan*/prefects, should be perceptible despite the very different nature of the sources may have an importance beyond the simple facts themselves, for it may render more likely the existence of specific, continental-type court offices in England, as suggested in Chapter 18. Similarly, the fact that the lower rank of officials is not visible in the Lombard kingdom should not necessarily be taken to indicate that it did not exist, particularly since it is was present in the Frankish world (in the guise of *domestici*).

The foregoing arguments suggest the presence of greater resemblances than have often been thought to exist between the structures of the royal courts in the four regions discussed. The same is also true of kingship itself, both in relation to the ways in which kings portrayed their power, and in connection with the activities of kings and their consorts. One of the best examples of this relates to the making (and content) of law. In all four regions the traditions established earlier in the post-Roman period were continued. This is perhaps clearest in the case of the Visigoths, whose legal history had begun in the fifth century with the issuing of a law code by Euric (based on Roman provincial law) and continued in the mid-sixth under Theudis. This meant that although Leovigild (and some of his successors) produced a complete code, it took the form of a revision of his predecessors' enactments, reacting to the new legal and political circumstances of his own time. The reactive nature of a high proportion of Visigothic law becomes more explicit in the seventh century, as individual provisions – sometimes termed *nouellae* – were promulgated in response to specific judicial cases, as were imperial rescripts. Merovingian legislative activity is much less well-attested during the seventh century, but appears to share some of these characteristics, entire law codes being reissued – especially for particular areas of the kingdom and for subject peoples – and also some supplementary measures being enacted in the form of capitularies, which might be considered as groups of rescripts.

The Lombards and the Anglo-Saxons, by contrast, did not enter the post-Justinianic period with any written law. The legislative activity of their kings is, however, little different from that of the Franks and Visigoths. In the case of the Lombards, Rothari's *Edict* (of Roman provincial character) formed the foundation upon which all later enactments built, in the same way as did Euric's or Leovigild's codes for the Visigoths. Later Lombard rulers did not reissue the entire *corpus*, but promulgated new measures as required: such provisions (which must have arisen at all times of year) were published (almost annually under Liutprand) in groups similar to those contained in the Frankish capitularies. Anglo-Saxon law proceeded on roughly similar lines: the codes of Hlothhere and Eadric, and of Wihtræd were supplements to Æthelberht's (Roman provincial type) edict, while that of Ine is a series of periodic enactments of the kind associated with Liutprand.[2]

The means by which kings pursued their legislative activities appear to have owed much to Roman traditions – to a mixing of provincial and imperial practices which had begun in the first 'barbarian' kingdoms. Similar borrowings are apparent in relation to the ways in which kings depicted their power and sought to claim legitimacy. Here, though, the period following the abortive Justinianic attempt to re-establish the western Empire saw a greater degree of evolution. The attack on the west, combined with the inevitable weakening of sentiment as the days of the last western emperor became increasingly distant, meant that 'barbarian' kings no longer saw themselves as part of the one great *imperium*, from whose leaders they could claim some kind of legitimation. New expressions of authority had to be found, and in the cases of the Visigoths and Lombards (who were for varying periods in conflict with the Empire) it may have been desirable for their rulers to claim parity with the emperors. One of the means by which this was achieved was through a theocratic interpretation of the king's position. There was not necessarily anything completely new in this – already in the sixth century the Franks had begun to portray their kings in Biblical terms – but part of the impetus for the development of the idea may have come from changing relations with the Empire, as well as from the need to assist kings (particularly in areas where the dynastic principle was weakest) to maintain their position. There was, however, a pre-condition for the evolution of the necessary body of ecclesiastical support – the monarchy had not only to be Christian, but also Catholic: this determined the earliest date at which theocratic doctrines could be enunciated in each of the kingdoms.

One of the vehicles for propaganda concerning the king's position was coinage. In the fifth and early sixth centuries, 'barbarian' kings imitated imperial gold coins in such a way as to indicate their subordination to the Empire; when, from the late sixth century onwards, they wished to proclaim their independence, they again did so (to varying degrees) by the same means. One way of achieving this could have involved the development of new designs, not dependent upon imperial types. Instead, however, kings chose to continue to imitate imperial coins, copying the reverse, rather than the obverse, and replacing the imperial bust with their own portraits. For all that the relationship with the Empire had changed, kings still operated in a 'Roman' world.

Similar adaptations of Roman/imperial traditions were made in the sphere of royal ceremonial, with all kingdoms displaying some aspects of the rituals of *aduentus*. These are perhaps clearest in the case of the Lombards, but the adoption of Toledo as a ceremonial capital in the Visigothic kingdom (particularly when juxtaposed with the imperial-type church councils held there) strongly suggests that similar rituals were practised. The evidence for the Merovingians is, predictably, less – it was not something to which the anti-Merovingians would have drawn attention – but there are hints: Einhard's depiction of Childeric III supplies one,[3] and the late sixth-century account of Chilperic I building amphitheatres is another.[4] Both have possible parallels in England, in the shape of Edwin's progress behind a standard, and the nature of the site at Yeavering.[5]

Using the sources in the way attempted here suggests that many of the perceived differences between the kingdoms arise from the varying lenses through which they have to be viewed; nevertheless, it is not the case that seventh-century royal government was uniform. The territories over which kings ruled were of widely differing scale, ranging from the comparatively minute Anglo-Saxon kingdoms, to the larger (and expanding) but disjointed Lombard lands; and upwards, though the very large and diverse Visigothic kingdom, to the vast area subject to Merovingian *imperium*. In addition, whereas the Franks were well established by the end of the sixth century, the Visigothic kings were only then coming to create their mature kingdom or *imperium*, while the Lombards were beginning to carve out their sphere of influence and establish their kingdom.

These factors – and others, such as the varying extent of urban life – affected the provincial structure of the kingdoms. In England, kingdoms were probably small enough for only one tier of provincial administration to have been needed – that of the *gerefan*/prefects, whose jurisdictions probably had some similarities to those of *comites ciuitatum* (though without the fully urban connotation). A kingdom the size of Lombard Italy required two types of provincial government – the predominantly civil, in the hands of the gastalds, and the military, in the hands of the *duces*. Although it was argued in Part III that the dominance of *duces* may often be over-estimated, it is likely that such military leaders were of greater importance in the kingdom's heartland than elsewhere in western Europe since they were the agents of the continuing conquest of Italy. In addition, the southern *duces*, whose territories were for much of the time physically separated from the central part of the kingdom, almost inevitably came to enjoy a relatively high degree of autonomy, and to be the superiors of the gastalds. Similar freedom of action may have come to be enjoyed by the provincial *duces* of Spain, whose spheres of jurisdiction were larger than those of their Lombard counterparts, and whose position may have evolved from that of war leader to provincial governor (over the *comites ciuitatum*) as the kingdom expanded into a kind of *imperium*. The pattern in the territories subject to Frankish *imperium* is less easy to discern, partly because it was not uniform. In the core of the kingdom there were *duces* – some of whose territories were not permanent, and who appear to have been war leaders – whose jurisdictions encompassed larger territories than those of *comites ciuitatum*; but not all areas seem to have been covered by them. In some of the larger regions – such as Aquitaine – *duces* may have become provincial governors of the kind suggested for Spain, while in the territories of the subject peoples to the east the *duces* appear to have been semi-autonomous, and were probably men who would have been described in an Anglo-Saxon context as *principes*, *subreguli*, or even *reges* who were subject to greater, *imperium*-wielding, kings.

Variations in provincial government are paralleled by differences in the detailed organisation of the royal court, though here the evidence is

176

particularly poor. Despite the broad degree of similarity between the courts, the precise titles of their officials seem to have varied, as does usage of terms such as *dux* and *comes*. This is particularly apparent between the Visigothic and Frankish courts, with the former seeming to rank a greater number of men as *comites* than the latter, but certainty on the point is unattainable owing to the variability and incompleteness of the evidence; even less is known of Lombard and Anglo-Saxon courtiers.

The differences were, however, variations on a theme, which appears to have been of essentially 'Roman' ancestry. This may not be particularly surprising in relation to the Visigoths and Franks, whose entry into the former Empire was effected in the fifth century, but may be less expected in the case of the Lombards, who only entered Italy in the 560s, and of the Anglo-Saxons. However, both those peoples had been settled inside the Roman world for some time before that, the Lombards since the 520s in Pannonia, and the Anglo-Saxons from the fifth century. This suggests that caution should be exercised in hypothesising about the earlier periods: the lack of evidence for the Lombards and Anglo-Saxons before the late sixth century cannot necessarily be taken as indicative of a failure to adopt 'Roman' traditions.

It could be argued that the 'Roman' elements of kingship result from the fact that the only model for Christian, Catholic, rulership was that provided by the Empire, and that the adoption and adaptation of Roman traditions was a sign of membership of the community of Catholic kings. Such a case could derive added strength from the high proportion of the sources that were written (whether with a religious purpose or not) by Catholic churchmen. An argument of that kind would, however, fail to take adequate account of fifth- and early sixth-century history, which shows that the Arian kings of the Burgundians, Vandals, Visigoths and, above all, the Ostrogoths, took over at least as many 'Roman' customs as their Catholic Frankish counterparts, and enjoyed the co-operation of some of their Roman (and Catholic) subjects.[6] It may, accordingly, be more likely that the broad similarities between the seventh-century kingdoms result from their common inheritance of 'Roman' institutions (which they may have been more disposed to adapt than to overthrow completely), and from their common need to define themselves (at different times and in varying ways) in terms of the Empire. This was as true of the period after the failure of the Justinianic re-conquest as of the fifth and sixth centuries, and is visible throughout the seventh century, despite the growth of diversity amongst the 'barbarian' kingdoms themselves as each adapted to its peculiar circumstances as the days of the western Empire became increasingly remote. As the Carolingians were to show, the definition of western kingship in terms of 'Roman' imperial traditions remained a powerful force even at the very end of the eighth century.

Maps

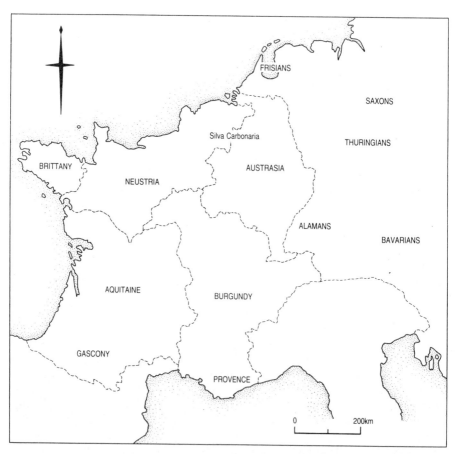

Map I. The *regnum Francorum* in the seventh century

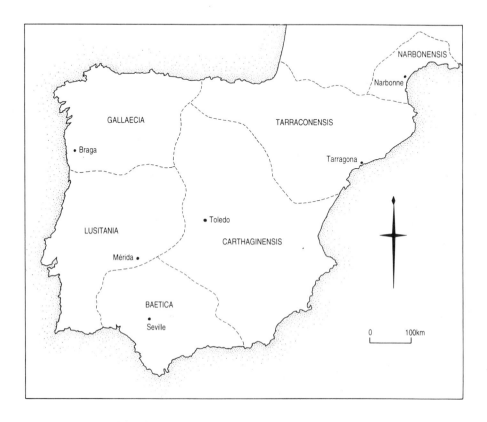

Map II. Visigothic Spain in the seventh century

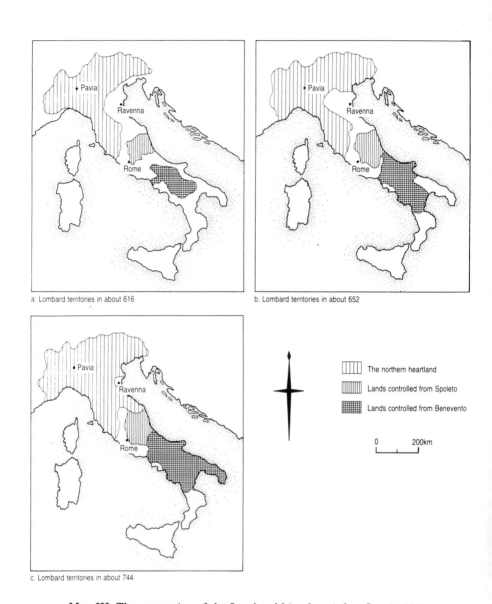

a. Lombard territories in about 616

b. Lombard territories in about 652

c. Lombard territories in about 744

The northern heartland

Lands controlled from Spoleto

Lands controlled from Benevento

0   200km

Map III. The expansion of the Lombard kingdom (after Conti 1990)

180

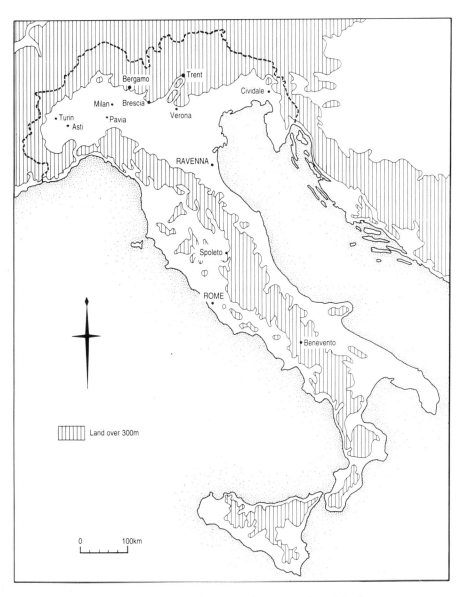

Map IV. Italy, showing the main places mentioned in the text

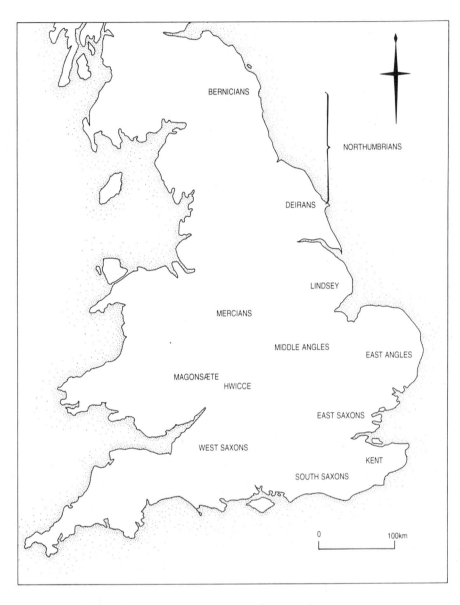

Map V. The main territories of early Anglo-Saxon England

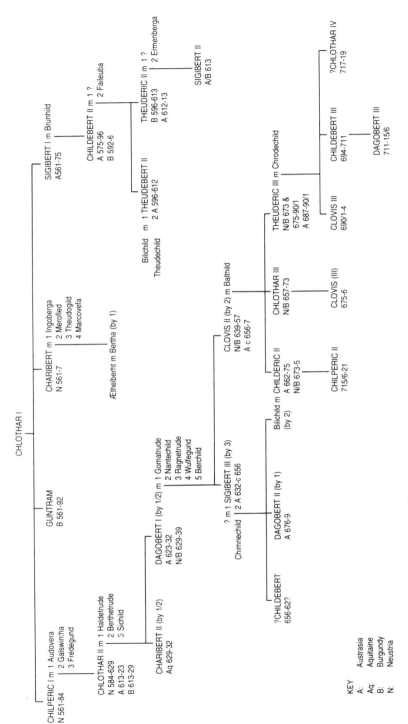

Table I. Simplified genealogy of the Merovingian dynasty, 561-721

CHLOTHAR I

CHILPERIC I m 1 Audovera
N 561-84   2 Galswintha
                  3 Fredegund

CHLOTHAR II m 1 Haldetrude
N 584-629   2 Berthetrude
A 613-23   3 Sichild
B 613-29

CHARIBERT II (by 1/2)
Aq 629-32

GUNTRAM
B 561-92

DAGOBERT I (by 1/2) m 1 Gomatrude
A 623-32   2 Nantechild
N/B 629-39   3 Ragnetrude
                     4 Wulfegund
                     5 Berchild

?CHILDEBERT
656-62?

DAGOBERT II (by 1)
A 676-9

? m 1 SIGIBERT III (by 3)
Chimnechild 2 A 632-c 656

CLOVIS II (by 2) m Bathild
N/B 639-57
A c 656-7

Biichild m CHILDERIC II
(by 2)   A 662-75
          N/B 673-5

CHILPERIC II
715/6-21

CHLOTHAR III
N/B 657-73

CLOVIS (III)
675-6

CHARIBERT m 1 Ingoberga
N 561-7   2 Merofled
              3 Theudogild
              4 Marcovefa

Æthelberht m Bertha (by 1)

Biichild   m 1 THEUDEBERT II
Theudechild 2 A 596-612

THEUDERIC III m Chrodechild
N/B 673 &
675/6-90/1
A 687-90/1

CLOVIS III
690/1-4

SIGIBERT I m Brunhild
A561-75

CHILDEBERT II m 1 ?
A 575-96   2 Faileuba
B 592-6

THEUDERIC II m 1 ?
B 596-613   2 Ermenberga
A 612-13

SIGIBERT II
A/B 613

CHILDEBERT III
694-711

DAGOBERT III
711-15/6

?CHLOTHAR IV
717-19

KEY
A: Austrasia
Aq: Aquitaine
B: Burgundy
N: Neustria

183

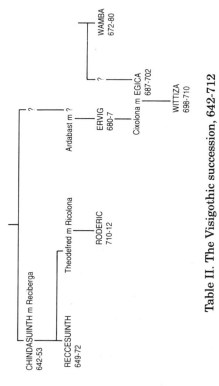

Table II. The Visigothic succession, 642-712

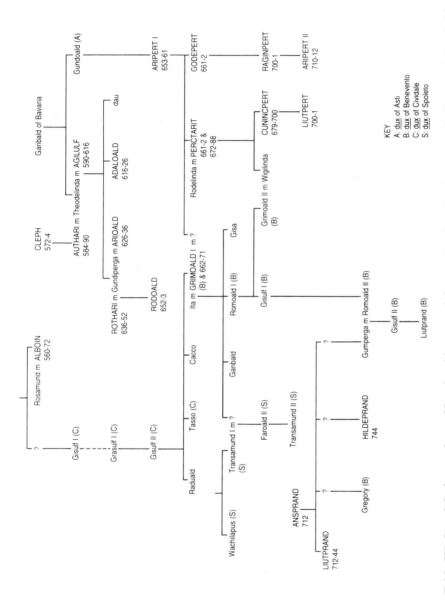

Table III. Simplified genealogy of Lombard kings and *duces* related to the dynasties of Alboin and Garibald

185

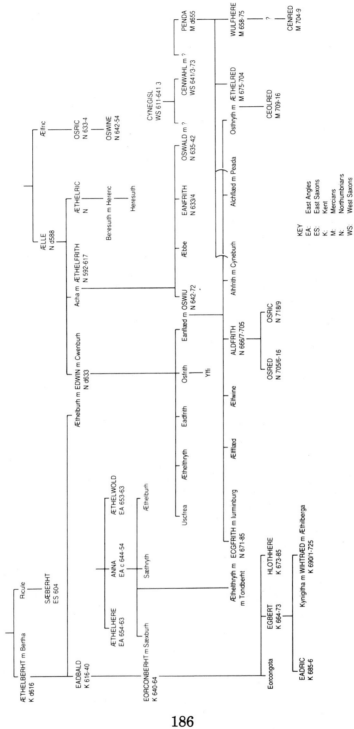

Table IV. Simplified genealogy showing selected inter-relationships between the rulers of early Anglo-Saxon England

186

Abbreviations

A.H.D.E. = *Anuario de historia del derecho español*
Aistulf = *Leges Aistulfi*
Atti ... = *Atti dei congressi internazionali di studi sull'alto medioevo*, Spoleto
Æthelberht = *Laws of Æthelberht*
Barcelona = Council of Barcelona, in J. Vives, *Concilios visigóticos e hispano-romanos*
Cap. Mer. = *Capitularia Merowingica*
C.D.L. = *Codice Diplomatico Longobardo*
C.E. = *Codex Eurici*
Ch.L.A. = *Chartae Latinae Antiquiores*
Chronicon s. Sophiae = *Chronicon Beneventani monasterii sanctae Sophiae*
Chron. Uult. = *Chronicon Uulternese del monaco Giovanni*
C.I. = *Codex Iustinianus*
C.Th. = *Codex Theodosianus*
D.A. = *Diplomata Arnulfingi*
Desid., *Ep.* = Desiderius of Cahors, *Epistolae*
D.M. = *Diplomata Merovingicorum*
Ep. = *Epistolae*
Ep. Austr. = *Epistolae Austrasicae*
Ep. Mer. = *Epistolae Aevi Merowingici Collectae*
Ep. Wis. = *Epistolae Wisigothicae*
Form. Andecau. = *Formulae Andecauenses*
Form. Wis. = *Formulae Wisigothicae*
Fort., *Carm.* = Fortunatus, *Carmina*
Fred. = Fredegar
Greg., *Dialogues* = Gregory the Great, *Dialogues*
Greg., *Reg.* = Gregory the Great, *Register Epistolarum*
Grimoald = *Leges Grimualdi*
H.E. = Bede, *Historia Ecclesiastica Gentis Anglorum*
H.G. = Isidore of Seville, *Historia Gothorum*
Historia Wambae = Julian of Toledo, *Historia excellentissimi Wambae regis de expeditione et uictoria, qua reuellantem contra se prouinciam Galliae celebri triumpho perdomuit*
H.L. = Paul the Deacon, *Historia Langobardorum*
Hlothhere and Eadric = *Laws of Hlothhere and Eadric*
Ine = *Laws of Ine*
L.H. = Gregory of Tours, *Decem libri historiarum*
L.H.F. = *Liber historiae Francorum*
Lib. Pont. = *Liber Pontificalis*
Liutprand = *Leges Liutprandi*
L.U. = *Liber iudicorum siue Leges Uisigothorum* ...
M.G.H. = *Monumenta Germaniae Historica*

Abbreviations

M.G.H., A.A. = *Monumenta Germaniae Historica, Auctores Antiquissimi*

M.G.H., Ep. = *Monumenta Germaniae Historica, Epistolae*

M.G.H., S.R.G. = *Monumenta Germaniae Historica, Scriptores Rerum Germanicarum*

M.G.H., S.R.L. = *Monumenta Germaniae Historica, Scriptores Rerum Langobardicarum et Italicarum saeculorum VI-IX*

M.G.H., S.R.M. = *Monumenta Germaniae Historica, Scriptores Rerum Merouingicarum*

Narbonne = Council of Narbonne, in J. Vives, *Concilios visigóticos e hispano-romanos*

N.I. = *Nouellae Iustiniani*

O.E.B. = *The Old English Version of Bede's Ecclesiastical History of the English People*

P.L. = *Patrologiae cursus completus ...* series *Latina* (ed. J.-P. Migne, 221 vols Paris 1844-1904)

Ratchis = *Leges Ratchis*

Rothari = *Edictum Rothari*

S = P.H. Sawyer, *Anglo-Saxon Charters: an annotated list and bibliography*, London

Saragossa = Council of Saragossa, in J. Vives, *Concilios visigóticos e hispano-romanos*

Settimane ... = *Settimane di studio del centro italiano di studi sull'alto medioevo*, Spoleto

Sid. Ap., *Ep.* = Sidonius Apollinaris, *Epistolae*

Toledo = Council of Toledo, in J. Vives, *Concilios visigóticos e hispano-romanos*

Uita Desid. Cad. ep. = *Uita Desiderii Cadurcae urbis episcopi*

Uita Desid. ep. Biturc. = *Uita sancti Desiderati episcopi Biturcensium*

Uita Germani Grand. = *Uita Germani abbatis Grandiuallensis*

U.P.E. = *Uitas Patrum Emeritensium*

Wihtræd = *Laws of Wihtræd*

Z.R.G., g.A. = *Zeitschrift der Savigny-Stiftung für Rechtsgeschichte, germanistische Abteilung*

Notes

Introduction

1. Fanning 1991, the significance of which (despite the title) extends well beyond England.

2. The leading account of the Merovingian kingdoms which avoids this is Wood 1994a.

Introduction to Part I

1. Einhard, *Uita Karoli Magni*, 1.

2. Wallace-Hadrill 1965, and 1975, p. 98.

Chapter 1

1. Briefly discussed in Barnwell 1992, pp. 91-3.

2. Wallace-Hadrill 1960, p. xxiii.

3. Wallace-Hadrill 1962, p. 83.

4. Wallace-Hadrill 1960, pp. xxiii-xxv; see also Wattenbach, Dümmler and Huf 1991, vol. 1 pp. 111-13.

5. Goffart 1963.

6. Goffart 1963, p. 221.

7. For a discussion of their relevance to the subject of fifth-century western imperial government, see Barnwell 1992, esp. pp. 7-8, 15, 38-40.

8. Wallace-Hadrill 1962, p. 75.

9. Goffart 1963, pp. 217-18; Wallace-Hadrill 1960, p. xxi; *idem* 1962, p. 75.

10. Fred., *cont.*, 34; Wallace-Hadrill 1960, p. xiii; Wood 1994a, p. 257.

11. Wood 1994a, p. 257.

12. See Gerberding 1987; for the possibility of female authorship, see Nelson 1990, p. 82.

13. For the dating of the lives, see Wattenbach, Dümmler and Huf 1991, vol. 1 pp. 120-35; Wood 1988, pp. 369-70 lists the lives by period; see also Wood 1994a, pp. 246-7, where the purpose of hagiography is discussed.

14. Wood 1994a, pp. 195-6.

15. Wood 1991b.

16. Wood 1988 – the arguments are summarised on p. 384.

17. See Part II for the Visigothic councils and the participation of the king and his courtiers.

18. Wood 1990, p. 70.

19. The letters are collected as the *Ep. Mer.*: nos 12-17 relate to the seventh century; of them two were written by popes to kings (12 and 13), while the remaining four were written by bishops, only one (15) being addressed to a king.

20. Some versions of the text, together with a discussion of the differing interpretations of it, are in Barnwell 1991.

21. This is argued for the *Formulae Andecauenses* by Wood 1986, p. 9, and for the *Formulae Marculfi* by Levillain 1923, pp. 90-1.

22. Wood 1986, p. 9.

23. Riché 1962, pp. 221-2; Brunner 1887-92, vol. 1 pp. 403-4.

24. Levillain 1923, pp. 21-3.

25. Marculf, *praefatio*.

26. Riché 1980, p. 176.

27. The originals are published in *Ch.L.A.* vols XIII and XIV; for a discussion of the numbers of *diplomata* which survive from the entire Merovingian period, see Brühl 1989, pp. 524-5.

28. Jusselin 1905 and 1907; Mentz 1911 disputed Jusselin's readings, but Jusselin 1913 is a defence of them; later, Mentz (1939 and 1942) discusssed the history of tironian notes and, in the 1942 work, reproduced his readings, but they have still not gained favour – see Ganz 1983, p. 62, and Bischoff 1990, p. 80 n. 203.

29. For the date of the *Lex Ribuaria*, see the review of the evidence in Schott 1979, p. 38; the *Pactus legis Alamannorum* is conveniently discussed in Schott 1978, cols 1881-2, where the literature is reviewed – cf. Schott 1979, pp. 39-40.

30. See Siems 1978, cols 1887-90; Schott 1979, pp. 40-1; McKitterick 1989, p. 68 n. 108.

Chapter 2

1. Fred. IV.17, 20, 21, 26, 27, 38.

2. Jonas, *Uita Columbani*, I.28 and *L.H.F.* 38 (cf. Fred. IV.38 for both); *L.H.F.* 37.

3. Fred. IV.68, 74.

4. Fred. IV.87.

5. Fred. IV.42.

6. Fred., *cont.*, 5, 10.

7. *Childeberti secundi decretio, Cap. Mer.*, pp. 15-17.

8. For the importance of the Marchfield, see Bachrach 1974.

9. For imperial rescripts and sixth-century Frankish capitularies, see Barnwell 1992, pp. 8-9, 14-18, 98-9, and the references there.

10. *Chlotharii II praeceptio, Cap. Mer.*, pp. 18-19; *Chlotharii II edictum, ibid.*, pp. 20-3

11. See Ewig 1976f, p. 463; Schmidt-Wiegand 1978, col. 1923. For the date, see Chapter 1, n. 29.

12. Wood 1990, p. 66.

13. *Passio Leudegarii I*, 7; cf. Wood 1994a, pp. 113-14.

14. Wood 1994a, p. 116.

15. For references to discussions of the dates of both, see Chapter 1 nn. 29-30.

16. Wallace-Hadrill 1962, pp. 214-16, and, esp., Murray 1994.

17. *Passio Leudegarii I*, 7: 'Interea Childerico rege expetiunt uniuersi, ut talia daret decreta per tria quam obtinuerat regna, ut uniuscuiusque patrie legem uel consuetudinem deberent sicut antiquitus, iudices conseruare, *et ne una prouintia rectores in aliis introirent ...*' cf. *Chlotharii II edictum*, 12, *Cap. Mer.*, p. 22: '*Et nullus iudex de aliis prouinciis aut regionibus in alia loca ordinetur*; ut, si aliquid mali de quibuslibet condicionibus perpetrauerit, de suis propriis rebus exinde quod male abstolerit iuxta legis ordine debeat restaurare' (my italics).

18. Barnwell 1992, pp. 97-8.

19. Wallace-Hadrill 1955, p. 442; *idem.* 1962, p. 214.

20. Wood 1993, pp. 174-5.

21. Wood 1993, esp. pp. 164-8, 176; this cannot be taken as evidence supportive of the thesis that royal law-making was more concerned with boosting the image of the king than with practical application (see Wormald 1977), since there is no regular pattern to the associations of imperial and Frankish material such as would have been likely had the king officially inspired them in order to gain prestige by the association of his enactments with those of the earlier emperors.

22. Discussed in Barnwell 1992, pp. 84, 95-6, 117-18, 135, 136-6.

23. Collins 1983a, pp. 27-30.

24. Grierson and Blackburn 1986, p. 120; cf. p. 85 (table 10).

25. Grierson and Blackburn 1986, pp. 128-31; Prou 1892, p. xxix.

26. E. James 1988, pp. 194-9.

27. Brühl 1967, pp. 200-7; Ewig 1976d, pp. 383-9; see also Chapters 7 and 11 below.

28. The fifteen places are: Châtou-sur-Seine (*Captonnacum*), *D.M.* 40 (not an original), 59 (=*Ch.L.A.* XIV.572); Clichy (*Clipiacus*), *D.M.* 14 (=*Ch.L.A.* XIII.551), 15 (not an original), 19 (=*Ch.L.A.* XIII.558); Compiègne (*Compendium*), *D.M.* 31 (not an original), 54-5 (not originals), 57 (=*Ch.L.A.* XIII.570), 63 (not an original), 67 (=*Ch.L.A.* XIV.577), 68 (=*Ch.L.A.* XIV.578), 70 (=*Ch.L.A.* XIV.581), 71 (not an original), 81-4 (=*Ch.L.A.* XIV.588-91), 85-6 (not originals), 87 (=*Ch.L.A.* XIV.593), 89 (not an original); Crécy (*Crisciacus*), *D.M.* 56 (not an original), 76 (=*Ch.L.A.* XIV.585); Etrépagny (*Stirpiniacus*), *D.M.* 10 (=*Ch.L.A.* XIII.552), 11 (=*Ch.L.A.* XIII.550), 38 (not an original); Luzarches (*Lusarca*), *D.M.* 49 (=*Ch.L.A.* XIII.567), 64 (=*Ch.L.A.* XIV.575); Maastricht* (*Traiectus*), *D.M.* 29 (not an original); Mâlay-le-Roi (*Masolacus*), *D.M.* 47 (=*Ch.L.A.* XIII.566), 48 (=*Ch.L.A.* XIII.565); Montmacq (*Mamaccas*), *D.M.* 75 (not an original), 77-8 (=*Ch.L.A.* XIV.586-7), 79 (not an original); Nîmes* (*Nemauso*), *D.M.* 42 (not an original); Paris* (*Parisius*), *D.M.* 88 (not an original); Quierzy (*Carraciacus*), *D.M.* 73 (=*Ch.L.A.* XIV.584); S.-Cloud (*Novi[g]entum*), *D.M.* 60-1 (=*Ch.L.A.* XIV.573-4), 69 (=*Ch.L.A.* XIV.579); Valenciennes* (*Ualencianae*), *D.M.* 66 (=*Ch.L.A.* XIV.576). Those marked with an asterisk are the towns. A survey (not exhaustive) of the other sources for the period from 594 to 721 suggests that there is evidence for at least fourteen other royal villas at which kings were periodically present; since the sources are generally so incomplete, there may have been a much larger number of sites. For royal villas in general, see Ewig 1976d, pp. 383-9.

29. Barbier 1990, pp. 251-8.

30. See Schramm 1954-78, vol. 1 pp. 317-18.

31. *Uita Eligii*, I.5.

32. *H.G.* 51; Sid. Ap., *Ep.*, I.2; see Barnwell 1992, pp. 72-4, and Chapter 7 below.

33. Schramm 1954-78, vol. 1 pp. 319-20.

34. The best account of these developments is Ewig 1976g, pp. 17-21.

35. Fort., *Carm.*, VI.2 lines 77-84; see, in general, Van Dam 1985, p. 197; Ewig 1988, pp. 138-9.

36. *Concilium Clippacense 626/627, praefatio, Concilia Galliae* vol. 2 p. 291.

37. *L.H.F.* 42.

38. *Ep. Austr.*, 2; Greg., *Reg.*, VI.5.

39. *Ep. Mer.*, 15; see Wallace-Hadrill 1971, pp. 47-50 for references to the more general Christian virtues of kings – *iustitia, pietas, patientia* and the like.

40. Marculf I.5; cf. I.25, and Supplement 6.

41. Wallace-Hadrill 1971, p. 50.

42. *D.M.* 10 (not an original;) *D.M.* 11 (=*Ch.L.A.* XIII.550); *D.M.* 47 (=*Ch.L.A.* XIII.566); *D.M.* 48 (=*Ch.L.A.* XIII.565); *D.M.* 53 (not an original); *D.M.* 57 (=*Ch.L.A.* XIII.570); *D.M.* 80 (not an original). Many other *diplomata* employ the same invocation elsewhere, usually right at the end where the place of issuing is recorded.

43. Gerberding 1987, pp. 48-9.

44. *Passio Leudegarii I*, 5, 19.

45. Stephen, *Uita Wilfridi*, 28.

46. *L.H.F.* 53; Fred., *cont.*, 10.

47. *Lex Ribuaria*, 36 (drawing on the *Edictus Chilperici*, 8, *Cap. Mer.*, p. 9); see also *Lex Ribuaria*, 42, 51.

48. *Lex Ribuaria*, 50.

49. Marculf I.1, 2.

50. Marculf I.12.

51. Marculf I.21, 25, 37.

52. Marculf I.34.

53. Tessier 1962, p. 17; cf. Pirenne 1934, pp. 168-9.

54. Barnwell 1992, p. 97.

55. Wallace-Hadrill 1962, p. 209.

56. This is clear from the opening formulae of the documents, e.g. 'Cum ante dies in nostri uel procerum nostrorum presencia Conpendio in palacio nostro resideremus ibique ueniens fimena nomene Acchildis Amalgario interpellauit dum dicerit ...' (*D.M.* 49 = *Ch.L.A.* XIII.567).

57. Fred. IV.44: '... cunctis illorum iustis peticionibus annuens preceptionebus roborauit' (J.M. Wallace-Hadrill's translation).

58. *D.M.* 83 (=*Ch.L.A.* XIV.590).

59. This is clear not only from the surviving *placita* (*D.M.* 34 [=*Ch.L.A.* XIII.561], 35 [=*Ch.L.A.* XIII.562], 59 [=*Ch.L.A.* XIV.572], 60 [=*Ch.L.A.* XIV.573], 64 [=*Ch.L.A.* XIV.575], 66 [*Ch.L.A.* XIV.576], 70 [=*Ch.L.A.* XIV.581], 73 [=*Ch.L.A.* XIV.584], 76-78 [*Ch.L.A.* XIV.585-587], 79 [not an original], and 83 [=*Ch.L.A.* XIV.590]), but also from Marculf I.25, 'Procolo de regis iuditio, cum de magna rem duo causantur simul', which states: 'Ergo cum nos in Dei nomen ibi in palatio nostro ad uniuersorum causas recto iuditio terminandas una cum domnis et patribus nostris episcopis uel cum plures obtimatibus nostris, illis episcopis, illi maiorem domus, illis ducibus, illis patriciis, illis referendariis, illis domesticis, illis siniscalcis, illis cobiculariis, et illi comes palati uel reliquis quam plures nostris fidelibus resederemus, ibique ueniens illi illo interpellauit, dum diceret ...'. See also Wood 1994a, pp. 261-2.

60. Balon 1968a, pp. 16-17.

61. Balon 1973, esp. pp. 7-11; on the Marchfield gatherings, see Bachrach 1974.

62. Fred. IV.54.

63. Fred. IV.89.

64. Gerberding 1987, p. 162.

65. Gerberding 1987, pp. 109-12.

66. *D.M.* 77 and 78 (=*Ch.L.A.* XIV.586 and 587); cf. *D.M.* 70 (=*Ch.L.A.* XIV.581), of 697.

67. Fouracre 1984b, pp. 10-11.

68. Anon., *Uita Ceolfrithi*, 32; see Wood 1994a, p. 268.

69. Wood 1994a, pp. 198-9.

70. *Uita Balthildis*, 4; see Nelson 1978, p. 74, and Stafford 1983, p. 99.

71. *Uita Audoini*, 16.

72. *D.M.* 29 (not an original); this is the only extant instance of two royal women signing a document of this kind.

73. Desideris of Auxerre, Fred. IV.19; Innocentius of Rodez, *L.H.* VI.38; perhaps Gregory of Tours, implied by Fort., *Carm.*, V.3 lines 11-15.

74. Fred. IV.24.

75. *Uita Eremberti*, 5; *Passio Leudegarii I*, 2, 3.

76. Fred IV.24, 27.

77. There is a list in *Uita Balthildis*, 9, but see also Nelson 1978, pp. 67-72.

78. *D.M.* 57 (=*Ch.L.A.* XIII.570).

79. *Uita Balthildis*, 10; for her patronage of Chelles, see especially caps 7 and

18, and the later *Uita Bertilae*, 7; cf. *D.M.* 33 (not an original), signed by both Balthild and Chlothar III.

80. Fred. IV.42.

81. *D.M.* 29.

82. Fred. IV.36; Jonas, *Uita Columbani*, I.18: 'Uerebatur enim, ne si abiectis concubinis reginam [Brunhild] aulae praefecisset, dignitates atque honoris suae modum amputasset'.

83. Jonas, *Uita Columbani*, I.19.

84. Nelson 1978, pp. 43-4.

85. Fred. IV.89.

86. *Uita Balthildis*, 5; Fred., *cont.*, 1.

87. Nantechild – *D.M.* 18 (=*Ch.L.A.* XIII.556); Balthild – *D.M.* 33, 38 (not originals).

88. *D.M.* 58 (not an original).

89. *D.M.* 28 and 25 (not originals), respectively.

90. Aega was placed in charge of Clovis II and ruled the palace and kingdom with the queen mother, Nantechild – see Fred. IV.79, 80.

Chapter 3

1. Barnwell 1992, pp. 101-2.

2. Fred. IV.38.

3. Fred. IV.36; Jonas, *Uita Columbani*, I.20.

4. Barnwell 1992, *passim*.

5. *Uita Eligii*, II.56.

6. *Uita Eligii*, II.20, 27.

7. Barnwell 1992, pp. 20-1.

8. *D.M.* 37 (=*Ch.L.A.* XIII.557), referring to Madeland and Amalbercth; 64 (=*Ch.L.A.* XIII.575), referring to Benedict and Chardoin; 66 (=*Ch.L.A.* XIV.576), referring to Chugobercth and Landric; 70 (=*Ch.L.A.* XIV.581), referring to Benedict and Ermedramn; cf. Marculf I.25, which lists the *seniscalc* as one of the types of official who could be present at the royal tribunal.

9. Tardif 1881, pp. 54-5, thought that they were the same as the *maiores domus*, but this cannot be so since both titles appear in forms which clearly demonstrate that they are not synonymous in Marculf I.25, the formula for a *placitum*, and a number of actual *placita*; while *maiores* appear singly, *seniscalces* appear in pairs.

10. Goffart 1982.

11. See Goffart 1982; Dagobert II, for example, imposed a 'humiliating' tax on the Franks – Stephen, *Uita Wilfridi*, 33; *Uita Eligii*, I.15 refers to a 'census publicus'.

12. Doehaerd 1949, pp. 32-3.

13. Gerberding 1987, pp. 165-6.

14. Fred. IV.75: Dagobert, 'tinsaurum quod suffecerit filium tradens ...'.

15. The evidence is discussed in Kaiser 1979, though the case for an episcopal takeover of this function is overstated.

16. *Lex Ribuaria*, 91; *D.M.* 82 (=*Ch.L.A.* XIV.589).

17. Fred. IV.67.

18. Although Rado, later a referendary of Clovis III, was in charge of *thesauri* (*Uita Audoini*, 1; *Uita Agili*, 19), his exact title is not recorded; even if he is assumed to have been a *thesaurarius*, these references reveal nothing of his functions beyond his association with treasure.

19. *Uita Desid. Cad. ep.*, 2, 5, 7; Desiderius was made bishop as a reward for his services while at the court – *ibid.*, 13-15; cf. *D.M.* 13 (not an original), which refers to his earlier career as *thesaurarius*. Desid., *Ep.*, II.2 shows abbot Bertegisel asking Desiderius for assistance in petitioning the king.

20. *Uita Eligii*, I.4. *D.M.* 19 (=*Ch.L.A.* XIII.558) and 21 (not an original), of Sigibert III's reign and, therefore, potentially within the same lifetime as the period referred to in the *Uita Eligii*, record the presence of an untitled Bobo; *D.M.* 22 (not an original), of the same period, records two men of this name, one a *dux*, and the other with no title: the latter could be the *thesaurarius*, but there is no way of being certain.

21. The only *camerarius* in the fourth book of Fredegar's *Chronicle* is Wandalmar (Fred. IV.4), but this relates to 585, a time before Gregory's work ended. Similarly absent are *aerarii*, who only appear, in the seventh century, in Marculf I.8.

22. For the sixth century, see Barnwell 1992, pp. 106-7.

23. That the omision not coincidental is perhaps indicated by their absence from the list of officials in Marculf's formula for a *placitum* – Marculf I.25.

24. Barnwell 1992, pp. 104-5.

25. Marculf I.25; *D.M.* 22 (not an original), 66 (=*Ch.L.A.* XIV.576) and 70 (=*Ch.L.A.* XIV.581).

26. The influence of *domestici* may be indicated by the fact that Arnulf is described in his *Uita* as 'domesticus adque consiliarius regis' under Theudebert II (*Uita Arnulfi*, 7), but extreme caution should be exercised in interpreting this, since the source is almost certainly an eighth-century document, projecting an image of powerful Arnulfings back into an earlier period – see Wood 1982, p. 69 n. 2.

27. *Lex Ribuaria*, 91.

28. *D.M.* 19 (=*Ch.L.A.* XIII.558); Pardessus, II.361.

29. Marculf I.39, II.52.

30. *Uita Eligii*, I.17.

31. Ganshof 1968, pp. 19, 36.

32. *D.M.* 57 (=*Ch.L.A.* XIII.570).

33. *D.M.* 66 (=*Ch.L.A.* XIV.576).

34. *D.M.* 67 (=*Ch.L.A.* XIV.577).

35. *D.M.* 70 (=*Ch.L.A.* XIV.581).

36. *D.M.* 71 (not an original).

37. Another courtier, Aghilus, though not undergoing as many transformations, may have been associated with the positions of *domesticus* and referendary in succession, though the latter title is not specifically applied to him: he signed *D.M.* 60 and 61 (=*Ch.L.A.* XIV.573 and 574) in a way usually associated with a referendary, and appears six years later (as Arghilus) in *D.M.* 70 (=*Ch.L.A.* XIV.581) as a *domesticus*.

38. Balon 1968a, pp. 1-22.

39. Fred. IV.44, 57, 75.

40. Classen 1956, pp. 53-4; cf. Levillain 1911, pp. 105-7; Honoré 1994, pp. 43-4.

41. Classen 1956, p. 53; Levillain 1911, pp. 113-16, though he differs from Classen in suggesting that it was only a memorandum, later used as the basis of the final draft, which was presented to the king.

42. *D.M.* 47 (=*Ch.L.A.* XIII.566), see Jusselin 1907, pp. 489-90; *D.M.* 48 (=*Ch.L.A.* XIII.565), see Jusselin 1907, pp. 488-9; *D.M.* 57 (=*Ch.L.A.* XIII.570), see Jusselin 1905, p. 366; *D.M.* 61 (=*Ch.L.A.* XIV.574), see Jusselin 1907, p. 497; *D.M.* 67 (=*Ch.L.A.* XIV.577), see Jusselin 1907, pp. 498-9; *D.M.* 70 (=*Ch.L.A.* XIV.581), see Jusselin 1907, p. 500; *D.M.* 71 (not an original), see Jusselin 1907, p. 500; *D.M.* 72 (=*Ch.L.A.* XIV.583), see Jusselin 1907, pp. 501-2.

43. Classen 1956, pp. 48-9; Levillain 1931, pp. 7-13.

44. *D.M.* 42 (not an original): 'Ut autem haec scriptio firma et stabilis in aeuum permaneat et a nullo nostrorum successorum sit permutanda, nostro nomine insigniri et anuli impressione iussimus sigillari'; *D.M.* 44 (also not an original): 'Et ut haec praesens auctoritas firmior sit, manu nostra uel anulo nostro subter eam decreuimus roborari'.

45. *Uita Agili*, 20; *Uita Ansberti*, 4 (cf. cap. 2); cf. *Uita Audoini*, 2, and *Uita Boniti*, 2; see also *Uita Desid. ep. Biturc.*, 2, which relates to the sixth century.

46. Levillain 1911, esp. p. 116. This interpretation can be carried further (though with less certainty), and has been applied to the case of Hamingus, whose name appears in isolation at the end of the *Edict of Paris* (*Cap. Mer.*, p. 23; see Bresslau 1912-58, p. 365), presumably by comparison with the *Decree* of Childebert II (*Cap. Mer.*, p. 17), at the end of which the name of Asclepiodotus appears with the *recognouit* formula.

47. *D.M.* 15 (not an original); Dado's career is one of the best-known of the seventh century: Fred. IV.78 confirms that he was a referendary in 635; a private charter, Pardessus II.275, provides the same evidence for 636; it is therefore likely that the association of his name with the *optolit* formula in *D.M.* 14 (not an original), of 631, occurred while he occupied the same office. For other references to his career, see Ebling 1974, no. 141.

48. *D.M.* 66 (=*Ch.L.A.* XIV.576); interpretation of this aspect of the document is not, however, entirely clear: although the name of Walderamn appears with the *recognouit* formula in cursive, the tironian notes contain another *recognouit* clause in which the name is that of Attalus.

49. See Classen 1956, pp. 51-3 and *idem* 1955, pp. 55-6. The parallels with Roman practice are not exact, since the referendary seems to have taken over some (but not all) of the functions earlier associated with the *magister libellorum* (master of petitions) – see Honoré 1994, pp. 43-4, and Wilcken 1920, pp. 6-7. For the non-identity of the referendary and the *magister*, see Bury 1910, followed by Boak 1915, pp. 102-3, and Teitler 1985, p. 285 n. 75, *contra* Mommsen 1910, p. 421.

50. See, for example, Bergmann 1976, pp. 18-19.

51. *D.M.* 66 (=*Ch.L.A.* XIV.576); cf. *D.M.* 35 (=*Ch.L.A.* XIII.562), where there are two; Marculf I.25; Fred. IV.78.

52. *N.I.* 10.

53. *D.M.* 70 (=*Ch.L.A.* XIV.581), 78 (=*Ch.L.A.* XIV.587), 79 and 94 (not originals).

54. Ganz 1983, p. 64, who sees it as the first step towards the ending of the office, which did not survive into the Carolingian period – see Levillain 1911, p. 108.

55. *D.M.* 78 (=*Ch.L.A.* XIV.587).

56. *D.M.* 30 (not an original), of 673: 'Childericus rex recognouit'.

57. *Uita Ansberti*, 4; *Uita Audoini*, 1; *Uita Boniti*, 2.

58. For imperial parallels, see *C.I.* XV.2 and *N.I.* 124; cf. Procopius, *De Bello Persico*, II.23.6, and *Historia Arcana*, XIV.11-12; see also *N.I.* 10 and 113.

59. Fred. IV.40.

60. Fred. IV.78.

61. *D.M.* 46 (not an original), and 48 (=*Ch.L.A* XIII.565).

62. Bury 1910, pp. 28-9.

63. Constantine VII, *De Ceremoniis*, 86.

64. *Uita Eligii*, II.56, cf. 20, 27.

65. *D.M.* 87 (=*Ch.L.A.* XIV.593), Jusselin 1907, p. 505.

66. *D.M.* 82 (=*Ch.L.A.* XIV.589); Jusselin 1907, p. 504, made nothing of the phrase in front of Ragamfred's name; Mentz 1942, p. 226 (whose readings are regarded with some suspicion – see Chapter 1, n. 28), thought it reads '[...]-uit decretante Raganfrido maiore domus' – an otherwise unknown formula.

67. *D.M.* 81 (=*Ch.L.A.* XIV.588), Jusselin 1907, p. 504; Mentz 1942, p. 207, produced an entirely different reading.
68. *D.M.* 84 (=*Ch.L.A.* XIV.591), Jusselin 1907, p. 505; cf. Mentz 1942, p. 226, who identifies the official as Ragamfred.
69. *D.M.* 77 (=*Ch.L.A.* XIV.586), Jusselin 1907, pp. 503-4.
70. Jusselin 1907, pp. 503-4; Ganz 1983, pp. 63-5.
71. Bury 1910, *contra* Mommsen 1910, p. 421. Bury was later supported by Boak 1915, pp. 102-3 and, more recently, by Teitler 1985, p. 285 n. 75.
72. *D.M.* 10 (=*Ch.L.A.* XIII.552); *D.M.* 85 (not an original); *D.M.* 40, of questionable authenticity, claims to have been written by Syggo, *diaconus*.
73. *D.M.* 46 (not an original).
74. A.H.M. Jones 1964, pp. 548, 572.
75. *Lex Ribuaria*, 62 gives clear evidence that *cancellarii* wrote documents, but it is not clear that the provision necessarily refers to royal officials; less equivocal is cap. 91, in which *cancellarii* appear in a list of royal officials who could act as judges.
76. Ganshof 1968, p. 20.
77. Classen 1956, p. 56; cf. *idem* 1955, pp. 84-7.
78. Riché 1962, p. 285; as Riché suggests, the source could have been either the *Lex Romama Uisigothorum* or a copy of the rescript itself.
79. Murray 1994.
80. Classen 1956, p. 57.
81. Riché 1962, pp. 284-5, comments on the quality of the Latin of the *diplomata*.
82. For tironian notes in Merovingian Gaul – and not only in the royal administration – see Ganz 1983.
83. *C.Th.* IX.19.3; see Götze 1965-6, pp. 4, 8-24, and Vezin 1980, where similar evidence for Visigothic documents is discussed – see Chapter 8 below.
84. Götze 1965-6, p. 8.
85. On sixth-century *maiores* see Barnwell 1992, pp. 102-3.
86. *Passio Leudegarii I*, 4: Ebroin, 'qui sub rege Chlothario tunc regebat palatium ...'; cf. Fort., *Carm.*, IV.13, line 5: 'ipse palatinam rexit [*sc.* Servilio] ...'.
87. Fred. IV.42.
88. McKitterick 1983, pp. 22-3; cf. Werner 1973, pp. 489-90. Schöne 1856, pp. 69-70, went so far as to see the position of *maior domus* as deriving from that of the Roman praetorian prefect, the highest-ranking and vice-imperial provincial governor.
89. Fouracre 1984a, p. 8.
90. Fred. IV.54.
91. Heidrich 1989, pp. 217-18.
92. The equation is suggested by *Uita Eligii*, II.56, cf. II.20, 27; see Barnwell 1992, pp. 102, 141-2.
93. Fred. III.58-9; for discussion of the case see Barnwell 1992, p. 103.
94. Heidrich 1989, p. 217.
95. Fred. IV.52.
96. Fouracre 1984a, p. 8, makes a similar suggestion.
97. Wunder 1991, pp. 47-51.
98. Fred. IV.61; see Wallace-Hadrill's translation, pp. 50-1 and the note there for one interpretation, and Wunder 1991, p. 52, for another.
99. Fred. IV.79-80; for explicit references to him as *maior*, see Fred. IV.84-5.
100. Fred. IV.62.
101. A.H.M. Jones 1964, p. 568; cf. Bury 1958, p. 33.
102. Fred. IV.86.
103. Fred. IV.88.

104. See the disagreement, in more general terms, between Heidrich 1965-6, p. 90, and Fouracre, 1984a, p. 9.

105. Fred. IV.89.

106. *L.H.F.* 43. For discussions of these events, see Wood 1994a, pp. 222-4; Ewig 1976b, pp. 206-10; Dupraz 1948, chapter 4; and, for a different chronology, Gerberding 1987, chapter IV.

107. *L.H.F.* 43; see Wood 1994a, p. 222.

108. *Passio Leudegarii I*, 4.

109. Wood 1994a, p. 238.

110. Heidrich 1989, pp. 218-20.

111. See Ewig 1976b, pp. 210-21.

112. Wood 1994a, p. 235.

113. *L.H.F.* 47; Fred., *cont.*, 4.

114. *L.H.F.* 48.

115. Gerberding 1987, pp. 93-4.

116. Fred., *cont.*, 5; Werner 1973, pp. 493-4.

117. Fouracre 1984b, pp. 6-7, 10-11; Gerberding 1987, pp. 94-109.

118. *D.M.* 70 (=*Ch.L.A.* XIV.581), and 77-8 (=*Ch.L.A.* XIV.586-7).

119. *L.H.F.* 49, 51; Fred., *cont.*, 7, 8.

120. Fred., *cont.*, 8; *L.H.F.* 51.

121. Fouracre 1984b, pp. 13-14.

122. *D.M.* 47 (=*Ch.L.A.*XIII.566) and 48 (=*Ch.L.A.* XIII.565), with Jusselin 1907, pp. 488-90, date from the minority of Theuderic III; *D.M.* 67 (=*Ch.L.A.* XIV.577) and 71 (not an original), with Jusselin 1907, pp. 498-500, from that of Childebert III. *D.M.* 72 (=*Ch.L.A.* XIV.583), with Jusselin 1907, pp. 501-2 is also of Childebert's reign but cannot be dated within it – it may, therefore, also belong to the period of minority. The only certain exception to the association of the phrase with minorities is *D.M.* 57 (=*Ch.L.A.* XIII.570) – see Jusselin 1905, p. 366.

123. See Marculf I.25, and the surviving *placita*; see also *Lex Ribuaria*, 91, which indicates that *maiores* could be judges.

124. Desid., *Ep.*, I.2.

125. *Uita Fursei*, 9, cf. *Uirtutes Fursei*, 5.

126. *Passio Praeiecti*, 22.

127. Marculf I.34.

128. Fred. IV.45.

129. Fred. IV.85.

130. *Uita Condedi*, 8.

131. Suggested by a private charter of 663, Pardessus II.348, in which three *maiores* are mentioned, against this see Heidrich 1989, pp. 220-2.

132. Heidrich 1965-6, esp. pp. 78-9.

Chapter 4

1. For this threefold division of *comites*, see Dill 1926, p. 142; cf. Fustel de Coulanges 1930, pp. 202-3. Bachrach 1972, pp. 80-1, omits those with specific offices in the court.

2. Irsigler 1969, pp. 128-9.

3. Barnwell 1992, pp. 107-8.

4. Fred. IV.30.

5. Fred. IV.40; although not explicitly a *comes stabuli* in this chapter, he is so decribed in cap. 42, relating to the same year (613).

6. Marculf I.25.

7. Fred. IV.90.

8. *Passio Leudegarii I*, 33; *Passio Praeiecti*, 26, which refers to Ebroin as *comes palatii* at the time of Leodegar's martyrdom – is this a mistake for *maior domus*?

9. The relevant ones are: *D.M.* 34-5 (=*Ch.L.A.* XIII.561-2), 59-60 (=*Ch.L.A.* XIV.572-3), 64 (=*Ch.L.A.* XIV.575), 70 (=*Ch.L.A.* XIV.581), 73 (=*Ch.L.A.* XIV.584), 76-8 (=*Ch.L.A.* XIV.585-7), 79 (not an original), and 83 (=*Ch.L.A.* XIV.590).

10. Marculf I.25, 37-8.

11. Tessier 1962, p. 36; Bergmann 1976, pp. 22-47.

12. *D.M.* 94 (not an original), of 726.

13. For the sixth century, see Barnwell 1992, p. 108, with pp. 25-6 for the fifth-century western imperial evidence.

14. *D.M.* 79 (not an original): '... inluster uir Ingobertus, qui ad uice itemque inluster uir Ratbertho, comite palate nostro, adestare uidebatur, testimoniauit ...'

15. *D.M.* 78 (=*Ch.L.A.* XIV.587).

16. *D.M.* 66 (=*Ch.L.A.* XIV.576) and 73 (=*Ch.L.A.* XIV.584).

17. *D.M.* 66 (=*Ch.L.A.* XIV.576), and 77 (=*Ch.L.A.* XIV.586).

18. On the synonymity of the two terms, see Fustel de Coulanges 1930, p. 203 and, more recently, Murray 1986; although Claude 1964 sees a difference between the titles in the sixth century (refuted by Murray), he accepted their identity for the seventh.

19. Fred. IV.87.

20. *Uita Eligii*, I.66.

21. *D.M.* 77 (=*Ch.L.A.* XIV.586).

22. *Uita Eligii*, I.50; I.55 describes him simply as 'graphio'.

23. Fred. IV.37 – they opposed the invasion of Alemannia, *c.* 610, 'cum citeris de ipso pago comitebus', implying that there were other *comites* stationed in the region; for Herpin, see also Fred. IV.43.

24. *Uita Eligii*, II.43.

25. *Uita Desid. Cad. ep.*, 2.

26. Those listed above are the only incontrovertible ones where the name, title and name of the place appear in a single reference; in a small number of other instances the relationship between the official and the place can be inferred – e.g., Genesius can be seen to have been *comes* in Auvergne by taking the evidence of chapters 14 and 15 of the *Passio Praeiecti* together.

27. See Lewis 1976, esp. pp. 387-9, and Wolfram 1988, pp. 213-14.

28. *D.M.* 66 (=*Ch.L.A.* XIV.576).

29. Marculf I.25.

30. *Lex Ribuaria*, 36, 51, 91.

31. Implicit in *Lex Ribuaria*, 54.

32. The charters which are addressed to named *comites* are *D.M.* 15 (not an original), 18 (=*Ch.L.A.* XIII.556), 23, 30 and 62 (not originals); several others are addressed to unnamed *comites*; whether the *comites* are named or not, they are often associated with other officials.

33. *D.M.* 25 (not an original).

34. Fustel de Coulanges 1930, pp. 222-3.

35. Marculf I.8, 28, 39, 40.

36. In the former category (from before 721) are *D.M.* 13 (not an original), 14 (=*Ch.L.A.* XIII.551), and 28 (not an original); in the latter are *D.M.* 38 (not an original), 51 (=*Ch.L.A.* XIII.568), 63, 74 and 86 (not originals); combinations of the two practices are found in *D.M.* 15 (not an original), 18 (=*Ch.L.A.* XIII.556), 44 (not an original). It is possible that there is a chronological progression in the formula used, with a gradual shift from named officials or specific offices to a more generic description of the addressees, though this need have no administrative significance.

37. *D.M.* 77 (=*Ch.L.A.* XIV.586).

38. *Form. Andecau.*, 50.

39. Marculf I.8: 'Praespicuae regalis in hoc perfectae conlaudatur clementia, ut inter cuncto populo bonitas et uigilantia requeratur personarum, nec facile cuilibet iudiciaria conuenit committere dignitatem, nisi prius fides seo strinuetas uideatur esse probata. Ergo dum et fidem et utilitatem tuam uidemur habere conpertam, ideo tibi accionem comitiae, ducatus aut patriciatus in pago illo, quem antecessor tuos illi usque nunc uisus est egisse, tibi ad agendum regendumque commissemus, ita ut semper erga regimine nostro fidem inlibata custodias, et omnis populus ibidem commanentes, tam Franci, Romani, Burgundionis uel reliquas nationis, sub tuo regimine et gubernatione degant et moderentur, et eos recto tramite secundum lege et consuetudine eorum regas, uiduis et pupillis maximus defensor appareas, latronum et malefactorum scelera a te seuerissimae repremantur, ut populi bene uiuentes sub tuo regimine gaudentes debeant consistere quieti; et quicquid de ipsa accione in fisci dicionibus speratur, per uosmet ipsos annis singulis nostris aerariis inferatur.'

40. Fred. IV.37, 87.

41. Barnwell 1992, pp. 110-11.

42. Claude 1964, pp. 28-9; Durliat 1979, esp. pp. 238-9.

43. Desid., *Ep.*, I.13, II.20.

44. *Passio Leudegarii I*, 2.

45. *Passio Leudegarii I*, 20.

46. E. James 1983; Wood 1983a, pp. 50-1 discusses the evidence for the activities of bishops in Clermont.

47. Seventh-century examples include: Ansebert* of Rouen (*Uita Ansberti*, 4); Aetherius of Lyons (*Uita Austrigisili*, I.5, and Fred. IV.22); Audoin* (=Dado) of Rouen (*Uita Audoini*, 2; *Uita Agili*, 20; *Uita Amandi*, I.17); Bonitus* of Clermont (*Uita Boniti*, 2); Desiderius of Cahors (*Uita Desid. Cad. ep.*, 2, 4, 7; cf. *D.M.* 13 [not an original]); Eligius of Noyon (*Uita Eligii*, I.4). Those marked with an asterisk were referendaries while at court, as are the sixth-century examples in Barnwell 1992, p. 208 n. 116.

48. Fred. IV.42.

49. Jonas, *Uita Columbani*, I.23.

50. *Uita Amandi*, 14; *Uita Germani Grand.*, 11.

51. Bachrach 1972, p. 89, seems to imply that this was new in the seventh century, but such is not the case – see Barnwell 1992, p. 111.

52. Fred. IV.85.

53. Fred. IV.77.

54. Fred. IV.87.

55. Fred. IV.87; this kind of possibility is discussed in Heidrich 1965-6, pp. 89-90.

56. Fred. IV.21.

57. Fred. IV.77.

58. E.g., *Lex Ribuaria*, 33, 34, 37, 75; Fred. IV.20, 37-8; *L.H.F.* 48, cf. Fred., *cont.*, 6.

59. Pardessus, II.348.

60. Marculf I.8.

61. Barnwell 1992, p. 112.

62. Fred. IV.68.

63. Fred. IV.77.

64. See Fred. IV. 73, relating to Venerandus who, according to the later *Gesta Dagoberti*, 29, may have been created *dux* and, therefore, have held a specific office; and Fred. IV.78, where eleven *duces* are listed as having participated in Dagobert's campaign against the Gascons – the meaning is not entirely clear, but it is likely that at least some of the men listed held the office of *dux*, since the passage also refers to *comites* who fought with no *dux* over them; this is difficult to understand if the *duces* are here simply military leaders. For a different interpretation, see Bachrach 1972, p. 87.

65. Fred. IV.8, 88; Fred., *cont.*, 27, referring to the 690s; *Lex Alamannorum*, Codex A, *incipit.*

66. Fred. IV.77, 87; cf. 68, 74-5; see also Wood 1994a, pp. 162-3.

67. Wood 1994a, pp. 161-2, cf. 116-17.

68. Fred. IV.13, 43.

69. Fred. IV.14, see also IV.18 and *L.H.* VIII.18, X.3; *Passio Leudegarii I*, 25; *L.H.F.* 48, cf. Fred., *cont.*, 6. For a discussion of the importance of Champagne in the politics of Neustria and Austrasia, see Rouche 1989, pp. 9-10.

70. Fred. IV.20, 37-8.

71. For the *ducatus* see Fred. IV.21; Fred., *cont.*, 10, cf. *L.H.F.* 53; possibly also Fred. IV.78 with 55; see also the preface and cap. 4 of the Council of Bordeaux of 663x675 – *Concilia Galliae*, vol. 2 pp. 312-13. The history of the area is discussed in Boussard 1973, pp. 10-11, Werner 1973, pp. 500-3, and Rouche 1979, esp. pp. 104-9.

72. Rouche 1989, pp. 9-10.

73. Jonas, *Uita Columbani*, I.14.

74. *Passio Desiderii et Reginfredi*, 9, 'dux regionis illius'.

75. *D.A.* 4.

76. Heidrich 1965-6, pp. 89-91 suggests something similar; see also Irsigler 1969, pp. 128-9 and Sprandel 1957, p. 52.

77. E.g., *D.M.* 14 (=*Ch.L.A.* XIII.551) and 62 (not an original), where the officials are named, and 28 and 30 (not originals), where they are not.

78. *D.M.* 14 (=*Ch.L.A.* XIII.551) and 18 (=*Ch.L.A.* XIII.556).

79. Fred. IV.90.

80. Fred. IV.78.

81. Lewis 1976, p. 392.

82. Marculf I.8; the text is at n. 39 above.

83. *Lex Ribuaria*, 51.

84. *D.M.* 13 (not an original; cf. *Uita Desid. Cad. ep.*, 13), 14 (=*Ch.L.A.* XIII.551), 15 (not an original), 18 (=*Ch.L.A.* XIII.556), 26, 28, 30, 42, 44 (none of which is an original), 48 (=*Ch.L.A.* XIII.565), 62 (not an original). See also Marculf II.49.

85. *D.M.* 29 (not an original).

86. Marculf I.25.

87. Lewis 1976, pp. 388-9, suggests that the *optimates*, who 'are clearly distinguished from named counts', may be *duces*.

88. Fred. IV.54, 58.

89. Fred. IV.67.

90. Fred. IV.73.

91. Heidrich 1965-6, p. 89. That the power of all *duces* – both in the frontier or non-Frankish areas and within the core of the *regnum Francorum* – was derived from the same late Roman source is argued by Werner 1973, pp. 194-5; for further detail on late Roman *duces*, see Barnwell 1992, pp. 38-41.

92. Heidrich 1965-6, p. 105.

93. Wood 1994a, p. 161.

94. Fred. IV.77, 87; see Werner 1973, pp. 497-9.

95. Fred. IV.68, 74-5, 77; see Wood 1994a, p. 162.

96. Fred. IV.87.

97. Wood 1994a, p. 163.

98. Wood 1994a, pp. 116-17, 162-3.

99. Geary 1988, p. 210.

100. Gerberding 1987, pp. 111-12.

101. Werner 1973, pp. 503-4; cf. pp. 501-3 for a suggestion that the Aquitanians were still classed as Franks, at least by those outside the kingdom.
102. Marculf I.25.
103. Barnwell 1992, p. 113, cf. pp. 43-7.
104. *Passio Praeiecti*, 23; *Passio Leudegarii I*, 9.
105. Fred. IV.29.
106. Fred. IV.78; cf. *Uita Eligii*, II.28.
107. Fred. IV.24; he later became Theuderic II's *maior domus* – Fred. IV.27.
108. The other seventh-century patricians are Alethius, Fred. IV.42-3, and Quolen, Fred. IV.18, but nothing is known of them; the latter may have been patrician in Provence since Fredegar's report of his appointment immediately precedes an account of plague in that area, but the connection is not conclusive, expecially since the chapter also refers to other parts of the kingdom.
109. *H.E.* III.19; *Uita Fursei*, 9; *Uirtutes Fursei*, 5; for other examples, see Heidrich 1965-6, pp. 93-8.
110. Marculf I.25; the text is in n. 39, above.
111. *Lex Ribuaria*, 51; *Passio Praeiecti*, 23-4; *Passio Leudegarii I*, 9.
112. Fred. IV.27.
113. Fred. IV.78 and, implicitly, IV.42.
114. Marculf II.49; *D.M.* 48 (=*Ch.L.A.* XIII.565).

Chapter 5

1. See Wood 1994a, pp. 257-8 for a summary of the account provided in the influential *Annales Mettenses Priores*.
2. *L.H.* V, *praefatio*.
3. Werner 1973, pp. 512-13.
4. *Lex Ribuaria*, 51, 91.

Introduction to Part II

1. For this kind of interpretation, see, in English, e.g., Dykes Shaw 1906, or Bachrach 1973, esp. pp. 12-13; for an exposition of varying interpretations see García Moreno 1975, chapter 1.
2. Collins 1989, esp. chapter 1.
3. Claude 1971a, pp. 208-9.
4. Ewig, 1969, pp. 69-70; cf. García Moreno 1974a, p. 7.
5. Claude 1971a, esp. p. 69; Sánchez-Albornoz y Menduiña 1971a, p. 184.

Chapter 6

1. Hillgarth 1966, p. 495.
2. K.B. Wolf 1990, p. 1.
3. Hillgarth 1970, pp. 266-9, 281-3, 308-9; cf. K.B. Wolf 1990, pp. 10-11.
4. Hillgarth 1970, pp. 296-8; on the *H.G.*, see also Reydellet 1970.
5. Váquez de Parga 1961, p. 105.
6. Hillgarth 1970, pp. 298-9.
7. K.B. Wolf 1990, pp. 19-21.
8. *H.G.* 1-4.
9. Hillgarth 1970, pp. 298-9.
10. Fontaine 1960, p. 70 n. 99.
11. *H.G.* 62-3.
12. Reydellet 1981, p. 526.
13. K.B. Wolf 1990, pp. 14-15.

14. Collins 1977, pp. 42-4; Brunhölzl 1990, p. 104.

15. *Historia Wambae*, 10, 25 and the *iudicium* liken the king to David; see also Braulio, *Ep.*, 37 and John of Biclaro, *s.a.* 589, p. 218. For a modern discussion, see Wallace-Hadrill 1971, pp. 53-5.

16. *Historia Wambae*, 1.

17. Collins 1977, pp. 47-8, *contra* Hillgarth 1970, p. 300, who sees it as propaganda for Wamba's reign.

18. Thompson 1969, p. 163; Fontaine 1980, pp. 118-25.

19. Hillgarth 1970, pp. 305-7.

20. Brunhölzl 1990, p. 94.

21. Diesner 1979, pp. 25-6.

22. They are *Ep. Wis.*, 2, 4, 7-9; the collection also includes three letters addressed to Sisebut – nos 3, 5 and 6.

23. For a summary of the history of the law code, see Nehlsen 1978, col. 1971.

24. Wilhelmsen 1978, p. 144, notes that some form of the word 'iudex' is found in every version of the title; cf. Collins 1983a, p. 125.

25. *L.U.* V.4.22.

26. Wilhelmsen 1978, p. 144.

27. *L.U.* IV.5.6.

28. For a similar observation, see Thomspon 1969, p. 127.

29. *L.U.* VII.5.1, cf 5.2 of Chindasuinth, which may have superseded the earlier law which had been inserted by Leovigild; the older law is closely paralleled by Paul, *Sententiae*, V.25.1.

30. *L.U.* II.1.25.

31. Canellas López 1979 provides a comprehensive collection of 231 documents which were produced in the Visigothic era, of which the vast majority are private. Of those private documents, some of the most significant are found in the collection of instruments inscribed on slate, fully edited in Velázquez Soriano 1989 (more accessibly, but partially and inaccurately, in Gómez Moreno 1966), and in five fragmentary instruments written on parchment – see Canellas López 1979, nos 119, 178, 192, 209, and 229, and, more fully, Mundó Marcet 1974.

32. Canellas López 1979, pp. 17-16, cf. Brunner 1887-92, vol. 1 pp. 402-3.

33. Canellas López 1979, no. 115.

34. The best accounts of the councils are Orlandis and Ramos-Lissón 1981, and Schwöbel 1982; but García Villada 1931, and Andrés Marcos 1929 are still useful.

35. See Hillgarth 1966, and Orlandis and Ramon-Lissón 1981, pp. 343-6; this matter is further discussed in Chapter 7.

Chapter 7

1. The literature on this is vast: see, for example, Barbero de Aguilera 1970; D'Abadal y de Vinyals 1960; Ferreirós 1970; Gallego Blanco 1974; Gibert 1969; Orlandis 1962a and 1962e; see also Claude 1971a, *passim*, and Collins 1983a, pp. 113-15.

2. Gibert 1969, p. 464; Collins 1983a, pp. 113-14; Collins 1989, pp. 9-10.

3. For an account of Chindasuith's attempts to secure his power, see Diesner 1979.

4. Gibert 1956, p. 464; Ferreirós 1970, p. 676; Claude 1971a, pp. 196-8.

5. Liuva I made Leovigild *consors regni* – John of Biclaro, *s.a.* 569, p. 212, and *H.G.* 48; Leovigild made Reccared I and Hermenegild *consortes regni* – John of Biclaro, *s.a.* 573, p. 213; Sisebut may have made Reccared II *consors regni* – see Claude 1971a, p. 92; Suinthila made Riccimer *consors regni* – *H.G.* 65; Chinthila nominated Tulga – Fred. IV.82; Chindasuinth made Reccesuinth *consors regni* – see Claude 1971a, p. 131, citing Braulio, *Ep.*, 31 and 37; Wamba nominated Ervig

– XII Toledo, p. 386; Ervig nominated Egica – *Laterculus regnum Visigothorum*, 49, p. 468; Ervig made Wittiza *consors regni* – *Chronicle of 754*, 58, p. 350, cf. *Chronicle of Alfonso III*, Roda Version, 4, p. 11. It is also possible that Roderic shared rule with Achila, though the relationship between the two men is unknown – see Collins 1989, pp. 32-3.

6. Claude 1971a, pp. 59-60; G. Wolf 1988, pp. 218-21.

7. John of Biclaro, *s.a.* 579, p. 215.

8. *L.U.* III.5.2.

9. Gibert 1956, pp. 552-7, argues that the former Roman provinces maintained their identity throughout the seventh century (cf. Claude 1970, p. 93), while as late as *c.* 544, Theudis was militarily active in Africa, perhaps trying to exert his authority throughout the former Roman Spanish diocese – *H.G.* 42, discussed in Barnwell 1992, p. 77.

10. *H.G.* 51, cf. *U.P.E.* V.6.22; on the significance of this, see Schramm, 1954-78, vol. I, pp. 317-18. In the fifth century, Theoderic II had used the magistrates' *sella*, rather than a throne – see Barnwell 1992, pp. 72-3. For a different view, see McCormick 1986, pp. 298-300.

11. Barnwell 1992, p. 118.

12. *Historia Wambae*, 27.

13. John of Biclaro, *s.a.* 578, p. 215; *H.G.* 51. The evidence concerning Reccopolis is conveniently gathered in Raddatz 1964, and Claude 1965. As with the throne, there is also a parallel here with the Vandals, Geiseric having founded the city of Hunericopolis – see Courtois 1955, p. 243.

14. See Collins 1980, pp. 212-13.

15. *L.U.* IX.1.21.

16. See Collins 1980, p. 198.

17. *Historia Wambae*, 3; the precise location of the villa is unknown, though it lies in the diocese of Salamanca – Ewig 1976d, p. 368.

18. See Mommsen's introduction to Isidore's *H.G.*, at p. 260, and Ewig 1976d, p. 368.

19. John of Biclaro, *s.a.* 590, pp. 219-20; see McCormick 1986, pp. 303-4.

20. *Historia Wambae*, 30; for the survival of similar techniques into the eighth century, see Collins 1989, p. 133.

21. For imperial practices, see McCormick 1986, pp. 35-111.

22. The standard work on Visigothic coins is Miles 1952, but see the important revisions to the chronology relating to Leovigild's reign proposed in Grierson and Blackburn 1986, pp. 46-51.

23. Miles 1952, pp. 44-6.

24. Collins 1983b, pp. 27-30; see also Barnwell 1992, pp. 95-6.

25. Miles 1952, pp. 23-9.

26. *L.U.* IV.2.19 (*misericordia*); II.1.8 (*pietas*).

27. XV Toledo, *tomus* of Egica, pp. 450 and 464.

28. XVI Toledo, 1, 2, pp. 497-500; see Claude 1971a, pp. 76-7. For other royal titles see Diaz y Diaz 1976b.

29. Miles 1952, p. 24; see also Saitta 1979, pp. 120-1 and n. 125.

30. Thompson 1969, pp. 70-3, citing Miles 1952, pp. 85, 108, 110, 111, 187, 190-2; cf. Grierson and Blackburn 1986, p. 50.

31. Ewig 1976g, p. 25 n. 97, notes that the phrase 'In Dei nomine' was first linked to the king's title in 653.

32. Collins 1980, pp. 204-5; Grierson and Blackburn 1986, p. 52.

33. *L.U.* III.5.2: 'Flauuius Reccaredus rex uniuersis prouinciis Domino ordinante ad regni nostri dicionem pertinentibus'.

34. V Toledo, 3.

35. Collins 1977, p. 47.

36. *Historia Wambae*, 2, 4.

37. *Historia Wambae*, 3.

38. Collins 1977, pp. 41-6.

39. *Epistola Pauli perfidi, qui tyrannice rebellionem in Gallias fecit Wambani principis magni*, one of the documents appended to Julian's *Historia Wambae*, p. 500: the letter begins, 'In nomine Domini Flauius Paulus unctus rex orientalis Wambani regi austro …'.

40. *Historia Wambae*, 8.

41. See McCormick 1986, p. 315, and the earlier literature cited there.

42. Esp. IV Toledo 75, p. 186 (on which see Orlandis and Ramos Lissón 1981, pp. 166-7), and XII Toledo, *tomus* of Ervig, p. 383; cf. the portrayal of Egica in XVI Toledo, p. 482.

43. Isidore, *Etymologiae*, III.51.4-6; see Anton 1972, pp. 269-71.

44. Hillgarth 1970, pp. 280-1.

45. Braulio, *Ep.*, 37: 'Unde caelorum regem et sedium omnium rectorem supplici prece deposcimus, qui et Moysi Iesum successorem, et in Dauid throno filium eius constituit Salomonem, ut clementer insinuet uestris animis ea quae suggerimus …'.

46. Braulio, *Ep.*, 32.

47. Braulio, *Ep.*, 35.

48. Thompson 1969, p. 188.

49. Sisebut, Letter to Isidore, lines 4-8:

> At nos congeries obnubit turbida rerum
> Ferratique premunt milleno milite; curae
> Legiferaeque crepant, latrant fora, classica turbant,
> Et trans Oceanum ferimur porro, usque niuosus
> Cum teneat Uasco nec parcat Cantaber horrens.

50. Collins 1983a, pp. 108-9.

51. Collins 1989, p. 99, notes that late seventh-century military undertakings seem to have been rare, but the extent to which this is a function of the lack of a good narrative source is unclear.

52. John of Biclaro, *s.a.* 570-572, pp. 212-15, and *s.a.* 585, p. 217.

53. *H.G.* 54.

54. *H.G.* 58.

55. *H.G.* 61: 'In bellicis quoque documentis ac uictoriis clarus. Astures enim rebellantes misso exercitu in dicionem suam reduxit. Roccones montibus arduis undique consaeptos per duces deuicit. De Romanis quoque praesens bis feliciter triumphauit …' The identity of the Ruccones is not known – see Thompson 1969, p. 161.

56. *H.G.* 62-4; similarly, Gundemar, *H.G.* 59.

57. Isidore, *Etymologiae*, IX.3.4-6: 'Reges a regendi uocati … Non autem regit, qui non corrigit. Recte igitur faciendo regis nomen tenetur, peccando amittitur. Unde et apud ueteres tale erat prouerbium: "Rex eris si recte facias: si non facias, non eris". Regiae uirtutes praecipue duae: iustitia et pietas. Plus autem in regibus laudatur pietas; nam iustitia per se seuera est.' Cf. his *Sententiae*, III.47.1, 48.5, 49.3, 50.6, 51.3-6.

58. *H.G.* 35, 51.

59. Collins 1983a, pp. 119-20. Of the kings whose laws are included in the *L.U.*, Ervig and Egica are also associated with conciliar legislation (XIII and XV Toledo), while of those in whose names no 'secular' laws survive, Sisenand and Chintila have such association (IV-VI Toledo).

60. *H.G.* 51.

61. *L.U.*, *supplementum*, I.2.

62. One of the clearest examples of this is *L.U.* IX.1.21, a Novel issued by Egica, which records the date and place at which it was promulgated.

63. See Barnwell 1992, esp. pp. 8-9, 11, 85-7.

64. García Gallo 1974, p. 455.

65. Orlandis and Ramos-Lissón 1981, pp. 343-6.

66. *L.U.* II.1.4, 1.10, 1.11, 1.13, 1.14.

67. *L.U.* VII.5.9.

68. *L.U.* II.1.13.

69. Barnwell 1992, pp. 85-6.

70. *L.U.* IX.2.8.

71. For a discussion of the issues concerning this, see Barnwell 1992, pp. 74-6.

72. For the continuation of essentially 'Roman' law beyond the Visigothic period, see D'Abadal y de Vinyals 1958, pp. 562-70; cf. Collins 1985 and 1986. Recognition of the 'Roman' nature of Visigothic law renders obsolete the debates concerning the date at which the principle of territoriality, as opposed to that of personality, of the law was established. The leading English-speaking exponent of the personality of the law well into the seventh century is P.D. King – see King 1972 and 1980; of the earlier counter-arguments, some of the most significant are to be found in García-Gallo 1936-41 (disputed by Merêa 1948, pp. 199-248) and 1974, and D'Ors 1956.

73. García-Gallo 1974, p. 404.

74. *Form. Wis.*, 13.

75. *Form. Wis.*, 14.

76. *Form. Wis.*, 1, 6, 7, 20.

77. *Form. Wis.*, 22; see García-Gallo 1936-41, pp. 244-5.

78. *Uita Fructuosi*, 15.

79. Collins 1983a, p. 127.

80. See VIII and XII Toledo.

81. Braulio, *Ep.*, 37.

82. For a discussion of such evidence as does exist, see Orlandis 1962d and Nelson 1991.

83. XIII Toledo, 5, pp. 421-2, cf. III Saragossa, 5, pp. 479-80.

84. III Saragossa, 5, pp. 479-80; XVII Toledo, 7, pp. 533-4.

85. III Toledo, p. 116.

86. Canellas López 1979, no. 115.

Chapter 8

1. Claude 1971a, pp. 118, 161-2; Gallego-Blanco 1974, p. 727.

2. *L.U.* II.1.1, 1.5; XII.2.14; see Sánchez-Albornoz y Menduiña 1971a, p. 227.

3. *Historia Wambae*, 9.

4. *Historia Wambae, iudicium in tyrannorum perfidia promulgatum*, 5.

5. XIII Toledo, 2, pp. 416-19; see Thompson 1969, p. 234.

6. Such men were all members of the *officium palatinum*, *palatii regis* or *aula regalis* (terms which are synonymous) – see Sánchez-Albornoz y Menduiña 1971a, pp. 178-80, and Thompson 1969, p. 252.

7. Specific titles are found in VIII, IX and XIII Toledo; III and XII Toledo simply list *uiri illustres*; XV and XVI Toledo list (with a single exception) men described as 'comites' or 'proceres'.

8. Canellas López 1979, no. 115.

9. John of Biclaro, *s.a.* 590, pp. 219-20.

10. Barnwell 1992, pp. 53-4.

11. Alderic, Nilacus, Transeric amd Wiliangus are 'comites et spatarii'; Torresarius is 'comes spatarius'; Sisimir is 'comes spatarius et dux'; Severinus is 'comes spatarius'. Transeric and Severianus also appear as 'comites' in XVI Toledo, where very few detailed titles are recorded.

12. VIII Toledo: Cuneifred; Canellas-López, no. 115: Eumensfred.

13. Sid. Ap., *Ep.*, I.2.

14. XVI Toledo, *Lex edita in confirmatione concilii*, pp. 517-18.

15. XIII Toledo; Gisclamund, the *comes stabuli* on that occasion also appears (like all the other courtiers) as 'comes' in XV Toledo.

16. On the importance of treasure in sixth-century Spain, see Claude 1972, p. 15, who comments on the prominence accorded to it by John of Biclaro; the position is unlikely to have changed in the succeeding century.

17. Canellas-López 1979, no. 115.

18. For an alternative view, see Thompson 1969, p. 216.

19. *Numerarii* were primarily financial officials: Isidore, *Etymologiae*, IX.4.19, states that 'numerarii uocati sunt, quia publicum nummum aerariis inferunt'; such a function is reflected in I Barcelona, *de fisco Barcinonensi*, p. 54, and XVI Toledo, *lex edita in confirmatione concilii*, p. 517. The laws indicate that they might also be expected to act as judges (*L.U.* II.1.27) and apprehend fugitives (*L.U.* IX.1.21), but such duties were laid upon all royal officials, no matter what their main function; cf. the position regarding *uilici* in XIII Toledo, *edictum de tributis relaxatis*, p. 436, *L.U.* VI.1.1, VIII.1.5, 1.9, IX.1.8, 1.9, X.1.16. For an interpretation, see King 1972, pp. 69-70.

20. I Barcelona, p. 54; for the history of the *de fisco Barcinonensi*, see Orlandis and Ramos-Lissón 1981, pp. 127-8.

21. See *L.U.* XII.1.2 and, by implication, the case of Theudemund, *spatarius*, discussed above.

22. *L.U.* XII.1.2.

23. Thompson 1969, p. 216.

24. For the Visigothic position, see García Moreno 1974a, pp. 62-5; for the fifth-century Empire, see Barnwell 1992, p. 29.

25. *L.U.* VII.2.10, which lays down a ninefold restitution for thefts from public *thesauri*, and which, as Zeumer noted on p. 292 of his edition, is drawn from Paul, *Sententiae*, V.27, where fourfold restitution is envisaged; see also Ervig's law, *de tributus relaxatis*, in XIII Toledo, p. 436, and *H.G.* 56.

26. For Roman *thesauri*, see A.H.M. Jones 1964, pp. 428-9; on the provinces, see Claude 1970, p. 93 (*pace* Silvestre and Guitérrez 1991), and Map II on p. 179. That the old provinces continued to have importance at least into the middle of the sixth century is suggested by the fact that Theudis had tried to gain control of Mauritania Tingitania, which had formed part of the Roman diocese of Spain – see Barnwell 1992, p. 77, and the references there. There is a parallel to the seventh-century significance of Roman provincial boundaries in Frankia, where Werner 1985a, pp. 31-2, has shown that the division between Austrasia and Neustria, which was marked by the *Silva Carbonaria*, lay on the boundary between the provinces of Germania II and Belgica II (see Map I on p. 178).

27. See García Moreno 1982, pp. 244-5; cf Orlandis and Ramos-Lissón 1981, p. 128.

28. Ervig, *de tributis relaxatis*, in XIII Toledo, pp. 435-7

29. Barnwell 1992, pp. 30-1.

30. Paul appears in VIII and IX Toledo (653 and 655, respectively), and Cixilla in XIII Toledo (683).

31. Canellas-López 1979, no. 115.

32. III Toledo, p. 108, and IV Toledo, 4, p. 189, cited by Claude 1971a, p. 70 n. 86.

33. *L.U.* VII.5.9.

34. Barnwell 1992, pp. 145-6.

35. Canellas-López 1979, p. 37, suggests that the *comes notariorum* was 'una réplica del "magister officiorum" romano', but the evidence for such a suggestion is unclear.

36. Vezin 1974, esp. p. 219, and 1980, pp. 73-4.

37. *Lex Theudi*, p. 469.

38. See *L.U.* II.1.19 and X.2.6, cited by Canellas-López 1979, pp. 86-7, where the archaeological evidence is also discussed.

39. VIII Toledo: Adulf, Afrila, Evantius, Fandila, Ubendarius (?= Wenedarius); XIII Toledo: Adeliubus, Egica, Reccared, Salamir, Sisebut, Suniefred, Wademir.

40. Canellas López 1979, no. 115.

41. The two are Adeliubus and Reccared.

42. The possible exception is Wademir whom García-Moreno 1974b, no. 161, suggests may have been the same as *dux* Wandemir who fought for Wamba against Paul (*Historia Wambae*, 15): the two names are, however, different.

43. Schade 1872-82, p. 777.

44. García Moreno 1974a, p. 132.

45. E.g. Claude 1970, p. 53; Sánchez-Albornoz y Menduiña 1971a, p. 184: 'la multiplicidad de *comites scanciarum* y *comites cubiculariorum* que aparecen entre los miembros del *officium Palatinum* concurrentes a los Concilios VIII y XIII de Toledo y la acumulación con tales títulos del de *dux* atestigua, a las claras, lo puramente honorífico de tales dignidades'.

46. Claude 1971a, p. 69: 'Für den *comes cubicular iorum* ist die Annahme eines oströmischen Vorbildes deshalb wahrscheinlich, weil dort die Verwaltung des *sacrum cubiculum*, der privaten wohnräume des Herrschers, zur Entstehung der Einrichtung der *cubicularii* geführt hatte, während aus den germanischen Reichen kein Parallelfall bekannt ist; wahrscheinlich was ihre Bedeutung geringer als am oströmischen Hof. Vielleicht übernahm man im Westgotenreich nur den Titel, ohne dass eine entsprechende Organisation geschaffen wurde.'

47. Sid. Ap., *Ep.*, I.2; see Wolfram 1988, p. 220.

48. John of Biclaro, *s.a.* 598, p. 218.

49. Barnwell 1992, pp. 78-9.

50. John of Biclaro, *s.a.* 587, p. 218, and 585, p. 217, respectively.

51. *H.G.* 54.

52. *H.G.* 58, cf. 61 for similar usage. It has been suggested that similar uncertainty attends Isidore's use of the term in his other works – see Diesner 1978a, p. 60.

53. *Historia Wambae*, 7.

54. *Historia Wambae*, 7, 12.

55. *Historia Wambae*, 10, 15.

56. XVII Toledo, *tomus* of Egica, p. 525.

57. *Uita Fructuosi*, 14; I disagree with King 1972, pp. 74-5, who thinks that this was a separate office, and that Claudius of Lusitania filled both positions.

58. John of Biclaro, *s.a.* 590, p. 218.

59. *U.P.E.* 17.

60. *L.U.* V.7.19; IX.2.8, 2.9.

61. XIII Toledo, *edictum de tributis relaxatis*, p. 436.

62. *L.U.* III.4.7.

63. *L.U.* IV.5.6.

64. *L.U.* VI.5.12.

65. *L.U.* II.1.18, 1.19, 1.24, 2.7; VI.4.3; XII Toledo, *tomus* of Ervig, p. 383.

66. For a similar suggestion concerning autonomy, see Gibert 1956, p. 578.

67. García Moreno 1974a, pp. 120-1; cf. Sprandel 1957, p. 55. The possible exception is *L.U.* III.4.17, which may be of Leovigild.

68. This also makes uncertain the suggestion of García Moreno 1974a, pp.

149-55, that the appearance of *duces* in the laws of Chindasuinth marks a militarisation of the government.

69. García Moreno 1974a, pp. 123-4, 145-6.

70. Great territorial officials performing symbolic service for kings are not unknown later in the middle ages: Widukind of Corvei, *Rerum gestum Saxonicarum libri tres*, II.1, records that Otto I made the German *duces* perform such service at his coronation; and there is an account of great magnates, including British kings, rowing the English king Edgar on the Dee in a symbolic act – 'Florence' of Worcester, *Chronicon*, pp. 142-3; see F.M. Stenton 1971, p. 369.

71. Fred. IV.78.

72. XII Toledo, *tomus* of Ervig, p. 383; *Historia Wambae*, 2; see Gibert 1956, p. 578.

73. *Uita Fructuosi*, 2.

74. The kind of interpretation offered here could also explain the status of Zerezindo, *dux*, who was buried at Villamartín (Vives, *Inscripciones*, no. 153): had he been a *dux prouinciae*, it is unlikely that the name of the province would not have been recorded.

75. *Historia Wambae*, 6.

76. For subjects not listed below, see *L.U.* II.3.10; IV.2.14; VIII.4.26; IX.1.20.

77. *L.U.* II.1.11; see also *L.U.* II.1.31, VI.1.1 and VII.1.5 for administration of the law.

78. *L.U.* III.4.17.

79. *L.U.* III.6.1.

80. *L.U.* VIII.4.29.

81. Narbonne, 4, p. 147, and 13, p. 149.

82. *L.U.* IX.2.1, 2.3, 2.5.

83. *L.U.* IX.2.6.

84. *L.U.* VIII.1.9.

85. Barnwell 1992, pp. 108-11.

86. Collins 1983a, p. 102. *L.U.* VIII.1.9 refers to *comites prouinciarum*: they are likely to be *comites ciuitatum* – i.e., the courtiers who were stationed in the provinces – though this cannot be proved.

87. One of the clearest examples is *L.U.* VII.4.2: 'Quotiens Gotus seu quilibet in crimine, aut in furtum aut in aliquo scelere, accusatur, ad corripiendum eum iudex insequatur. Quod si forte ipse iudex solus eum conprehendere uel distringere non potest, a comite ciuitatis querat auxilium, cum sibi solus sufficere non possit'; cf. *L.U.* II.1.31.

88. *L.U.* III.4.17: '... si iudex per neglegentium, aut forte redemtus, talia uitia requirere aut contestari uel distringere noluerit, a comite ciuitatis C flagella suscipiat et XXX solidos reddat ei, cui a nobis fuerit ordinatum'.

89. *L.U.* II.2.7.

90. E.g. *L.U.* II.1.15, 1.27, 1.30; II.2.7; IV.5.6; V.4.19; VI.5.12; VII.1.5; VIII.1.5, 5.6; IX.1.21, 2.8, 2.9; XI.1.2; XII.1.2; XIII Toledo, *edictum de tributis relaxatis*, p. 436.

91. Some of the laws listed in n. 90 may be to *comites ciuitatum*. Valderic signed XIII Toledo in 683 as *comes* of Toledo, but five years later appears in the signature list of XV Toledo simply as 'comes', as do all the other signatories.

92. King 1972, p. 55.

93. Leo II, *Ep.*, VI (*a.* 683).

94. Braulio, *Uita Aemiliani*, 14.

95. *Uita Fructuosi*, 15.

96. *Comites et proceres*: Babilo, Astald, Eured amd Froila at VIII Toledo; *comites proceres*: Aunemund and Teudemund at XVI Toledo; *proceres*: Theudila, Audemund and Trasimir at XIII Toledo. That the last three were also *comites* may be suggested by the fact that a Teudila appears as *comes* in XV Toledo, where all the courtiers are accorded this title without further elaboration: given that this is only five years after XIII Toledo (held in 683), it is possible that Teudila is the Theudila of XIII.

97. Sánchez-Albornoz y Menduiña 1971a, pp. 196-9.

98. *Historia Wambae*, 7.

99. *Historia Wambae, iudicium in tyrannorum perfidi promulgatum*, 5.

100. See XIII Toledo, 2, pp. 416-19, and Thompson 1969, p. 234.

101. Most clearly in *L.U.* IX.2.9; see Merêa 1948, p. 263.

102. XIII Toledo, *lex in confirmatione*, p. 416; cf. *L.U.* XII.1.3.

103. *L.U.* IX.2.9.

104. *L.U.* IX.2.8.

105. King 1972, pp. 58-9; cf. Sánchez-Albornoz y Menduiña 1971a, pp. 202-3, who sees them as living on their estates or at court, but as having special military duties.

106. Sánchez-Albornoz y Menduiña 1942, vol. 1 p. 107; Gamillscheg 1934-6, vol. I p. 356; cf. Wolfram 1988, pp. 101-2.

107. Sánchez-Albornoz y Menduiña 1942, vol. 1 p. 107; Gamillscheg 1935-6, vol. I p. 356; Diesner 1969, pp. 15-16; cf. Wolfram 1988, pp. 101-2, 242.

108. See, most clearly, *L.U.* IX.2.9.

109. *L.U.* III.6.1; VIII.1.5; XII.1.2.

110. *L.U.* II.1.24.

111. *Form. Wis.*, 39.

112. *L.U.* II.1.4, 1.27.

113. *L.U.* IX.2.8, cf. 2.9.

114. XIII Toledo, *edictum de tributis relaxatis*, p. 436.

115. *L.U.* IV.5.6.

116. *L.U.* IX.1.21.

117. *L.U.* II.1.16; IX.2.1, 2.3, 2.4, 2.5, 2.9.

118. E.g. Brunner 1887-92, vol. I p. 133; King 1972, pp. 73-4, and esp. pp. 81-2, has a more complex explanation of the relationship.

119. *C.E.* 322 and *L.U.* IV.2.14; see Claude 1971b, p. 184.

120. Mayer 1925-6, vol. II p. 137; Gamillscheg 1932, p. 140; Claude 1971b, pp. 182-3.

121. Schade 1872-82, p. 171.

122. Schade 1872-82, p. 930, cf. p. 99; Feist 1939, pp. 497-8.

123. Schade 1872-82, p. 930, cf. p. 104; Feist 1939, p. 496. The term is the same as that in *thiudans*, the title of the great Gothic leaders, such as Athanaric, in the fourth century – see Feist 1939, pp. 496-7, and Skeat 1868, col. 226.

124. Wolfram 1988, p. 219.

125. The association is so close that Mayer 1925-6, vol. II pp. 132, 137-8, even suggests that *tiufadus* and *uicarius* should be seen as equivalents, though there does not seem to be enough evidence to support such a contention.

126. See Claude 1971b, pp. 185-6, and García Moreno 1974a, pp. 150-1.

127. E.g. *L.U.* I.2.26, II.1.30, 3.10; VI.1.5; VIII.1.9; III Toledo, 17, p. 130, and 21, p. 132.

128. *L.U.* V.4.8; VI.2.4, 5.12; VIII.5.6; IX.1.9; XII.3.20, 3.26; III Toledo, 18, p. 131.

129. E.g. *L.U.* II.4.5; III.6.1; IV.4.1; VI.3.7, 4.4; IX.1.6; XII.1.2, 3.7, 3.25, 3.27; III Toledo, 16, p. 130.

130. *Form. Wis.*, 40; *L.U.* IX.1.6 and X.1.16.

131. *L.U.* III.2.2 and VI.3.7; possibly also VIII.1.9.

132. See Sánchez-Albornoz y Menduiña 1971c, pp. 84-5, on *Form. Wis.*, 40, and Mayer 1925-6, vol. II pp. 129-32. It has been suggested that the *iudex ciuitatis* represents a Roman official who was gradually replaced by the Gothic *comes*, perhaps with the *iudex* having civil authority and the *comes* military (Thompson 1969, pp. 139-42, followed by Collins 1983a, pp. 102-3 and Collins 1989, pp. 189-90). While there is some evidence for such a state of affairs in Ostrogothic Italy (Barnwell 1992, pp. 57-8; for the possibility of something similar in the Lombard kingdom, see Chapter 12 below), and it is not impossible that the Visigothic *iudex ciuitatis* was heir to the Roman *iudex ordinarius*, the Visigothic evidence is not such as to permit of any certainty; even if such a situation did pertain in the early days of the kingdom, it is unlikely to have been more than a transitional arrangement, and it is not reasonable to suppose that all the unpecified *iudices* or the late laws were attached to cities.

133. Thompson 1969, p. 140, citing *L.U.* II.1.31.
134. King 1972, pp. 79-81.

Chapter 9

1. E.g. Stroheker 1965c, pp. 230-2; García Moreno 1974a, p. 7: ' ... en toda la organización del reino de Toledo es enorme y fundamental la impronta tardo romano y bizantina; ... en la gran reorganización que debío llevar a cabo Leovigildo, fue su modelo siempre presente Bizancio ... en definitiva, el reino visigodo no puede comprenderse si no es dentro de la "Spätantike" o Antigüedad Tardia.'
2. For a similar conclusion, though reached by a different route, see Claude 1971c, p. 70: 'Die westgotischen Hofämter zeigen eine eigentümliche Mischung germanischer, römischer und autochthoner Elemente. Der oströmische Einfluss ging nicht sehr tief, während die alten germanischen Hausämter grössere Bedeutung hatten.'
3. Collins 1980, pp. 198-9.

Introduction to Part III

1. For a detailed discussion, see Part III of Barnwell 1992, esp. chapter 15.

Chapter 10

1. Goffart 1988b, p. 344.
2. Bullough 1986, esp. pp. 99-101, and Zanella 1990, esp. pp. 82-4; on Paul's understanding of the terms *gens* and *natio*, see Morghen 1974, p. 17.
3. Goffart 1988b, pp. 353-6.
4. Goffart 1988b, p. 430.
5. On Paul's association with the Beneventan court, see Belting 1962, esp. pp. 168-9, though Goffart 1988b, p. 336 n. 28, and p. 339, advocates caution in accepting all of Belting's case; on Paul's position at the court of Desiderius, see Wattenbach, Dümmler and Huf 1991, vol. 1 pp. 181-2.
6. Goffart 1988b, pp. 399-407; cf. Krüger 1981.
7. Bullough 1986, pp. 88-90.
8. Goffart 1988b, pp. 329-32.
9. Bullough 1986, p. 90; Leicht 1952, p. 59.
10. Sutherland 1975, p. 393.
11. See, for example, *H.L.* III.35, on Theodelinda, and *H.L.* IV.47 (cf. Fred. IV.70) concerning Gundiperga (both discussed below); see also *H.L.* III.32 on Authari's 590-1 campaign in southern Italy, and Waitz's note there.
12. Bullough 1986, esp. pp. 95-6.
13. Gardiner 1983.
14. Fasoli 1965, pp. 24-5; Wattenbach, Dümmler and Huf 1991, vol. 1 p. 179.

15. Perhaps a larger number than are found in the *Register*, which was not compiled until 794 and may have been an extract from a greater *corpus* – see Noble 1990, p. 91.

16. Brunhölzl 1990, pp. 61-3.

17. Noble 1985, pp. 348-9.

18. Brühl 1973, p. 63.

19. Noble 1985.

20. Autpert, *Uita Paldionis, Tatonis et Tasonis*.

21. Brühl 1979, p. 98. The documents of the Spoletan *duces* are published in *C.D.L.* IV.i; private documents from the duchy are in *C.D.L.* V.

22. So Zielinski 1972; Kurze 1973 argued that Gregory was not a trustworthy copyist, but Zielinski 1976 provides a stout defence of him and is supported by Brühl 1983, esp. pp. 240-1.

23. Brühl 1971, p. 11; Zielinski 1972, pp. 6-7; on the *Chronicon s. Sophiae*, see also Smidt 1910. There is no modern edition of the ducal documents of Benevento (one will ultimately form *C.D.L.* IV.ii); the private documents are in *C.D.L.* V.

24. Brühl 1979, p. 97; Bresslau 1912-58, vol. 1 p. 353. The private documents form *C.D.L.* I and II; the royal ones are in *C.D.L.* III.i.

25. E.g. Buchner 1953, pp. 34-5; Tagliaferri 1990, p. 361.

26. See Barnwell 1992, pp. 74-6, 85-6, 96-8, 139 and 173-4.

27. Collins 1991b, pp. 200-1.

Chapter 11

1. Hallenbeck 1982, p. 12, for example, sees a gradual growth of royal power as one of the major themes of Lombard history.

2. *H.L.* II.32, cf. III.16; Fred. IV.45.

3. R. Schneider 1972, p. 24.

4. For a discussion of some possible interpretations, see Fröhlich 1980, pp. 105-16.

5. Wickham 1981, pp. 37-8; on the difference between rebellion and revolution, see Gluckman 1966, pp. 27-53. For contrary views, see Gasparri 1978 and Jarnut 1982; for a review of interpretations, see Harrison 1993, pp. 5-6.

6. *H.L.* III.16; see Wickham 1981, p. 3; Hallenbeck 1982, p. 7; Tabacco 1989, p. 94.

7. Fred. IV.45.

8. Wickham 1981, pp. 31-2.

9. Besta 1927-9, vol. I p. 140.

10. Jarnut 1982, pp. 45-6.

11. See Liutprand, Prologues to laws of 713, 717, 721, 724, 726 and 729; Ratchis, 1, and Prologue to laws of 746; Aistulf, Prologues to laws of 750 and 755.

12. Liutprand, Prologue to laws of 713: 'cor regis in mano Dei est, atestante sapientissimo Salomonem, qui ait: Sicut impitus aquae, ita cor regis in mano Dei'; the Biblical reference is to Proverbs 12.1, in the *Uersio antiqua*.

13. Rothari, 2.

14. *Carmen de synodo Ticinensi*, p. 191.

15. *Laudes Mediolanensis ciuitate*, verse 18; on the date, see Colombo 1931, esp. pp. 72-5.

16. *In ecclesia beati Anastasi*, XII.10-14:

> Talibus unde meas tendens ad sidera palmas
> Uocibus oro: 'Dei fili, pro plebe fideli,
> Qui regis angelicos coetus, qui cuncta gubernas,
> Fac, precor, ut crescat mecum catholicus ordo,
> Et templo concede isti ut Salomoni locutus'.

See Badini 1980, esp. pp. 294-5.

17. *H.L.* III.16, 28, 30.
18. Gasquet 1887, p. 69.
19. See *C.D.L.* III.i.2, 3, 5-8, 12-15, 19, 22, 24, 27, 28; see also Wolfram 1967, pp. 92-3, Gasparri 1983, p. 86, and, more generally, Hodgkin 1880-99, vol. V p. 234.
20. Brühl 1973, pp. 71-2.
21. Rothari, 242: 'Si quis sine iussionem regis aurum figurauerit aut moneta confinxerit, manus ei incidatur'; for other apsects of royal regulation of coinage, see Grierson and Blackburn 1986, pp. 60-1.
22. Wroth 1911, pp. 136-7; Arslan 1990, p. 164; Grierson and Blackburn 1986, pp. 56-7.
23. Arslan 1990, p. 164; Grierson and Blackburn 1986, pp. 58-9.
24. *H.L.* V.6-12; see Diesner 1976a, esp. pp. 34-5.
25. McCormick 1986, pp. 289-93.
26. *H.L.* V.41; a similar ceremonial triumph may have been celebrated earlier by *Dux* Romoald of Benevento – *H.L.* V.10; cf. McCormick 1986, p. 294.
27. *H.L.* V.36; see Ward Perkins 1984, pp. 167-9.
28. G. Wolf 1988, pp. 221-5.
29. *H.L.* IV.30.
30. *H.L.* II.28.
31. Ewig 1976d, pp. 373-4.
32. Bognetti 1968d; Fasoli 1965, p. 53.
33. Ewig 1976d, pp. 373-4.
34. *H.L.* II.27.
35. *H.L.* II.31.
36. *H.L.* III.30.
37. *H.L.* III.35.
38. *H.L.* III.31.
39. *H.L.* IV.3.
40. For the importance of treasure in the Lombard kingdom, see John of Biclaro, *s.a.* 573, p. 213; for a general discussion of treasure in early medieval kingdoms, see Claude 1973.
41. *H.L.* IV.21, 22; Adaloald, son of Agilulf and Theodelinda, was born there – IV.25.
42. *C.D.L.* III.i.1.
43. According to *H.L.* IV.21; see Ward Perkins 1984, p. 170.
44. See Darmstädter 1896, p. 163, Fasoli 1965, p. 88, and Ward Perkins 1984, p. 169.
45. Brühl 1968, pp. 369-70; for the events of 661, see *H.L.* IV.51.
46. Ewig 1976d, pp. 374-5.
47. Christie 1995, pp. 161-2.
48. Brühl 1968, pp. 372-3.
49. *H.L.* V.1.
50. *H.L.* V.33.
51. *H.L.* V.38.
52. *H.L.* V.39.
53. Brühl 1972, pp. 56-7, and 1969, p. 191.
54. Rothari, Prologue; Aistulf, laws of 750, Prologue.
55. Brühl 1969, pp. 191-3.
56. *C.D.L.* III.i.15 and 23, respectively.
57. Brühl 1968, pp. 357-9.
58. Brühl 1968, p. 359.
59. *H.L.* III.35: '... uir strenuus et bellicosus et tam forma quam animo ad regni gubernacula coaptatus.'

60. *H.L.* II.8, cf. Marius, *s.a.* 569, p. 238.
61. *H.L.* III.32.
62. *H.L.* III.18.
63. *H.L.* IV.8; for Agilulf's qualities as warrior, see above.
64. *H.L.* IV.28.
65. *H.L.* V.6-9.
66. *H.L.* VI.49, 54.
67. Zanella 1990, p. 75.
68. *Carmen de synodo Ticinensi*, p. 190 – Cunincpert was
    Elictus gente a Deo ut regeret
    Langibardorum [*sic*], rebelles conpescuit,
    Bello prostrauit Alexo [= Alahis] nequissimo,
    Semidiruta nuncupata Motina
    Urbe pristino decore restituit.
On the rebellion, see *H.L.* V.38.
69. Rothari, 20.
70. Rothari, 23.
71. Rothari, 21.
72. Rothari, 22.
73. Rothari, 20.
74. *H.L.* IV.42, V.33.
75. Rothari, 189.
76. Liutprand, 25.
77. *C.D.L.* III.i.4, 6, 12, 13, 22.
78. On the 'Germanic' nature of Lombard law see the summary provided by Dilcher 1978; cf., for example, Buchner 1953, pp. 34-5, and Wickham 1981, pp. 36-7, though both do recognise some Roman influence. Slightly greater emphasis is laid on the Roman content by Brunner 1887-92, vol. I pp. 369-70; Besta 1952; Vismara 1981, esp. pp. 168-9, 176-7; Astuti 1975, p. 677; Tagliaferri 1990, p. 361; see also Paradisi 1968, p. 3, and, particularly, Drew 1987, p. 804.
79. Rothari, 386.
80. *H.L.* IV.42.
81. Collins 1983a, pp. 27-30; Barnwell 1992, pp. 75-6.
82. See the discussion in Barnwell 1992, pp. 85-6, 96-9, 139.
83. Rothari, 243.
84. Rothari, 386.
85. The best exposition of this view is Mor 1972; Wickham 1981, p. 69, is more cautious.
86. Rothari, 367.
87. The fact that there is an eighth-century abbreviation of Justinian's legislation (Julian's *Epitome latina nouellarum Iustiniani*) is not evidence for the continued existence of Roman, as opposed to Germanic, law in Lombard Italy (and, therefore of the personality of the law), as suggested by Mor 1972, since it is imperial, rather than provincial, law; the position in the Lombard kingdom may have been similar to that in the early sixth-century Visigothic kingdom, where both Euric's *Code* and the *Lex Romana Uisigothorum* were in force, and in early sixth-century Burgundy, where the *Liber constitutionum* and *Lex Romana Burgundionum* had simultaneous validity. Similarly, the evidence of Liutprand, 91, which stipulates that all charters were to be written '... siue ad legem Langobardorum ... siue Romanorum' cannot be taken to imply personality of the law, since the two terms could be alternative expressions for the same provisions, or relate to provincial and imperial law, respectively.
88. Rothari, Prologue, and 386.

89. See Collins 1991b, p. 200, and Brunner 1887-92, vol. I p. 368, who notes the parallel between Rothari's Prologue and *N.I.* 7.

90. Liutprand, Prologue to laws of 725; cf. Liutprand, Prologue to laws of 726, and, for example, Grimoald, Preface; also Liutprand, Prologue to laws of 713, and caps 11, 12 (both *a.* 717), 59, 62 (both *a.* 724), 87 (*a.* 727), 106 (*a.* 729), 118, 120, and 128 (all *a.* 731), Ratchis, 6, and Aistulf, 10, 11 (both *a.* 755).

91. *Liber constitutionum*, LII.1.

92. Liutprand in 713, 717, every year from 720 to 729 (inclusive), 731, and annually from 733 to 735; Ratchis in 745 and 746; Aistulf in 750 and 755. This quest to keep the law up to date is an effective counter to the argument of Bognetti (1968c, pp. 130-1) that the issuing of law was (despite the injunctions of, e.g., Rothari, 386, and the Epilogues to Liutprand's laws of 713, 717 and 721, and the Prologues to the same king's laws of 731) only intended to have a psychological effect by increasing the king's prestige; *ibid.*, p. 125, is likely to be correct, however, when he suggests that it is 'Utopian' to believe that the provisions were adhered to in all parts of the kingdom all the time.

93. Classen 1956, p. 86.

94. Rothari, 386; Grimoald, Prologue; Liutprand, Prologues to the laws of 713, 717, 720, 721, 724, 726, 727-729, 731 and 735; Ratchis, Prologue, and Prologue to laws of 746.

95. Liutprand, Prologue to the laws of 713, states that the laws were made on the eve of 1 March; the Prologues to all the other laws of Liutprand (except those of 733, for which no prologue survives), and to those of Aistulf and Ratchis, refer to 1 March itself. Apart from the laws of 733, the only exceptions to this pattern are the laws of Rothari (issued on 22 November), and of Grimoald (issued in July).

96. Mor 1961, p. 11.

97. Besta 1927-9, vol. I p. 201.

98. Most of the available evidence is collected in Morosi 1936; see also Leicht 1923, pp. 12-13, and Jarnut 1982, pp. 50-1.

99. *H.L.* III.35.

100. *Origo gentis Langobardorum*, 6; *H.L.* IV.3, 8, 13, 27.

101. Fred. IV.70; *H.L.* IV.47 is mistaken in believing it to have been Radoald, Rothari's son, who married Gundiperga, but the principle would still have been the same.

102. Fred. IV. 71.

103. *H.L.* II.29.

104. *H.L.* V.1.

105. *H.L.* VI.50.

106. Mor 1993, pp. 191-2.

107. *L.H.* IX.25; *H.L.* III.28.

108. Fred. IV.45.

109. For the clearer case of Bertha and Æthelberht of Kent, see Chapter 16.

110. *H.L.* IV.20; for their release, see IV.28.

111. *H.L.* V.8.

112. *H.L.* II.28.

113. *H.L.* IV.5, 8, 9; cf. Greg., *Reg.*, IV.2, 4, 33.

114. Greg., *Reg.*, IV.5.

115. Fasoli 1965, p. 93.

116. *Ep. Austr.*, 8.

117. *H.L.* IV.41; see von Pflugk-Harttung 1887, p. 87.

118. See *C.D.L.* III.i.2.

119. *H.L.* IV.21, 22.

120. *H.L.* IV.47 (which wrongly states that Gundiperga was the wife of Rodoald).

121. *H.L.* V.34.
122. Theodore, *Ep.*, VI.
123. *C.D.L.* III.i.24.
124. *C.D.L.* III.i.31, 33, 36-8, 40-4.
125. The other royal charters from before the reign of Desiderius are *C.D.L.* III.i.1, 3, 5, 7, 8, 14, 15, 18, 19, 23, 24, 27, 28.

Chapter 12

1. The clearest exposition of this view is Wickham 1981, esp. pp. 33, 37-8, 44, 47, 159; cf. Harrison 1993, *passim.*
2. *H.L.* III.18, 19.
3. *H.L.* IV.8.
4. *H.L.* IV.3, 13; *Origo gentis Langobardorum*, 6.
5. *H.L.* IV.27.
6. Fred. IV.50, cf. 69; Fredegar states that Taso was *dux* in Tuscany, but Wallace-Hadrill 1960, p. 58 n. 1, notes that *H.L.* IV.38 places him (in relation to another incident) in Cividale.
7. *H.L.* V.36, 38-41.
8. *H.L.* IV.42.
9. *H.L.* IV.51.
10. *H.L.* VI.18.
11. Wickham 1981, p. 42.
12. Gasparri 1978, p. 20.
13. *H.L.* II.9.
14. *H.L.* IV.40; Fred. IV.38.
15. *H.L.* IV.51.
16. *H.L.* VI.55.
17. *H.L.* VI.55-8.
18. *H.L.* VI.51.
19. See, for example, *H.L.* III.32; IV.10, 16, 38-46, 50; V.16-18, 23, 24; VI.2.
20. Gasparri 1978, p. 24, believes, for example, that under Perctarit and Cunincpert, if at no other time, all *duces* were royal appointees. The older tradition of seeing *duces* as 'the old aristocratic clan chiefs' persists, however – most recently, for example, in Christie 1995, p. 115.
21. *H.L.* III.8; *L.H.* IV.44.
22. *H.L.* VI.54.
23. *Ep. Austr.*, 40; *H.L.* III.1, 8, 9, 13, 27; IV.16, 37; V.7, 10, 36; VI.1, 24, 25, 27, 44, 45, 52, 54; *L.H.* IV.44; *Lib. Pont.*, 87.2, 91.16, 92.15.
24. *H.L.* II.9.
25. The known *duces* are: Euin, 574-595 (*H.L.* II.32; III.9, 10, 27; IV.1, 10); Gaidoald, 595-603 (*H.L.* IV.10, 27); Alahis, under Cunincpert (*H.L.* V.36, 38-41). The dates in this and similar succeding notes should be treated as the widest possible range for each *dux*, and not necessarily as the full dates of their periods of office.
26. The known *duces* are: Agilulf, before 590 (*H.L.* III.30); Arioald, 616-626 (Fred. IV.49, 50); Garipald, *c.* 661/2 (*H.L.* IV.51); Raginpert, *c.* 700 (*H.L.* IV.51, VI.18).
27. The known *duces* are, Alichis, *c.* 574 (*H.L.* II.32); Rothari, before 636 (Fred. IV.70); Gaidoald, *c.* 706-730 (*H.L.* VI.50); Adelchis, 766 (*C.D.L.* III.i.38).
28. The known *duces* are, Willari, *c.* 574 (*H.L.* II.32); Gaidulf, *c.* 596 (*H.L.* IV.3, 13); Rotharit, *c.* 700 (*H.L.* VI.18-20).
29. For a complete set of references, see Gasparri 1978.
30. *H.L.* IV.40, 48; cf. *Origo gentis Langobardorum*, 6, and Fred. IV.34.

Darmstädter 1896, p. 251, assumed that the *ducatus* was hereditary, and that it might therefore have come to an end with Aripert's accession to the throne in 653, since its lands could have merged with those of the crown.

31. *Origo gentis Langobardorum*, 6; *H.L.* IV.13.

32. *Ep. Austr.*, 40, 41.

33. *C.D.L.* I.16.

34. *Lib. Pont.*, 94.48-51.

35. The only other reference to a *dux* in Tuscany occurs in Fred. IV.50 and 69, but the Taso to whom he refers is likely to be the same as that referred to in *H.L.* IV.38, who was, in reality, *dux* of Cividale – see Wallace-Hadrill 1960, p. 58 n. 1.

36. See, for example, Wickham 1981, pp. 41-2.

37. Rothari, 6.

38. Rothari, 23.

39. Rothari, 21, 25.

40. Rothari, 22.

41. Rothari, 20.

42. Rothari, 24.

43. *H.L.* IV.1.

44. *Lib. Pont.*, 93.11, 15, 16; 97.5. Stabilis, *dux* (location, if any, unknown), was also used as an envoy between the king, Desiderius, and the Papacy – *Lib. Pont.*, 97.20.

45. *C.D.L.* I.113.

46. *C.D.L.* I.21.

47. *C.D.L.* III.i.113.

48. *H.L.* II.32; Wickham 1981, p. 31.

49. The known *duces* are: Faroald, 576-590/1 (*H.L.* III.13); Ariulf, 590/1-600/1 (*H.L.* IV.16; Greg., *Reg.*, II.7, 33, 45; V.36); Teudelapius, 600/1 – *c.* 653 (*H.L.* IV.16, 50); Atto *c.* 653 – *c.* 663 (*H.L.* IV.50); Transamund I and Wachilapus, both in the period *c.* 663-703x705 (*H.L.* IV.51; VI.30); Faroald, 703x705-719/20 (*H.L.* VI.30, 44); Hilderic, 739 (*H.L.* VI.55); Transamund II, 719/20-742x744 (*H.L.* VI.44, 55, 57; *Lib. Pont.*, 92.15); Agiprand, 742x744-745 (*H.L.* VI.57; *Lib. Pont.*, 93.11); Lupus, 745-751 (*C.D.L.* III.i.23; IV.i.3-13); Alboin, 757/8 (*C.D.L.* V.24-7; *Codex Carolinus*, 11, 17); Gisulf, 759/60-761/2 (*C.D.L.* IV.i.14-16, cf. V.28-32); Theodicius, 761/2-773 (*C.D.L.* IV.i.17, 18, 20, 22; cf. V.34-37, 50-4, 56-63; *Lib. Pont.*, 96.5, 15; 97.5); Hildeprand (*C.D.L.* IV.i.23; see Gasparri 1978, pp. 84-5).

50. The known *duces* are: Zotto, 569x571-589x591 (*H.L.* III.32; IV.18); Arichis I, *c.* 590 – *c.* 640 (*H.L.* IV.18-19, 39, 42-4); Aio, 640-641/2 (*H.L.* IV.42-44, 46); Raduald, 641/2-646/7 (*H.L.* IV.39, 44, 46); Grimoald I, 646/7-671 (*H.L.* IV.39, 46, 51; V.7); Romoald I, 671-687 (*H.L.* IV.51; V.7, 10; VI.1, 2); Grimoald II, 687-689 (*H.L.* VI.2); Gisulf I, 689-706 (*H.L.* VI.2, 27, 39; *Lib. Pont.*, 87.2; *Chron. Uult.*, doc. 9); Romoald II, 706-731/2 (*H.L.* VI.39, 55; *C.D.L.* V.ii); Gregory, 732-739/40 (*H.L.* VI.55, 56); Godescalc, 739/40-742 (*H.L.* VI.56-8); Gisulf II, 742-751 (*H.L.* VI.55, 57, 58; *C.D.L.* V.iii, iv; *Chron. Uult.*, docs 15, 16, 18); Liutprand, 754 (*Chron. Uult.*, doc. 32; *Chron. s. Sophiae*, I.24); Arichis II, 758-787 (*C.D.L.* V.v-viii, x, xi; see Gasparri 1978, pp. 98-100).

51. The *H.L.* is very uninformative – see III.32, 33; IV.18; see also Hallenbeck 1982, p. 6.

52. Bognetti 1967d.

53. Greg., *Reg.*, II.45.

54. The evidence for the Byzantine connections of Faroald, Ariulf and Zotto is conveniently summarised in Brown 1984, p. 71; for a sceptical view of imperial involvement in the foundation of the *ducatus*, see Collins 1991b, pp. 190-1.

55. *H.L.* V.16.

56. *H.L.* VI.57; cf. *Lib. Pont.*, 92.15.

57. See, for a clear example, Hallenbeck 1982, esp. at pp. 13, 27-8.
58. *H.L.* VI.44.
59. *Lib. Pont.*, 92.15, 93.2-5; *H.L.* VI.55.
60. Gasparri 1978, p. 81, citing *C.D.L.* III.i.23, and V.16; see also Gasparri 1983, pp. 101-2, and Wickham 1981, p. 44.
61. *Codex Carolinus*, 11.
62. Gasparri 1978, pp. 91-2.
63. *H.L.* VI.55; for Audelahis, see Gasparri 1978, pp. 92-3.
64. *H.L.* VI.56
65. Gasparri 1978, pp. 86-8.
66. Grierson and Blackburn 1986, pp. 58, 66-72.
67. Grierson and Blackburn 1986, pp. 58, 63-4.
68. *H.L.* IV.51.
69. Gasparri 1983, p. 186.
70. Belting 1962.
71. Rothari, 375; Liutprand, 59.
72. See, for example, Leicht 1923, pp. 16-17; Bognetti 1966, p. 264; Collins 1991b, pp. 189-90.
73. For example: Hodgkin 1880-99, vol. VI pp. 577-8; Mor 1952; Wickham 1981, pp. 41-2; Tabacco 1989, p. 102; Christie 1995, p. 115.
74. *C.D.L.* III.i.44.
75. *C.D.L.* III.i.6, 44.
76. Hodgkin 1880-99, vol. VI p. 577.
77. Gasparri 1978, p. 20, reaches the same conclusion.
78. *H.L.* V.29, which recounts how Alzeco, a *dux* of the Bulgars, arrived in Italy looking for a homeland; he was given land upon which to settle on condition that he changed his title from that of *dux* to that of gastald.
79. Rothari, 375; Liutprand, 59.
80. Rothari, 210, 271.
81. Rothari, 221.
82. Rothari, 189.
83. Rothari, 15.
84. Rothari, 23, 24; see Leicht 1923, p. 21.
85. See for example: *C.D.L.* III.i.1, 5, 8, 14, 15, 19, 22-4, 28 (all royal documents); IV.1.3, 5-8, 10, 13 (all Spoletan); *Chron. s. Sophiae*, doc. I.22, and *Chron. Uult.*, doc. 32 (both Beneventan). For other involvement with landed property, see Liutprand, 78.
86. *Lib. Pont.*, 91.7.
87. *Lib. Pont.*, 93.11.
88. *C.D.L.* II.163.
89. *C.D.L.* IV.i.14; V.20; although these relate to the *ducatus* of Spoleto, there is no reason to suppose that gastalds could not act in this way in the north, or in Benevento.
90. *C.D.L.* V.1.
91. For example, *C.D.L.* I.38 and II.137 from the north; V.11, 29, 47, 56 from Spoleto.
92. For example, *C.D.L.* IV.i.1, 2, 4, 5, 7, 9-11, 13, 16-18 (ducal); V.2-7, 12, 14, 15, 19, 22, 23, 25-8, 30-3, 35, 37-43; 46-9, 52, 54, 56, 57 (private); cf. V.vii, viii, from Benevento (private).
93. Besta 1927-9, vol. I pp. 166-8, who is sceptical about the use of gastalds to check the power of the *duces*; Darmstädter 1896, pp. 278-9; Gamillscheg 1934-6, vol. II p. 66; Gasparri 1983, pp. 90-3; Tabacco 1989, p. 102.
94. This view was espoused by Mor 1952.

95. See, for example, *C.D.L.* I.50; II.163; III.i.4, 6, 13, 44; IV.i.12, 16-18; V.1, 3-5, 19, 20, 22, 23-8, 31-3, 35, 37-43, 46-9, 52, 54, 56, 57, 62, 63, vii; *Stephani II bulla.*

96. One of the clearest examples is *C.D.L.* III.i.6, which refers to: 'Curti nostre Placentine, hubi preesse inuenitur Daghibertus gastaldius noster, et curti nostre Parmisiane, hubi Immo gastaldus noster esse inuenitur.'

97. Bognetti 1966, pp. 362-7.

98. See, for example, Hodgkin 1880-99, vol. VI pp. 575-6; Gasparri 1978, p. 21; Brogiolo 1990, p. 130.

99. The only route which has been suggested by which this is etymologically possible sees the *gast* element as being related to the modern Dutch *kaste*, meaning a granary – see Braccini 1995, pp. 1085-8.

100. Bognetti 1966, p. 264.

101. Bognetti 1966, p. 264; for further discussion, see also Gamillscheg 1934-6, vol. II pp. 141-2.

102. *H.L.* II.32 and III.16; for a discussion of these passages, see Goffart 1980, pp. 176-86.

103. Barnwell 1992, pp. 151-2, 157-8.

104. Some of the most important of the laws relating to *iudices* are: Rothari, 25, 35, 150, 244, 260, 264; Liutprand, 18, 25-8, 44, 78, 80, 81, 83, 85; Ratchis, 4, 5.

105. This is implied by Christie 1995, p. 115.

106. Sánchez-Albornoz y Menduiña 1959, p. 374.

107. For the etymology of the word, see Braccini 1995, pp. 1108-10.

108. The subordinate position of *sculdahis* is implicit in many laws, including three of Rothari's provisions which refer to gastalds (Rothari, 15, 189, 221), but is explicit in Liutprand, 25, 26, 44, and Ratchis, 1.

109. *Centenarii* were certainly subordinate to *iudices* – Ratchis, 1; see Jarnut 1982, p. 52; on *centenarii* see F. Schneider 1914, pp. 173, 178, and Hartmann 1897-1903, vol. II.ii p. 39.

110. Rothari, 251.

111. Liutprand, 44.

112. Liutprand, 25, 26, 28; Ratchis, 1.

113. Rothari, 35; Liutprand, 85.

114. Rothari, 15.

115. Rothari, 189, 221.

116. Liutprand, 83; Aistulf, 7.

117. *H.L.* VI.24.

118. *C.D.L.* III.i.6; IV.i.12, 14, 15; similar evidence is found in private documents – see *C.D.L.* II.262, V.8, 34, 61.

119. *C.D.L.* IV.i.1 (ducal) and V.39 (private).

120. *C.D.L.* I.57; II.248; V.2-4, 6, 7, 12, 14-19, 23, 24, 29, 36, 49, 50, 53, 58, 62, 73.

121. Previdi 1973, pp. 636-7 and 658-61, argues that *sculdahis* were not tied to specific territories. His case rests on two main points. (a) Simply because a *sculdahis* signed a document in a given place does not mean that he had *territorial* jurisdiction there; this may be true, but it seems to run counter to a statement that a *sculdahis* was 'rector loci' (*H.L.* VI.24; cf. Cavanna 1967, pp. 383, 422-4). (b) A *sculdahis* was not directly dependent on his gastald in a rigidly hierarchical fashion, since Spoletan *duces* (*C.D.L.* IV.i.12; V.20) could use them as, presumably, could the king. This thesis is used to explain the absence of *sculdahis* from the immunity clauses of charters – see below.

122. *C.D.L.* I.24; II.141; V.17, 27.

123. *C.D.L.* I.19.

124. *C.D.L.* III.i.6.

125. *C.D.L.* I.113.

126. Niermeyer 1976, pp. 943-4; the evidence is *C.D.L.* I.19: '... iam senex scario regis de curte dicitur Sexanio.'

127. The word *scario* is derived from the root *(un-)skarjan*; (cf. O.E. *(a-)scierian*) meaning to separate or divide, suggesting that it could relate to a division of the army; see Feist 1939, p. 534, Schade 1872-82, p. 789, and Braccini 1995, pp. 1115-16.

128. Fred. IV.37, 74; see Bachrach 1972, p. 81. Meyer 1877, p. 303, suggested a relationship to the army.

129. *C.D.L.* I.18.

130. Aistulf, 20.

131. Meyer 1877, p. 292.

132. Meyer 1877, p. 304, suggested that *scariones* were court ushers or messengers – but the basis for this is not certain.

133. For pertinent comments on this, see Brown 1984, p. 40.

134. Rotili 1990, p. 133.

135. So Bierbrauer 1990 (esp. p. 113) in relation to Trent.

136. Tagliaferri 1990, p. 102, suggesting that the *dux* of Cividale had jurisdiction in the territories of the Roman municipalities of Aquileia, Concordia, Zuglio Carmico and Cividale.

137. See Chapter 8, n. 26.

Chapter 13

1. Gregory the Great used the term in this sense in relation to Pronulf who, with King Authari, witnessed the flood of the Tiber in 591 – *Dialogues*, III.xix.1-2; for other accounts of the flood, see *L.H.* X.1; *H.L.* III.23-4.

2. See, for example, *C.D.L.* III.i.1, 5, 8, 14, 15, 19, 22-4, 27, 28; IV.i.3, 5, 8, 13; the list is not exhaustive.

3. See Meyer 1877, p. 293; Brunner 1887-92, vol. I p. 142; Mayer 1909, vol. I pp. 440-1; Gamillscheg 1934-6, vol. II pp. 185-6; Feist 1939, p. 200; Diesner 1976b; Fasoli 1965, p. 149, produces evidence from a glossary, that *gasindii* are equated with 'qui in palacio regis custodiunt'. *Gasindius* comes from the same root – *gasintha* – as the O.E. *gesith*, on which see Chapter 17, and is found in some of Marculf's formulae, where it means simply 'companion' – Marculf I.23, 24, 32. *Gasindius* has sometimes (Besta 1927-9, vol. I pp. 150-1; Bognetti 1968a, p. 476; Diesner 1978b, p. 20) been interpreted as being the equivalent of the Visigothic *gardingus*, or the Frankish *domesticus*, but there is no etymological justification for this.

4. Ratchis, 14.

5. Liutprand, 62.

6. *C.D.L.* II.155, 226; III.i.36.

7. *C.D.L.* I.48; II.163, 226, 229, 293; Ratchis, 11.

8. *C.D.L.* II.262; IV.i.12.

9. *C.D.L.* I.14, 17, 48; II.155, 226, 229; V.1.

10. *C.D.L.* V.i; Ratchis, 10; on *gasindii* in general, see Wickham 1981, pp. 134-6. It is in this context that the references in Marculf's *Formulae* should be seen – see n. 3, above.

11. *H.L.* III.9.

12. *H.L.* IV.51; V.16.

13. Wolfram 1967, pp. 190-1, suggests that *comites* were military officials; according to him once the kingdom and *ducatus* were established they may have become unnecessary.

14. Bertolini 1968a, p. 489, makes a similar suggestion – though with a wider application – arguing that the term did no more than describe high-ranking public officials, and was adopted under Byzantine influence. Gregory the Great has a similar usage, relating to a 'comes urbis Centumcellensis' (Civita Vecchia) in Roman territory – *Dialogues*, IV.xxviii.1.

15. Greg., *Reg.*, V.6.

16. *C.D.L.* I.49.

17. Niermeyer 1976, p. 124.

18. Ratchis, 12.

19. *C.D.L.* II.226.

20. *C.D.L.* II.257. For the suggestion that they were butlers, see Brühl 1968, pp. 377-80; the term could therfore be related to the Gothic *skaftjan*, 'to prepare'; the alternative suggestion, noted in the *C.D.L.* edition, may derive from a fourteenth-century manuscript of the *H.L.* (Oxford, Magdalen College Lat. 14), which, alone among the manuscripts, states, in V.2, that *scaffard* and *uestiarius* are equivalents.

21. Hartmann 1897-1903, vol. II.ii p. 47.

22. *C.D.L.* I.48, where the signatory is specifically described as 'uesterarius regie potestatis'; V.6, 7.

23. *Lib. Pont.*, 97.5.

24. *C.D.L.* III.i.6.

25. *H.L.* II.28.

26. *H.L.* II.28 (the murder of Alboin); VI.38 (an abortive plot against Liutprand).

27. *H.L.* II.9; VI.6.

28. *C.D.L.* V.8.

29. Hartmann 1897-1903, vol. II.ii, p. 47; Brühl 1968, p. 377.

30. *C.D.L.* III.i.4, 6, 13; V.8.

31. A.H.M. Jones 1964, pp. 372-3.

32. Brühl 1968, p. 337. Meyer 1877, p. 304, thought it meant 'judge', taking it to be a compound of *stol* ('seat') and *sitan* ('to sit'), meaning 'one who sat on the seat of judgement'; attractive though his linguistic argument is, however, there is nothing in the evidence for the activities of *stolesaz* to provide positive support for it.

33. Wickham 1981, p. 159.

34. Rothari, 150.

35. Hartmann 1897-1903, vol. II.ii p. 47 stated that the *maior domus* was clearly ('offenbar') identical with the *stolesaz*, sometimes seen as a financial official; Darmstädter 1896, p. 276, in the same vein, saw the *maior* as head of the financial administration. Brühl 1968, p. 377, thought that the *infertor* of the *Liber Papiensis* was the *seniscalc*, and wondered (cf. Besta 1927-9, vol. I p. 152) if he was the same as the *maior*.

36. See Chapter 3 n. 9.

37. *C.D.L.* II.163; III.i.13.

38. *C.D.L.* I.17; the outcome was confirmed by Liutprand the following year, in *C.D.L.* III.i.12.

39. The following discussion is based on the evidence for the royal writing office; many of its features were replicated in the chanceries of the *duces* of Spoleto and Benevento, but, although the approporiate references are supplied in the notes, for reasons of clarity the text only exceptionally makes explicit mention of them. For a full discussion of the Spoletan writing office, see Bullough 1971.

40. *C.D.L.* III.i.8, 12, 13, 15, 19, 27, 28, 31, 33, 35, 37, 38, 40, 41, 44, see also p. 280; IV.i.1-13, 22; *Chron. s. Sophiae*, docs I.21-4; *Chron. Uult.*, doc. 32.

41. *C.D.L.* III.i.7, 14, 18, 22, 23, 39, 42, 43; IV.i.15.

42. This may also lie behind the Epilogue to Liutprand's laws of 713, which refers to the role of a notary in producing the written version.

43. *C.D.L.* III.i.13; cf. p. 280 of the same volume, which refers to an account of a (now lost) charter of 755 in a document of 898.

44. The formula which denotes this is: 'ex dicto domni regis per *n.* scripsi ego *n.* (notarius)'. This is found in *C.D.L.* III.i.13, where the intermediary is Seno, 'illuster uir'; for notaries as intermediaries, see *C.D.L.* III.i.12, 15, 22, 31, and for referendaries, *C.D.L.* III.i.8, 19, 28, 33 (see also 24). Some of the documents issued by the Spoletan and Beneventan *duces* do not appear to have involved an intermediary of any kind – see *C.D.L.* IV.i.4, 5, 8, 9, 12, 13, 14, 17, 22; *Chron. s. Sophiae*, docs I.23, 24, and *Chron. Uult.*, doc. 32.

45. The formula is: 'ex dicto domni regis et ex dictatu *n.* scripsi ego *n.* (notarius)'; *C.D.L.* III.i.6, 7, 18 (on which see Brühl 1970, pp. 129-30), 27, 39 (in all these cases, the dictator is a notary, but in view of the fact that another formula – in n. 46 below – recorded that referendaries could fulfil this role this is probably no more than a reflection of the small number of surviving documents); IV.i.3, 6, 7, 10, 11; 15. A similar procedure is envisaged by a slightly different formula in *Chron. s. Sophiae*, doc. I.22, from Benevento.

46. The formula is: 'ex dicto domni regis per *n.* et ex ipsius dictatu scripsi ego *n.* (notarius); *C.D.L.* III.i.14, 37, 38, 40-4.

47. Wattenbach 1958, pp. 420-1, 457-61; Classen 1956, p. 82.

48. *C.D.L.* III.i.6 records the presence of Albinus, referendary, at an enquiry into a boundary dispute between Parma and Piacenza, and the same document was dictated by Teoderacus, also referendary.

49. *C.D.L.* III.39, *a.* 767 (notary); 40, 41, *a.* 771, 772 (referendary); he is likely to be the same as the Andreas (referendary) of 43, *a.* 770x772; the same may be true of Sissinus, who appears in III.i.22 and 23 as a notary, and in 35 as a referendary, but the time-span is in this instance twenty-one years, rendering it less certain that the references are to same man.

50. *C.D.L.* I.17, 18 (in this case the *notarius regis* was a witness); II.137, 155.

51. *C.D.L.* I.18 (where there are two such men, one a witness, the other the writer), 36; II.226.

52. Particularly since Gumpert features as a *notarius regis* in 761 (*C.D.L.* II.155) and as a *notarius regiae potestatis* in 769 (*C.D.L.* II.226) – though it is not impossible that his office changed in the intervening eight years.

53. Schiaparelli 1932, pp. 18-24.

54. This is implied in Conti 1972, p. 167, and 1982, pp. 119-20.

55. *C.D.L.* I.21.

56. *C.D.L.* I.19, 20; III.i.13.

57. *C.D.L.* III.i.6.

58. *H.L.* IV.35.

59. *Lib. Pont.*, 97.20, 23.

Chapter 14

1. For balanced comments on this, see Brown 1984, pp. 40-1.

2. Greg., *Dialogues*, III.xxxviii.3.

3. Tagliaferri 1965, p. 27.

Introduction to Part IV

1. Campbell 1986a, p. 130.

Chapter 15

1. Despite the large amount of more recent scholarship concerning Bede, Campbell 1966 remains one of the best introductions; the papers in Hamilton Thompson 1935, though dated, probably represent the best of their generation.

2. See, most memorably, Wormald 1978 p. 68: 'Previous generations of historians were ready to welcome him [Bede] into their own ranks ... Historians are now readier to admit that his is only one view of what was happening in seventh-century Britain, and it is not necessarily the most revealing just because it was the opinion of the cleverest man of the age'; cf. Dumville 1977b, pp. 191-2.

3. For this thesis, see Goffart 1988b, chapter IV; Kirby 1983, pp. 110-12, by contrast, suggests that variations in the accounts of Wilfrid's career may derive at least as much from the possibility that Bede and Stephen had different sources of information (Hexham and Ripon, respectively), than from their personal feelings towards the bishop.

4. On the centrality of the English, see esp. Cowdrey 1981, though Kirby 1993 emphasises a wider perspective, in which the English were also the agents of salvation for the other inhabitants of the British Isles.

5. McClure 1983; Ward 1990, esp. chapter 5.

6. This is explicit in the Preface; see also Ward 1990, p. 88.

7. Ward 1990, p. 88.

8. Goffart 1988b, pp. 241-2; Campbell 1989a, p. 18.

9. *H.E.* V.23-4.

10. Goffart 1988b, pp. 250-3.

11. McClure 1984 suggests that Bede was the author, and that his *Uita Ceolfrithi* represents a later expansion and revision of it, but the case is not conclusive – see Goffart 1988b, p. 277 n. 195.

12. The anonymous *Uita* had earlier been adapted by Bede into a verse meditation – see Lapidge 1989.

13. On the authorship of the last, see Kirby 1981, pp. 102-4.

14. Goffart 1988b, pp. 264-70, argues that the *Life of St Gregory* and the anonymous *Life of St Cuthbert* are precursors of what he perceives as Bede's preoccupation with presenting an anti-Wilfridian view of Northumbrian history.

15. See Picard 1982, esp. pp. 166-9.

16. This is especially true of Bede and Stephen – see n. 3 above; on Bede and Adomnán, see Picard 1984.

17. Kirby 1983, pp. 105-6.

18. See O'Sullivan 1978, the papers in Lapidge and Dumville 1984, and Higham 1994, chapter 5.

19. F.M. Stenton 1971, p. 4; Miller 1975, p. 261; O'Sullivan 1978, pp. 180-1 (who defends the usefulness of the text, seemingly on the grounds that without it 'a whole nation, a whole century, must be silent to us'); Higham 1994, esp. chapters 1 and 3.

20. Sims-Williams 1983, pp. 7-15.

21. R.H.C. Davis 1971.

22. Dumville 1976-7, pp. 352-3.

23. Sisam 1953; Dumville 1976.

24. It is possible that such was the date of their introduction to England, but there is also argument in favour of a date earlier in the sixth century – see, for example, Chaplais 1973a, esp. pp. 32-3, and 1973c; Wormald 1984, esp. p. 14; Kelley 1990, pp. 40-3; see also Chapter 18, below, for further discussion of this.

25. Chaplais 1973a, p. 33.

26. Wormald 1984, p. 9; Chaplais 1973a, pp. 33-6.

27. Chaplais 1973b, pp. 67-9; Wormald 1984, p. 19.

28. Wallace-Hadrill 1971, pp. 37-9.

Chapter 16

1. McClure 1983, pp. 87-8, citing *H.E.* II.16 and I Kings 4.21, 24-5.

2. Discussed – though without reference to Bede's story – in Chadwick 1907, p. 257.

3. Hill 1975, pp. 40-3; McClure 1983, pp. 88-9, where a parallel is drawn between Bede's description of the Battle of the Winwæd (*H.E.* III.24) and the battle in which Absalom was killed (II Samuel 18.8, the textual parallel being with the Vulgate).

4. *H.E.* I.34.

5. *H.E.* IV.21, 26.

6. *H.E.* II.9, 20.

7. *H.E.* III.9.

8. *H.E.* III.24.

9. *H.E.* IV.16.

10. *H.E.* III.7.

11. *H.E.* IV.21.

12. *H.E.* II.20, III.7, 9, 18, 24.

13. *H.E.* III.18.

14. *H.E.* III.14.

15. Chadwick 1905 pp. 273-4; for a different interpretation, see Yorke 1983, pp. 7-8.

16. *H.E.* IV.26.

17. *H.E.* III.1.

18. *H.E.* II.20.

19. *H.E.* IV.23.

20. *H.E.* II.15.

21. *H.E.* IV.15.

22. Felix, *Uita Guthlaci*, 49, 52.

23. *H.E.* IV.16; Dumville 1979, p. 19.

24. *H.E.* III.18.

25. *H.E.* V.19, 24 (*s.a.* 704).

26. *H.E.* III.21.

27. Yorke 1983 provides a full discussion of the issues, but not all the cases she cites are equally convincing.

28. See also *H.E.* III.8; Yorke 1983, p. 7.

29. Goscelin of Canterbury, *Uita Mildrethae*, 5; see Rollason 1982, pp. 37-8; Yorke 1983, pp. 6-7.

30. S 13, 14.

31. S 10.

32. *H.E.* V.8.

33. *H.E.* IV.12, and Plummer's note.

34. Kirby 1991, p. 49; cf. the older discussion in Chadwick 1905, pp. 289-90.

35. S 1165.

36. See Blair 1989, pp. 105-7; Wormald 1983, p. 112.

37. Stephen, *Uita Wilfridi*, 19.

38. S 53.

39. S 1429.

40. Kirby 1991, p. 12.

41. *H.E.* III.30.

42. S 1169; Stephen, *Uita Wilfridi*, 40.

43. In the words of Campbell 1979a, the overkings would have tried to ensure that subject rulers had, 'as little of the *rex* and as much of the *comes* about them as possible'.

44. The most significant contributions to the debate over the last forty years have been made in Drögereit 1952; Stengel 1960; John 1966 (esp. pp. 1-63); F.M. Stenton 1970c; Vollrath-Reichelt 1971; Yorke 1981; Wormald 1983; Fanning 1991; Kirby 1991 (esp. pp. 14-20); Keynes 1992; Higham 1995.

45. *H.E.* II.5. The problems are compounded by the fact that the *Anglo-Saxon Chronicle, s.a.* 829, contains a copy of Bede's list, with the addition of Ecgberht of the West Saxons, describing such men as 'bretwalda' (in version A, 'brytenwealdan'); as the term does not occur in any of the earlier sources, and, although applied to earlier rulers, only has specific relevance to the ninth century, it is not discussed here *per se.*

46. Fanning 1991, pp. 17-18, citing the cases of the Northumbrians Ecgfrith (*H.E.* IV.12), Aldfrith and Osred (both *H.E.* V.18), the Mercians Wulfhere, Æthelred I and Æthelbald (all *H.E.* V.24), and the West Saxons Cædwalla (*H.E.* IV.12) and Ine (*H.E.* V.7).

47. The earliest documents to use the term in an Anglo-Saxon context are Aldhelm's *Carmina ecclesiastica* – III, 1.9, 11.3, 11.35-8 – and Adomnán's *Uita Columbae* – 9a, pp. 198-200. In the case of Aldhelm, the term – used in relation to West Saxon kings – may have been chosen for a variety of reasons: it could reflect the same kind of overlordship as Bede's usage, or it could have been used for poetic reasons, particularly in relation to Cædwalla, who is said to have relinquished the 'imperium mundi sceptrumque' in order to become a monk – Aldhelm could have been seeking to draw attention to the scale of his sacrifice, and in any case the word *regnum* had been used in the previous line. Adomnán is the only author (and he was not English) to use the word *imperator* (of Oswald): see Byrne 1973, pp. 256-9.

48. Fanning 1991, pp. 7-15, *contra* Yorke 1981, p. 7, and McClure 1983, pp. 97-8. See also, for discussion in relation to the Northumbrian instances, Stancliffe 1995, pp. 49-58.

49. *Contra*, in particular, Higham 1992a and 1995; attractive as is Higham's thesis concerning overlordships being coterminous with the late Roman provinces of Britain, there are too many contrary indications for the case to be sustainable.

50. There are some parallels between Bede's usage and that of the eighth-century Papacy – see R. Davis 1992, pp. xi-xiii.

51. For a discussion of Frankish overlordship – though expressed as hegemony rather than *imperium* – see Wood 1992

52. Fanning 1991, pp. 24-5; Wood 1983b, p. 14.

53. Keynes 1992, pp. 109-10; Higham 1995, esp. chapters 1 and 2.

54. F.M. Stenton 1970c; Higham 1992a.

55. *H.E.* II.5.

56. *H.E.* II.5.

57. F.M. Stenton 1971, p. 59; Wood 1983b, esp. pp. 12, 15-16.

58. *H.E.* II.5.

59. So, most recently and cogently, Wormald 1995, pp. 970-4.

60. Wallace-Hadrill 1971, pp. 33-40; for another view, though, see Charles-Edwards 1983, pp. 48-9.

61. Wallace-Hadrill 1971, pp. 37-8; Lohaus 1974, pp. 17-18; Jolliffe 1933, pp. 111-12.

62. Æthelberht, 25.

63. *Codex Eurici*, 310.

64. The best discussion of *bucellarii* in English is Liebeschuetz 1991, pp. 43-8; for a detailed discussion of the Anglo-Saxon evidence, and further references, see Barnwell 1996.

65. Æthelberht, 26.

66. F.M. Stenton 1971, p. 303; cf. p. 315.

67. Chadwick 1907, p. 73; for the Frankish evidence, see *Pactus legis Salicae,*

35.8, 36.1, 42.4, 50.1, 87.1-2; *Pactus Childeberti I et Chlotarii I, Cap. Mer.*, c. 8; *Lex Ribuaria*, 40.5; 65.1; see also Fustel de Coulanges 1889, pp. 401-2, and Grahn-Hoek 1976, pp. 65-6. For Lombard *aldiones*, see the Lombard laws, *passim*.

68. Applebaum 1972, pp. 257-8; Finberg 1972, p. 386; Myres 1986, p. 142; for evidence of the continued existence of *laeti* in Gaul see Bachrach 1972, pp. 21, 79.

69. For the Frankish parallel, see Wallace-Hadrill 1971, p. 38; the Visigothic instance is in *L.U.* IV.5.5 (issued by Leovigild).

70. John 1964, esp. chapter 1; Campbell 1989b, p. 25.

71. Such consultation was not restricted to law-making – see, for example, *H.E.* II.9, 13; Bede, *Uita Ceolfrithi*, 9; Stephen, *Uita Wilfridi*, 10, 34, 58; S 7, 8, 10, 18, 45.

72. Wormald 1995, pp. 980-3.

73. Vollrath-Reichelt 1971, pp. 21-6.

74. S 9 (of Eadric of Kent, 686); 14 (of Oswine of Kent, 690); 235 (of Cædwalla of Wessex, 685x687); 1787 (an incomplete charter of Swæfred of Essex, *c.* 706x *c.* 709); 102 (of Æthelbald of Mercia, 716-17).

75. *H.E.* II.16.

76. Deanesly 1943, pp. 138-9.

77. Raw 1992, pp. 172-3, where *Elene* lines 76, 123-4, are cited in relation to Constantine.

78. For a discussion of the standard in relation to Bede's passage, see Schramm 1968, p. 71; more generally, see Campbell 1982, pp. 66-7, and 1992, pp. 91-3.

79. For the use of standards at an *aduentus*, see Ammianus Marcellinus, XVI.10.4-10, esp. at 6-7, and the discussion in Matthews 1989, pp. 231-3.

80. See Wallace-Hadrill 1965.

81. Ammianus Marcellinus, XVI.10.13.

82. Hope-Taylor 1977, pp. 119-22, 241-4.

83. Brooks 1984, pp. 24-5.

84. Blagg 1982, p. 52.

85. West Yorkshire Archaeology Service press release, 'Excavations at Catterick racecourse 1995' (8 Sept. 1995), and report in *The Times*, 9 Sept. 1995, p. 4; see also *British Archaeology*, 9 (Nov. 1995); for the mass baptism, see *H.E.* III.14, and, for other references to Catterick, II.14, 20.

86. *H.L.* IV.30.

87. *L.H.* V.17.

88. Bede, *Uita Cuthberti*, 27; for similar usage relating to Bamburgh, see *H.E.* III.6, 12, 16; on the significance of the term *ciuitas* in this context, see Campbell 1979b, p. 37.

89. Campbell 1979b, p. 43.

90. The two terms seem to be synonymous, at least as used by Bede – Campbell 1979b, pp. 44-5.

91. *H.E.* III.21, 22.

92. *H.E.* II.14.

93. *H.E.* II.14.

94. *H.E.* II.14.

95. *H.E.* III.22.

96. Stephen, *Uita Wilfridi*, 38.

97. *Uita Gregorii*, 15.

98. Anon., *Uita Cuthberti*, IV.8; for a suggestion that Carlisle was the former capital of Rheged, see Cramp 1995, p. 7.

99. *H.E.* II.16.

100. Hlothhere and Eadric, 16.

101. White 1990, p. 7.

102. Barker n.d., pp. 16-18.

103. For a cautious suggestion concerning Carlisle, see Cramp 1995, p. 7.

104. Kenyon 1948, p. 8.

105. Wacher 1974, p. 375.

106. M.J. Jones and Gilmour 1980, pp. 61-2; Stocker 1993, pp. 117-19.

107. Gilmour 1979; M.J. Jones and Gilmour 1980, Stocker 1993, pp. 117-19; Stafford 1985, p. 87.

108. Rodwell 1984.

109. Blair 1988, pp. 40-50, demonstrates that although minster churches are often found in former Roman towns, the royal sites with which they are associated are sometimes set at a distance. This is not, however, necessarily at variance with the suggestion made here.

110. Biddle 1964. pp. 203-11; *idem* 1972, p. 116, and 1975, pp. 237-40, where it is argued that the early palace was associated with the Roman *basilica*.

111. *H.E.* III.7.

112. *Contra* Yorke 1982, who suggests that Winchester only became a royal centre in the eighth century.

113. Bidwell 1979, pp. 110-12.

114. Merrifield 1965, pp. 62 and 78 n. 60; on the early development of the forum, see Philp 1977.

115. Vince 1990, pp. 59-60.

116. See Bassett 1989a; Darville 1988; Hooke 1985, pp. 76-7; Myres 1986, pp. 157-8; Pretty 1989, pp. 174-5.

117. For an exploration of some of the issues raised by this in relation to revenue extraction, see Barnwell 1996.

118. On Burgundian residences, see Barnwell 1992, p. 87 and the references there; on the Vandals, *ibid.*, pp. 118-20; for Italy, see Chapter 11 above.

119. Esmonde Cleary 1989, esp. pp. 130-61.

120. Wightman 1978, esp. p. 113.

121. For comments with similar implications, see Blair 1992, pp. 241-2.

122. Stephen, *Uita Wilfridi*, 39: '... rex cum regina sua per ciuitates et castellos uicosque cotidie gaudentes et epulantes in pompa saeculari circumeuntes.'

123. *H.E.* II.9.

124. *H.E.* III.11.

125. *H.E.* III.15.

126. *H.E.* IV.19.

127. See Stafford 1983, pp. 73-4.

128. *H.E.* IV.19.

129. *H.E.* III.8.

130. Felix, *Uita Guthlaci*, 48.

131. Bede, *Uita Cuthberti*, 23, 24; cf. Anon., *Uita Cuthberti*, III.6.

132. Bede, *Uita Cuthberti*, 27, 28.

133. *Uita Balthildis*, 10.

134. *L.H.* V.39; IX.39.

135. *H.E.* II.20.

136. *H.E.* V.24; on her relationship to Oswald of the Northumbrians, see *H.E.* III.11.

137. Stephen, *Uita Wilfridi*, 24.

138. *H.E.* II.12.

139. Greg., *Reg.*, XI.35; *H.E.* II.11.

140. Stephen, *Uita Wilfridi*, 2, 3; *H.E.* V.19.

141. Stephen, *Uita Wilfridi*, 22.

142. S 16, 19 (the latter with an identical witness list to S 21).

143. S 15.

144. S 42.

145. S 15, 18.
146. S 16.
147. S 42; see F.M. Stenton 1971, p. 58.
148. Bede, *Uita Cuthberti*, 27, 28.
149. *H.E.* II.20.
150. *H.E.* III.24.
151. *H.E.* II.9; cf. *L.H.* VI.45.
152. *H.E.* IV.3.
153. *H.E.* IV.22.

Chapter 17

1. Campbell 1979a, p. 3.
2. Thacker 1981, pp. 203-4.
3. *H.E.* III.21; the suggestion is strengthened by the fact that the *O.E.B.* describes Peada as 'ætheling'.
4. Stephen, *Uita Wilfridi*, 34.
5. Stephen, *Uita Wilfridi*, 60.
6. *H.E.* III.24.
7. S 8.
8. S 18.
9. *H.E.* IV.19.
10. Stephen, *Uita Wilfridi*, 60.
11. *H.E.* V.24.
12. The following remarks may be equally applicable to the *eorlas* found in the Kentish laws, but the evidence is too scanty for there to be any certainty; *eorlas* are discussed by Chadwick 1905, p. 102, and Loyn 1992, pp. 77-8, though the conclusions of both must remain tentative.
13. E.g. *H.E.* IV.3 refers to St Peter as 'apostolorum princeps', which the *O.E.B.* renders as 'aldor thara apostola'; cf. *H.E.* III.17 (=*O.E.B.* III.14) and IV.18 (=*O.E.B.* IV.20). A parallel usage may be found in the *O.E.B.*'s rendering of *metropolis* as *ealdorburg* ('chief town') – see Campbell 1979b, p. 43.
14. Loyn 1992, p. 75; Campbell 1979a, p. 7; for the origins of the later more definite usage of *ealdorman*, see Yorke 1995, p. 84.
15. Ine, Prologue.
16. For an interpretation of the evolution of the word, see Yorke 1995, p. 84.
17. Ine, 45.
18. Ine, 50.
19. Ine, 36.
20. As thought by Chadwick 1905, p. 284.
21. Bosworth and Toller 1898, p. 836.
22. *H.E.* I.13, 21.
23. *H.E.* III.19; this does not mean, however (*pace* Thacker 1981, pp. 215-17, expanded upon by Yorke 1990, p. 171), that *patricii* in eighth-century Northumbria may have had similarities with Frankish *maiores domus*.
24. S 252; the witness list is suspect, but the text seems less so.
25. Aldhelm, *Ep.*, 10 (13).
26. S 9.
27. For examples other than those already cited, see S 8, 9, 15, 18, 1787.
28. S 7, 10.
29. S 1787.
30. *H.E.* II.9; 13.
31. *H.E.* II.13.
32. Stephen, *Uita Wilfridi*, 11.

33. A phrase used by Stephen, *Uita Wilfridi*, 24.

34. Adomnán, *Uita Columbae*, 8b.

35. Chadwick 1905, p. 334.

36. *H.E.* IV.13.

37. *H.E.* III.3.

38. *H.E.* II.13.

39. Bede, *Chronica maiora*, 590: 'His temporibus multi Anglorum gentis nobiles et ignobiles, uiri et feminae, duces et priuati, diuini amoris instinctu de Brittania Romam uenire consueuerant.'

40. S 102.

41. S 1173.

42. *H.E.* IV.15.

43. *H.E.* III.24.

44. *H.E.* IV.26.

45. *H.E.* V.24; on the identity of Berht and Berctfred, see Wallace-Hadrill 1988, p. 202.

46. *H.E.* III.24.

47. Stephen, *Uita Wilfridi*, 36.

48. Stephen, *Uita Wilfridi*, 18.

49. Anon., *Uita Cuthberti*, I.7.

50. Bede, *Uita Cuthberti*, 15, cf. 16, 31.

51. *H.E.* III.14.

52. Bede, *Epistola ad Ecgbertum*, 13.

53. Stephen, *Uita Wilfridi*, 40.

54. *H.E.* IV.1.

55. Stephen, *Uita Wilfridi*, 60.

56. *H.E.* V.24.

57. *H.E.* II.16.

58. Stephen, *Uita Wilfridi*, 38.

59. Stephen, *Uita Wilfridi*, 36.

60. Stephen, *Uita Wilfridi*, 37.

61. Stephen, *Uita Wilfridi*, 36.

62. Campbell 1979b, pp. 37-41, 43.

63. Thacker 1981, pp. 210-11.

64. Thacker 1981, p. 211.

65. Anon., *Uita Cuthberti*, IV.8.

66. Levison 1946, pp. 125-6.

67. The traditional view is that the two terms are not related – see Chadwick 1905, p. 228 n. 1; Skeat 1884, *sub* 'reeve' – but this has now been questioned – see Braccini 1995, pp. 1089-93.

68. *H.E.* II.16 = *O.E.B.* II.13.

69. Ælfric, *Glossary*, 87.

70. Hlothhere and Eadric, 16.

71. Wihtræd, 22.

72. Ine, 73.

73. *H.E.* V.4.

74. Anon., *Uita Cuthberti*, IV.7.

75. *H.E.* V.4 – not only is Puch's villa described as 'uilla comitis', but another *comes*, Addi, is stated to have built a church (see *H.E.* V.5); Bede, *Epistola ad Ecgbertum*, 11.

76. Bede, *Uita Cuthberti*, 25; Anon., *Uita Cuthberti*, IV.7; *H.E.* V.5 – where 'puer' means 'servant', as in the *pueri regis* of continental sources such as *Pactus legis Salicae*, 13.7 and 54.2, and the Burgundian *Liber constitutionum* LXVI.

77. *H.E.* III.22.

78. *H.E.* I.25.

79. *H.E.* III.21.

80. S 53.

81. *H.E.* IV.22.

82. The term is related to the Gothic *ge-* (or *ga-*)*sintha* (Bosworth and Toller 1898, p. 442), and hence to the Lombard *gasindius* – see Chapter 13; cf. Feist 1939, p. 200, and Skeat 1868, col. 101. On the equation of *comes* and *gesith*, see Larson 1904, p. 82.

83. Ine, 51.

84. Ine, 63, cf. 50.

85. Wihtræd, 5; Ine, 51.

86. Loyn 1955, esp. p. 538, though he suggests a different development.

87. Thacker 1981, p. 207.

88. The only evidence which seems, at first sight, to contradict this is a passage in the anonymous *Uita Ceolfrithi* (cap. 34), which refers to a time when Ceolfrith's father held the 'officium comitatus', but that need imply no more than that he was a *gesithcund* man who was a member of the court.

89. Loyn 1955 and 1992, on the other hand, sees *gesith* as replacing *eorl*, during the second half of the seventh century.

90. See, for example, *H.E.* II.13; III.6, 14.

91. S 102.

92. E.g. *H.E.* II.13; III.3.

93. Bede, *Uita Ceolfrithi*, 8.

94. Bede, *Uita Ceolfrithi*, 1.

95. Diesner 1980, p. 18. Something similar is implied by Bede, *Epistola ad Ecgbertum*, 13.

96. *H.E.* III.14.

97. *H.E.* IV.3.

98. *H.E.* II.9; other *milites* appear in contexts in which they could be seen as bodyguards, though they could be no more than retainers – see *H.E.* II.20; III.1, 3, 14, 24; Stephen, *Uita Wilfridi*, 47.

99. F.M. Stenton 1970a, p. 401.

100. Chadwick 1905, pp. 335-8, where it is suggested that *milites* were young men in the same way as is suggested above for *ministri*.

101. Brunner 1887-92, vol. I pp. 141-2; F.M. Stenton 1971, p. 488.

102. Little 1889, esp. p. 724.

103. Ine, 45.

104. Chadwick 1905, pp. 340-3, 346-7.

105. Loyn 1955, pp. 540-1; part of his argument is derived from his observation that the *thegn*, like a foreigner, could clear his name by taking an oath at the altar, which he suggested might imply that the *thegn* was usually away from home.

106. This seems to be the situation envisaged by the Épinal glossary, which gives *gesith* as the equivalent of *optimas*, and *assecula* and *minister turpitudinis* for *thegn* – see Little 1889, p. 724.

107. See Chadwick 1905, pp. 156-7, where the two groups are characterised as *dugoth* and *geogoth*, respectively.

108. Chadwick 1905, p. 334.

Chapter 18

1. For a detailed study, see Lohaus 1974.

2. The early exponent of the theory that the Jutes were Franks was Jolliffe 1933, passim, but esp. pp. 102-11; the more recent literature is large, and no attempt is made to cite all the relevant authorities here – see, for example, Evison

1965, Myres 1970, p. 170, Wallace-Hadrill 1971, pp. 23-6, and, more recently, Hawkes 1982 (esp. p. 72) with the references there.

3. *H.E.* I.25.

4. These are most fully explored in Wood 1991a: what follows is partial, being restricted to some of the most obvious and significant cases.

5. *H.E.* III.18, cf. II.15.

6. Werner 1985b, p. 42.

7. For example, Sæthryth and Æthelburh, daughters of Anna of the East Angles, were abbesses at Faremoutiers-en-Brie; Earcongota, grand-daughter of Eadbald of Kent (and, therefore, great grand-daughter of Erchinoald) also went there; Hereswith, mother of the East Anglian king, Aldwulf, went to Chelles – *H.E.* III.8, IV.23; for a full discussion, see Wood 1991a, pp. 6-7.

8. This is not restricted to Leudhard, who travelled to England with Bertha (*H.E.* I.25), but also relates to Agilberht and his nephew, Leuthar, in the kingdom of the West Saxons (*H.E.* III.7), and to the Burgundian, Felix, in that of the East Angles (*H.E.* II.15, III.18): for these, and other ecclesiastical contacts, see Wood 1991a.

9. F.M. Stenton 1971, p. 59; Wood 1983b, pp. 15-16; *pace* Levison 1946.

10. The clearest example is Greg., *Reg.*, VI.49, to Theudebert II and Theuderic II; see Wood 1983b, p. 12, and Wood 1994b.

11. Wood 1991a.

12. *H.L.* V.33.

13. *H.L.* V.37.

14. Campbell 1986b, pp. 133-4.

15. Æthelberht, 7; Ine, 33.

16. S 1 (Rochester) and 2-4 (Canterbury).

17. Deanesly 1941, 1941-2, and 1941-3.

18. Levison 1946, Appendix I.

19. Morris 1995.

20. For an account of the document, see Deanesly 1941, pp. 53-8.

21. Levison 1946, pp. 174-5 (cf. M.R. James 1907, p. 2), suggesting that this was the case for S 2 and 3, but that S 4 was written in a different script, which was an imitation of uncial; Deanesly 1941, pp. 53-6, at first thought the script was an earlier Merovingian one (at least in relation to S 3) but later (1941-3, p. 101 n. 3) amended her view, stating that it was 'half-cursive', and of a type found in some ninth-century Anglo-Saxon manuscripts: it is characteristic of Levison's handling of the subject that, although he cites the later paper in this context, he attacks Deanesly on the basis of her original statement.

22. The case for an Augustinian introduction is best stated by Chaplais 1973c; cf. 1973a, esp. pp. 32-3. The best detailed discussion of the origins of the English charter is Wormald 1984, while Kelley 1990, pp. 40-3, provides a coherent and summary critique of the arguments, highlighting their inconclusive nature.

23. *H.E.* I.33.

24. It reads:

> Ego Æthilberhtus rex Anglorum hanc donacionem meam signo
>   sanctae crucis propria manu confirmaui.
> Ego Augustinus gratia Dei archiepiscopus libenter
>   subscripsi.
> Ego Ædbaldus regis filius faui.
> Ego Hamgisilus dux laudaui.
> Ego Hocca comes consensi.
> Ego Angemundus referendarius approbaui.
> Ego Graphio comes bene dixi.
> Ego Tangisilus regis optimas confirmaui.

Ego Pinca consensi.

Ego Geddi corroboraui.

25. As in the following, concerning whose authenticity there is a degree of certainty: S 8, 9-19, 21; though Scharer 1982 thinks S 10, 13, 15, 17 and 18 to be forgeries, and S 21 to be interpolated.

26. Levison 1946, p. 176.

27. Even Deanesly (1941-3, p. 105) had to admit that this smacks of scribal error at the least.

28. Deanesly 1941, p. 65 thought that this was a contraction of *pincerna*, and was therefore the title of another official known from the Merovingian court; Levison 1946, p. 220, however, did not believe that such a contraction was possible, and thought it more likely that the *p* was a misreading of *wyn* (*w*), making the name 'Winca', which is a known place-name element.

29. Levison 1946, pp. 181, 184-6.

30. Morris 1995, p. 94, makes a similar suggestion, though he also thinks that the longer list may be of the same date.

31. Morris 1995, pp. 94-5.

32. Morris 1995, esp. pp. 97-8, reaches a similar conclusion.

33. Levison 1946, p. 221; for the writing of charters, see Chaplais 1973a, p. 36, and Wormald 1984, p. 9.

34. The fact that there are no outward marks of the procedure, such as are found in the tironian notes of the Merovingian documents, or as would be implied by the use of a seal (Chaplais 1973a, p. 33), cannot be taken to indicate that no verification process existed.

35. Morris 1995, p. 95, came near to understanding the true nature of the referendary's position, though without discussing the comparative evidence.

36. It is possible that changes of a similar nature may have occurred in the Merovingian *diplomata* – see Chapter 4 n. 36.

37. *H.E.* II.16.

38. Campbell 1986a, p. 130; for an exploration of some aspects of this question not covered here, see Barnwell 1996.

39. For recent surveys see Higham 1992b and Dark 1994 – though I would not necessarily agree with all the conclusions of either.

40. E.g. Morris 1973, pp. 132-3; Myres 1986, p. 14; Bachrach 1988, p. 135.

41. Cramp 1995; on Bernicia, see Jackson 1953, pp. 701-5.

42. Coates 1989-90; Yorke 1995, p. 49.

Conclusion

1. Wood 1977a, p. 4.

2. The nature of Ine's code is shown in Wormald 1995, which also discusses the relationship of Anglo-Saxon to continental law-making; the important results of Wormald's research present both similarities and contrasts with those presented here.

3. Wallace-Hadrill 1965.

4. *L.H.*, V.17.

5. *H.E.* II.16; Hope-Taylor 1977, pp. 119-22, 241-4.

6. Barnwell 1992.

Bibliography

Primary sources

The following list contains selected editions of primary sources; translations are not generally cited.

Adomnán, *Uita Columbae*, ed. and trans. A.O. and M.O. Anderson, London 1961
Aldhelm, *Carmina ecclesiastica*, ed. R. Ehwald, *M.G.H., A.A.* XV, Berlin 1919
Aldhelm, *Epistolae*, ed. R. Ehwald, *M.G.H., A.A.* XV, Berlin 1919
Alfonso III, *Chronicle*, ed. J. Prelog, Frankfurt am Main 1980
Ammianus Marcellinus, *Rerum gestarum libri qui supersunt*, ed. and trans. J.C. Rolfe, 3 vols London and Harvard 1935-40
Anglo-Saxon Chronicle, ed. D. Whitelock, D.C. Douglas and S.I. Tucker, London 1961
Annales Mettenses Priores, ed. B. von Simson, *M.G.H., S.R.G. in usum scholarum separatim editi*, Hanover 1905
Anon., *Uita Ceolfrithi*, ed. (as *Historia abbatum*) C. Plummer, *Venerabilis Bedae opera historica*, 2 vols Oxford 1896
Anon., *Uita sancti Cuthberti*, ed. and trans. B. Colgrave, Cambridge 1940
Autpert, *Uita Paldonis, Tatonis et Tasonis Uulternensium*, ed. G. Waitz, *M.G.H., S.R.L.*, Hanover 1878
Ælfric, *Glossary*, ed J. Zupitza, Berlin 1966
Bede, *Chronica maiora ad a. DCCXXV*, ed. T. Mommsen, *M.G.H., A.A.* XIII, Berlin 1898
Bede, *Epistola ad Ecgbertum episcopum*, ed. C. Plummer, *Venerabilis Bedae opera historica*, 2 vols Oxford 1896
Bede, *Historia ecclesiastica gentis Anglorum*, ed. C. Plummer, *Venerabilis Bedae opera historica*, 2 vols Oxford 1896; also ed. B. Colgrave and R.A.B. Mynors, Oxford 1969
Bede, *Uita Ceolfrithi*, ed. (as *Historia abbatum*), C. Plummer, *Venerabilis Bedae opera historica*, 2 vols Oxford 1896
Bede, *Uita sancti Cuthberti*, ed. and trans B. Colgrave, Cambridge 1940
Bibliorum sacrorum latinae versiones antiquae, ed. P. Sabatier, 3 vols 1751
Braulio, *Epistolae*, ed. J. Madoz, Madrid 1941
Braulio, *Uita sancti Aemiliani confessoris*, in *P.L.* LXXX
A. Canellas López, *Diplomática Hispano-Visigoda*, Saragossa 1979
Capitularia Merowingica, ed. A. Boretius, *M.G.H., Leges, sectio II t. I*, Hanover 1883
Carmen de synodo Ticinensi, ed. L. Bethmann and G. Waitz, *M.G.H., S.R.L.*, Hanover 1878
Cartularium Saxonicum: a collection of charters relating to Anglo-Saxon history, ed. W. de G. Birch, 3 vols London 1885-93; other editions of charters, notably those sponsored by the British Academy, have also been consulted as appropriate.

Bibliography

Chartae Latinae Antiquiores, 1954-

Chronica rerum Visigothorum, ed. K. Zeumer, *M.G.H., Leges, sectio I t. I*, Hanover and Leipzig 1902

Chronicle of 754, ed. T. Mommsen, in *Continuationes Bizantina Arabica et Hispani, M.G.H., A.A.* XI, Berlin 1894

Chronicon Beneventani monasterii sanctae Sophiae, ed. F. Ughelli, *Italia sacra*, X Venice 1722

Chronicon Uulternese del monaco Giovanni, ed. V. Federici, 3 vols Rome 1925-38

Codex Carolinus, ed. W. Gundlach, *M.G.H., Ep.* III, Berlin 1892

Codex Eurici, ed. K. Zeumer, *M.G.H., Leges, sectio I t. I*, Hanover and Leipzig, 1902

Codex Iustinianus, ed. P. Krueger, Berlin 1900

Codex Theodosianus, ed. T. Mommsen, *Theodosiani libri XIV cum constitutionibus sirmondianis*, Berlin 1905; see also the translation by C. Pharr *et al.*, *The Theodosian Code and Novels and the Sirmondian constitutions*, Princeton 1952

Codice Diplomatico Longobardo, 5 vols Rome 1929-; vols I-II ed. L. Schiaperelli; vols. III-IV.i ed. C. Brühl; vol V ed. H. Zielinski (= *Fonti per la storia d'Italia pubblicate dall'Istituto storico italiano* 62-6)

Concilia Galliae a. 511-a. 695, ed. C. de Clerq, Turnholt 1963 (= *Corpus Christianorum series Latina* CXLVIIIa)

Constantine VII Porphyrogenitus, *De ceremoniis aulae Byzantinae*, ed. J.J. Reiski, 2 vols Bonn 1829-30 (in *Corpus Scriptorum Historiae Byzantinae*)

Constantius, *Uita Germani episcopi Autissiodorensis*, ed. R. Borius, Paris 1965 (= *Sources chrétiennes* 112)

De Liutprando rege, ed. G. Waitz, *M.G.H., S.R.L.*, Hanover 1878

Desiderius of Cahors, *Epistolae*, ed. W. Arndt, *M.G.H., Ep.* III, Berlin 1892

M.C. Diaz y Diaz, 'Los documentos hispano-visigóticos sobre pizarra', *Studi medievali* 3rd ser VII (1966) pp. 75-107

Diplomata Arnulfingi (=*Diplomata maiorum domus regiae*), ed. G.H. Pertz, *M.G.H., Diplomata imperii I*, Hanover 1872

Diplomata Merovingicorum (=*Diplomata regum Francorum e stirpe Merowingica*), ed. G.H. Pertz, *M.G.H., Diplomata imperii I*, Hanover 1872

Edictum Rothari, ed. F. Bluhme, *M.G.H., Leges (in folio)* IIII, Hanover 1868; see also C. Azzara and S. Gasparri, ed. and trans., *Le leggi dei Longobardi: storia, memoria e diritto di un popolo germanico*, Milan 1992

Einhard, *Uita Karoli Magni*, ed. O. Holder-Egger, *M.G.H., S.R.G. in usum scholarum separatim editi*, 6th edn. Hanover 1911

Elmham (Thomas), *Historia monasterii sancti Augustini Cantuariensis*, ed C. Hardick, London 1858 (Rolls Series)

Epistolae Aevi Merowingici Collectae, ed. W. Gundlach, *M.G.H., Ep.* III, Berlin 1892

Epistolae Austrasicae, ed. W. Gundlach, *M.G.H., Ep.* III, Berlin 1892; see also the edition by M. Rochais, Turnholt 1957 (= *Corpus Christianorum series Latina* CXVII.1)

Epistolae Langobardicae collectae, ed. W. Gundlach, *M.G.H., Ep.* III, Berlin 1892

Epistolae Wisigothicae, ed. W. Gundlach, *M.G.H., Ep.* III, Berlin 1892

Epistola Pauli perfidi, ed. W. Levison, *M.G.H., S.R.M.* V, Hanover and Leipzig 1910

Felix, *Uita sancti Guthlaci*, ed. and trans. B. Colgrave, Cambridge 1956

Felix of Toledo, *Uita sancti Iuliani Toletani episcopi*, in *P.L.* XCVI

'Florence' (= John) of Worcester, *Chronicon*, ed. B. Thorpe, London 1848

Formulae Andecauenses, ed. K. Zeumer, *M.G.H., Leges, sectio V*, Hanover 1886

Formulae Aruernensis, ed. K. Zeumer, *M.G.H., Leges, sectio V*, Hanover 1886

Formulae Biturcenses, ed. K. Zeumer, *M.G.H., Leges, sectio V*, Hanover 1886

Formlae Marculfi, ed. K. Zeumer, *M.G.H., Leges, sectio V*, Hanover 1886

Formulae Turonensis, ed. K. Zeumer, *M.G.H., Leges, sectio V*, Hanover 1886

Bibliography

Formulae Wisigothicae, ed. K. Zeumer, *M.G.H., Leges, sectio V*, Hanover 1886

Fortunatus (Venantius Honorius Clementianus), *Carmina*, ed. F. Leo, *M.G.H., A.A.* IV.i, Berlin 1881

Fredegar, *Chronicle*, ed. B. Krusch, *M.G.H., S.R.M.* II, Hanover 1888; for Book IV and the continuations, see also J.M. Wallace-Hadrill, *The Fourth Book of the Chronicle of Fredegar with its continuations*, London 1960

Gesta Dagoberti I regis Francorum, ed. B. Krusch, *M.G.H., S.R.M.* II, Hanover 1888

M. Gibbs, *Early Charters of the Cathedral Church of St Paul, London*, London 1939 (= Camden 3rd ser LVIII)

Gildas, *De excidio et conquestu Britanniae ac flebili castigatione in reges, principes et sacerdotes*, ed. T. Mommsen, *M.G.H., A.A.* XIII, Berlin 1898; see also M. Winterbottom, ed. and trans., *Gildas: The Ruin of Britain and other works*, Chichester 1978

M. Gómez-Moreno, *Documentación goda en pizarra: studio y transcripción*, Madrid 1966

Goscelin of Canterbury, *Uita Deo dilectae uirginis Midrethae*, ed. D. Rollason, *The Mildrith Legend: a study in early medieval hagiography in England*, Leicester 1982

Gregory of Tours, *Decem libri historiarum*, ed. B. Krusch and W. Levison, *M.G.H., S.R.M.* I.i, Hanover 1937-51

Gregory the Great, *Dialogues*, ed. A. de Vogüé, 3 vols Paris 1978-80 (= *Sources chrétiennes* 251; 260; 265)

Gregory the Great, *Register Epistolarum*, ed. P. Ewald and L.M. Hartmann, *M.G.H., Ep.* I and II, Berlin 1891-99.

Historia Brittonum, ed. T. Mommsen, *M.G.H., A.A.* XIII, Berlin 1898; see also J. Morris, ed. and trans., *Nennius: British History and the Welsh Annals*, Chichester 1980

In ecclesia beati Anastasi quam construxit Leutbrandus rex in Italia, ed. F. Dümmler, *M.G.H., Poetae latinae medii aevi* I, Berlin 1881

Isidore of Seville, *Chronica maiora*, ed. T. Mommson, *M.G.H., A.A.* XI, Berlin 1894

Isidore of Seville, *Etymologicarum siue Origines libri XX*, ed. W.M. Lindsey, 2 vols Oxford 1911

Isidore of Seville, *Historia Gothorum*, ed. T. Mommson, *M.G.H., A.A.* XI, Berlin 1894

Isidore of Seville, *Historia Sueborum*, ed. T. Mommsen, *M.G.H., A.A.* XI, Berlin 1894

Isidore of Seville, *Historia Vandalorum*, ed. T. Mommsen, *M.G.H., A.A.* XI, Berlin 1894

Isidore of Seville, *Sententiae*, in *P.L.* LXXXIII

John of Biclaro, *Chronicle*, ed. T. Mommsen, *M.G.H., A.A.* XI, Berlin 1894

Jonas, *Uita Columbani abbatis discipulorum eius*, ed. B. Krusch, *M.G.H., S.R.M.* IV, Hanover 1902

Julian, *Epitome latina nouellarum Iustiniani*, ed. G. Haenel, Leipzig 1873

Julian of Toledo, *Historia excellentissimi Wambae regis de expeditione et uictoria, qua reuellantem contra se prouinciam Galliae celebri triumpho perdomuit*, and the associated *Insultatio uilis storici in tyrannidem Galliae*, and *Iudicium in tyrannorum perfidia promulgatum*, ed. W. Levison, *M.G.H., S.R.M.* V, Hanover and Leipzig 1910

Justinian, *Nouellae*, ed. R. Schöll and G. Kroll, 8th edn Berlin 1963

Laudes Mediolanensis ciuitate: uersum de Mediolano ciuitate, ed. E Dümmler, *M.G.H., Poetae latinae medii aevi* I, Berlin 1881

Laws of Æthelberht, ed. F. Liebermann, *Die Gesetze der Angelsächsen*, vol. 1 Halle 1903

Bibliography

Laws of Hlothhere and Eadric, as *Laws of Æthelberht*
Laws of Ine, as *Laws of Æthelberht*
Laws of Wihtræd, as *Laws of Æthelberht*
Leges Aistulfi, as *Edictum Rothari*
Leges Grimualdi, as *Edictum Rothari*
Leges Liutprandi, as *Edictum Rothari*
Leges Ratchis, as *Edictum Rothari*
Leo II, *Epistolae*, in *P.L.* XCVI
Lex Baiuuariorum, ed. E. von Schwind, *M.G.H., Leges, sectio I t. V.ii*, Hanover 1926
Lex Ribuaria, ed. F. Beyerle and R. Buchner, *M.G.H., Leges, sectio I t. III.ii*, Hanover 1954
Lex Romana Burgundionum, ed. L.R. de Salis, *M.G.H., Leges, sectio I t. II.i*, Hanover 1892
Lex Romana Uisigothorum, ed. G. Haenel, Berlin 1849
Lex Thiudi, ed. K. Zeumer, *M.G.H., Leges, sectio I t. I*, Hanover and Leipzig 1902
Liber constitutionum, ed., L.R. de Salis, *M.G.H., Leges, sectio I t. II.i*, Hanover 1892
Liber historiae Francorum, ed. B. Krusch, *M.G.H., S.R.M.* II, Hanover 1888
Liber iudicorum siue Lex Uisigothorum edita ab Reccesvindo rege a. 654 renovata ab Ervigio rege a. 681, accedunt (suis locis insertae) leges nouellae et extrauagantes, ed. K. Zeumer, *M.G.H., Leges, sectio I t. I*, Hanover and Leipzig 1902
Liber Pontificalis, ed. L. Duchesne, 3 vols Paris 1955-7
Marius of Avenches, *Chronicle*, ed. T. Mommson, *M.G.H., A.A.* XI, Berlin 1894
A. Mundó Marcet, *Los diplomas visigodas originales en pergamino, transcripción y commentario con un regesto de documentos de la época visigoda*, Barcelona 1974
The Old English Version of Bede's Ecclesiastical History of the English People, ed. T. Millar, 4 vols London 1890-98
Origo gentis Langobardorum, ed. G. Waitz, *M.G.H., S.R.L.*, Hanover 1878
Pactus legis Alamannorum, ed. K. Lehman, *M.G.H., Leges, sectio I t. V.i*, Hanover 1888
Pactus legis Salicae, ed. K.A. Eckhardt, *M.G.H., Leges, sectio I t. IV.i*, Hanover 1962
J.M. Pardessus, ed., *Diplomata, chartae, epistolae, leges ...*, 2 vols Paris 1843-9 repr. 1969
Passio Desiderii episcopi et Raginfridi diaconi martyrum Alsegaudiensium, ed. W Levison, *M.G.H., S.R.M.* VI, Hanover and Leipzig 1913
Passio Leudegarii episcopi et martyris Augustodunensis I, ed., B. Krusch, *M.G.H., S.R.M.* V, Hanover 1910
Passio Praeiecti episcopi et martyris Aruerni, ed. B. Krusch, *M.G.H., S.R.M.* V, Hanover 1910
Paul, *Sententiae*, in *Fontes iuris romani anteiustiniani*, vol. 2 Florence 1968
Paul the Deacon, *Historia Langobardorum*, ed. G. Waitz, *M.G.H., S.R.G, in usum scholarum separatim editi*, Hanover 1878
Paul the Deacon, *Historia Romana*, ed. A. Crivellucci, Rome 1913 (= *Fonti per la storia d'Italia pubblicate dall'Istituto storico italiano* 51)
Procopius, *De Bello Persico*, ed. J. Haury, *Procopius, opera omnia*, 3 vols Leipzig 1905-13
Procopius, *Historia Arcana*, as Procopius *De Bello Persico*
Il regesto di Farfa di Gregorio di Catino, ed. I. Giorgi and U. Balzani, 5 vols Rome 1879-92
Sidonius Apollinaris, *Epistolae*, ed. A Loyen, 2 vols Paris 1970
Sisebut, *Letter to Isidore*, ed. A. Bährens, *Poetae latini minores*, vol. 5 Leipzig 1883
Sisebut, *Uita uel passio sancti Desiderii*, ed. B. Krusch, *M.G.H., S.R.M.* III, Hanover 1896
Stephani II papae bulla qui decernit contra episcopum Senensem quasdam paro-

Bibliography

chias spectare ad ecclesiam Arretinam a. 752, ed. L. Muratori, *Antiquitates Italiae medii aevi*, vol. 6 Milan 1942

Stephen, *Uita sancti Wilfridi episcopi*, ed. and trans B. Colgrave Cambridge 1927

Taio, *Sententiarum libri quinque*, in *P.L.* LXXX

Theodore, *Epistolae*, in *P.L.* LXXXVII

Vegetius, *Epitoma rei militaris*, ed C. Lang, Leipzig, 1885

I. Velázquez Soriano, *El Latín de las pizarras visigóticas*, 2 vols Madrid 1989

Uirtutes Fursei abbatis Latiniacensis, ed. B. Krusch, *M.G.H., S.R.M.* IV, Hanover 1902

Uita Amandi, ed. B. Krusch, *M.G.H., S.R.M.* V, Hanover 1910

Uita Aniani episcopi Aurelianensis, ed. B. Krusch, *M.G.H., S.R.M* III, Hanover 1896

Uita Ansberti episcopi Rotomagensis, ed. W. Levison, *M.G.H., S.R.M.* V, Hanover 1910

Uita Audoini episcopi Rotomagensis, ed. W. Levison, *M.G.H., S.R.M* V, Hanover 1910

Uita Austrigisli episcopi Biturigi, ed. B. Krusch, *M.G.H., S.R.M.* IV, Hanover 1901

Uita Bertilae abbatissae Calensis, ed. W. Levison, *M.G.H., S.R.M.* VI, Hanover and Leipzig 1913

Uita Bertini episcopi Aruerni, ed. B. Krusch, *M.G.H., S.R.M.* VI, Hanover and Leipzig 1913

Uita Condedi anchoretae Belcinnacensis, ed. W. Levison, *M.G.H., S.R.M* V, Hanover 1910

Uita Desiderii Cadurcae urbis episcopi, ed. B. Krusch, *M.G.H., S.R.M.* IV, Hanover 1902

Uita Eligii episcopi Nouiomagensis, ed. B. Krusch, *M.G.H., S.R.M.* IV, Hanover 1902

Uita Eremberti episcopi Tolosani, ed. W. Levison, *M.G.H., S.R.M.* V, Hanover 1910

Uita Fursei abbatis Latiniacensis, ed. B. Krusch, *M.G.H., S.R.M.* IV, Hanover 1902

Uita Germani abbatis Grandiuallensis, ed. B. Krusch, *M.G.H., S.R.M.* V, Hanover 1910

Uita Gregorii Magni, ed. and trans, B. Colgrave, Cambridge 1985

Uita sanctae Balthildae, ed. B. Krusch, *M.G.H., S.R.M.* II, Hanover 1888

Uita sancti Agili abbatis, in *Acta Sanctorum, Augusti VI*

Uita sancti Arnulfi, ed. B. Krusch, *M.G.H., S.R.M.* II, Hanover 1888

Uita sancti Desiderati episcopi Biturcensium, in *Acta Sanctorum, Maii II*

Uita sancti Fructuosi, ed. F.C. Noak, Washington 1946

Uitas Patrum Emeritensium, ed. J.N. Garvin, Washington 1946

J. Vives, *Concilios visigóticos e hispano-romanos*, Barcelona and Madrid 1963

J. Vives, *Inscripciones cristianas de la España romana y visigoda*, Barcelona 1942

D. Whitelock, *English Historical Documents, vol. 1: c. 500-1042*, 2nd edn London 1979

Widukind of Corvei, *Rerum gestarum Saxonicum libri tres*, ed. P. Hirsch and H.-E. Lohmann, *M.G.H., S.R.G. in usum scholarum separatim editi*, 5th edn Hanover 1935

Secondary works

Andreolli, M.P., 1966. 'Un pagina di storia Longobarda: "Re Ratchis" ', *Nuova rivista di storia* L pp. 281-327

Andrés Marcos, T., 1929. *Constitución, transmisión y ejercicio de la monarquía visigoda en los concilios de Toledo*, Salamanca

Anton, H.H., 1972. 'Der König und die Reichskonzilien im westgotischen Spanien', *Historisches Jahrbuch* 92 pp. 257-81

Bibliography

Applebaum, S., 1972. 'Roman Britain', in H.P.R. Finberg (ed.), *The Agrarian History of England and Wales, vol. 1.2: A.D. 43-1042*, Cambridge pp. 3-277

Arslan, E.A., 1990. 'Le monete', in Menis 1990 pp. 164-5

Astuti, G., 1974. 'Spirito del diritto longobardo: il processo ordalico', *Atti del congresso internazionale sul tema: la civiltà dei Longobardi in Europa*, Rome pp. 85-100 (= *Problemi attuali di scienza e di cultura: Accademia nazionale dei Lincei CCCLXXI*)

Astuti, G., 1975. 'Influssi romanistici nelle fonti del diritto longobardo', *Settimane ... XXII: La cultura antica nell'occidente latino dal VII all'XI secolo* pp. 653-95

Atsma, H. (ed.), 1989. *La Neustrie. Les Pays au nord de la Loire de 650 à 850: colloque historique international*, 2 vols Sigmaringen

Bachrach, B.S., 1972. *Merovingian Military Organisation, 481-751*, Minneapolis

Bachrach, B.S., 1973. 'A reassessment of Visigothic Jewish policy, 589-711', *American Historical Review* 78 pp. 11-34

Bachrach, B.S., 1974. 'Was the Marchfield part of the Frankish constitution?', *Medieval Studies* 36 pp. 128-85

Bachrach, B.S., 1988. 'Gildas, Vortigern and constitutionality in sub-Roman Britain', *Nottingham Medieval Studies* XXXII pp. 126-40

Badini, A., 1980. 'La concezione delle regalità in Liutprando e le inscrizioni delle chiesa di s. Anastasio a Corteolona', *Atti ...*, 6 pp. 283-302

Balon, J., 1968a. 'Les arrêts de la cour palatine; reflets de la civilisation mérovingienne', *Anciens Pays et assemblées d'états* 48 pp. 1-22

Balon, J., 1968b. 'Le plaid royal de Valenciennes, 28 février 693', *Anciens Pays et assemblées d'états* 47 pp. 1-35

Balon, J., 1973. 'Aux origines du régime parlementaire dans le monde moderne: les assemblées législatives franques et leurs réalisations', *Anciens Pays et assemblées d'états* 62 pp. 5-19

Barbero de Aguilera, A., 1970. 'El pensamiento político visigodo y las primeras unciones regias en la Europa medieval', *Hispania* 115 pp. 245-326

Barbier, J., 1985. 'Palais et terres du fisc en Neustrie', in Périn and Feffer 1985 pp. 67-70

Barbier, J., 1989. 'Aspects du fisc en Neustrie (IVe – Xe siècles). Résultats d'une recherche en cours', in Atsma 1989 vol. 1 pp. 129-42

Barbier, J., 1990. 'Le système palatial franc: genèse et fonctionnement dans le nord-ouest du *regnum*', *Bibliothèque de l'École des Chartes* 148 pp. 245-99

Barker, P.A., n.d. *Wroxeter Roman City: excavations 1966-1980*, London

Barker, P.A. (ed.), 1990. *From Roman Viroconium to medieval Wroxeter: recent work on the site of the Roman city of Wroxeter*, Worcester

Barnwell, P.S., 1991. ' "Epistola Hieronomi de gradus Romanorum": an English school book', *Historical Research* 64 pp. 77-86

Barnwell, P.S., 1992. *Emperor, Prefects and Kings: the Roman West 395-565*, London and Chapel Hill

Barnwell, P.S., 1996. 'Hlafæta, ceorl, hid and scir: Celtic, Roman or Germanic?', *Anglo-Saxon Studies in Archaeology and History* 9

Bartolini, F., 'Problemi di diplomatica longobardi', *Atti del 1° congresso internazionale de studi longobardi*, Spoleto pp. 29-36

Bassett, S., 1989a. 'Churches in Worcester before and after the conversion of the Anglo-Saxons', *Antiquaries Journal* LXIX pp. 225-56

Bassett, S., 1989b. 'In search of the origins of Anglo-Saxon kingdoms', in Bassett 1989c pp. 3-27

Bassett, S. (ed.), 1989c. *The Origins of Anglo-Saxon Kingdoms*, Leicester

Bastier, J., 1979. 'Droit wisigothique et droit germanique', *Mélanges offerts à Jean Dauvillier*, Toulouse pp. 47-64

237

Bibliography

Belfort, A. de, 1892-5. *Description générale des monnaies mérovingiennes*, 5 vols Paris

Belting, H., 1962. 'Studien zum beneventanischen Hof im 8. Jahrhundert', *Dumbarton Oaks Papers* 16 pp. 143-93

Benveniste, E., 1969. *Le Vocabulaire des institutions indo-européennes*, 2 vols Paris

Bergmann, W., 1976. 'Untersuchungen zu den Gerichtsurkunden der Merowingerzeit', *Archiv für Diplomatik* 22 pp. 1-186

Berschin, W., 1989. '*Opus deliberatione ac perfectum*: why did the Venerable Bede write a Second Prose Life of St Cuthbert?', in Bonner, Rollason and Stancliffe 1989 pp. 95-102

Bertini, L., 1973. 'I gastaldi longobardi di Siena', *Atti* ..., 5 pp. 681-6

Bertolini, O., 1968a. 'Ordinamenti militari e strutture sociali dei Longobardi in Italia', *Settimane ... XV: Ordinamenti militari in occidente nell'alto medioevo* pp. 429-607

Bertolini, O., 1968b. 'Le relazione politiche di Roma con i ducati di Spoleto e di Benevento nel periodo del dominio Longobardo', in *idem*, *Scritti scelti de storia medievale*, 2 vols Livorno vol. 2 pp. 681-92

Bertolini, O., 1972. *Roma e i Longobardi*, Rome

Besta, E., 1927-9. *Il diritto pubblico italiano*, 3 vols Padua

Besta, E., 1952. 'Le fonti dell'editto de Rotari', *Atti del 1° congresso internazionale de studi longobardi*, Spoleto pp. 51-69

Beyerle, F., 1928. 'Die *Lex Ribuaria*', *Z.R.G., g.A.* 48 pp. 264-378

Beyerle, F., 1929. 'Die süddeutschen Leges und die merovingische Gesetzgebung', *Z.R.G., g.A.* 49 pp. 264-434

Beyerle, F., 1935. 'Die Gesetzbuch Ribuariens', *Z.R.G., g.A.* 55 pp. 1-80

Beyerle, F., 1955. 'Die Formel-Schulbuch Markulfs', *Aus Verfassungs- und Landesgeschichte. Festschrift zum 70. Geburtstag Theodor Mayer dargebracht von seinen Freunden und Schülern*, 2 vols Lindau und Konstanz vol. 2 pp. 365-89

Beyerle, F., 1956. 'Die beiden süddeutschen Stammesrechte', *Z.R.G., g.A.* 63 pp. 84-104

Bianchi, D., 1953. 'Per il testo della "Historia Langobardorum" di Paolo Diacono', *Atti* ..., 2 pp. 121-37

Biddle, M., 1964. 'Excavations at Winchester, 1962-3: second interim report', *Antiquaries Journal* XLIV pp. 188-219.

Biddle, M., 1972. 'Excavations at Winchester, 1970: ninth interim report', *Antiquaries Jounral* LII pp. 93-131

Biddle, M., 1975. 'Winchester: the development of an early capital', in H. Jankuhn, W. Schlesinger and H. Steuer (eds), *Vor- und Frühformen der europäischen Stadt in Mittelalter: Bericht über ein Symposium in Reinhausen bei Göttingen*, 2 vols Göttingen vol. 1 pp. 229-62

Bidwell, P.T., 1979. *The Legionary Bath-house and Basilica and Forum at Exeter, with a summary account of the legionary fortress*, Exeter

Bierbrauer, V., 1990. 'Il ducato di Tridentum', in Menis 1990 pp. 113-16

Bischoff, B., 1990. *Latin Palaeography: antiquity and the middle ages*, Cambridge

Blagg, T.F.C., 1982. 'Roman Kent' in Leech 1982 pp. 51-60

Blair, J., 1988. 'Minster churches in the landscape', in D. Hooke (ed.), *Anglo-Saxon Settlements*, Oxford pp. 35-58

Blair, J., 1989. 'Frithuwold's kingdom and the origins of Surrey', in Bassett 1989c pp. 97-107

Blair, J., 1992. 'Anglo-Saxon minsters: a topographical review', in J. Blair and R. Sharpe (eds), *Pastoral Care before the Parish*, Leicester, London and New York pp. 226-66

Boak, A.E.R., 1915. 'The Roman *magistri* in the civil and military service of the Empire', *Harvard Studies in Classical Philology* XXVI pp. 73-162

Bibliography

Bognetti, G.P., 1966. 'Il gastaldato longobardo e i giudicati de Adaloaldo, Arioaldo e Pertarido nella lite fra Parma e Piacenza', in *idem* 1966-8 vol. 1 pp. 219-74

Bognetti, G.P., 1966-8. *L'età longobarda*, 4 vols Milan

Bognetti, G.P., 1967a. 'Il ducato longobardo di Spoleto', in *idem* 1966-8 vol. 3 pp. 485-505

Bognetti, G.P., 1967b. 'L'influsso delle istituzioni militari romane sulle istituzioni longobarde del secolo VI e la nature della "fara" ', in *idem* 1966-8 vol. 3, pp. 1-46

Bognetti, G.P., 1967c. 'I ministri romani dei re longobardi e un'opinione di Alessandro Manzoni', in *idem* 1966-8 vol. 3 pp. 47-66

Bognetti, G.P., 1967d. 'Tradizione longobarda e politica bizantina nelle origini del ducato di Spoleto', in *idem* 1966-8 vol. 3 pp. 441-75

Bognetti, G.P., 1968a. 'La costituzione e l'ordinamento dei primi stati barbarici nell'Europa occidentale dopo le invasioni nelle Romania', in *idem* 1966-8 vol. 4 pp. 455-71

Bognetti, G.P. 1968b. 'Frammenti di uno studio sulla composizione dell'Editto di Rotari', in *idem* 1966-8 vol. 4 pp. 585-609

Bognetti, G.P., 1968c. 'L'Editto di Rotari come espediente politico di una monarchia barbarica', in *idem* 1966-8 vol. 4 pp. 113-35

Bognetti, G.P., 1968d. 'Teoderico di Verona e Verona longobarda capitale di Regno', in *idem* 1966-8 vol. 4 pp. 339-77

Bonner, G., Rollason, D., and Stancliffe, C. (eds), 1989. *St Cuthbert, his cult and his community to A.D. 1200*, Woodbridge

Bosworth, J., and Toller, T.N., 1898. *An Anglo-Saxon Dictionary*, Oxford

Boussard, J., 1973. 'L'ouest du royaume franc aux VIIe et VIIIe siècles', *Journal des savants*, pp. 3-27

Braccini, G.P., 1995. 'Termini germanici per il diritto e la giustizia: sulle tracce dei significati autentici attraverso etimologie vecchie e nuove', *Settimane ... XLII: La giustizia nell'alto medioevo* pp. 1053-207

Bresslau, H., 1912-58. *Handbuch der Urkundenlehre für Deustchland und Italien*, 2 vols Leipzig and Berlin; repr. Berlin 1960

Brogiolo, G.P., 1990. 'Il problema della continuità', in Menis 1990 p. 130

Brooks, N.P., 1974. 'Anglo-Saxon Charters: the work of the last twenty years', *Anglo-Saxon England* 3 pp. 211-32

Brooks, N.P., 1984. *The Early History of the Church at Canterbury*, Leicester

Brooks, N.P., 1989a. 'The creation and early structure of the kingdom of Kent', in Bassett 1989c pp. 55-74

Brooks, N.P., 1989b. 'The formation of the Mercian kingdom', in Bassett 1989c pp. 159-70

Brown, T.S., 1984. *Gentlemen and Officers: imperial administration and aristocratic power in Byzantine Italy, AD 554-800*, London

Brühl, C., 1967. 'Remarques sur les notions de "capitale" et de "résidence" pendant le haut moyen âge', *Journal des savants* pp. 193-215

Brühl, C., 1968. *Fodrum, Gistum, Servitum Regis: Studien zu dem wirtschaftlichen Grundlagen des Königtums im Frankenreich und in den fränkischen Nachfolgestaaten Deutschland, Frankreich und Italien vom 6. bis zur Mitte des 14. Jahrhunderts*, 2 vols Cologne and Graz

Brühl, C., 1969. 'Das "Palatium" von Pavia und die "Honorantiae Civitatis Papiae" ', *Atti ...*, 4 pp. 189-220

Brühl, C., 1970. *Studien zu den langobardischen Königsurkunden*, Tübingen

Brühl, C., 1971. 'Chronologie und Urkunden der Herzöge von Spoleto', *Quellen und Forschungen* LI pp. 1-92

Brühl, C., 1972. 'Langobardische Königsurkunden als Geschichtsquelle', *Studi storici in onore de Ottorino Bertolini*, 2 vols Pisa vol. 1 pp. 47-72

Bibliography

Brühl, C., 1973. 'Zentral- und Finanzverwaltung im Franken- und Langobarden-reich', *Settimane ... XX: I problemi dell'occidente nel secolo VIII* pp. 61-94

Brühl, C., 1979. 'Die Urkunden der Langobarden: Überlieferung und Probleme', *Jahrbuch für internationale Germanistik* XI.1 pp. 93-9

Brühl, C., 1983. 'Überlegungen zur Diplomatik der spoletinischen Herzogs-urkunde', *Atti ...*, 9 pp. 231-49

Brühl, C., 1989. 'Das merowingische Königtum im Spiegel seiner Urkunden', in Atsma 1989 vol. 1 pp. 523-33

Brunhölzl, F., 1990. *Histoire de la littérature latine du moyen âge, I.1: l'époque mérovinginenne*, Louvain

Brunner, H., 1887-92. *Deutsche Rechtsgeshichte*, 2 vols Leipzig

Brunner, H., 1888. 'Zur Geschichte des Gefolgswesens', *Z.R.G., g.A.* 9 pp. 210-19

Buchner, R., 1953. *Die Rechtsquellen*, Weimar (= Supplement to W. Wattenbach and W. Levison, *Deutschlands Geschichtsquellen im Mittelalter, Vorzeit und Karolinger*)

Bullough, D.A., 1971. 'The writing-office of the Dukes of Spoleto in the eighth century', in *idem* and R.L. Storey (eds), *The Study of Medieval Records: essays in honour of Kathleen Major*, Oxford pp. 1-21

Bullough, D.A., 1986. 'Ethnic history and the Carolingians: an alternative reading of Paul the Deacon's *Historia Langobardorum*, in C. Holdsworth and T.P. Wiseman (eds), *The Inheritance of Historiography, 350-900*, Exeter pp. 85-106

Bury, J.B., 1910. 'Magistri scriniorum, antigraphês and rhepherendarioi', *Harvard Studies in Classical Philology* XXI pp. 23-9

Bury J.B., 1958. *History of the Later Roman Empire: from the death of Theodosius I to the death of Justinian*, New York (repr.)

Byrne, J.F., 1973. *Irish Kings and High-Kings*, London

Caggiano, A., 1982. 'L'amministrazione periferica longobarda in Puglia: gastaldi e gastaldati', *Vetera Christianorum* 19 pp. 361-72

Campbell, J., 1966. 'Bede', in T.A. Dorey (ed.), *The Latin Historians*, London pp. 159-90

Campbell, J., 1979a. *Bede's reges and principes*, Jarrow

Campbell, J., 1979b. 'Bede's words for places', in P.H. Sawyer (ed.), *Names, Words and Graves: early medieval settlement*, Leeds pp. 34-55

Campbell, J., 1982. *The Anglo-Saxons*, Oxford

Campbell, J., 1986a. 'The Age of Arthur', in *idem*, *Essays in Anglo-Saxon History*, London pp. 121-30

Campbell, J., 1986b. 'Early Anglo-Saxon society according to written sources', in *idem*, *Essays in Anglo-Saxon History*, London pp. 131-8

Campbell, J., 1989a. 'Elements in the background to the Life of St Cuthbert and his early cult', in Bonner, Rollason and Stancliffe 1989 pp. 3-19

Campbell, J., 1989b. 'The sale of land and the economics of power in early England: problems and possibilities', *Haskins Society Journal* 1 pp. 23-37

Campbell, J., 1992. 'The impact of the Sutton Hoo discovery on the study of Anglo-Saxon history', in Kendall and Wells 1992 pp. 79-101

Campos, J., 1960. *Juan de Biclaro obispo de Gerona: su vida y su obra*, Madrid (= Consejio superior de investigaciones científicas, *Estudios* XXXII)

Canellas López, A., 1979. *Diplomática Hispano-Visigoda*, Saragossa

Carlot, A., 1903. *Étude sur le domesticus franc*, Liège. (= *Bibliothèque de la faculté de philosophie et lettres de l'Université de Liège*, fasc. XIII)

Carver, M.O.H., 1989. 'Kingship and material culture in early Anglo-Saxon East Anglia', in Bassett 1989c pp. 141-58

Carver, M.O.H. (ed.), 1992. *The Age of Sutton Hoo: the seventh century in north-western Europe*, Woodbridge

Cavanna, A., 1967. *Fara, sala, arimannia nella storia di un vico longobardo*, Milan

Bibliography

Cavanna, A., 1968. 'Nuovi problemi intorno alle fonti dell'Editto de Rotari', *Studia et documenta historiae et iuris* XXXIV pp. 269-361

Chadwick, H.M., 1905. *Studies on Anglo-Saxon Institutions*, Cambridge

Chadwick, H.M., 1907. *The Origin of the English Nation*, Cambridge

Chaplais, P., 1973a. 'The origin and authenticity of the royal Anglo-Saxon diploma', in Ranger 1973 pp. 28-42

Chaplais, P., 1973b. 'Some early Anglo-Saxon diplomas on single sheets: originals or copies?', in Ranger 1973 pp. 63-87

Chaplais, P., 1973c. 'Who introduced charters into England?', in Ranger 1973 pp. 88-107

Charles-Edwards, T.M., 1972. 'Kinship, status and the origins of the hide', *Past and Present* 56 pp. 3-33

Charles-Edwards, T.M., 1983. 'Bede, the Irish and the Britons', *Celtica* XV pp. 42-52

Charles-Edwards, T.M., 1989. 'Early medieval kingships in the British Isles', in Bassett 1989c pp. 28-39

Christie, N., 1991., 'Invasion or invitation? The Longobard occupation of northern Italy, AD 568-9', *Romanobarbarica* 11 pp. 79-108

Christie, N., 1995. *The Lombards: the ancient Longobards*, Oxford

Chrysos, E.K., 1989. 'Legal concepts and patterns for the barbarians' settlement on Roman soil', in Chrysos and Schwarcz 1989 pp. 12-23

Chrysos, E.K., and Schwarcz, A. (eds), 1989. *Das Reich und die Barbaren*, Vienna and Cologne (= *Veröffentlichungen des Instituts für österreichische Geschichtsforschung* 29)

Classen, P., 1955. 'Kaiserrescript und Königsurkunde: diplomatische Studien zum römisch-germanischen Kontinuitäts-problem, I. Teil', *Archiv für Diplomatik* 1 pp. 1-87

Classen, P., 1956. 'Kaiserrescript und Königsurkunde: diplomatische Studien zum römisch-germanischen Kontinuitäts-problem, II. Teil', *Archiv für Diplomatik* 2 pp. 1-115

Claude, D., 1964. 'Untersuchungen zum frühfränkischen Comitat', *Z.R.G., g.A.* 81 pp. 1-79

Claude, D., 1965. 'Studien zu Reccopolis 2: die historische Situation', *Madrider Mitteilungen* 6 pp. 165-94

Claude, D., 1970. *Geschichte der Westgoten*, Stuttgart

Claude, D., 1971a. *Adel, Kirche und Königtum im Westgotenreich*, Sigmaringen (= *Vorträge und Forschungen*, Sonderband 8)

Claude, D., 1971b. 'Millenarius und thiuphadus', *Z.R.G., g.A.* 88 pp. 181-90

Claude, D., 1972. 'Gentile und territoriale Staatsideen im Westgotenreich', *Frühmittelalterliche Studien* 6 pp. 1-38

Claude, D., 1973. 'Beiträge zur Geschichte der frühmittelalterlichen Königsschätze', *Early Medieval Studies* 7 pp. 5-24 (= *Antikvariskt Arkiv* 54)

Claude, D., 1977. 'The oath of allegience and the oath of the king in the Visigothic kingdom', *Classical Folia* 30 pp. 3-26

Claude, D., 1988. 'Der Millenarius', in Wolfram and Schwarcz 1988 pp. 17-20

Coates, R., 1989-90. 'On some controversy surrounding *Gewissae / Gewissei, Cerdic* and *Ceawlin*', *Nomina* 13 pp. 1-11.

Colgrave, B., 1963. 'The earliest life of St Gregory the Great, written by a Whitby monk', in N.K. Chadwick (ed.), *Celt and Saxon: studies in the early British border*, Cambridge pp. 119-37

Collins, R., 1977. 'Julian of Toledo and the royal succession in late seventh-century Spain', in Sawyer and Wood 1977 pp. 30-49

Collins, R., 1980. 'Mérida and Toledo, 550-585', in E. James 1980 pp. 189-219

Collins, R., 1983a. *Early Medieval Spain: unity and diversity, 400-1000*, London

Collins, R., 1983b. 'Theodebert I, "Rex Magnus Francorum" ', in Wormald, Bullough and Collins 1983 pp. 7-33

Collins, R., 1985. 'Sicut lex Gothorum continet: law and charters in ninth- and tenth-century León and Catalonia', *English Historical Review* C pp. 487-512

Collins, R., 1986. 'Visigothic law and regional custom in disputes in early medieval Spain', in Davies and Fouracre 1986, pp. 85-104

Collins, R., 1989. *The Arab Conquest of Spain, 710-797*, Oxford

Collins, R., 1990. 'Literacy and the laity in early medieval Spain', in McKitterick 1990 pp. 109-33

Collins, R., 1991a. '¿Donde estaban los arrianos en el año 589?', *Concilio III de Toledo: XIV centenario 589-1989*, Toledo pp. 211-22

Collins, R., 1991b. *Early Medieval Europe, 300-1000*, Basingstoke and London

Colombo, A., 1931. 'Il "Versum de Mediolana Civitate" dell'anonimo Liutprandeo e la importanza della metropoli Lombarda nell'alto medioevo', *Miscellanea di studi Lombardi in onore di Ettore Verga*, Milan pp. 69-105

Conti, P.M., 1972. 'L'uso dei titoli onorari ed aulici nel regno longobardo', *Studi storici in onore di Ottorino Bertolini*, 2 vols Pisa vol. 1 pp. 105-76

Conti, P.M., 1982. ' "Exceptores" e "cives". Consuetudine e diritto nelle città dell'Italia longobarda', *Studi medievali* 3rd ser. XXIII pp. 101-50

Conti, P.M., 1990. 'Il quadro storico-politico', in Menis 1990 pp. 92-6

Courtois, C., 1955. *Les Vandales et l'Afrique*, Paris

Cowdrey, H.E.J., 1981. 'Bede and the "English People" ', *Journal of Religious History* 11 pp. 501-23

Cramp, R., 1995. 'The making of Oswald's Northumbria', in C. Stancliffe and E. Cambridge (eds), *Oswald: Northumbrian King to European Saint*, Stamford pp. 1-32

D'Abadal y de Vinyals, R., 1958. 'A propos du legs visigothique en Espagne', *Settimane ... V: Caratteri del secolo VII in occidente* pp. 541-85

D'Abadal y de Vinyals, R., 1960. *Del reino de Tolosa al reino de Toledo*, Madrid

D'Abadal y de Vinyals, R., 1965. 'La monarquia en el regne de Toledo', *Homenaje a Jamie Vicens Vives*, 2 vols Barcelone vol. 1 pp. 191-200

Dark, K.R., 1994. *Civitas to Kingdom: British political continuity, 300-800*, London and New York

Darmstädter, P., 1896. *Das Reichsgut in der Lombardei und Piemont (568-1250)*, Strassburg

Darvill, T., 1988. 'Excavations in the site of the early Norman castle at Gloucester, 1983-4', *Medieval Archaeology* XXXII pp. 1-49

Davies, W., 1977. 'Annals and the origin of Mercia', in A. Dornier (ed.), *Mercian Studies*, Leicester pp. 17-29

Davies, W., and Fouracre, P. (eds), 1986. *The Settlement of Disputes in Early Medieval Europe*, Cambridge

Davis, R., 1992. *The Lives of the Eighth-century Popes (Liber Pontificalis)*, Liverpool

Davis, R.H.C., 1971. 'Alfred the Great: propaganda and truth', *History* 56 pp. 169-82

Deanesly, M., 1941. 'Early English and Gallic minsters', *Transactions of the Royal Historical Society* 4th ser. XXIII pp. 25-70

Deanesly, M., 1941-2. 'Canterbury and Paris in the reign of Æthelberht', *History* 26 pp. 97-104

Deanesly, M., 1941-3. 'The Court of King Æthelberht of Kent', *Cambridge Historical Journal* VII pp. 101-14

Deanesly, M., 1943. 'Roman traditionalist influence among the Anglo-Saxons', *English Historical Review* LVIII pp. 129-46

Bibliography

Debus, H.K., 1967. 'Studien zu merowingischen Urkunden und Briefen. Untersuchungen und Text: I', *Archiv für Diplomatik* 13 pp. 1-106

Debus, H.K., 1968. 'Studien zu merowingischen Urkunden und Briefen. Untersuchungen und Text: II', *Archiv für Diplomatik* 14 pp. 1-192

Diaz y Diaz, M.C., 1976a. 'La Lex Visigothorum y sus manuscritos: un ensayo de reinterpretación', *A.H.D.E.* XLIV pp. 163-223

Diaz y Diaz, M.C., 1976b. 'Titulaciones regias en la monarquía visigoda', *Revista portuguesa de historia* 16 pp. 133-41

Diesner, H.-J., 1969. 'König Wamba und der westgotische Frühfeudalismus', *Jarhrbuch der österreichischen Byzantinistik* 18 pp. 7-35

Diesner, H.-J., 1976a. 'Byzanz, Rom und die Langobarden', *Jahrbuch der österreichischen Byzantinistik* 25 pp. 31-45

Diesner, H.-J., 1976b. 'Zur langobardischen Sozialstruktur: Gasindii und Verwandtes', *Klio* 58 pp. 140-4

Diesner, H.-J., 1978a. *Isidor von Sevilla und das westgotische Spanien*, Berlin (= *Abhandlungen der sächsischen Akademie der Wissenschaften zu Leipzig, philologisch-historische Klasse* 67.3)

Diesner, H.-J., 1978b. 'Westgotische und langobardische Gefolgschaften und Untertanenverbände', *Sitzungsberichte der sächischen Akademie der Wissenschaften zu Leipzig, philologisch-historische Klasse* 120.2

Diesner, H.-J., 1979. 'Politik und Ideologie im Westgotenreich von Toledo: Chindasvind', *Sitzungsberichte der sächsischen Akademie der Wissenschaften zu Leipzig, philologisch-historische Klasse* 121.2

Diesner, H.-J., 1980. 'Fragen der Macht- und Herrschaftsstruktur bei Beda', *Akademie der Wissenschaften und der Literatur, Abhandlungen der geistes- und sozialwissenschaftlichen Klasse* (Mainz) 1980.3

Dilcher, G., 1978. 'Langobardisches Recht', in Erler, Kaufmann and Schmidt-Wiegand 1971-

Dill, S., 1926. *Roman Society in Gaul in the Merovingian Age*, London

Doehaerd, R., 1949. 'La Richesse des mérovingiens', *Studi in onore de Gino Luzzatto*, 4 vols Milan vol. 1 pp. 30-46

D'Ors, A., 1956. 'La territorialidad del derecho de los visigodos', *Settimane ... III: I Goti in occidente – problemi* pp. 363-408

Drew, K.F., 1967. 'The barbarian kings as lawgivers and judges', in R.S. Hoyt (ed.), *Life and Thought in the Early Middle Ages*, Minneapolis pp. 7-29

Drew, K.F., 1987. 'Another look at the origins of the middle ages: a reassessment of the role of the Germanic kingdoms', *Speculum* 62 pp. 803-12.

Drögereit, R., 1952. 'Kaiseridee und Kaisertitel bei den Angelsachsen', *Z.R.G., g.A.* 69 pp. 24-73

Dumville, D.N., 1975-6. ' "Nennius" and the *Historia Brittonum*', *Studia Celtica* 10/11 pp. 78-95

Dumville, D.N., 1976. 'The Anglian collection of royal genealogies and regnal lists', *Anglo-Saxon England* 5 pp. 23-50

Dumville, D.N., 1976-7. 'On the north British section of the *Historia Brittonum*', *Welsh History Review* 8 pp. 345-54

Dumville, D.N., 1977a. 'Kingship, Genealogies and Regnal Lists', in Sawyer and Wood 1977 pp. 72-104

Dumville, D.N., 1977b. 'Sub-Roman Britain: history and legend', *History* 62 pp. 173-92

Dumville, D.N., 1979. 'The Ætheling: a study in Anglo-Saxon constitutional history', *Anglo-Saxon England* 8 pp. 1-33

Dumville, D.N., 1989a. 'Essex, Middle Anglia and the expansion of Mercia in the south-east Midlands', in Bassett 1989c pp. 123-40

243

Dumville, D.N., 1989b. 'The origins of Northumbria: some aspects of the British background', in Bassett 1989c pp. 213-22

Dupraz, L., 1948. *Contribution à l'histoire du Regnum Francorum pendant le troisième quart du VIIe siècle*, Fribourg

Durliat, J., 1979. 'Les attributions civiles des évêques mérovingiens: l'exemple de Didier, évêque de Cahors (630-655)', *Annales du Midi* XCI pp. 237-54

Durliat, J., 1988. 'Le salaire de la paix dans les royaumes barbares (V^e-VIe siècles)', in Wolfram and Schwarcz 1988 pp. 21-72

Dykes Shaw, R., 1906. 'The fall of Visigothic power in Spain', *English Historical Review* XXI pp. 209-28

Eagles, B.N., 1989. 'Lindsey', in Bassett 1989c pp. 202-12

Ebling, H., 1974. *Prosopographie der Amtsträger des Merowingerreiches von Chlothar II (613) bis Karl Martell (741)*, Munich

Engel, A., and Serrure, R., 1964. *Traité numismatique du moyen âge*, 3 vols Bologna

Erler, A., Kaufmann, E., and Schmidt-Wiegand, R. (eds), 1971-. *Handwörterbuch zur deutschen Rechtsgeschichte*, Berlin

Esmonde Cleary, S., 1989. *The Ending of Roman Britain*, London

Evans, J., 1965. 'St Germanus in Britain', *Archaeologia Cantiana* LXXX pp. 175-85

Evison, V.I., 1965. *The Fifth-century Invasions South of the Thames*, London

Ewig, E., 1969. 'La monocratie dans l'Europe occidentale du Ve au Xe siècle', *Recueils de la Société Jean Bodin, XXI: La Monocratie*, 2 vols Brussels pp. 57-105

Ewig, E., 1976a. 'Das Fortleben römischer Institutionen in Gallien und Germanien', in *idem* 1976e vol. 1 pp. 409-34

Ewig, E., 1976b. 'Die fränkischen Teilreiche im 7. Jahrhundert (613-714)' in *idem* 1976e vol. 1 pp. 172-230

Ewig, E., 1976c. 'Die fränkischen Teilungen und Teilreiche (511-613)', in *idem* 1976e vol. 1 pp. 114-71

Ewig, E., 1976d. 'Résidence et capitale pendant le haut moyen âge', in *idem* 1976e vol. 1 pp. 362-408

Ewig, E., 1976e. *Spätantikes und fränkisches Gallien: gesammelte Schriften (1952-73)*, 2 vols Munich

Ewig, E., 1976f. 'Die Stellung Ribuariens in der Verfassungsgeschichte des Merowingerreiches', in *idem* 1976e vol. 1 pp. 450-71

Ewig, E., 1976g. 'Zum christlichen Königsgedanke im Frühmittelalter', in *idem* 1976e vol. 1 pp. 3-71

Ewig, E., 1983. *Die Merowinger und das Imperium*, Opladen (= Rheinisch-Westfälische Akademie der Wissenschaften, *Vorträge* G261)

Ewig, E., 1988. *Die Merowinger und das Frankenreich*, Stuttgart, Berlin and Cologne

Fanning, S.C., 1981. 'Lombard Arianism reconsidered', *Speculum* 56 pp. 241-58

Fanning, S.C., 1991. 'Bede, *Imperium*, and the Bretwaldas', *Speculum* 66 pp. 1-26

Fasoli, G., 1965. *I Longobardi in Italia*, Bologna

Feist, S., 1939. *Vergleichendes Wörterbuch der gotischen Spräche*, 3rd edn Leiden

Ferreirós, A.I., 1970. 'Notas en torno a la sucesión al trono en el reino visigodo', *A.H.D.E.* XL pp. 53-82

Finberg, H.P.R., 1972. 'Anglo-Saxon England to 1042', in *idem* (ed.), *The Agrarian History of England and Wales, vol. 1.2: A.D. 43-1042*, Cambridge pp. 383-532

Fontaine, J., 1960. 'Théorie et pratique du style chez Isidore de Séville', *Vigiliae Christianae* 14 pp. 65-101

Fontaine, J., 1980. 'King Sisebut's *Vita Desiderii* and the political function of Visigothic hagiography', in E. James 1980 pp. 93-129

Foot, S., 1993. 'The Kingdom of Lindsey', in Vince 1993 pp. 128-40

Bibliography

Fouracre, P., 1984a. 'Merovingians, mayors of the palace, and the notion of a "low-born" Ebroin', *Bulletin of the Institute of Historical Research* 57 pp. 1-14

Fouracre, P., 1984b. 'Observations on the outgrowth of Pippinid influence in the "regnum Francorum" after the Battle of Tertry (687-715)', *Medieval Prosopography* 5 pp. 1-31

Fouracre, P., 1986. ' "Placita" and the settlement of disputes in later Merovingian Francia', in Davies and Fouracre 1986 pp. 123-43

Fouracre, P., 1990. 'Merovingian history and Merovingian hagiography', *Past and Present* 127 pp. 3-38

Fröhlich, H., 1980. *Studien zu langobardischen Thronfolge von dem Anfängen bis zur Eroberung des italienischen Reiches durch Karl den Grossen*, 2 vols Tübingen

Fustel de Coulanges, N.D., 1889. *Histoire des institutions politiques de l'ancienne France, 4: L'Alleu et le domaine rural pendant l'époque mérovingienne*, Paris

Fustel de Coulanges, N.D., 1930. *Histoire des institutions politiques de l'ancienne France, 3: La Monarchie franque*, 6th edn Paris

Gallego-Blanco, E., 1974. 'Los concilios de Toledo y la sucesión al trono visigodo', *A.H.D.E.* XLIV pp. 723-39

Gamillscheg, E., 1932. 'Historia lingüística de los visigodos', *Revista de filología española* XIX pp. 117-50 and 229-60

Gamillscheg, E., 1934-6. *Romania Germanica: Sprach und Siedlungsgeschichte der Germanen auf dem Boden des alten Römerreichs*, 3 vols Berlin and Leipzig

Ganshof, F.L., 1968. *Frankish Institutions under Charlemagne*, New York

Ganz, D., 1983. 'Bureaucratic shorthand and Merovingian learning', in Wormald, Bullough and Collins 1983 pp. 58-75

Ganz, D., and Goffart, W., 1990. 'Charters earlier than 800 from French collections', *Speculum* 65 pp. 906-32

García-Gallo, A., 1936-41. 'Nacionalidad y territorialidad del derecho en la época visigoda', *A.H.D.E.* XIII pp. 168-264

García-Gallo, A., 1940. 'Notas sobre el reparto de tierras entre visigodos y romanos', *Hispania* 4 pp. 40-63

García-Gallo, A., 1974. 'Consideración crítica de los estudios sobre la legislación y la costumbre visigodas', *A.H.D.E.* XLIV pp. 343-464

García Moreno, L.A., 1971. Algunos aspectos fiscales de la península Ibérica durante el siglo V', *Hispania antiqua* 1 pp. 233-56

García Moreno, L.A., 1974a. 'Estudios sobre la organización administrativa del reino visigodo de Toledo', *A.H.D.E.* XLIV pp. 5-155

García Moreno, L.A., 1974b. *Prosopografia del reino visigodo de Toledo*, Salamanca (= *Acta Salamanticensia iussu senatus universitas edicta. Filisófia y letras* 77)

García Moreno, L.A., 1975. *El fin del reino visigodo de Toledo: decadencia y catástrofe. Una contribución a su crítica*, Madrid

García Moreno, L.A., 1982. 'Imposición y política fiscal en la España visigoda', *Historia de la hacienda española (época antigua y medieval); homenaje al profesor García de Valdeavellano*, Madrid pp. 261-300

García Moreno, L.A., 1983. 'El termino "sors" en el "Liber Iudicum": de nuevo el problema de la division de las tierras entre Godos y provinciales', *A.H.D.E.* LIII pp. 137-75

García Moreno, L.A., 1989. *Historia de España visigoda*, Madrid

García Moreno, L.A., 1991. 'La coyuntura política del III Concilio de Toledo. Una historia larga y tortuosa', *Concilio III de Toledo: XIV centenario 589-1989*, Toledo pp. 271-96

García Moreno, L.A., 1994. Gothic survivals in the Visigothic Kingdoms of Toulouse and Toledo', *Francia* 21 pp. 1-15.

Bibliography

García Villada, Z., 1931. 'El gobierno de la nación y los concilios generales y provinciales en tempo de los visigodos', *Estudios ecclesiasticos* X pp. 500-23

Gardiner, K., 1983. 'Paul the Deacon and Secundus of Trento', in B. Croke and A.M. Emmett (eds), *History and Historians in Late Antiquity*, Sydney pp. 147-54

Gasparri, S., 1978. *I duchi longobardi*, Rome (= Istutito storico italiano per il medioevo, *Studi storici*, fasc. 109)

Gasparri, S., 1983. 'Il ducato longobardo di Spoleto – istituzioni, poteri, gruppi dominanti', *Atti ...,* 9 pp. 77-122

Gasparri, S., 1986. 'Strutture militari e legami di dipendenzia in Italia in età longobardo e carolingia', *Rivista storica italiana* XCVIII pp. 664-726

Gasquet, A., 1887. 'Le royaume lombard: ses relations avec l'empire grec et avec les Francs', *Revue historique* XXXIII pp. 58-92

Geary, P.J., 1988. *Before France and Germany: the creation and transformation of the Merovingian world*, Oxford

Gelling. M., 1992. *The West Midlands in the Early Middle Ages*, Leicester, London and New York

Gerberding, R.A., 1987. *The Rise of the Carolingians and the Liber Historiae Francorum*, Oxford

Gibert, R., 1956. 'El reino visigodo y el particularismo español', *Settimane ... III: I Goti in occidenti – problemi* pp. 537-83

Gibert, R., 1968. 'La fundación del reino visigótico: una perspectiva histórico-jurídica', *Album J. Balon*, Namur pp. 1-25

Gibert, R., 1969. 'La sucesión al trono en la monarquía española', *Recueils de la Société Jean Bodin, XXI: La Monocratie*, 2 vols Brussels pp. 447-546

Gibert, R., 1980. 'Prenotariado visigótico', *Cuadernos de historia de España* LXIII-LXIV pp. 12-43

Gilmour, B., 1979. 'The Anglo-Saxon church at St Paul-in-the-Bail, Lincoln', *Medieval Archaeology* XXIII pp. 214-18

Gluckman, M., 1966. *Custom and Conflict in Africa*, Oxford

Götze, J., 1965-6. 'Die Litterae Elongatae. Ein Beitrag zur Formengeschichte und Herkunft der mittelalterlichen Urkundenschrift', *Archiv für Diplomatik* 11-12 pp. 1-70

Goffart, W., 1963. 'The Fredegar problem reconsidered', *Speculum* 38 pp. 206-41

Goffart, W., 1972. 'From Roman taxation to medieval seigneurie: three notes', *Traditio* XLVII pp. 165-87 and 373-94

Goffart, W., 1980. *Barbarians and Romans A.D. 418-584: the techniques of accommodation*, Princeton

Goffart, W., 1982. 'Old and new in Merovingian taxation', *Past and Present* 96 pp. 3-21

Goffart, W., 1988a. 'After the Zwettl Conference: comments on the "Techniques of Accommodation" ', in Wolfram and Schwarcz 1988 pp. 72-85

Goffart, W., 1988b. *The narrators of barbarian history (A.D. 550-800): Jordanes, Gregory of Tours, Bede and Paul the Deacon*, Princeton

Goffart, W., 1990. 'The *Historia Ecclesiastica*: Bede's agenda and ours', *Haskins Society Journal* 2 pp. 29-45

Goubert, P., 1946. 'Influences byzantines sur l'Espagne wisigothique', *Revue des études byzantines* IV pp. 111-34

Grahn-Hoek, H., 1976. *Die fränkische Obersicht im 6. Jahrhundert: Studien zu ihrer rechtlichen und politischen Stellung*, Sigmaringen (= *Vorträge und Forschungen*, Sonderband 21)

Graus, F., 1965. *Volk, Herrscher und Heiliger im Reich der Merowinger: Studien zur Hagiographie der Merowingerzeit*, Prague

Grierson, P., and Blackburn, M., 1986. *Medieval European Coinage, with a cata-*

Bibliography

logue of the coins in the Fitzwilliam Museum, Cambridge, vol. 1: the early middle ages (5th to 10th centuries), Cambridge

Hallenbeck, J.T., 1982. Pavia and Rome: the Lombard monarchy and the papacy in the eighth century, Philadelphia (= Transactions of the American Philosophical Society 72.4)

Hallenbeck, J.T., 1989. 'King Desiderius as surrogate "Patricius Romanorum": the politics of equilibrium 757-768', Studi medievali 3rd ser. XXX pp. 49-64

Hamilton Thompson, A. (ed.), 1935. Bede: his life, times and writing, Oxford

Harrison, D., 1993. The Early State and the Towns: forms of integration in Lombard Italy A.D. 568-774, Lund

Hartmann, L.M., 1897-1903. Geschichte Italiens im Mittelalter, 2 vols Gotha.

Hartmann, L.M., 1901. 'Notare der langobardischen Könige', Mitteilungen der Instituts für österreichische Geschichtsforschung, Ergänzungsband VI pp. 17-24

Hawkes, S.C., 1982. 'Anglo-Saxon Kent, c. 425-725', in Leech 1982 pp. 64-78

Hawkes, S.C., 1989. 'The south-east after the Romans: the Saxon settlement', in V.A. Maxfield (ed.), The Saxon Shore: a handbook, Exeter pp. 78-95 (= Exeter Studies in History, 25)

Heidrich, I., 1965-6. 'Titulatur und Urkunden der arnulfingischen Hausmeier', Archiv für Diplomatik 11-12 pp. 71-279

Heidrich, I., 1989. 'Les Maires du palais neustriens du milieu du VIIe au milieu du VIIIe siècle', in Atsma 1989 vol. 1 pp. 217-29

Higham, H.J., 1992a. 'King Cearl, the Battle of Chester and the origins of Mercian "Overkingship" ', Midland History XVII pp. 1-15

Higham, N.J., 1992b. Rome, Britain and the Anglo-Saxons, London

Higham, N.J., 1994. The English Conquest: Gildas and Britain in the fifth century, Manchester

Higham, N.J., 1995. An English Empire: Bede and the early Anglo-Saxon kings, Manchester

Hill, R.M.T., 1975. 'Holy Kings: the bane of seventh-century society', Studies in Church History 12 pp. 39-43

Hillgarth, J.N., 1966. 'Coins and Chronicles: propaganda in sixth-century Spain and the Byzantine background', Historia 15 pp. 493-508

Hillgarth, J.N., 1970. 'Historiography in Visigothic Spain', Settimane ... XVII: La storiografia altomedievale pp. 261-311

Hodgkin, T., 1880-99. Italy and her Invaders, 8 vols Oxford

Honoré, T., 1994. Emperors and Lawyers, 2nd edn Oxford

Hooke, D., 1985. The Anglo-Saxon Landscape: the kingdom of the Hwicce, Manchester

Hope-Taylor, B., 1977. Yeavering: an Anglo-British centre of early Northumbria, London

Irsliger, F., 1969. Untersuchungen zur Geschichte des frühfränkischen Adels, Bonn (= Rheinisches Archiv, Veröffentlichungen des Instituts für geschichtliche Landeskunde des Rheinland und der Universität Bonn, 70)

Jackson, K.H., 1953. Language and History in Early Britain, Edinburgh

Jackson, K.H., 1963. 'On the northern British section in Nennius', in N.K. Chadwick (ed.), Celt and Saxon: studies in the early British border, Cambridge pp. 20-62

James, E. (ed.), 1980. Visigothic Spain: new approaches, Oxford

James, E., 1982. The Origins of France: from Clovis to the Capetians, 500-1000, London

James, E., 1983. ' "Beati pacifici": bishops and the law in sixth-century Gaul', in J. Bossy (ed.), Disputes and Settlements: law and human relations in the West, Cambridge pp. 25-46

James, E., 1988. The Franks, Oxford

Bibliography

James, M.R., 1907. *A Descriptive Catalogue of the Manuscripts in the Library of Trinity Hall*, Cambridge

Jarnut, J., 1972. *Prosopographische und sozialgeschichtliche Studien zum Langobardenreich in Italien*, Bonn

Jarnut, J., 1982. *Geschichte der Langobarden*, Stuttgart

John, E., 1964. *Land Tenure in Early England: a discussion of some problems*, Leicester

John, E., 1966. *Orbis Britanniae and other studies*, Leicester

Jolliffe, J.E.A., 1933. *Pre-feudal England: the Jutes*, London

Jolliffe, J.E.A., 1961. *The Constitutional History of Medieval England from the English Settlement to 1485*, 4th edn London

Jones, A.H.M., 1964. *The Later Roman Empire, 284-602: a social, economic and administrative survey*, 3 vols Oxford

Jones, M.E., 1988. 'The appeal to Aetius in Gildas', *Nottingham Medieval Studies* XXXII pp. 141-55

Jones, M.J., 1993. 'The latter days of Roman Lincoln', in Vince 1993 pp. 14-28

Jones, M.J., and Gilmour, B.J.J., 1980. 'Lincoln, principia and forum: a preliminary report', *Britannia* XI pp. 61-72

Jusselin, M., 1905. 'Notes tironiennes dans les diplômes', *Bibliothèque de l'École des Chartes* 66 pp. 361-89

Jusselin, M., 1907. 'Notes tironiennes dans les diplômes mérovingiens', *Bibliothèque de l'École des Chartes* 68 pp. 481-508

Jusselin, M., 1913. 'La transmission des ordres à la chancellerie mérovingienne d'après les souscriptions et notes tironiennes', *Bibliothèque de l'École des Chartes* 74 pp. 66-73

Kaiser, R., 1979. 'Steuer und Zoll in der Merowingerzeit', *Francia* 7 pp. 1-17

Kampers, G., 1979. *Personengeschichtliche Studien zum Westgotenreich in Spanien*, Münster

Kelly, S., 1990. 'Anglo-Saxon lay society and the written word', in McKitterick 1990 pp. 36-62

Kendall, C.B., and Wells, P.S., 1992. *Voyage to the Other World: the legacy of Sutton Hoo*, Minneapolis

Kent, J.P.C., 1960. 'From Roman Britain to Saxon England', in R.H.M. Dolley (ed.), *Anglo-Saxon Coins: studies presented to F.M. Stenton on the occasion of his 80th birthday*, London pp. 1-22

Kenyon, K.M., 1948. *Excavations at the Jewry Wall Site, Leicester*, Oxford

Keynes, S., 1992. 'Rædwald the Bretwalda', in Kendall and Wells 1992 pp. 103-23

King, P.D., 1972. *Law and Society in the Visigothic Kingdom*, Cambridge

King, P.D., 1980a. 'The alleged territoriality of Visigothic law', in B. Tierney and P. Linehan (eds), *Authority and Power: studies in medieval law and government presented to Walter Ullman on his 70th birthday*, Cambridge pp. 1-11

King, P.D., 1980b. 'King Chindasvind and the first territorial law-code of the Visigothic kingdom', in E. James 1980 pp. 131-57

King, P.D., 1988. 'The barbarian kingdoms', in J.H. Burns (ed.), *The Cambridge History of Medieval Political Thought, c. 350-c. 1450*, Cambridge pp. 123-53

Kirby, D.P., 1983. 'Bede, Eddius Stephanus and the "Life of Wilfrid" ', *English Historical Review* XCVIII pp. 101-14

Kirby, D.P., 1991. *The Earliest English Kings*, London

Kirby, D.P., 1993. *Bede's Historia ecclesiastica gentis anglorum: its contemporary setting*, Jarrow

Krüger, K.H., 1981. 'Zur "beneventanischen" Konzeption der Langobardengeschichte des Paulus Diaconus', *Frühmittelalterliche Studien* 15 pp. 18-35

Kurze, W., 1973. 'Zur Kopiertätigkeit Gregors von Catino', *Quellen und Forschungen* LIII pp. 407-56

Bibliography

Lapidge, M., 1989. 'Bede's Metrical *Vita S. Cuthberti*', in Bonner, Rollason and Stancliffe 1989 pp. 77-92

Lapidge, M., 1993. *Bede the Poet*, Jarrow

Lapidge, M., and Dumville, D.N. (eds), 1984. *Gildas: new approaches*, Woodbridge

Larson, L.M., 1904. *The King's Household in England before the Norman Conquest*, Madison

Lear, F.S., 1951. 'The public law of the Visigothic Code', *Speculum* 26 pp. 1-23

Leech, P.E. (ed.), 1982. *Archaeology in Kent to A.D. 1500: in memory of Stuart Eborall Rigold*, London.

Leicht, P.S., 1923. 'Gli elementi romani nella costituzione longobarda', *Archivio storico italiano*, LXXXI pp. 5-24

Leicht, P.S., 1950. 'König Ahistulfs Heeresgesetze', *Miscellanea Academica Berolinensia: Gesammelte Abhandlungen zur Feier das 250 Jährigen Bestehens der deutschen Akademie der Wissenschaften zu Berlin*, 2 vols Berlin vol. II.1 pp. 97-102

Leicht, P.S., 1953. 'Paolo Diacono e gli altri scrittori delle vicende d'Italia nell'età carolingia', *Atti ...*, 2 pp. 57-74

Levillain, L., 1911. 'La souscription de chancellerie dans les diplômes mérovingiens', *Le Moyen Age* XXIV pp. 89-124

Levillain, L., 1923. 'Le formulaire de Marculf et la critique moderne', *Bibilothèque de l'École des Chartes* 84 pp. 21-91

Levillain, L., 1931. 'La formule "bene valiat" et le sceau dans les diplômes mérovingiens', *Bibliothèque de l'École des Chartes* 92 pp. 5-22

Levison, W., 1946. *England and the Continent in the Eighth Century*, Oxford

Levison, W., and Lowe, H., 1953. *Deutschlands Geschichtsquellen im Mittelalter, Vorzeit und Karolinger, II.Heft.* Weimar

Lewis, A.R., 1976. 'The dukes in the *regnum Francorum*, A.D. 550-751', *Speculum* 51 pp. 381-410

Liebeschuetz, J.H.W.G., 1991. *Barbarians and Bishops: army, church, and state in the age of Arcadius and Chrysostom*, Oxford

Little, A.G., 1889. 'Gesiths and thegns', *English Historical Review* IV pp. 723-9

Löfstedt, B., 1976. 'Ein textcritischen Problem in den langobardischen Gesetzen', *Z.R.G., g.A.* 93 pp. 319-21

Lohaus, A., 1974. *Die Merowinger und England* Munich (= *Müncher Beiträge zur Mediävistik und Renaissance-Forschung* 19)

Loyn, H.R., 1955. 'Gesiths and thegns in Anglo-Saxon England from the seventh to the tenth centuries', *English Historical Review* LXX pp. 529-49

Loyn, H.R., 1984. *The Governance of Anglo-Saxon England, 500-1087*, London

Loyn, H.R., 1992. 'Kings, Gesiths and Thegns', in Carver 1992 pp. 75-9.

McClure, J., 1983. 'Bede's Old Testament Kings', in Wormald, Bullough and Collins 1983 pp. 76-98

McClure, J., 1984. 'Bede and the Life of Ceolfrid', *Peritia* 3 pp. 71-84

MacCormack, S.G., 1981. *Art and Ceremony in Late Antiquity*, Berkeley

McCormick, M., 1986. *Eternal Victory: triumphal rulership in late antiquity, Byzantium and the early medieval west*, Cambridge

McKitterick, R., 1983. *The Frankish Kingdoms under the Carolingians, 751-987*, London

McKitterick, R., 1989. *The Carolingians and the Written Word*, Cambridge

McKitterick, R. (ed.), 1990. *The Uses of Literacy in Early Medieval Europe*, Cambridge

Markus, R.A., 1975. *Bede and the Tradition of Ecclesiastical Historiography*, Jarrow

Martindale, J. (ed.), 1992. *The Prosopography of the Later Roman Empire, vol. III: 527-641*, Cambridge

Bibliography

Matthews, J., 1989. *The Roman Empire of Ammianus*, London

Mayer, E., 1909. *Italienische Verfassungsgeschichte von der Gothenzeit bis zur Zunftherrschaft*, 2 vols Leipzig

Mayer, E., 1925-6. *Historia de las instituciones sociales y políticas de España y Portugal durante los siglos V a XIV*, 2 vols Madrid

Menis, G.C. (ed.), 1990. *I Longobardi*, Milan

Mentz, A., 1911. 'Beiträge zur Geschichte der tironischen Noten', *Archiv für Urkundenforschung*, 3 pp. 1-38

Mentz, A., 1939. 'Die tironischen Noten. Eine Geschichte der römischer Kurzschrift. Erster Teil', *Archiv für Urkundenforschung* 16 pp. 287-384

Mentz, A., 1942. 'Die tironischen Noten. Eine Geschichte der römischer Kurzschrift. Zweiter Teil', *Archiv für Urkundenforschung* 17 pp. 155-303

Merêa, P., 1948. *Estudos de direito visigótigo*, Coimbra

Merrifield, R., 1965. *The Roman City of London*, London

Meyer, C., 1877. *Sprache und Sprachdenkmäler der Langobarden: Quellen, Grammatik, Glossar*, Paderborn

Miles, G.C., 1952. *The Coinage of the Visigoths of Spain, Leovigild to Achila II*, New York

Miller, M., 1975. 'Bede's use of Gildas', *English Historical Review* XC pp. 241-61

Miller, M., 1976-7. 'Starting to write history: Gildas, Bede and Nennius', *Welsh History Review* 8 pp. 456-65

Mommsen, T., 1910. 'Ostgotische Studien', in *idem*, *Gesammelte Schriften* VI pp. 362-84

Mor, C.G., 1933. 'La successione al trono nel diritto pubblico longobardo', *Studi in onore de Federico Cammeo*, 2 vols Padua vol. 2 pp. 177-200

Mor, C.G., 1952. 'I gastaldi con potere ducale nell'ordinamento pubblico longobardo', *Atti del 1° congresso internazionale de studi longobardi*, Spoleto pp. 409-15

Mor, C.G., 1958. 'Lo stato longobardo nell VII secolo', *Settimane ... V: Caratteri del secolo VII in occidente* pp. 271-307

Mor, G.C., 1961. 'Modificazione strutturali dell'Assemblea nazionale longobarda nel secolo VIII', *Album Helen Maud Cam*, Louvain pp. 1-12

Mor, G.C., 1972. 'Il diritto romano nel sistema giuridico longobardo del secolo VIII', *Atti della Accademia nazionale de Lincei* 8th ser., *Rendiconti: Classe di scienze morali, storiche e filogiche* XXVII pp. 3-16

Mor, G.C., 1974. 'Prime osservazioni sul notariato langobardo', *Mélanges Roger Prubenas*, Montpellier pp. 569-77 (= *Recueil de mémoires et travaux publié par la société d'histoire du droit et des institutions des anciens pays de droit écrit*, fasc. 9)

Mor, G.C., 1975. 'Appunti sull'amministrazione cittidina in età longobarda', *Studi in memoria de Enrico Guicciardi*, Padua pp. 261-78

Morghen, R., 1974. 'La civiltà dei Longobardi nella "Historia Langobardorum" di Paolo Diacono', *Atti del convegno internazionale sul tema: la civiltà dei longobardi in Europa* Rome pp. 9-23 (= *Problemi attuali di scienza e di cultura: Accademia nazionale dei Lincei* CCCLXXI)

Morosi, C., 1936. 'L'Assemblea nazionale del regno longobardo-italico', *Rivista de storia del diritto italiano* IX pp. 248-90 and 434-75

Morris, J., 1973. *The Age of Arthur*, London

Morris, J., 1995. *Arthurian Sources, vol. 2: Annals and Charters*, Chichester

Mundó Marcet, A., 1974. *Los diplomas visigodas originales en pergamino, transcripción y commentario, con un regesto de documentos de la época visigoda*, Barcelona

Murphy, F.X., 1952. 'Julian of Toledo and the fall of the Visigothic kingdom in Spain', *Speculum* 27 pp. 1-27

Bibliography

Murray, A.C., 1986. 'The position of the *Graphio* in the constitutional history of Merovingian Gaul', *Speculum* 61 pp. 787-805

Murray, A.C., 1988. 'From Roman to Frankish Gaul: "Centenarii" and "Centenae" in the administration of the Merovingian kingdoms', *Traditio* XLIV pp. 59-100

Murray, A.C., 1994. 'Immunity, nobility and the *Edict of Paris*', *Speculum* 69 pp. 18-39

Musset, L., 1975. *The Germanic Invasions: the making of Europe A.D. 400-600*, London

Myres, J.N.L., 1986. *The English Settlements*, Oxford

Nehlsen, H., 1978. 'Lex Visigothorum', in Erler, Kaufmann and Schmidt-Wiegand 1971-

Nelson, J.L., 1978. 'Queens as Jezebels: the careers of Brunhild and Balthild in Merovingian history', in D. Baker (ed.), *Medieval Women*, Oxford pp. 31-77

Nelson, J.L., 1990. 'Perceptions du pouvoir chez les historiennes du haut moyen âge', in M. Rouche and J. Heuclin (ed.), *La Femme au moyen âge*, Mauberge pp. 75-83

Nelson, J.L., 1991. 'A propos des femmes royales dans les rapports entre le monde wisigothique et le monde franc à l'époque de Reccared', *Concilio III de Toledo: XIV centenario 589-1989*, Toledo pp. 465-76

Niermeyer, J.F., 1976. *Mediae Latinitatis Lexicon Minus*, Leiden

Noble, T.F.X., 1984. *The Republic of St Peter: the birth of the Papal State, 680-825*, Philadelphia

Noble, T.F.X., 1985. 'A new look at the "Liber Pontificalis"', *Archivum historiae pontificiae* 23 pp. 347-58

Noble, T.F.X., 1990. 'Literacy and the papal government in late antiquity and the early middle ages', in McKitterick 1990 pp. 82-108

Orlandis, J., 1956. 'El cristianismo en el reino visigodo', *Settimane ... III: I Goti in occidenti – problemi* pp. 153-71

Orlandis, J., 1962a. 'Algunas observaciones en torno a la "tirania" de san Heremenegildo', in Orlandis 1962c pp. 3-12.

Orlandis, J., 1962b. 'La iglesia visigoda y los problemas de la sucesión al trono en el siglo VII', in Orlandis 1962c pp. 43-55

Orlandis, J., 1962c. *El poder real y la sucesión al trono en la monarquía visigoda*, Rome (= *Estudios Visigóticos III*, which is *Cuadernos del instituto juridico español* 16)

Orlandis, J., 1962d. 'La reina en la monarquía visigoda', in Orlandis 1962c pp. 102-23

Orlandis, J., 1962e. 'La sucesión al trono en la monarquía visigoda', in Orlandis 1962c pp. 57-102

Orlandis, J., 1962f. 'En torno a la noción visigoda de tiranía', in Orlandis 1962c pp. 13-42

Orlandis, J., 1971. 'Los hispano-romanos el la aristocracia visigótica del siglo VII', *Revista portuguesa de historia* 13 pp. 189-96

Orlandis, J., 1977. *Historia de España: la España visigótica*, Madrid

Orlandis, J., 1991. 'El significado del III Concilio de Toledo en la Historia Hispánica y Universal', *Concilio III de Toledo: XIV centenario 589-1989*, Toledo pp. 325-32

Orlandis J., and Ramos-Lissón, D., 1981. *Die Synoden auf der iberischen Halbinsel bis zum Einbruch des Islam (711)*, Paderborn, Munich and Zurich

O'Sullivan, T.D., 1978. *The De Excidio of Gildas: its authenticity and date*, Leiden

Paradisi, B., 1968. 'Il prologo e l'epilogo dell'editto di Rotari', *Studia et documenta historiae et iuris* XXXIV pp. 1-31

Paravicini, W., and Werner, K.F. (eds.), 1980. *Histoire comparée de l'administration*

Bibliography

(IVe-XVIIIe siècles): actes du XIVe colloque historique franco-allemand de l'Institut Historique Allemand de Paris, Zurich and Munich

Périn, P., 1989. 'Paris mérovingien, *sedes regia*', *Klio* 71 pp. 487-502

Périn, P., and Feffer, L.-C. (eds), 1985. *La Neustrie: Les Pays au nord de la Loire de Dagobert à Charles le Chauve (VIIe-IXe siècles)*, Créteil

Philp, B.J., 1977. 'The *Forum* of Roman London, 1968-9', *Britannia* VII pp. 1-64

Picard, J.-M., 1982. 'The Purpose of Adomnán's *Vitae Columbae*', *Peritia* 1 pp. 160-77

Picard, J.-M., 1984. 'Bede, Adomnán, and the writing of history', *Peritia* 3 pp. 50-70

Pirenne, H., 1934. 'De l'état de l'instruction des laïques à l'époque mérovingienne', *Revue bénédictine* XLIV pp. 164-77

Pretty, K., 1989. 'Defining the Magonsæte', in Bassett 1989c pp. 171-83

Previdi, E.S., 1973. 'Lo "sculdahis" nel territorio longobardo di Rieti (sec. VIII e IX): dall'amministrazione longobarda a quella franca', *Studi medievali* 3rd ser. XIV pp. 627-76

Prou, M., 1892. *Les Monnaies mérovingiennes*, Paris

Raddatz, K., 1964. 'Studien zu Reccopolis I: die archäologischen Befunde', *Madrider Mitteilungen* 5 pp. 213-33

Ranger, F. (ed.), 1973. *Prisca Munimenta: studies in archival and administrative history presented to A.E.J. Hollaender*, London

Raw, B., 1992. 'Royal power and royal symbols in *Beowulf*', in Carver 1992 pp. 167-74

Reinhart, W., 1951 'Über die Territorialität der westgotischen Gesetzbücher', *Z.R.G., g.A.* 68 pp. 348-54

Reydellet, M., 1970. 'Les intentions idéologiques et politiques dans la *Chronique* d'Isidore de Séville', *Mélanges d'archéologie et d'histoire de l'École française de Rome* LXXXII pp. 363-400

Reydellet, M., 1981. *La Royauté dans la littérature latine de Sidoine Apollinaire à Isidore de Séville*, Rome

Richards, M.P., 1986. 'The manuscript contexts of the Old English Laws: tradition and innovation', in P.E. Szarmach (ed.), *Studies in Earlier Old English Prose*, New York pp. 171-92

Richardson, H.G., and Sayles, G.O., 1966. *Law and Legislation from Æthelberht to Magna Carta*, Edinburgh

Riché, P., 1962. *Éducation et culture dans l'occident barbare, VIe-VIIIe siècle*, Paris

Riché, P., 1965. *Enseignement du droit en Gaule du VIe au XIe siècle*, Milan (= *Ius romanum medii aevi*, pars I 5b *bb*)

Riché, P., 1980. 'La formation des scribes dans le monde mérovingien et carolingien', in Paravicini and Werner 1980 pp. 75-80

Rodwell, W., 1984. 'Churches in the landscape: aspects of topography and planning', in M.L. Faull (ed.), *Studies in Late Anglo-Saxon Settlement*, Oxford pp. 1-23

Rollason, D.W., 1982. *The Mildreth Legend: a study in early medieval hagiography in England*, Leicester

Rosenthal, J.T., 1975. 'Bede's use of miracles in the Ecclesiastical History', *Traditio* XXXI pp. 328-35

Rotili, M., 1990. 'Una città d'età longobarda: Benevento', in Menis 1990 pp. 131-6

Rouche, M., 1979. *L'Aquitaine des Wisigoths aux Arabes: naissance d'une région, 418-781*, Paris

Rouche, M., 1989. 'Remarques sur la géographie historique de la Neustrie (650-850)', in Atsma 1989 vol. 1 pp. 1-23

Saitta, B., 1979. 'Un momento di disagregazione nel regno visigoto di Spagna: la rivolta di Ermenegildo', *Quaderni Catanesi di studi classici e medievali* 1 pp. 81-134

Bibliography

Sánchez-Albornoz y Menduiña, C., 1942. *En torno a los orígines del feudalismo*, 3 vols Mendoza

Sánchez-Albornoz y Menduiña, C., 1959. 'El gobierno de las ciudades en España del siglo V al X', *Settimane ... VI: La città nell'alto medioevo* pp. 359-91

Sánchez-Albornoz y Menduiña, C., 1962. 'Pervivencia y crisis de la tradición jurídica romana en la España Goda', *Settimane ... IX: Il passaggio dall'antichità al medioevo in occidente* pp. 128-99

Sánchez-Albornoz y Mednuiña, C., 1971a. 'El aula regia y las asambleas políticas de los Godos', in *idem* 1971b pp. 149-252

Sánchez-Albornoz y Menduiña, C., 1971b. *Estudios Visigodos*, Rome

Sánchez-Albornoz y Menduiña, C., 1971c. 'Ruina y extinción del municipio romano en España e instituciones que le reemplazan', in *idem* 1971c pp. 9-147

Sawyer, P.H., 1968. *Anglo-Saxon Charters: an annotated list and bibliography*, London

Sawyer, P.H., and Wood, I.N. (eds), 1977. *Early Medieval Kingship*, Leeds

Schade, O., 1872-82. *Altdeutsches Wörterbuch*, 2 vols Halle

Scharer, A., 1982. *Die angelsächsische Königsurkunde im 7. und 8. Jahrhundert*, Vienna, Cologne and Graz

Schiaperelli, L., 1932. 'Note diplomatiche sulle carte longobarde', *Archivio storico italiano* XC pp. 3-34

Schiaperelli, L., 1933. 'Note diplomatiche sulle carte longobarde', *Archivio storico italiano* XCI pp. 3-66

Schiaperelli, L., 1934. 'Note diplomatiche sulle carte longobarde', *Archivio storico italiano* XCII pp. 3-55

Schmidt-Wiegand, R., 1978. 'Lex Ribuaria', in Erler, Kaufmann and Schmidt-Wiegand 1971-

Schneider, F., 1914. *Die Reichsverwaltung in Toscana von der Gründung des Langobardenreiches bis zum Ausgang der Staufer (568-1268), vol. 1: Die Grundlagen*, Rome

Schneider, R., 1972. *Königswahl und Königserhebung im Frühmittelalter*, Stuttgart

Schöne, G., 1856. *Die Amtsgewalt der fränkischen maiores domus*, Braunschweig

Schott, C., 1978. 'Lex Alamannorum', in Erler, Kaufmann and Schmidt-Wiegand 1971-

Schott, C., 1979. 'Der Stand der Leges-Forschung', *Frühmittelalterliche Studien* 13 pp. 29-55

Schramm, P.E., 1954-78. *Herrschaftszeichen und Staatssymbolik: Beiträge zu ihrer Geschichte vom dritten bis zum sechzehnten Jahrhundert*, 4 vols Stuttgart

Schramm, P.E., 1968. ' "Mythos" des Königtums', in *idem, Kaiser, König und Päpste: Gesammelte Aufsätze zur Geschichte des Mittelalters, Bd 1: Von der Spätantike bis zum Tode Karls des Grossen (814)*, Stuttgart pp. 68-78

Schwöbel, H., 1982. *Synode und König im Westgotenreich: Grundlagen und Formen ihrer Beziehung*, Cologne and Vienna

Selle-Hosbach, K., 1974. *Prosopographie merowingischer Amtsträger in der Zeit von 511-613*, Bonn

Siems, H., 1978. 'Lex Baiuuariorum', in Erler, Kaufmann and Schmidt-Wiegand 1971-

Silvestre, H.A., and Gutiérrez, F.J.J., 1991. 'Sobre la provincia en el reino Hispano-Visigodo de Toledo', *Concilio III de Toledo: XIV centenario 598-1989*, Toledo pp. 387-92

Sims-Williams, P., 1983. 'Gildas and the Anglo-Saxons', *Cambridge Medieval Celtic Studies* 6 pp. 1-30

Sisam, K., 1953. 'Anglo-Saxon royal genealogies', *Proceedings of the British Academy* XXXIX pp. 287-346

253

Bibliography

Skeat, W.W., 1868. *A Moeso-Gothic Glossary*, London

Skeat, W.W., 1884. *The Concise Dictionary of English Etymology*, repr. Ware 1993

Smidt, W., 1910. *Das Chronicon Beneventani monasterii s. Sophiae: eine quellen-kritische Untersuchung*, Berlin

Sprandel, R., 1957. 'Dux und Comes in der Merowingerzeit', *Z.R.G., g.A.* 74 pp. 41-84

Stafford, P.A., 1983. *Queens, Concubines and Dowagers: the king's wife in the early middle ages*, London

Stafford, P.A., 1985. *The East Midlands in the Early Middle Ages*, Leicester

Stancliffe, C., 1995. 'Oswald, "Most Holy and Most Victorious King of the Northumbrians"', in *idem* and E. Cambridge (eds), *Oswald: Northumbrian King to European Saint*, Stamford pp. 33-83

Stengel, E.E., 1960. 'Imperator und Imperium bei den Angelsachsen', *Deutsches Archiv für Erforschung des Mittelalters* 16 pp. 15-72

Stenton, D.M. (ed.), 1970. *Preparatory to Anglo-Saxon England: being the collected papers of Frank Merry Stenton*, Oxford

Stenton, F.M., 1955. *The Latin Charters of the Anglo-Saxon period*, Oxford

Stenton, F.M., 1970a. 'The East Anglian kings of the seventh century', in D.M. Stenton 1970 pp. 394-402

Stenton, F.M., 1970b. 'Lindsey and its kings', in D.M. Stenton 1970 pp. 127-35

Stenton, F.M., 1970c. 'The supremacy of the Mercian kings', in D.M. Stenton 1970, pp. 48-66

Stenton, F.M., 1971. *Anglo-Saxon England*, 3rd edn Oxford

Stocker, D., 1993. 'The early church in Lincolnshire', in Vince 1993 pp. 101-22

Stroheker, K.F., 1965a. *Germanentum und Spätantike*, Zurich and Stuttgart

Stroheker, K.F., 1965b. 'Leowigild', in *idem* 1965a pp. 134-91

Stroheker, K.F., 1965c. 'Das spanische Westgotenreich und Byzanz', in *idem* 1965a pp. 207-45

Sutherland, J.N., 1975. 'The idea of revenge in Lombard society in the eighth and tenth centuries: the cases of Paul the Deacon and Liudprand of Cremona', *Speculum* 50 pp. 391-410

Tabacco, G., 1989. *The Struggle for Power in Medieval Italy*, Cambridge

Tagliaferri, A., 1965. *I Longobardi nella civiltà e nell'economia italiana del primo medioevo*, Milan

Tagliaferri, A., 1990. 'Il ducato di Forum Iulii', in Menis 1990 pp. 102-3 and 358-63

Tardif, J., 1881. *Études sur les institutions politiques et administratives de la France: période mérovingienne*, Paris

Tarradell, M., 1978. 'El govern de la pre-Catalunya sota l'imperi Romà i el regne visigòtic', *Cuadernos de historia economica de Cataluna* 18 pp. 9-21

Teitler, H.C., 1985. *Notarii and Exceptores: an enquiry into the role and signifi-cance of shorthand writers in the imperial and ecclesiastical bureaucracy of the Roman Empire (from the early Principate to c. 450 A.D.)*, Amsterdam

Tessier, G., 1962. *Diplomatique royale française*, Paris

Thacker, A.T., 1981. 'Some terms for noblemen in Anglo-Saxon England, c. 650-900', *Anglo-Saxon Studies in Archaeology and History* 2 pp. 201-23

Thompson, E.A., 1960. 'The conversion of the Visigoths to Catholicism', *Notting-ham Medieval Studies* IV pp. 4-35

Thompson, E.A., 1969. *The Goths in Spain*, Oxford

Todd, M., 1992. *The Early Germans*, Oxford

Van Dam, R., 1985. *Leadership and Community in Late Antique Gaul*, Berkeley and Los Angeles

Váquez de Parga, L., 1961. 'Notas sobre la obra historica de san Isidoro', *Isidoriana* pp. 99-105

Bibliography

Vezin, J., 1974. 'Documents wisigothiques récemment découverts', *Journal des savants* pp. 218-22

Vezin, J., 1980. 'L'influence des actes des hautes fonctionnaires romaines sur les actes de Gaule et d'Espagne au VIIe siècle', in Paravicini and Werner 1980 pp. 71-4

Vince, A., 1990. *Saxon London: an archaeological investigation*, London

Vince, A. (ed.), 1993. *Pre-Viking Lindsey*, Lincoln

Vismara, G., 1981. 'Il diritto in Italia nell'alto medioevo', *La cultura in Italia fra tardo antico e allo medioevo*, 2 vols Rome vol. 1 pp. 165-79

Vollrath-Reichelt, H., 1971. *Königsgedanke und Königtum bei den Angelsachsen bis zur Mitte des 9. Jahrhunderts*, Cologne and Vienna

von Pflugk-Harttung, J., 1887. 'Die Thronfolge in Langobardenreiche', *Z.R.G., g.A.* 8 pp. 66-88

Wacher, J., 1974. *The Towns of Roman Britain*, London

Waitz, G., 1896. *Abhandlungen zur Deutsches Verfassungs- und Rechtsgeschichte*, Göttingen

Waitz, G., 1953-5. *Deutsche Verfassungsgeschichte*, 8 vols repr. Kiel

Wallace-Hadrill, J.M., 1955. Review of F. Beyerle and R. Buchner (eds), *M.G.H. Legum sectio I t. III pars II: Lex Ribuaria*, in *English Historical Review* LXX pp. 440-3

Wallace-Hadrill, J.M., 1960. *The Fourth Book of the Chronicle of Fredegar with its Continuations*, London

Wallace-Hadrill, J.M., 1962. *The Long-haired Kings*, London

Wallace-Hadrill, J.M., 1965. Review of A.H.M. Jones, *The Later Roman Empire, 284-602: a social, economic and administrative survey* (1964), in *English Historical Review* 80 pp. 785-90

Wallace-Hadrill, J.M., 1971. *Early Germanic Kinghip in England and on the Continent*, Oxford

Wallace-Hadrill, J.M., 1975. 'Gregory of Tours and Bede: their views on the personal qualities of kings', in *idem*, *Early Medieval History*, Oxford pp. 96-114

Wallace-Hadrill, J.M., 1983. *The Frankish Church*, Oxford

Wallace-Hadrill, J.M., 1988. *Bede's Ecclesiastical History of the English People: a historical commentary*, Oxford

Ward, B., 1990. *The Venerable Bede*, London

Ward-Perkins, B., 1984. *From Classical Antiquity to the Middle Ages: urban public buildings in northern and central Italy A.D. 300-850*, Oxford

Wattenbach, W., 1958. *Das Schriftswesen im Mittelalter*, 4th edn Graz

Wattenbach, W., Dümmler, E., and Huf, F., 1991. *Deutschlands Geschichtsquellen im Mittelalter: Frühzeit und Karolinger*, 2 vols, Kettwig

Werner, K.F., 1973. 'Les Principautés périphériques dans le monde franc du VIIIe siècle', *Settimane ... XX: I problemi dell'occidente nel secolo VIII* pp. 483-514

Werner, K.F., 1980. 'Missus – Marchio – Comes: entre l'administration centrale et l'administration locale de l'empire carolingien', in Paravicini and Werner 1980 pp. 191-239

Werner, K.F., 1985a. 'Qu'est'ce que la Neustrie?', in Périn and Feffer 1985 pp. 29-38

Werner, K.F., 1985b. 'Les rouages de l'administration', in Périn and Feffer 1985 pp. 41-6

White, R., 1990. 'Excavations in the site of the Baths basilica', in Barker 1990 pp. 3-7

Wickham, C.J., 1981. *Early Medieval Italy: central power and local society, 400-1000*, London

Wickham, C.J., 1986. 'Land disputes and their social framework in Lombard-Carolingian Italy, 700-900', in Davies and Fouracre 1986 pp. 105-24

Wightman, E.M., 1978. 'Peasants and potentes: an investigation of social structure

Bibliography

and land tenure in Roman Gaul', *American Journal of Ancient History* 3 pp. 97-128

Wightman, E.M., 1985. *Gallia Belgica*, London

Wilcken, U., 1920. 'Zu den Kaiserreskripten', *Hermes* 55 pp. 1-41

Wilhelmsen, A., 1978. 'Punishment for criminal offences in the Visigothic code', *Classical Folia* 32 pp. 141-52

Wolf, G., 1988. 'Mittel der Herrschaftssicherung in den Germanenreichen des 6. und 7. Jahrhunderts', *Z.R.G., g.A.* 105 pp. 214-38

Wolf, K.B., 1990. *Conquerors and Chroniclers of Early Medieval Spain*, Liverpool

Wolfram, H., 1967. *Intitulatio I: Lateinische Königs- und Fürstentitel bis zum Ende des 8. Jahrhunderts*, Graz, Vienna and Cologne (= *Mitteilungen der Instituts für österreichische Geschichtsforschung* Ergänzungsband XXI)

Wolfram, H., 1988. *History of the Goths*, Berkeley

Wolfram, H., and Schwarcz, A. (eds), 1988. *Anerkennung und Integration. Zu den wirtschaftlichen Grundlagen der Völkerwanderungszeit 400-600. Berichte des Symposions der Kommission für Frühmittelalterforschung 7. bis 9. Mai 1986 Stift Zwettl, Niederösterreich* (= Österreichische Akademie der Wissenschaften, philosophisch-historische Klasse, Denkschriften 193)

Wood, I.N., 1977a. 'Introduction', in Sawyer and Wood 1977 pp. 1-5

Wood, I.N., 1977b. 'Kings, kingdoms and consent', in Sawyer and Wood 1977 pp. 6-29

Wood, I.N., 1982. 'The *Uita Columbani* and Merovingian hagiography', *Peritia* 1 pp. 63-80

Wood, I.N., 1983a. 'The ecclesiastical politics of Merovingian Clermont', in Wormald, Bullough and Collins 1983 pp. 34-57

Wood, I.N., 1983b. *The Merovingian North Sea*, Alingsås

Wood, I.N., 1984. 'The end of Roman Britain: continental evidence and parallels', in Lapidge and Dumville 1984 pp. 1-25

Wood, I.N., 1986. 'Disputes in late fifth- and sixth-century Gaul: some problems', in Davies and Fouracre 1986 pp. 7-22

Wood, I.N., 1988. 'Forgery in Merovingian hagiography', in *Monumenta Germaniae Historica, Schriften 33.5: Fälschungen im Mittelalter*, Hanover pp. 369-84

Wood, I.N., 1990. 'Administration, law and culture in Merovingian Gaul', in McKitterick 1990 pp. 63-81

Wood, I.N., 1991a. 'The Franks and Sutton Hoo', in *idem* and N. Lund (eds), *People and Places in Northern Europe, 500-1600: essays in honour of Peter Hayes Sawyer*, Woodbridge pp. 1-14

Wood, I.N., 1991b. 'Saint-Wandrille and its hagiography', in *idem* and G.A. Loud (eds), *Church and Chronicle in the Middle Ages: essays presented to John Taylor*, London pp. 1-14

Wood, I.N., 1992. 'Frankish hegemony in England', in Carver 1992 pp. 235-41

Wood, I.N., 1993. 'The Code in Merovingian Gaul', in J. Harries and I.N. Wood (eds), *The Theodosian Code: studies in the imperial law of late antiquity*, London pp. 161-77

Wood, I.N., 1994a. *The Merovingian Kingdoms, 450-751*, London

Wood, I.N., 1994b. 'The Mission of Augustine of Canterbury to the English', *Speculum* 69 pp. 1-17

Wormald, P., 1977. '*Lex scripta* and *verbum regis*: legislation and Germanic kingship from Euric to Cnut', in Sawyer and Wood 1977, pp. 105-38

Wormald, P., 1978. 'Bede, "Beowulf" and the conversion of the Anglo-Saxon aristocracy', in R.T. Farrell (ed.), *Bede and Anglo-Saxon England*, Oxford pp. 32-95

Wormald, P., 1983. 'Bede, the *Bretwaldas* and the origins of the *gens Anglorum*', in *idem*, D. Bullough and R. Collins 1983, pp. 99-129

Bibliography

Wormald, P., 1984. *Bede and the Conversion of England: the charter evidence*, Jarrow

Wormald, P., 1986. 'Celtic and Anglo-Saxon Kingship: some further thoughts', in P.E. Szarmach (ed.), *Sources of Anglo-Saxon Culture*, Kalamazoo pp. 151-83

Wormald, P., 1995 ' "Inter cetera bona ... genti suae": law-making and peace-keeping in the earliest English kingdoms', *Settimane ... XLII: La giustizia nell'alto medioevo* pp. 963-93

Wormald, P., Bullough, D.A., and Collins, R. (eds), 1983. *Ideal and Reality in Frankish and Anglo-Saxon Society: studies presented to J.M. Wallace-Hadrill*, Oxford

Wroth, W., 1911. *Catalogue of the coins of the Vandals, Ostrogoths and Lombards and of the emperors of Thessalonica, Nicaea and Trebizond in the British Museum*, London

Wunder, H., 1991. 'Zur Entmachtung der austrasischen Hausmeiers Pippin', in K. Herbers, H.H. Kortüm amd C. Servatius (eds), *Ex ipsis rerum documentis: Beiträge zur Mediävistik. Festschrift für Harald Zimmermann zum 65. Geburtstag*, Sigmaringen pp. 39-54

Yorke, B.A.E., 1981. 'The vocabulary of Anglo-Saxon overlordship', in *Anglo-Saxon Studies in Archaeology and History* 2 pp. 171-200

Yorke, B.A.E., 1982. 'The foundation of the Old Minster and the status of Winchester in the seventh and eighth centuries', *Proceedings of the Hampshire Field Club and Archaeological Society* 38 pp. 75-83

Yorke, B.A.E., 1983. 'Joint kingship in Kent c. 560 to 785', *Archaeologia Cantiana* XCIX pp. 1-19

Yorke, B.A.E., 1990. *Kings and Kingdoms of Early Anglo-Saxon England*, London

Yorke, B.A.E., 1993. 'Fact or fiction? The written evidence for the fifth and sixth centuries A.D.', *Anglo-Saxon Studies in Archaeology and History* 6 pp. 45-50

Yorke, B.A.E., 1995. *Wessex in the Early Middle Ages*, London and New York

Zanella, G., 1990. 'La legittimazione del potere regale nelle "Storie" di Gregorio di Tours e Paolo Diacono', *Studi medievali* 3rd ser. XXXI pp. 55-84

Zielinski, H., 1972. *Studien zu dem spoletinischen "Privaturkunden" des 8. Jahrhunderts und ihrer Überlieferung im Regestum Farfense*, Tübingen

Zielinski, H., 1976. 'Gregor von Catino und das Regestum Farfense', *Quellen und Forschungen* LV-LVI pp. 361-404

Glossary of Terms for Legal Documents

The text contains many terms which may be unfamiliar to non-specialists: those relating to royal officials are elucidated in the appropriate place; but those relating to various types of legal enactment, which are only used in passing, are briefly defined below.

Capitulary. A collection of decrees which supplemented the main law codes; often arising from decisions made in assemblies of nobles, or in response to cases which had been referred to the king.

Charter. A document recording the transfer of rights to property, or the confirmation of a transfer made on an earlier occasion.

Diploma. The most formal kind of **charter** or *placitum*, issued by emperors, kings, popes and some *duces*.

Edict. A legal pronouncement issued by a Roman emperor on his own initiative (contrast with **rescript**), or by a highly placed provincial administrator.

Formulary. A collection of a wide range of official documents or sections of documents, often with references to specific people or places removed, to be used as models for the compilation of new documents.

Imperial Law (Roman). Law made by Roman emperors, and issued as **edicts** or **rescripts**; the subject of an extensive Classical juristic literature. In the later Roman Empire, much imperial law was codified by Theodosius II and Justinian I, the former being the source for much of the *Leges Romanae* of the Burgundians and Visigoths (which existed alongside codes based on **provincial law**).

Placitum. A document which recorded the final resolution of a legal case.

Provincial Law (Roman); also known as **Vulgar Law**. Legal customs of the provinces of the Roman Empire, which were not always in agreement with **imperial law**. This kind of law was never properly codified in the Roman period, but survives embedded in later 'barbarian' law codes, which it greatly influenced.

Rescript. An answer issued in the name of a Roman emperor to a case which officials had referred to him. Such documents were published in order that the principles they contained could be applied as widely as possible.

Index

This index is intended to be a guide to the principal discussions of the main themes and sources, rather than to be comprehensive.

259